# THE ARCHAEOLOGY
# OF
# EARLY MEDIEVAL IRELAND

# THE ARCHAEOLOGY OF EARLY MEDIEVAL IRELAND

*Nancy Edwards*

Routledge
Taylor & Francis Group

LONDON AND NEW YORK

First published 1990
First published in paperback 1996
by B. T. Batsford Ltd.

Reprinted 1999, 2000, 2002, 2004
by Routledge
2 Park Square, Milton Park, Abingdon, Oxon, OX14 4RN

Simultaneously published in the USA and Canada
by Routledge
270 Madison Ave, New York NY 10016

Transferred to Digital Printing 2006

*Routledge is an imprint of the Taylor & Francis Group*

*British Library Cataloguing in Publication Data*
A catalogue record for this book is available from the British Library

*Library of Congress Cataloging in Publication Data*
A catalog record for this book has been requested

ISBN 0–415–22000–9

**Publisher's Note**
The publisher has gone to great lengths to ensure the quality of this reprint
but points out that some imperfections in the original may be apparent

Printed and bound by CPI Antony Rowe, Eastbourne

**For Huw**

# CONTENTS

# ILLUSTRATIONS

# A NOTE ON RADIOCARBON DATES

The problems and inherent inaccuracies of radio-carbon dating are now well-known. In this book all radiocarbon dates quoted have been calibrated using the most recent calibration curve accepted by the International Radiocarbon Conference in 1986 (Stuiver, M. and Pearson, G. W. 1986 'High precision calibration of the radiocarbon timescale, AD 1950–500 BC', *Radiocarbon* 28: 805–38). In the text all radiocarbon dates are given as calendar years BC or AD using a 2 sigma range which means that there is only a 1 in 20 chance of the true date falling outside that range. For the general reader each date is first given as falling within a range of centuries. This does not mean that the archaeological event took place during the entire period quoted but *at some point* during it. For the more specialist reader this is followed in brackets by the precise 2 sigma calibrated data range. For easy reference the laboratory number of each date is given in the relevant endnote.

# Preface

This book has been written in response to the need for an up-to-date introduction to the archaeology of early medieval Ireland. Such a synthesis will, I hope, be of use, not just to those with an interest in archaeology, but also to those working in related disciplines, such as early Irish history, law and literature. I would also like to think that it is written in such a way as to be of interest to the general reader. A book of this kind should certainly not be seen as definitive. Instead I can only hope that it may inspire others to embark on research into this fascinating period of Irish archaeology.

The time-span covered by this book, essentially the fifth to the twelfth centuries, has been referred to by a variety of terms, the most common being 'early Christian', 'early historic', 'early medieval' and 'Dark Age' though others, such as the 'later Iron Age', have also been used. 'Early medieval' is preferred here.

After considerable thought it was decided on the whole not to include site location maps in this book. This is because of the great number of sites mentioned and because much more work has been done in some parts of Ireland than in others, making the compilation of meaningful distribution maps almost impossible. Instead sites are listed in the index together with the county in which they are located.

This book has not been easy to write. I have, nevertheless, enjoyed the challenge. However the project could never have been undertaken without the help of many friends and colleagues. First, I would like to thank those who have read and commented upon drafts of different chapters: John Bradley, Ewan Campbell (who also calibrated the radiocarbon dates for me), Tom Fanning, Ann Hamlin (who has also helped in many other

ways). Alan Lane, Jim Lang and Mick Monk. The mistakes and misconceptions which remain are, of course, my own.

Secondly, I would like to thank all those who facilitated my sabbatical leave in Ireland during the autumn of 1985 and made it such an academically stimulating and pleasurable experience. I am particularly grateful to Charles Doherry, who made available both his college room and his house while he was on sabbatical leave in Canada, and those who made me feel so welcome at University College Dublin. I would also like to thank the staff of the National Museum of Ireland and Ulster Museum for generous access to their collections and Siobhán de hÓir, Fergus Kelly, Chris Lynn and Betty O'Brien for help in various ways.

Thirdly, I would like to thank my students at University College Bangor over the years. It was they who made me aware of the need for this book and helped me to refine many of my ideas on the subject. I am also grateful to the staff of the college Arts Library who have gone to much trouble to find material for me.

Fourthly, I am pleased to acknowledge financial assistance from the British Academy, without which my sabbatical leave in Ireland would have been impossible, and the Society for Medieval Archaeology, who made a very welcome contribution towards the cost of the line drawings.

Finally, this book would not be what it is without the assistance of two people. First, I would like to thank Jean Williamson for her skilful and sensitive illustrations and secondly, my husband, Huw Pryce, for his constant help and encouragement, especially in the final stages when the going got tough.

Nancy Edwards
August 1989

# Preface to the Paperback Edition

It is now over six years since this book originally went to press. The paperback edition provides a welcome opportunity to mention some of the more important research and excavation which have taken place and been published in the meantime.

Amongst the more general works, Harold Mytum's *The Origins of Early Medieval Ireland* (London 1992) seeks to explain the changes which took place in the early centuries AD and resulted in the wealth of the Irish archaeological evidence for the period before the Viking invasions. Various aspects of the Iron Age and early centuries AD have also been recently reviewed in *Emania* 13 (1995). The quarterly *Archaeology Ireland* is a valuable guide to recent discoveries, research and discussion concerning the whole period. J. P. Mallory and T. E. McNeill provide a useful regional survey in *The Archaeology of Ulster: From colonisation to plantation* (Belfast 1991). The listing and description of early medieval sites of all kinds have proceeded apace with the publication by the Office of Public Works of several county archaeological inventories and the *Archaeological Survey of County Louth* (Dublin 1991). The *North Kerry Archaeological Survey* (Dingle 1995) has also recently appeared.

Research on aspects of the economy and technology have brought some very interesting results. The vital role of cattle in early medieval Irish society has been studied by both Nerys Patterson in *Cattle Lords and Clansmen: The social structure of early Ireland* (2nd edn London/NotreDame 1994) and A. T. Lucas in *Cattle in Ancient Ireland* (Kilkenny 1989). Environmental evidence currently being studied from the raised rath at Deer Park Farms, Co. Antrim, highlights the potential of waterlogged sites for preserving early medieval plant and animal remains (H. K. Kenward and E. P. Alison 1994 'A Preliminary View of the Insect Assemblages from the Early Christian Rath Site at Deer Park Farms, Northern Ireland' in J. Rackham (ed.) *Environment and Economy in Anglo-Saxon England*, CBA res. rep. 89, 89–107). The use of vertical as well as horizontal watermills has now

been established (Colin Rynne 1989 'The Introduction of the Vertical Watermill into Ireland: Some recent archaeological evidence' *Med. Arch.* 33, 21–31), as has the manufacture of glass (J. Henderson 1988 'The Nature of the Early Christian Glass Industry in Ireland: Some evidence from Dunmisk fort' *U.J.A.* 51, 115–26). B. G. Scott has made a study of Irish iron technology including that of the early middle ages in *Early Irish Ironworking* (Belfast 1990).

Turning to ornamental metalworking, there have been two important exhibition catalogues which contain several recent and significant discoveries: Susan Youngs' (ed.) *The Work of Angels: Masterpieces of Celtic metalworking, 6th to 9th centuries AD* (London 1989), which also includes an interesting section by P. T. Craddock on metalworking techniques, and Cormac Bourke's *Patrick: The archaeology of a saint* (Belfast 1993). Peter Harbison's *The High Crosses of Ireland: An iconographic and photographic survey* (Bonn 1992) is also worthy of note, as is *The Age of Migrating Ideas: Early medieval art in Northern Britain and Ireland* edited by R. M. Spearman and J. Higgitt (Stroud 1993).

Since 1989 there has been considerable progress in our understanding of the Viking impact on Ireland. The closely datable stratigraphy of the Dublin Viking levels is particularly important and has wider implications. Fascicules of the *Medieval Dublin Excavations 1962–81* have continued to appear, notably P. F. Wallace's study of *The Viking Age Buildings of Dublin* (Dublin 1992) and Thomas Fanning's *Viking Age Ringed Pins from Dublin* (Dublin 1994). Our knowledge of other Viking Age towns has greatly increased through excavation and there is a developing interest in what archaeology can tell us about the intermixing of the Viking and native populations. Several aspects of recent research on the Vikings in Ireland are summarised in *Archaeology Ireland* 9 (3) Autumn 1995.

Nancy Edwards
November 1995

# CHAPTER 1

# The Roman Impact

This book is concerned with the archaeology of Ireland in the early middle ages; that is, the period between the advent of Christianity, which had taken place by the early decades of the fifth century, and the settlement of the Anglo-Normans in the late twelfth century. The material remains of Ireland in this period are of great interest, since they include large numbers of surviving settlement and ecclesiastical sites (though only a small proportion of these have been investigated archaeologically), artefacts of considerable variety and richness ranging from everyday objects to precious relics, and the remains of Viking towns as revealed in the recent Dublin excavations. This is also the period when Ireland first emerges into history and we can begin to learn about the Irish from their own writings. It is therefore possible to draw upon documentary sources in order to illuminate the archaeological evidence.

The beginning of the period is particularly difficult to define in archaeological terms. This is because our knowledge of the Irish Iron Age which preceded it is still very unsatisfactory. We know almost nothing of Iron Age settlement and burial though major complexes of monuments connected with royal and ritual use, including some earlier than the Iron Age, have been investigated at Navan, Co. Armagh, Dún Ailinne, Co. Kildare, Tara, Co. Meath and Cruachan, Co. Roscommon. But the majority of the archaeological evidence consists of unassociated finds of La Tène decorated metalwork, which are only located across the northern two-thirds of the country. The first phase, consisting mainly of aristocratic warrior equipment, swords, scabbards, spearbutts and pieces of horse harness, may probably be dated to the third or second centuries BC. A later phase, perhaps spanning c.50 BC to the first or second century AD, includes bowls, discs, torques, brooches and the enigmatic Cork horns

and 'Petrie Crown', all decorated with compass-drawn spiral ornament, sometimes raised into high relief. Some pieces of stone sculpture, such as the famous spiral-carved Turoe stone, Co. Galway, are also of Iron Age date.[1] But the general paucity of archaeological evidence for the Irish Iron Age means that it is currently impossible to reconstruct a coherent picture of the period. It is therefore extremely difficult to determine the nature and extent of continuity between the Iron Age and the early middle ages.

A consideration of the Roman impact on Ireland in the first to fifth centuries AD is also crucial to our understanding of the subsequent period. Ireland was never part of the Roman Empire, though there are some indications that an invasion may have been contemplated. Tacitus reports that in AD 81/2 his father-in-law Agricola, the governor of Britain, occupied 'that part of Britain which looks towards Ireland' and he was of the opinion 'that Ireland could be overpowered and held with one legion and a moderate contingent of auxiliaries',[2] but there is no substantial evidence to suggest that such a campaign was ever launched. Nevertheless the proximity of Ireland to Roman Britain and to a lesser extent Gaul led to the establishment of a variety of contacts which were to prove of lasting importance.

The archaeological evidence is not easy to interpret. Indeed, the number of identifiably Roman artefacts seems remarkably small. Only 20 per cent of Roman coin finds are likely to have arrived in Ireland in antiquity. Equally the majority of Roman pottery, mainly single sherds of Samian ware, sometimes pierced or shaped, has been found on early medieval or later sites including well-stratified contexts in Dublin. Why this is so is unclear, but Samian could have been brought back by travellers as souvenirs, amulets or relics, though it may also have been imported for use as

*1  Ireland: provinces and counties.*

a colouring agent or even as an ingredient for medicines. Otherwise the archaeological evidence consists of a few burials showing signs of Roman contact; an interesting range of metalwork from Newgrange, Co. Meath; two late Roman hoards from Balline, Co. Limerick and Ballinrees, Co. Derry (2); occasional groups of Roman artefacts as, for example, from the hill-fort at Freestone Hill, Co. Kilkenny; and a variety of stray finds including brooches, toilet implements (though these are often difficult to distinguish from native copies), a bronze skillet from Rathlin Island, Co. Antrim, a bronze ladle from Bohermena, Co. Meath and a slate oculist's stamp from Golden Bridge, Co. Tipperary. The majority of Roman artefacts have come to light on the flat coastal plain between the River Boyne and the Wicklow mountains and along the north-east coast, both areas with easy access to Britain, but there is also a sprinkling of late Roman objects from Munster.[3]

But what is the significance of these finds and what can they, together with other evidence, tell us about the nature of contacts between Ireland and the Roman Empire? To begin with, some first-century objects associated with burials suggest the presence of British refugees who had fled to Ireland in the wake of the Roman invasion in AD 43. A wealthy grave group found near Donaghadee, Co. Down, which may have accompanied the cremated remains of a woman, included 150 glass beads, two glass bracelets and several copper-alloy objects. Although none of these are Roman, parallels may be identified in the Somerset area of southern England suggesting that a group of refugees may have found their way from there to Ulster. Similarly, a group of crouched inhuma-

**2** *Part of the late Roman silver hoard from Ballinrees, Co. Derry (Copyright: the Trustees of the British Museum).*

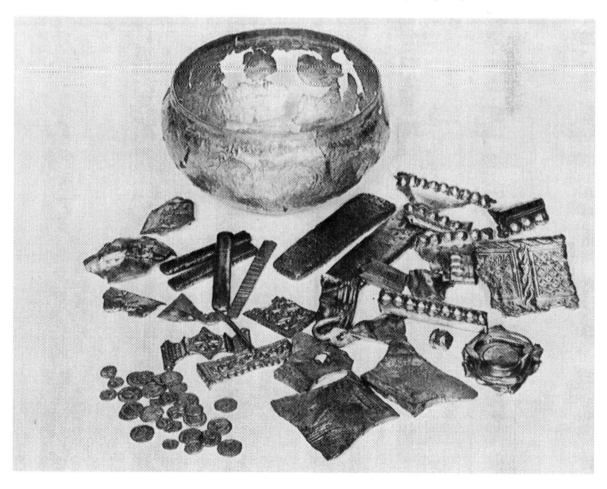

tions from Lambay Island, Co. Dublin, included what appears to have been a warrior grave accompanied by a sword, shield boss and sheet copper-alloy plaques which might have been attached to the shield. Amongst other finds were five copper-alloy fibulae of Roman type. The grave goods suggest that the refugees may have fled to Ireland from Yorkshire, perhaps via north Wales, but the brooches also demonstrate contacts with early Romanized areas of south-east England.[4] A second group of inhumations from Bray Head, Co. Wicklow, may represent slightly later immigrants. The bodies were laid out in long-cists orientated east/west with one or two coins of Trajan (97–117) or Hadrian (117–38) placed on or beside the breast, indicating some contact with Roman burial customs. However, the only known grave of purely Roman type is a second-century cremation, probably female, from Stonyford, Co. Kilkenny. It consisted of a green glass urn containing human bones, a glass cosmetic holder and a circular bronze mirror. The significance of the cremation is not altogether clear, though Warner has suggested it could indicate the presence of a Roman trading station, since it is located only a short distance from the navigable River Nore.[5]

In general there is surprisingly little archaeological evidence for Roman trade with Ireland. However, the few Roman objects so far recognized as having been deposited in antiquity may represent only the tip of the iceberg. Contemporary documentary sources certainly suggest trade contacts. The map of Ireland in Ptolemy's *Geographica* (compiled around the second century) includes names and locations of tribes, rivers and other places. He seems to have been drawing upon the work of an earlier Greek geographer, Philemon, who, it has been suggested, gathered his information from traders visiting Ireland probably in the years immediately preceding the Claudian invasion of Britain in AD 43. Forty years later Tacitus tells us the Romans were now better informed about Ireland 'thanks to the trade of merchants'.[6]

Some 25 Roman coins, mainly of high value, and several gold ornaments together spanning the entire Roman period have been found outside the Neolithic passage grave at Newgrange, some near the entrance, others in the vicinity of the surviving arc of the stone circle and at the foot of other standing stones. They seem to have been deposited either singly or in groups as votive offerings demonstrating the continuing sanctity of the site.

How this material was originally acquired is unclear but it is interesting to note that most of the more valuable coins may be dated to the late third and fourth centuries and could therefore represent the spoils of Irish raids on Roman Britain.[7]

Indeed, from the late third century onwards Ireland seems to have had increasing contacts with Roman Britain. Irish raiders, together with others from Scotland and the Continent, contributed to and took advantage of the gradual weakening of Roman control to plunder the wealth of the province. The most famous victim of these raids was St Patrick, who was enslaved in Ireland for six years during the first half of the fifth century. In Britain the most graphic archaeological evidence of Irish raiding may be seen in the years around the Barbarian Conspiracy of 367 when many villas south of the Bristol Channel were attacked.[8] In Ireland two important hoards of Roman metalwork give an indication of the booty captured. The Ballinrees hoard (2) when found originally comprised over 6kg (12½lbs) of silver ingots and plate and 1,701 coins. The ingots included both the cow-hide shaped type, two of which were stamped with Latin inscriptions, and bar-shaped examples. The plate was mainly fragmentary, having been cut up ready for the melting pot. The coins, *siliquae*, many of which had been clipped, span the fourth and early fifth centuries. The latest, a *siliqua* of Honorius datable to 419–23 and in virtually mint condition, suggests the hoard was deposited during the 420s. The late fourth-century Balline hoard is much smaller. It consists of four cow-hide shaped silver ingots, two fragmentary, and three pieces of silver plate. A stamp on one of the ingots bearing the inscription EX OFFI[CINA] ISATIS 'from the workshop of Isatis' is paralleled on a similar ingot from Richborough fort in Kent.[9]

At some point, either in the late Roman period or in the decades following the official Roman withdrawal, Irish raiding led to a series of settlements along the western seaboard of Britain.[10] The most important of these resulted in the emergence of the kingdom of Dalriada centred on Argyll in Scotland and the kingdom of Dyfed in south-west Wales, but there is also some evidence for settlement in south-west Scotland, north Wales, Cornwall and Devon. It is impossible to estimate the numbers of people involved. On the one hand they were taking advantage of the power vacuum created by the contraction of Roman control; on the other they were responding to the changing political situation in Ireland itself, whereby the expansion of the Uí Néill eastwards out of Connacht ultimately brought about the displacement of some other, less powerful tribes. The Irish settlements in western Britain retained contacts with their homeland and were probably instrumental in the transfer of many aspects of Roman culture across the Irish Sea in the immediate post-Roman period.

In archaeological terms the Roman impact on Ireland during the Roman period seems remarkably slight. But the long-term consequences were formative in the shaping of Ireland in the early middle ages. The conversion of the Irish to Christianity, the official religion of the late Roman Empire, was particularly important. It resulted not only in the Christian sites and objects which are so characteristic of early medieval Irish archaeology but also in the introduction of Latin as the language of the Church. It is also in the late fourth or early fifth centuries that we can begin to detect in the ogham inscriptions (see p. 103) the first signs of literacy amongst the Irish. The Church fostered the subsequent expansion of book-learning and the wealth of early medieval literature and manuscript illumination which sprang from it. The impact of Roman artefacts and technology on early medieval Ireland is more difficult to gauge but is likely to have been significant. It has been suggested that the expansion of agriculture detectable in pollen diagrams around the beginning of the early medieval period was the result of the introduction of a heavier plough, probably from Roman Britain (see p. 62). Equally many of the early medieval techniques of ornamental metal- and glass-working, for example millefiori, were introduced from the Roman world. Other early medieval artefacts of probable Roman origin include barrel padlocks, skillets and strainers; Irish swords were also influenced by Roman types.[11] Thus at the beginning of our period we are dealing with an Iron Age society which was being transformed as a result of contact with the Roman world.

# CHAPTER 2

# Settlement: Ring-Forts

Early medieval Irish settlement was essentially rural. There were no towns in the usual sense of the word until the foundation of the Viking trading ports in the ninth and tenth centuries, and the only native centres of population, which may have carried out some of the functions of urban communities, were the larger monasteries. Instead the fragmented nature of the landscape gave rise to scattered farmsteads and other non-nucleated settlements.

## Landscape

As Estyn Evans has so graphically shown, the key to the personality of Ireland is its landscape.[1] Unlike other European countries, Ireland has no central mountainous area; instead the uplands are mainly coastal and contrast sharply with the poorly drained central lowlands (3). This fragmentation of the high land, together with the diversity of the landscape, is the major product of a complex geographical history. The mountains seldom rise above 900 m (3,000 ft) and yet they achieve a remarkable variety: to the east, the more hospitable roundish ridges of the Mournes and the older granite of the Wicklows; to the west, the wilder undulating pinnacles of Macgillycuddy's Reeks, the bare peaks of Mount Brandon and Croagh Patrick, the flat limestone escarpment of Ben Bulbin and the precipitous cliffs of Slieve League. Many of the rivers follow tortuous courses. They rise in the central plains and trace sluggish paths through the lowlands, often broadening into lakes or marshes, and then quickening near the coast to cut their way through the uplands to the sea. The Shannon, for example, rises in the hills of Cavan/Leitrim and winds slowly southwards through Lough Ree, gathering tributaries in its wake, to cross through the quiet watery lands below Athlone and flow through Lough Derg, before shooting the rapids to its estuary.

The traveller in Ireland is immediately aware of great variety in the landscape. From Dublin Bay in the east, passing through the rich pastures of Meath, we journey northwards into the borderlands of Ulster. The country closes in, a maze of small lakes, streams and low, rounded hills, the glacial drumlins which stretch in a broad curving band from Dundalk to Donegal Bay. Beyond are the lowlands around Lough Neagh, the Sperrin Mountains and the spectacular coastal scenery of Antrim; to the north-west the harsh and rocky landscape of Donegal. Or we may travel westwards following the ancient routes along the raised gravel eskers into the heartland of Ireland. We cross the Shannon and then turn north-west towards the distant mountain backdrop of West Connacht with its expanses of blanket bog interrupted by brown peaty lakes. Alternatively, we continue west towards the bare limestone karst of the Burren or the sandstone and shale lowlands of west Clare. Again, we leave Dublin Bay, skirting the Wicklow mountains and crossing the flat, sandy plain of the Curragh, before turning south to follow the courses of the Barrow, Nore and Suir through fertile farmlands down to Waterford Harbour. We then head westwards into Munster through a patchwork of hills and valleys. Beyond are the lakes and mountains of south-west Ireland which stretch towards a ragged coastline projecting far out into the Atlantic.[2]

It is clear that such a diverse landscape, together with variations in climate and soil, will have had a profound effect upon the development of settlement types and settlement patterns. We should expect, for example, adaptations to different environments: to drumlin country, to lake and marsh or coastal sand-dune. We should also be aware of differing building styles and changes in materials according to their availability; the use of hazel rods or oak planks, drystone or sod walling. It is only then that we

**3** *Ireland: physical features.*

may begin to reconstruct a picture of early medieval settlement in Ireland.

## Social and political organization

To place the archaeological evidence for settlement in perspective, it is of equal importance to learn something of the social and political organization of Ireland in this period. We catch our first glimpse in a series of law tracts which were committed to writing during the seventh and eighth centuries. The product of a class of learned jurists, these texts are highly schematic, and it is not altogether clear to what extent the organization they describe is an ideal rather than a reality. It is also unclear how much applies to the period when they were written down and how much is, in fact, the enshrinement of older customary practices which had already gone out of use.[3]

The society depicted appears highly fragmented but at the same time there was some sense of Ireland as a wider community.[4] The land was divided into small units, each occupied by a *túath*, which may best be translated as a tribe.[5] A second element was the kin, which, at the beginning of the period, was the *derbfine*, and included all men who had shared a common agnatic great-grandfather. However, by the eighth century, the size of the kin had decreased from a four- to three-generation group or *gelfine* consisting of men with a common agnatic grandfather. The kin owned land jointly and it was responsible for the behaviour of its members. The Irish were also polygamous. A woman belonged to her father's or her husband's kin according to her marital status and the nature of the conjugal bond.

Hierarchy and status were all-important in Irish society as portrayed in the laws. Daily life was based upon complex personal relationships between lords and clients at every level. At the upper end of the scale there were three grades of king or *rí*: the king of the *túath*, the king of three or four *túatha*, and the king over kings. At this stage there was no king of all Ireland and the powers of kingship were comparatively limited. Below this were various noble grades, who included artists and craftsmen as well as warriors, the lowest grade of which had ten clients. Clients might be free or base. Free clients included several grades of farmer, the *bóaire* or strong farmer and the *ócaire* or small farmer, for example, who rented cattle from their lord, paid him food render and gave him personal service. The base client would

have worked his lord's land. At the bottom of the scale there were hereditary serfs, who were bound to the soil and could not leave their land, and slaves, who were the property of their lord.[6]

Recent scholarship,[7] based upon evidence from historical sources other than the law tracts, has shown that Irish society in the early middle ages was far from static: in fact, those who wrote down the laws may have done so in response to social change. There seems to have been a decline in tribal feeling and the importance of the *túath*. Instead we see the rise of powerful dynasties such as the Uí Néill in the north and the Éoganacht in the south who rapidly expanded their territorial claims at the expense of neighbouring kingdoms. In such circumstances petty kings became mere lords and the new dynastic kings, with the aid of their retinues, exercised increasingly wide powers. By the tenth century there were perhaps a dozen over-kingdoms but by the mid-twelfth century this number had been further reduced. The lower echelons of society were also changing. Amongst the common people the distinction between free and base client became blurred and there was an increase in the lower grades, perhaps because of a rise in the population.

## The nature of the evidence

There has been more work done on settlement than any other aspect of the archaeology of early medieval Ireland. However, we are still very far from obtaining a complete picture. The beginnings of an interest in the subject may be traced back to the second quarter of the nineteenth century when the Ordnance Survey of Ireland, in addition to compiling maps, set out to record archaeological monuments for the first time.[8] Unfortunately, the archaeological element of the survey was soon abandoned, but it had laid the foundations for antiquarian research well into the twentieth century. Two men should be mentioned in connection with early medieval settlement whose work is yet to be superseded. W.G. Wood-Martin made a detailed study of crannogs or lake-dwellings (published in 1886)[9] and, at the turn of the century, T.J. Westropp surveyed large numbers of ring-forts in western Ireland and attempted an assessment of their date, typology and structural features.[10]

The first major archaeological excavations on early medieval settlement sites took place in the 1930s and 1940s. The American Harvard expedition under the direction of Hugh Hencken dug the stone fort at Cahercommaun, Co. Clare, and a series of crannogs, including Lagore, Co. Meath. S.P. Ó Ríordáin and his colleagues excavated a variety of ring-forts, mainly in Co. Cork and Co. Limerick. These excavations produced a rich array of structures and artefacts which demonstrated the wealth of early medieval settlement archaeology. In Northern Ireland a great increase in the number of settlement sites investigated was fostered by the initiation of the Archaeological Survey of County Down in the 1950s[11] and this included the excavation of less prestigious sites which gave a better idea of the wide range of settlement evidence. Rescue archaeology also began around this time, mainly as a result of agricultural improvements which encouraged the destruction of archaeological sites, particularly ring-forts, which were beginning to lose the superstitious associations which had protected them.

Over the last 25 years settlement archaeology in Northern Ireland has been dominated by rescue considerations, though the response in the Republic has been much more limited. The results of minor excavations on sites immediately prior to or in the course of destruction have sometimes been difficult to assess, but more recent intensive excavation of threatened sites using modern scientific techniques has produced some very interesting results. In the Republic we are also beginning to see the fruits of survey in the recent publication of work on early medieval settlement sites in Co. Donegal, the Barony of Ikerrin in north-east Tipperary and the Dingle Peninsula of Co. Kerry.[12]

But the evidence for early medieval settlement archaeology remains extremely patchy. In some areas, particularly Co. Down and Co. Antrim, there have been a considerable number of excavations backed up by extensive archaeological survey. This means that it is possible to say quite a lot about variations in settlement types and settlement patterns over a relatively small area. However, comparatively little work has been done in Co. Clare, for example, since the time of Westropp, and what is typical of Co. Down and Co. Antrim is not necessarily typical of Co. Clare where the landscape is very different. The archaeologist should therefore be wary of using Co. Down and Co. Antrim to generalize about the whole of Ireland, though this will to a certain extent be inevitable where no other evidence is yet available.

## The problem of chronology

The establishment of an agreed chronology for the settlement archaeology of early medieval Ireland has been the cause of recurrent and often heated argument. Though the close dating of some sites is now, for the first time, becoming a reality, there is still a considerable way to go before there is a chance of solving many of the more complex issues. In the 1930s and 1940s, when there were few clear chronological markers and when scientific dating techniques were yet to be invented, archaeologists naturally turned to the documentary sources, especially the annals (terse accounts of events listed year by year), as a means of dating the sites they excavated. In particular, the crannog at Lagore, a site well-known in the annals as *Loch Gabair*, the seat of the kings of southern Brega, offered the possibility of close dating by comparison of the archaeological and historical evidence. The stratigraphy of the site, as interpreted by Hencken, closely mirrored the course of events described in the annals. Thus Lagore was a place of importance by the time a battle was recorded near the lake in 676 and the Viking raid of 934 signalled the final destruction of the crannog.[13] The dating of sites not mentioned in the sources was then achieved by comparison with the rich artefactual assemblage from Lagore. Alternatively, if decorated metalwork was present (for which some kind of chronological framework had been established based on a few fixed points such as its appearance in ninth-century Viking graves in Norway) the date range might be narrowed to one or two centuries. For example, Hencken dated Cahercommaun to the ninth century on the basis of the decorated metalwork which included a silver brooch found in one of the souterrains. This was supported by the general similarity of the artefacts to those from Lagore.[14]

More recently, there has been persistent criticism of such methods of assigning sites to the early middle ages. Firstly, modern research on the annals has shown that they are not to be totally relied on, especially for the period before the late seventh century, and that they are subject to chronological and scribal errors as well as later interpolations.[15] Equally, sites could have been occupied for some considerable time before or after they are mentioned in the documents. This has made archaeologists wary of combining historical and archaeological evidence, a fear which has sometimes led them to ignore the former entirely.

Secondly, there has been criticism of the use of decorated metalwork as a dating tool since the chronology for it has largely been established using art-historical comparison because the fixed chronological markers are so few (see p. 133). In particular, the tendency to assign large amounts of metalwork to the eighth century has led to the suggestion that there is something radically wrong with early medieval Irish chronology.[16] Thirdly, the improvement of archaeological techniques has given rise to a reassessment of the original interpretation of some earlier excavations. The stratigraphy of Lagore, for example, has recently been the subject of a much-needed reappraisal.[17]

The problems facing those working on other periods of Irish archaeology have also helped to sow the seeds of doubt, especially the virtual absence of late Bronze Age and Iron Age settlement sites. This has encouraged a tendency to push types of site common in the early middle ages, such as ring-forts and crannogs, backwards in an attempt to fill the void. The controversy which has surrounded Cahercommaun is a good illustration of this. Barry Raftery rightly criticized the dating of the site to the ninth century largely on the strength of the silver brooch, especially since its stratigraphical context did not rule out a later deposition. However he went on to imply that, since he interpreted Cahercommaun as a hill-fort and since many of the artefacts would not be out of place in a much earlier period, it might be Iron Age and he suggested that 'a number of other Irish sites, hitherto dated to the second half of the first millennium AD may well have to be back-dated by at least half a millennium'.[18] At the other end of the period there were also those who suggested extensive use of ring-forts into the later middle ages in areas outside Anglo-Norman control.[19]

This controversy, leading sometimes to widely differing dates for the same site, has caused considerable confusion. But to what extent are such doubts justified? In retrospect it seems that, while early medieval Irish settlement chronology will require considerable refinement in the future, the radical redating which has been suggested by some is largely a red herring. As far as the documentary sources are concerned, once the problems are realized and the danger of too slavish a correlation between the history and archaeology avoided, there seems little reason to doubt that particular sites were in use approximately during the period when they are mentioned in the annals and not several centuries before. The close correlation suggested by excavation between events described by Bede and the archaeological stratigraphy of the royal estate buildings at Yeavering in Northumbria in the sixth and seventh centuries[20] has demonstrated the potential for combining historical and archaeological research in the early medieval period in England and offers an interesting model for future work; but whether such close co-operation between the two disciplines is possible with the Irish evidence is unknown.

Our knowledge of the early medieval artefactual assemblage has also improved and, though sites cannot be closely dated from the finds alone, both decorated metalwork, and now pottery, found in stratified contexts will give a good indication. The recognition on Irish sites of imported pottery from the Mediterranean and France, which can be dated comparatively closely within the fifth- to early eighth-century period, has been an important breakthrough (see p. 68). For example, five sherds of E ware have recently been identified as very probably from the earliest occupation horizon at Lagore[21] suggesting a date in the early medieval period rather than before for the foundation of the site. In the north-east native souterrain ware (see p. 73) is common on ring-fort and other sites, and in some instances its stratigraphical relationship has shown that it came into use after imported pottery had ceased to be used. At Rathmullan, Co. Down, for example, E ware was found only in the earliest occupation level while the upper layers produced a considerable quantity of souterrain pottery but no E ware.[22] More generally, the increasing number of ring-forts and other sites excavated over the last 30 years, though often individually of limited importance, together lend support to the chronology of earlier excavations. The artefactual assemblages from these sites, which frequently include imported pottery and/or souterrain ware, are very similar to that of Lagore, though usually much less rich.[23] Thus it is becoming possible to identify other artefacts as characteristic of early medieval sites: copper-alloy and iron ringed pins, lignite bracelet fragments, double-sided antler combs, and lathe-turned bone or stone spindle whorls are just a few examples of very common finds.

Scientific dating techniques are also beginning to play their part and now offer the exciting prospect of refining the chronological framework very considerably in the future. Radiocarbon dating has been used surprisingly little in Ireland on sites of potentially early medieval date; the first example was the ring-fort at Raheenamadra, Co. Limerick in 1960–1.[24] However, where samples have been taken, they have fairly consistently provided a date range during the second half of the first millennium AD rather than earlier or later. For example, three radiocarbon determinations from the ring-fort at Killyliss, Co. Tyrone, (cal. AD 580–780, 680–990 and 770–995) have suggested a late sixth- to tenth-century date.[25] Problems with the accuracy of radiocarbon dating are well-known and this has led to experiments with other techniques. Of particular interest for early medieval Irish archaeology is the rapid development of the dendrochronological programme at Belfast conducted by M.G.L. Baillie and J. Pilcher. The Irish tree-ring chronology is now complete back to 5289 BC and for the first time it is becoming possible to provide precise calendrical dates for sites with waterlogged oak where timbers with a sufficient number of rings survive and where at least part of the sapwood is still present.[26] For example, the post palisade surrounding the crannog at Island MacHugh, Co. Tyrone, has been dated to the beginning of the seventh century and roof timbers from the souterrain at Coolcran ring-fort, Co. Fermanagh to AD 822 ± 9.[27] Such precise dates from waterlogged sites are nothing short of revolutionary, and there is also hope for sites without waterlogged wood, since new high-precision radiocarbon dates can normally be calibrated to within a century.[28]

All in all we are now in a position to begin to construct a chronological framework for early medieval Irish settlement archaeology. This cannot be so very different from that suggested by early excavations, but it is now backed up by much more historical and archaeological data, an increased understanding of the artefacts, and new scientific dating techniques. This leaves little to support a radically earlier dating for sites like Cahercommaun where the majority of artefacts suggest early medieval occupation; the stone axes, the saddle querns and perhaps some of the large number of rubbing and polishing stones[29] are far more likely to be remnants of earlier prehistoric activity on the same site.

## Ring-forts

Ring-forts, or enclosed homesteads, are the most characteristic type of Irish early medieval settlement. They are also the commonest field monument in Ireland. It is impossible to calculate precise numbers but area surveys give some idea of their abundance. For example, 1,300 have been recorded in Co. Down and in Co. Donegal, a much less fertile area, 684. In a recent survey of the Barony of Ikerrin, north-east Tipperary, an area of 28,328 hectares (70,000 acres), ring-forts made up 72 per cent of the monuments listed, 205 examples in all.[30] Many ring-forts were first recorded on large-scale Ordnance Survey maps in the last century. While a significant proportion of these survive intact, many others, though still traceable on the ground, have been severely modified; some survive merely as crop marks on aerial photographs, others not at all. In Co. Kerry it has been estimated that as many as 44 per cent of those marked on the Ordnance Survey maps may have been destroyed, though the record appears better in Co. Fermanagh where it has been estimated that less than 10 per cent have been lost. In the past ring-forts were partially protected by local superstition which tended to preserve their enclosures, though not necessarily their interiors, from cultivation (4). However, loss of superstition, and the fact that ring-forts are frequently sited on good agricultural land, has meant their regular destruction in recent times. Their very abundance means that few are protected monuments. The picture is not entirely gloomy. Many new discoveries of ring-forts are now being reported, mainly as a result of aerial survey which reveals them as crop-mark sites. In Co. Louth, for example, the number of ring-forts recorded has been increased by 35.5 per cent in addition to those on the Ordnance Survey maps as a result of the detailed study of aerial photographs.[31]

Only a tiny fraction of known ring-forts has been excavated, probably somewhere in the region of 200 sites. The evidence of ring-forts gained from survey alone is, inevitably, severely limited and many features can only be clarified by excavation. Superficial observation can be positively misleading. The excavation of a suspected ring-fort at Craigboy, Co. Down, revealed that it was probably a Bronze Age ring cairn while another at Gallanagh, Co. Tyrone, was a tree-ring, the product of nineteenth-century landscaping.[32]

**4** *Univallate earthen ring-fort, Lismore Fort, Smarmore, Co. Louth (Copyright: Cambridge University Committee for Aerial Photography).*

### Terminology and classification

Not everyone would agree that 'ring-fort' is the correct term to describe the great variety of enclosed homesteads it encompasses, since their defensive role is disputed and they are certainly not forts in the accepted military sense. However, it has come to be regarded as the most acceptable term because of more general problems in classification. In the early middle ages such sites were known by a number of different names: *ráth, líos, caiseal, cathair* and *dún,* elements which are frequently incorporated into modern place-names. *Ráth* and *líos* seem to refer to earthen ring-forts, *ráth* indicating the enclosing bank and *líos* the open space within. *Ráth* is a common place-name element in east and south-east Ireland and is also found in the west and south-west, though it is rare

in the north; *líos,* however, is infrequently found in the south and south-east, but is common elsewhere. *Caiseal* and *cathair* refer to stone-walled ring-forts. *Caiseal* is commonly found in the north-west while *cathair* is the usual term in the west and south-west. *Dún,* a less usual term implying a site of some prestige, is found throughout Ireland. It applies not only to prominently sited ring-forts but also to hill-forts and promontory forts which are not ring-forts at all. Some archaeologists have attempted to utilize these terms, particularly the anglicized forms 'rath' and 'cashel', to describe particular types of enclosed homesteads, but this classification is not entirely satisfactory since the boundaries between the different groups are not always clear-cut.[33]

There have been various attempts to classify ring-forts based on the number, composition and strength of the enclosure(s), the size of the area enclosed and the siting of the monument[34] but, unfortunately, none of these are completely

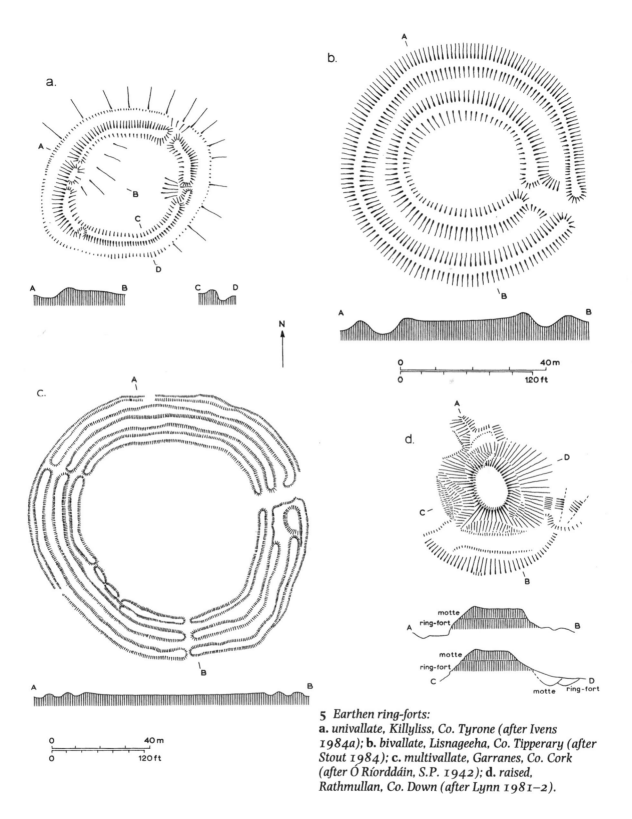

**5** *Earthen ring-forts:*
**a.** *univallate, Killyliss, Co. Tyrone (after Ivens 1984a);* **b.** *bivallate, Lisnageeha, Co. Tipperary (after Stout 1984);* **c.** *multivallate, Garranes, Co. Cork (after Ó Ríordáin, S.P. 1942);* **d.** *raised, Rathmullan, Co. Down (after Lynn 1981–2).*

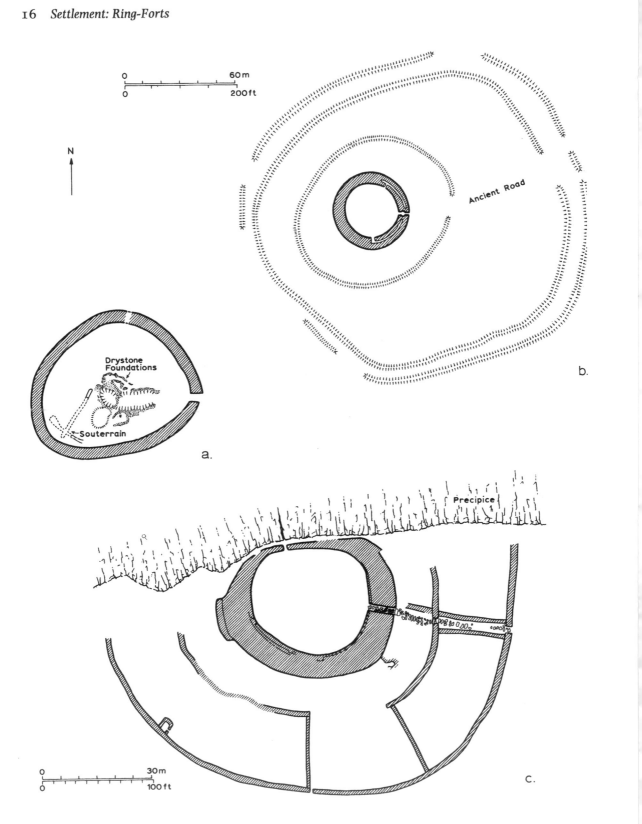

0    60 m
0    200 ft

N

Drystone
Foundations

Souterrain

a.

Ancient Road

b.

Precipice

0    30 m
0    100 ft

c.

7 *Stone-walled ring-forts:*
**a.** *Drumena, Co. Down (after Archaeological Survey of Northern Ireland 1966);* **b.** *Griannán of Aileach, Co. Donegal (after Lacy et al 1983);*
**c.** *Cahercommaun, Co. Clare (after Hencken 1938).*

the more general chronological problems already discussed. Were ring-forts the product of a long tradition, perhaps stretching back into the late Neolithic or early Bronze Age? Did they come into use during the Iron Age or were they an innovation at the beginning of the early middle ages? Were they a native invention or were they introduced from outside as a result of contacts with Britain or the Continent? These are just some of the questions which have been raised. There are no definitive answers but a discussion of the evidence does suggest that some solutions seem more likely than others.

The possibility that ring-forts formed a continuous settlement tradition from the late Neolithic or early Bronze Age onwards arose because a small number of southern Irish sites resembling stone ring-forts have produced very early dating evidence. At Knockadoon, Lough Gur, Co. Limerick, excavation of stone enclosures J, K and L revealed settlement and burial activity dated by pottery and radiocarbon to the late Neolithic and early Bronze Age and two stone enclosures from Aughinish Island, Co. Clare, produced artefacts from the late Bronze/early Iron Age overlap.[47] At Carrigillihy, Co. Cork, the excavator dated the first phase, a curvilinear stone enclosure with an oval stone hut, to the Bronze Age on the basis of a bronze awl and some rather nondescript pottery which appeared similar to that from Knockadoon, and a mid-Bronze Age date has recently been confirmed by radiocarbon. The second phase, however, a sub-square house built in the ruins of the enclosure and separated from Phase 1 by only a thin sterile layer, would seem, on artefactual evidence, to be early medieval.[48]

Evidence from other sites is less convincing. Ring-fort 5 at Cush, Co. Limerick, which was originally interpreted as earlier than the Bronze Age cremation urns found within it, may now be seen as similar to Letterkeen, Co. Mayo, where the site of a Bronze Age cemetery was later used for a ring-fort. The recent suggestion that Cush is Iron Age on the basis of the integration of the ring-forts with the field system and adjacent tumuli would seem to be equally unfounded since the artefacts,

apart from some residual prehistoric material, are of early medieval type.[49] Similarly, the prehistoric finds from Carraig Aille 1 and 2, Co. Limerick, like those from Cahercommaun, may be seen in terms of pre-ring-fort activity. The Rath of Feerwore, Co. Galway, has often been seen as Iron Age, but the stratigraphy suggests that the ring-fort overlies the Iron Age material which is perhaps associated with the nearby Turoe stone. A short cist containing a cremation, which was originally thought to have been dug into the ring-fort bank, is now interpreted as probably from under it. Thus there is now no proof of an Iron Age date for the ring-fort phase on this site.[50] Possibly the earliest datable ring-fort is the Rath of Synods at Tara, Co. Meath. Full assessment of this important site must await the final publication of the excavation report but in its earliest phases the site seems to have been an Iron Age ritual complex comparable with Navan, Co. Armagh, and Dun Ailinne, Co. Kildare. This was later replaced by a ring-fort which appears to have had stratified Roman artefacts dating to the second century AD.[51]

Caulfield has suggested that some ring-forts (and also crannogs) in southern Ireland were Iron Age settlements of a non-La Tène culture, since distinctive La Tène artefacts are confined to the north. The expansion of ring-forts throughout Ireland would therefore coincide with the political upheavals of the fourth and fifth centuries AD when Uí Néill influence spread northwards and eastwards.[52] But, as we have seen, although there may have been some enclosures which resembled ring-forts in prehistoric Ireland, there is no reason to accept their continuity from the late Neolithic onwards. With the possible exception of the Rath of Synods at Tara, evidence for their Iron Age use is also practically non-existent.

By contrast, Lynn has complained that the problems of the Irish Iron Age have distracted attention from the period of special interest, the fifth and sixth centuries AD, when ring-forts, sometimes dated by imported pottery, were becoming the characteristic settlement type. He has suggested that improved iron technology and new farming methods reached Ireland as a result of increased contact with late and sub-Roman Britain and that the evolution of the ring-fort is somehow a product of this.[53] This is an attractive theory since what little evidence we have would tend to support it. Pollen analysis has demonstrated a rapid growth in agriculture around the beginning of the early middle ages, probably as a result of the introduction of the coulter plough from Roman Britain (see p. 62). Ring-forts are certainly very common in the drumlin country of the Ulster border where the soils could only have been exploited by a heavier plough.[54]

Whether ring-forts are a native development is unclear, though it is now possible to glean something of their forerunners by examining pre-ring-fort activity. Evidence of occupation under ring-forts is quite common though, unfortunately, the remains of specific structures are rare. Indications of an open settlement may be suggested at Croft Road, Co. Down, and at Ballyhenry 2, Co. Antrim, where the remains of a substantial later prehistoric curvilinear building were uncovered.[55] Settlements surrounded by palisades or more flimsy wooden fences also seem likely. At Oldcourt, Co. Cork, there were traces of a feature under the bank which might be interpreted as a palisade trench. A small group of stake-holes beneath the ring-fort interior at Lisdoo, Co. Fermanagh, might be seen in terms of a hill-top palisade and at Coolcran, Co. Fermanagh, a line of stake-holes may have formed a perimeter fence. Some ring-forts were preceded by a simple ditched enclosure. At Millockstown, Co. Louth, for example, the earliest phase of occupation was enclosed by a narrow ditch approximately 60 m (197 ft) in diameter.[56] Sites such as these, if they had not been overlaid by a more obvious monument, would normally leave little mark upon the landscape and are therefore unlikely to be found except, perhaps, through aerial photography. But the enclosure element which seems to be indicated by these palisades and small ditches may have increased in importance with the resulting evolution of the ring-fort. It remains more difficult to speculate upon the relationship between ring-forts and hill-forts, especially the stone forts of western Ireland traditionally ascribed to the Iron Age.

Alternatively, it has recently been suggested that a possible origin for ring-forts in comparable sites in Roman Britain is worthy of closer scrutiny.[57] Parallels were originally sought with Iron Age farms in southern England such as Little Woodbury.[58] But, as a result of the increased attention given to Iron Age and native Romano-British farmsteads in recent years, it is obvious that the best parallels are to be made with sites in parts of western and northern Britain where Roman influence was weaker. In the south-west the occupation of settlements called *rounds*

between the first century BC and the sub-Roman period is especially interesting. These are farmsteads enclosed by a curvilinear bank and ditch with a varying number of round huts in the interior and sometimes a *fogou*, or underground passage, the equivalent of the Irish souterrain. There are also cellular stone courtyard houses, sometimes enclosed by drystone walls, which may be stone versions of rounds.[59] In south-west Wales late Iron Age and early Roman period enclosed farmsteads, such as Walesland Rath and Whitton Lodge, may also be compared with ring-forts, and there are now some indications of the possible re-occupation of such sites after the Roman withdrawal.[60] In south-west Scotland the excavation of Boonies, a farmstead constructed at the beginning of the Roman period, provides another parallel. Further north *dúns*, or stone-walled enclosures, which were constructed during the Iron Age and later, perhaps as late as the early middle ages, may be the equivalent of Irish cashels.[61]

The difficulty arises, however, when we try to ascertain the significance of these comparisons. It would be tempting to think that the enclosed homesteads of western Britain did influence the evolution of Irish ring-forts, a theory which is strengthened by the known close contacts either side of the Irish Sea at the end of the Roman period. But such a hypothesis remains difficult to prove at present. It is equally likely that the enclosed homesteads of western Britain and Ireland are the product of similar agricultural advances and a comparable social structure.

There has also been considerable controversy about how long ring-forts remained in use. Barrett and Graham expressed the opinion that ring-forts were not only the characteristic settlement type of the early middle ages, but that they also continued to be constructed and remained an important element in the rural settlement pattern in the centuries after the Anglo-Norman invasion, particularly in areas where there was little Anglo-Norman influence. Indeed, in areas of Anglo-Norman settlement such as Co. Meath, ring-forts may have been systematically destroyed.[62] On reflection, however, there seems little to support such a view. While it is true that native settlements datable to the centuries after the Anglo-Norman invasion have remained elusive, with the resulting concentration on colonial plantations, excavations of ring-forts have yet to produce substantial evidence for later medieval occupation.

In areas of Anglo-Norman settlement, such as

Co. Down, some ring-fort sites were re-utilized to build motte-and-bailey castles or ringworks; others may have been taken over for non-military purposes. For example, the final thirteenth-century phase at Ballynarry included a stone structure which might be interpreted as an English-style hall building, perhaps the residence of some Anglo-Norman bailiff.[63] Evidence of continued native use of ring-forts in Ulster is slight, but equally there is nothing to suggest their deliberate destruction. In some instances the final phase of native ring-fort occupation may have extended into the thirteenth century, or a ring-fort originally in use considerably earlier may have been reoccupied. But often only a few sherds of everted-rim cooking pot or Anglo-Norman green-glazed or coarse ware, sometimes unstratified, bear witness to such later activity. Occasionally, a little more survives; the secondary occupation at Ballyfounder consisted of a small rectangular timber-framed building, a few other post-holes and occupation debris dated to the thirteenth century by Anglo-Norman pottery.[64] However, there is no evidence of ring-fort use in this area after the thirteenth century and no indication of ring-fort construction after the Anglo-Norman conquest. In some cases the issue has been further complicated by the failure to distinguish ring-forts from Anglo-Norman ringworks, even after excavation. For example, the problematic site of Pollardstown, Co. Kildare, which was originally thought to be a ring-fort, but, where the artefactual assemblage was of twelfth- to fourteenth-century date, has now been reinterpreted as an Anglo-Norman ringwork.[65]

In parts of western Ireland, for example Co. Clare, where there was little Anglo-Norman penetration, it remains more difficult to tell whether ring-forts continued in use during the later middle ages since so little excavation has taken place. At Béal Ború, it was shown that the ring-fort was occupied during the eleventh century on the evidence of two Hiberno-Norse coins, and a documentary reference suggests that it may have been destroyed in 1116.[66] However, as a result of limited excavations at Thady's Fort and Garrynamona, it has been claimed that ring-forts continued to be built until the end of the middle ages and, indeed, as late as the early modern period.[67] While aspects of the stratigraphy of these sites remain unclear, at Thady's Fort at least the finds, which were of late medieval or early modern date, were associated, not with the construction of

the ring-fort, but with the house, which is obviously late. Nevertheless there remains the possibility that some ring-forts were occupied long after the majority went out of use. Cahermacnaghten, for example, was used by the O'Davoren family as a law school during the seventeenth century.[68] Other ring-forts on the Burren remained the sites of farms into modern times, but there is nothing to prove that they have any direct relationship with the stone enclosures adjacent or surrounding them.

Evidence for the occupation of ring-forts significantly after the Anglo-Norman invasion is therefore slight. While excavations in the west may bring new material to light which could radically change such an interpretation, this seems unlikely in Ulster, where more extensive excavation has taken place. It is interesting to note that place-name evidence suggests that elements such as *ráth* and *caiseal* were losing currency throughout Ireland from the thirteenth century onwards to be replaced by other native habitation terms such as *baile*, meaning homestead.[69]

### Siting, enclosures and entrances

Most ring-forts functioned primarily as farms, so suitable land was a major factor in their siting. A recent survey of the relationship between ring-forts and particular soil types in the Barony of Ikerrin, Co. Tipperary, has shown that peats and shallow rendzina soils were almost completely avoided because they were of poor quality. A related factor was altitude. Land near sea-level and valley bottoms does not seem to have been favoured. In Ikerrin 49 per cent of the ring-forts were found to be between 91.5 m (300 ft) and 152 m (500 ft) OD and another 37 per cent between 152 m (500 ft) and 214.5 m (700 ft) OD but very few were found above this altitude. Nearer the coast the picture is slightly different. In Skibbereen, Co. Cork, most ring-forts were sited on good agricultural land between 30.05 m (100 ft) and 122 m (400 ft) OD and only 20 per cent were found above this height. Although no precise figures exist for Co. Down, a glance at the survey shows a similar distribution, with stone-walled ring-forts making up a large proportion of sites above 152 m (500 ft) OD.[70]

While it is clear that a prominent position with a good view of the surrounding countryside was favoured for the siting of ring-forts, defence does not always seem to have been a primary consideration. Typical locations are the summits of

drumlins or other small hillocks and promontories, but a considerable number are found on
hillslopes or in open country overlooked by higher
ground. Sometimes their position was of strategic
importance. For example, the large multivallate
earthen ring-fort at Garranes, Co. Cork, was
probably located with reference to the route
across the hills linking the Bandon, Bride and Lee
valleys; and Béal Ború, Co. Clare, is situated on a
gravel spur overlooking the point where the
Shannon issues from Lough Derg, an important
river crossing.[71] In many instances prestige must
also have played its part; some ring-forts, particularly raised and platform raths and some cashels,
are visible from a considerable distance.

As we have seen, ring-fort enclosures are characterized by their number and the great variety of
their construction, the details of which can frequently only be recovered through excavation.
Building materials must usually have been what
was immediately available. Ring-fort banks were
primarily composed of upcast from the ditch.
Sometimes they appear merely to be of a simple
dump construction, but in many instances the
make-up is more complicated. At Garryduff 1, Co.
Cork, a univallate ring-fort, a particularly interesting sequence has been established. First, the line
of the ditch was marked and the turf stripped and
piled along the inner edge of the cutting.
Secondly, sandstone was excavated from the ditch
and built up to form a flat rock-chip platform at
the base of the bank. Above this a layer of soil
with rock chips was formed which was trampled
in the construction process. An inner revetment
wall of stones was then built against which the
bank material was heaped and an outer revetment wall was added along parts of the circuit to
prevent the bank from slipping into the ditch.
More trample layers indicate that the height of the
bank was built up in stages. It finally measured at
least 4.1 m (13 ft 6 in) wide and survived to a
height of over 1.25 m (4 ft). The outer ditch was
wide and shallow with some traces of a counter-
scarp bank.[72]

Enclosure banks with inner and/or outer stone
revetments similar to those just mentioned occur
frequently. Turf walls could also be constructed to
fulfil the same purpose and traces have sometimes
been found as, for example, at Raheenamadra, Co.
Limerick.[73] Revetments of timber, wooden palisades and fences are more difficult to detect but
sufficient evidence has accumulated to indicate
that they must have been relatively common. At

Knockea, Co. Limerick, inner and outer palisade
slots were excavated with the bank material piled
between them; the excavator has suggested that
the whole structure might have been consolidated
by connecting horizontal timbers passing through
the core of the bank. At Narraghmore, Co. Kildare,
a multivallate ring-fort, a trench was found along
the inner slope of the inner bank which had held a
series of large posts kept in place by packing
stones. A stockade of this kind would have held
the bank in position and added an extra measure
of protection. A similar palisade defined by single
post-holes rather than a continuous slot has been
excavated at Castleskreen 2, Co. Down, and at
Drumee, Co. Fermanagh, a post-hole on the inner
edge of the trench indicated that further diagonal
bracing must have been required to keep the
vertical timbers in place and stop the palisade
from bulging under the weight of the bank
material. At Lismahon, Co. Down, a raised rath,
the mound was held in position by a complex
timber revetment with internal and external
bracing, and at Corliss, Co. Armagh, a substantial
wooden fence was erected to prevent the bank
from sliding into the ditch.[74]

Fences were also sometimes placed along the
top of the ring-fort bank to increase the height.
Usually the only indication is a line of post-holes
along the top of the bank, as at Lissachiggel, Co.
Louth, but at Killyliss, Co. Tyrone, the actual
fence, a light wattle hurdle woven round a framework of split-oak rails, round poles and saplings,
was found because it had fallen into the waterlogged ditch. The legal texts suggest that such
fences may have been topped by a crest of blackthorn, and possible archaeological evidence for an
enclosure bank surmounted by a brushwood fence
or hedge has been excavated in the first phase of
the raised rath at Gransha, Co. Down.[75]

On the whole ring-fort ditches have received
less attention. The fact that they are frequently
waterlogged has, in the past, proved an obstacle to
excavation. But, with more modern techniques,
the potential importance of the environmental
evidence, together with the chance preservation
of organic artefacts, is beginning to be realized.
Ditches vary greatly in size and shape; flat-
bottomed, 'U'-shaped and 'V'-shaped sections are
all represented. In most cases they seldom rise
above 3 m (10 ft) in width and 2 m (6 ft 7 in) in
depth. Some, however, are more formidable: for
example the inner ditch of the bivallate ring-fort
at Lisdoo, Co. Fermanagh, was 7.5–8 m (24 ft

7 in–26 ft 3 in) wide and nearly 2 m (6 ft 7 in) deep while that at Lissue, Co. Antrim, was 5 m (16 ft 5 in) wide and 2.2 m (7 ft 3 in) deep.[76] There is rarely a berm between the bank and ditch and frequently the ditch gradually filled up with slip. Sometimes there is evidence of recutting once the ditch had silted up as at Ballypalady 2, Co. Antrim. Occasionally more unusual features have been recovered. A narrow slot had been cut at the bottom of the ditch at Knockea, perhaps to aid drainage. At Killyliss organic material was interpreted as a wattle lining intended as a revetment to prevent slippage, and the presence of watermites and caddis-fly larvae in the fill demonstrated that there had been open water in the bottom of the ditch throughout the period of occupation.[77]

There have also been fewer excavations of stone-walled ring-forts. The majority of simpler cashel enclosures may be represented by Drumena, Co. Down (**6, 7a**), where the wall is substantial, 2.7–3.6 m (8 ft 10 in–11 ft 10 in) thick, carefully constructed, with an inner and outer drystone facing with larger stones in the lower courses and a rubble core.[78] However, some stone-walled ring-forts, particularly in the west, have much more impressive enclosures with a variety of associated features. For example, at Carraig Aille 2, Co. Limerick, excavation revealed a wall approximately 4 m (13 ft) thick and surviving to a maximum height of just over 1 m (3 ft 3 in). But it was obvious that the enclosure had originally been considerably higher, perhaps 2–3 m (6 ft 7 in–9 ft 10 in), since excavation showed that six flights of steps had been constructed along the inner wall face to give access to some kind of wall walk near the top. More complete evidence of these features survives at the Grianán of Aileach, Co. Donegal (**7b**), but there was considerable nineteenth-century reconstruction and it is difficult to tell precisely how much is original. Here the exterior wall face is battered and the interior rises in three terraces to a height of approximately 5 m (16 ft 5 in). Access is provided by stone stairways set into the wall of each terrace. The Grianán of Aileach also has two passages built within the thickness of the cashel wall which possibly fulfil a similar function to souterrains (see below). At Leacanabuaile, Co. Kerry (**9d**), access to the souterrain was obtained through an aperture in the floor of a wall chamber. At Cahercommaun (**7c**) there are three stone enclosures, the outer two linked by radial walls. The inner is much more massive than the outer two and has various

wall niches rather than wall passages and two wall walks on the inner face but no evidence of steps. Perhaps access to the terraces was gained by ladders. At some point a bulge had appeared on the western side of the outer wall face and a buttress had been built to prevent its collapse. Vertical masonry joints are a characteristic of the outer enclosures. Whether these represent the work of different labour gangs is unclear. A similar feature was noted at Carraig Aille 2 but, because the joints were not visible through the whole thickness of the wall, it was thought to be purely fortuitous.[79]

Turning to ring-fort entrances, again the emphasis on defence is variable. It is interesting that there is a clear preference for orientation towards the east whatever the lie of the land. Where statistics are available it can be shown that almost two-thirds face approximately east if slight variations to the north-east and south-east are included.[80] The most usual surface evidence is a passage through the bank or stone wall and a causeway across the ditch, but excavation can produce some indications of constructional detail. For example, at Oldcourt, Co. Cork, a univallate earthen ring-fort, the entrance consisted of a passageway under 2 m (6 ft 7 in) wide through the bank surfaced with a rough cobbled paving, presumably to minimize the build-up of mud. On the south side there was a short palisade trench indicating a timber revetment to prevent the bank from slipping; to the north a stake-hole suggested the position of a wooden gate. The passage then broadened onto the causeway, approximately 3 m (9 ft 10 in) wide made up of large boulders and clay which had been built across the continuous ditch.[81] However, some entrances were more formidable. At Garryduff 1 there was a system of four substantial post-holes linked by palisade trenches which narrowed the passage to form a strong asymmetrical entranceway closed by a wooden gate. The excavator suggested that such a structure would have been sufficient to support a wooden gate-tower, perhaps similar to that which has been interpreted as forming part of the post-Roman defences at the hill-fort of South Cadbury, Somerset in south-west England. At Duneight, Co. Antrim, a palisade trench 14.95 m (49 ft) long was revealed which guarded the approach to the causeway across the inner ditch to prevent outflanking between the inner and outer enclosures.[82] The entranceways excavated at the multivallate ring-forts of Garranes and Ballycatteen, Co. Cork, are particularly impressive. The better preserved example at Garranes was defended by up to five wooden gates, though not all of these were necessarily in use at the same time, and the passage through the inner bank was further strengthened by palisade slots which narrowed the entrance and prevented slippage. At Ballycatteen the passageway was flanked by a stone revetment on one side, a timber palisade on the other. The elaborate double gateway through the inner bank was linked to a timber revetment set against the inner bank face and, like Garryduff I, it would have been sufficiently strong to have supported some kind of superstructure.[83] Occasionally other features survive. At Seacash, Co. Antrim, the causeway across the ditch had been widened at a late stage in its occupation or, perhaps, even after abandonment. Eight oak posts were set on the eastern side of the causeway and the intervening space was then filled with brushwood. Evidence for a rare example of a wooden bridge across the ditch rather than the usual causeway is preserved at Lissue, Co. Antrim.[84]

The major question which arises from this consideration of siting, enclosures and entrances is the extent to which ring-forts may be regarded as defended homesteads. Certainly, the majority of simple univallate ring-forts would have been unable to withstand any concerted attack. The enclosures seem to have been primarily designed to protect the inhabitants from robbers and marauders and to keep out wild animals, such as wolves. In some instances settlement continued on sites where the enclosure was in considerable disrepair and at Carraig Aille 2 occupation extended beyond the enclosure, access being provided by a gap in the wall, and parts of it were even built over. Environmental evidence from Seacash suggests that the ditch became overhung by trees and bushes, the resulting shade a haven for primroses, and that it quickly silted up, the high phosphate content indicating that it was probably used for the disposal of rubbish.[85]

However, a small proportion of univallate ring-forts, the more impressive cashels and larger multivallate sites do seem to have had a greater concern for defence, probably because the inhabitants were wealthier. Where excavation has taken place, the sites with considerable regard for defence are those with unusually rich artefacts. For example, at Garranes, a likely royal site, and at Garryduff I, there was extensive evidence for ornamental metal-working which may have led

to the need for increased protection. The enclosures and entrances described on these sites could undoubtedly have withstood a sudden attack and there was probably little need for protection against a prolonged offensive; weapons are rare finds on ring-fort sites. It is also likely, because of the highly-stratified nature of early medieval Irish society, that it was important to demonstrate power, prestige and wealth. For the upper echelons one of the most visible means of displaying these was by constructing, with the aid of base-client and slave labour, an imposing residence set in a prominent position with formidable enclosures and a highly-fortified entrance.

### Houses

The difficulties encountered in the search for associated ring-fort structures during earlier excavations are well expressed by S.P. Ó Ríordáin's description of Garranes: 'The areas excavated in the interior of the fort revealed numerous post-holes, very varied as to depth and diameter, but in no case was it possible to recover the plan of the houses which these post-holes represented'.[86] The eastern house at Uisneach, Co. Westmeath, is one of the few examples of a well-preserved structure from an early excavation.[87] Even with modern techniques, the evidence for internal structures is frequently fragmentary, partly because of subsequent disturbance, but usually because the buildings, which were often of wattles or planks, have left little trace in the archaeological record. However, sufficient material has now been accumulated, including a few unusually well-preserved examples, to enable the recognition of at least two radically different building plans and to make some kind of chronological distinction between them. There is much less evidence for the overall layout of ring-fort interiors, mainly because their total excavation is rare, but chance discoveries do give some idea of the range of possibilities.

Many ring-fort structures which functioned as domestic dwellings were round wicker or post-and-wattle buildings (8) with no separate roof supports. Sometimes traces of the base of the walling survive, particularly if the structure is waterlogged or has been destroyed by fire, but sometimes the only clue to the original ground-plan is a shallow curvilinear drainage gully which had been dug to catch the drops of rain from the eaves. The central structure at Dressogagh Rath, Co. Armagh, is a good example of a circular post-

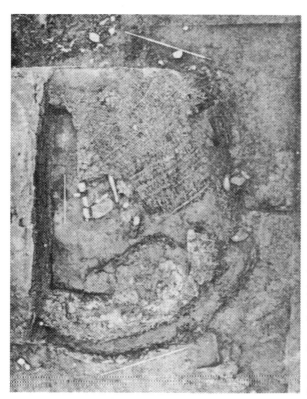

**8** *Deer Park Farms, Co. Antrim. In the main part of the picture are the well-preserved remains of a waterlogged round house (Structure Eta). At the bottom is a double row of wicker walling and at the top the inner wall has collapsed inwards. In the centre of the house is a hearth with traces of a bedding area against the wall to the bottom. The jambs of the communicating door to an adjacent round house (Structure Theta) may be seen on the right. These waterlogged remains contrast sharply with the stake-holes and post-holes which are all that survive of a later round house at the left of the picture (Crown copyright, reproduced with the permission of the Controller of Her Majesty's Stationery Office).*

and-wattle house in two phases with an adjacent curvilinear annexe (**9a**). During excavation the first features of the house and annexe to emerge were the drainage gullies, 100–250mm (4–9¾ in) deep with steep sides and flat bottoms; hearths were also located towards the centre of each structure. Then very faint traces of two shallow 'V'-sectioned slots were distinguished delineating successive phases of the walls of the house approximately 7 m (23 ft) in diameter, but no indications of walling were found in the annexe. These slots were punctuated by post-holes approximately 1 m (3 ft 3 in) apart, and enough charred remains survived to show that the walls had been built of wickerwork panels held in place between spaced posts with the bottoms of the panels set in the slots. Although the excavator suggested that the roof might have been supported by a central post, in the light of subsequent excavations, it seems more likely that it would have simply rested on the tops of the walls.[88]

Variations on this theme have been uncovered elsewhere. For example, at Grange, Co. Limerick, traces of a single wattle hut approximately 5 m (16 ft 5 in) in diameter were excavated. It had stood on a clay platform and indications of the ground-plan survived as a circular band of colour on the clay surface. The hut had been destroyed by fire and the only remains were fragments of charred wood and burnt clay which, it was suggested, were the collapsed wattle walls. The entrance to the north-west was marked by a gap with a charred lintel or threshold timber.[89] Recent excavations of a raised rath at Deer Park Farms, Co. Antrim, have revealed a complex series of phases and structures. The five wicker round houses in the Phase 1 univallate ring-fort, datable to the seventh and eighth centuries, were particularly well-preserved because of waterlogging. Structure Eta (**8**), which faced east towards the entrance, had an internal diameter of approximately 5.4 m (17 ft 9 in). The double walls were made of stout hazel uprights around which smaller hazel rods were woven in a spiralled fashion. The gap between the walls was filled with organic material, probably straw, moss and heather, which would have acted as insulation. Part of the inner wall, which had collapsed inwards, survived to almost 3 m (9 ft 10 in) in height. Some evidence for the internal arrangements also remained, including a stone-lined central hearth and a woven wattle bedding area set against the wall. At one phase in its existence

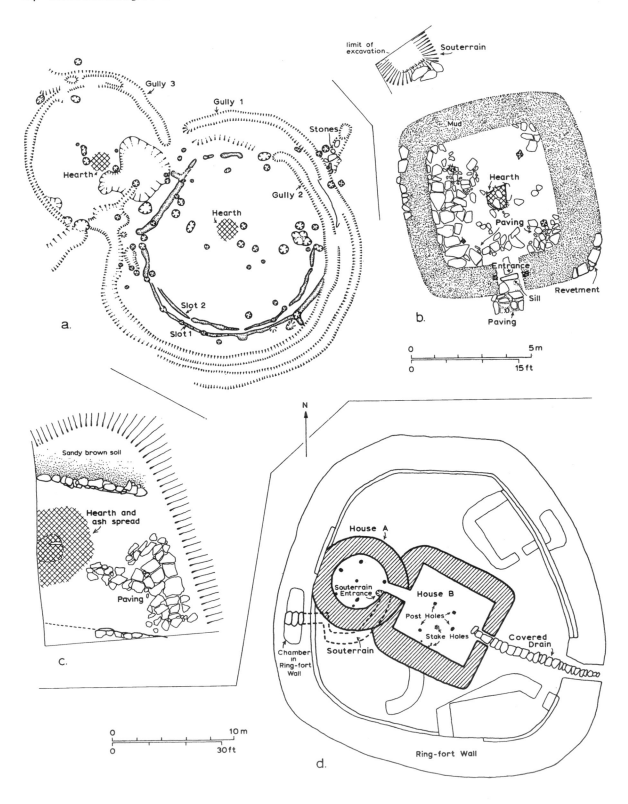

a.

Gully 3

Gully 1

Stones

Hearth

Gully 2

Hearth

Slot 2

Slot 1

limit of excavation

Souterrain

b.

Mud

Hearth

Paving

Entrance

Sill

Revetment

Paving

0        5 m

0        15 ft

c.

Sandy brown soil

Hearth and ash spread

Paving

0        10 m

0        30 ft

d.

N

House A

Souterrain Entrance

House B

Post Holes

Stake Holes

Chamber in Ring-fort Wall

Souterrain

Covered Drain

Ring-fort Wall

9 *Ring-fort structures:*
a. *Dressogagh, Co. Armagh (after Collins 1966);*
b. *Whitefort, Co. Down (after Waterman 1956a);*
c. *Rathmullan, Co. Down (after Lynn 1981–2);*
d. *Leacanabuaile, Co. Cork (after Ó Ríordáin, S.P. and Foy 1943).*

there was a communicating door between this house and Structure Theta to the west. Dendrochronology has shown that the oak door jambs of the latter were felled in AD 648.[90]

The second major building type was rectangular or sometimes square in plan. The construction techniques also differ from the round houses already described, since more extensive use was made of clay, stone and larger timbers, with the consequent need for more sophisticated carpentry. A very good example of this type was found at White Fort cashel, Drumarood, Co. Down (9b). Before excavation the house was visible as a platform approximately 7.6 m (25 ft) square with rounded corners, and a gap on the south side suggesting the position of the original doorway which faced the enclosure entrance. Upon investigation it was shown that the house consisted of two phases and that the upper was by far the better preserved. At the beginning of Phase 2 a stone revetment was added to the house platform to prevent slippage. The interior of the building was indicated by large stone paving slabs, some of which had been subsequently removed. Traces of thick mud walls were found in the form of a low bank between the edge of the floor and the stone revetment. A gap in the bank on the south side indicated the entrance lined with stone paving; two post-holes showed the position of the door. Inside, four post-holes forming the corners of a square suggested that the roof had been supported by four posts. The only other surviving feature was the central stone-lined hearth. At the time an attempted reconstruction showed a square house with low mud walls, the width of which had been reduced by benches cut into their thickness around the circumference of the interior. The timber-framed roof covered with turf or thatch rested on the walls while the four internal posts supported a central raised roof with openings to admit light and permit the smoke to escape.[91] In hindsight, such a reconstruction may be too sophisticated and some features, for example the clerestory, the pedimented doorway and the wall benches, must remain unproven; but it does demonstrate that quite substantial structures may have left comparatively little behind in the archaeological record.

There is evidence elsewhere for a variety of related constructional techniques. The Phase 3 building at Rathmullan (9c) is one of several examples of a rectangular house constructed on stone footings. The walling consisted of large flat boulders, the uneven external surfaces of which were held in position by an earthen revetment. It seems likely that these stone foundations would have supported a wooden superstructure set into horizontal sole-plates, thereby reducing to some extent the effect of rising damp on the timberwork. Alternatively, the ends of the rafters could have rested directly on the footings, but this is a less persuasive solution since the headroom within would have been severely restricted. The interior was paved towards the eastern end, possibly indicating the entrance area, and there was a central hearth. At Carraig Aille 2 there were several rectangular buildings with rather more substantial stone footings and paved floors. The house at Béal Ború is of special importance since it can be dated to the eleventh century by a Hiberno-Norse coin. It measured 4 m × 2.5 m (13 ft 2 in × 8 ft 3 in) internally and the walling consisted of stout posts 200–400 mm (7⅞ in–15¾ in) in diameter; those on the western end had been set into a shallow trench. There were no indications of the wall infill or the roof structure. The doorway, facing south, was entered through some kind of porch with stone paving immediately inside it and, again, there was a central hearth.[92]

At the moment it is not generally possible to recognize regional differences in these round and rectangular houses. The one exception is the drystone 'beehive' hut or *clochán* found in rocky districts of western Ireland. There has been a tendency to concentrate scholarly attention on examples from religious sites, such as Skellig Michael, Church Island and Reask, Co. Kerry (see p. 116, **54b, 54c, 55c**), but identical structures are also found in obviously secular contexts including stone-walled ring-forts, though few have been excavated. The main characteristics may be described as follows. Both round and square ground-plans have been noted. The walls are of drystone construction – limestone is an ideal material – fairly smooth on the inside face but of rougher appearance on the outside. Sometimes there is a low stone curb or *annulus* around the exterior or slabs protrude on the outer wall surface which may have kept a layer of sods in position to improve insulation. Alternatively, the lower part of the wall is sometimes lined inside and out with upright slabs. An important characteristic of this drystone-walling technique is the use of corbelling to form the roof. Successive courses are carefully laid so as to project slightly inwards and in this way a solid stone domed roof is constructed. In many instances, however, the corbelling is partial and a roof of thatch or sods would have been supported on wooden posts resting either on the top of the wall or set into the floor of the hut. Other features include door jambs, frequently made from erect monoliths, openings to let the light in, paving on the floor and cupboards built into the thickness of the wall.

House A at Leacanbuaile, Co. Kerry, is a good example of a round *clochán* from an excavated ring-fort site (**9d**). It is situated against the wall on the far side of the enclosure, the doorway facing the entrance. The walls are up to 1.5 m (5 ft) thick and they are corbelled from a height of 1.2 m (4 ft). However, the roof does not seem to have been of solid stone. Five post-holes around the perimeter of the interior would tend to suggest that they supported a timber-framed roof possibly capped with thatch. An aperture in the floor near the entrance gave access to the souterrain. While House A was still standing, House B, a sub-rectangular structure measuring internally 7.1 m (23 ft 4 in) × 6.15 m (20 ft 2 in) was built abutting against it. The walls, which survived to a maximum of 1.5 m (5 ft) high, are up to 1.83 m (6 ft) thick and constructed to an excellent finish. Post-holes cut into the floor may indicate roof supports. A drain dug into the clay and covered with slabs runs from the doorway of the house to the ring-fort entrance.[93]

It has been noted that in the case of Leacanabuaile the rectangular house is secondary to the round one. The same pattern has been recognized elsewhere and sufficient evidence has now accumulated to suggest that this is an important chronological marker.[94] The change from round to rectangular is demonstrated particularly well at Rathmullan, where four successive phases of ring-fort occupation have been preserved. Phases 1 and 2 have round houses while the Phase 3 house is rectangular. Activity on this site spans a considerable period: Phase 1 may be dated between the late sixth and early eighth centuries on the basis of Class E imported pottery, and Phases 2, 3 and 4 are associated with souterrain ware, evolving

from plain to cordoned types. Phase 4, however, is hardly earlier than the eleventh or twelfth centuries since the construction of the Anglo-Norman motte followed on immediately with no apparent break in occupation.[95] It is difficult at present to be precise about when the change from round to rectangular dwellings took place, but the sequence at Rathmullan is paralled elsewhere in eastern Ulster and a date in the eighth or ninth centuries seems likely at least for this part of the country. This suggests that houses described in the late seventh- or eighth-century law tract *Críth Gablach* are round rather than rectangular, as has sometimes been surmised.[96]

Why did this change take place? Certainly, at this late stage Roman influence, which has been considered important in the activation of a similar sequence in western Britain, would seem to be irrelevant. Equally, the introduction of Viking building techniques in the latter part of the ninth

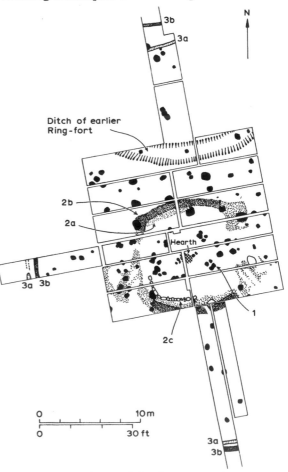

Ditch of earlier Ring-fort

10   *Lissue, Co. Antrim (after Bersu 1947).*

and tenth centuries probably came too late and, although Viking houses do have rectilinear plans, they are not otherwise directly comparable. However, one possible source of inspiration is the influence of rectangular church buildings. The historical sources make it clear that many were constructed of wattles but by the eighth century some larger buildings, for example Kildare and Rahan, were more sophisticated structures of jointed timbers and boards (see p. 122). It is possible that these developments spilled over into secular architecture.[97]

It has been suggested that there is a third major building type, a huge round house covering the entire area of the ring-fort enclosure with the roof supported on concentric rings of sturdy posts. The evidence for this is based upon one site, Lissue, Co. Antrim, a large univallate ring-fort excavated by Bersu in the late 1940s. Unfortunately, only a preliminary excavation report was published[98] and controversy has continued to surround Bersu's interpretation of what was found. The site had been intensively occupied over a considerable length of time and it is obvious that there were many phases of rebuilding; indeed the later ring-fort overlay an earlier, smaller one. In the middle of the site at least three structural phases were located (10). At the centre was a hearth and 2 m (6 ft 7 in) from this a concentric oval ring of post-holes (1), some earlier than others. Some 3 m (9 ft 10 in) beyond again was a curvilinear depression in two phases (2a, b), a third, indicated by a stone setting (2c), in the south-west corner. Various post-holes were found outside the curvilinear depressions, and narrow trenches opened up to the north, south and west indicated two or more phases of palisade trench (3a, b) on the inner side of the ring-fort bank. Bersu did not believe that these palisade trenches were anything to do with the enclosure bank. Instead, he interpreted what he had found with reference to enclosed sites he had previously excavated at Ballykeigan A and B and at Ballanorris in the Isle of Man. He suggested that he had uncovered at least three phases of a round house over 40 m (131 ft) in diameter with a central hearth, up to six concentric rings of posts supporting the roof and an exterior wall represented by the palisade trenches. The curvilinear depressions and stone setting formed a partition wall separating the occupation area into two zones.

A detailed reconsideration must await publication of the final report, but there are many problems with this interpretation, not least that no satisfactory parallels have come to light since.[99] Indeed, the considerable number of more recent ring-fort excavations would suggest that timber palisades acting as bank revetments are quite common. Furthermore, the curvilinear depressions (2a, b) may represent different phases of round houses similar to those already described; it is quite usual for the doorway to face the ring-fort entrance. Other post-holes could represent further phases of similar structures using different building techniques and on different alignments. The stone setting (2c) even presents the possibility of a rectangular structure. Consequently, the idea of a massive round house involving the roofing of the entire ring-fort enclosure now seems unlikely.

At the moment we know almost nothing of the internal arrangements of any of these house types. The most common surviving feature is a central hearth, usually stone-lined, often with stake-holes either side indicating the presence of pot-hangers used during cooking. Documentary references would suggest benches (*imdae*) of planks with straw which could perhaps be curtained off in some way to provide sitting and sleeping areas. Examples of bedding areas which fit this description have recently been located set against the walls of some of the Phase 1 houses at Deer Park Farms (8). Food storage is also mentioned in the sources but it is not altogether clear whether this was done within the dwelling itself or in a separate outhouse.[100] In time further excavation, particularly on waterlogged sites with well-preserved organic and environmental evidence, or possibly with the aid of detailed phosphate analysis, may provide more clues.

We also know surprisingly little about how the houses were organized within ring-forts because so few have been totally excavated. In many cases, for example Dressogagh and Whitefort, there was a single house towards the centre of the enclosure and sometimes, as at Dromore, Co. Antrim, there are indications of a second round house in addition to the central one.[101] Certainly, more than one house is to be expected in the case of larger ring-forts and this may affect the overall organization of the interior. For example, at Carraig Aille 2, the surviving traces of round huts would seem to suggest that several were grouped around the periphery of the enclosure. A similar arrangement is sometimes evidenced with rectilinear structures as, for example, at Shane's Castle, Co. Antrim.[102]

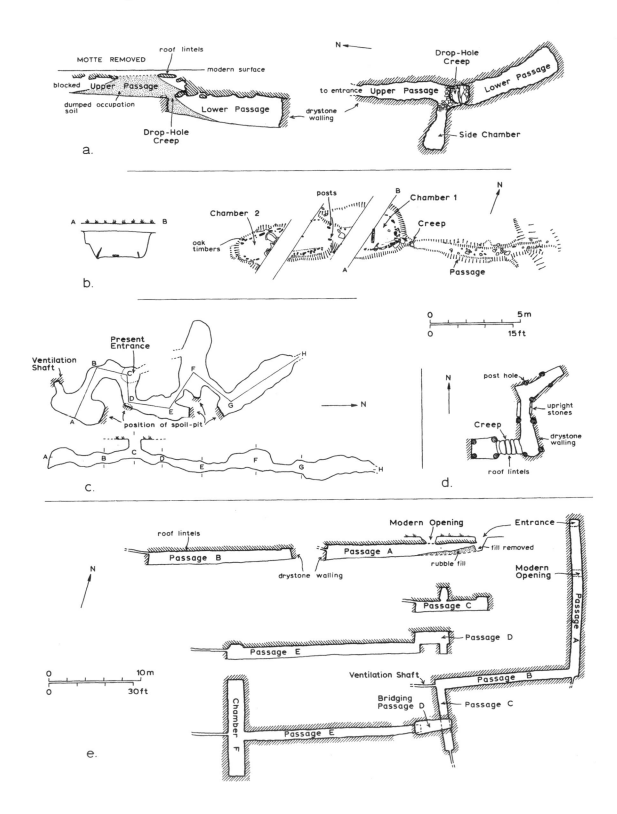

a.

b.

c.

d.

e.

11 *Souterrains:*
a. *Rathmullan, Co. Down (after Lynn 1981–2);*
b. *Coolcran, Co. Fermanagh (after Williams 1985a);*
c. *Keelnameela, Co. Cork (after Twohig 1971);*
d. *Ballycatteen, Co. Cork (after Ó Ríordáin, S.P. and Hartnett 1943);* e. *Donaghmore, Co. Louth (after Rynne 1959).*

---

## Souterrains

Souterrains, or man-made underground or semi-subterranean passages and chambers (11), are frequently found within ring-forts. However these curious structures are also a feature of a wide variety of other early medieval sites, including promontory forts, open settlements and ecclesiastical sites. Many are directly associated with domestic structures and some, for example Leacanbuaile, Co. Kerry (9d), and Ballywee, Co. Antrim (18d), were entered directly from the house. Upwards of 1,000 examples have so far been recorded,[103] many as isolated monuments uncovered by heavy machinery during agricultural improvement, house or road construction; as a result their broader archaeological context has often been lost. In some areas, such as Six Mile Water, Co. Antrim, west of Dundalk, Co. Louth, and Co. Cork, souterrains seem particularly abundant. However, such clusters may be misleading since some techniques of souterrain building leave more evidence in the archaeological record than others.

Two very different building techniques have been recognized. The method employed was determined by the local geology. In areas where the souterrain was to be dug into earth rather than solid rock or clay the open trench method, usually with drystone walling, was used. First, a deep straight-sided trench was dug large enough to contain the souterrain. Once the trench was complete, the drystone walls were built up within the trench around some kind of temporary centering. The gaps between the sides of the trench and the souterrain walls were then filled in and stone lintels placed to form the souterrain roof. This could then be covered with earth so that the souterrain was invisible above ground.[104]

Alternatively, the souterrain was constructed wholly or partly above ground, either dug into the make-up of a raised or platform rath or built as part of the ring-fort enclosure. A souterrain employing this type of building technique was dug into Phase 3 of the raised rath at Rathmullan (11a). This consisted of an upper passage 7 m (23 ft) long, leading from the entrance, which was not excavated. At the far end was a small side-chamber and the passage terminated with a vertical shaft in the floor, known as a 'drop-hole creep', leading down to a second, more spacious passage over 6 m (19 ft 8 in) long.[105] This is a comparatively simple example. In many instances a number of passages may be joined by creeps, of which there are several different designs. The most usual are simple constrictions, including the lowering of the headroom, making it difficult to pass from one passage to the next. Variations include drop-hole creeps and, at Donaghmore, Co. Louth, a particularly complex example (11e), there is a vertical creep through the roof of the souterrain giving access to an upper bridging passage (D) which then drops down again into a further gallery.

Other constructional details found in this kind of souterrain include evidence for wooden doors closing creeps, recesses beyond creeps which could have acted as 'guard chambers', corbelled chambers, ventilation shafts, drains and platforms in souterrains liable to flooding, small wall cupboards and occasionally shelves or benches.[106] Often the passage slopes gradually down from the entrance but access may sometimes be gained via a vertical shaft, possibly originally equipped with a wooden ladder. Occasionally, as at Killyglen, Co. Antrim, there is a second opening beyond the ring-fort enclosure, in this case beside a nearby stream.[107]

An interesting alternative to the drystone-walling technique has been uncovered at Coolcran, Co. Fermanagh (11b), where waterlogged conditions preserved a wooden souterrain. A narrow passage 6.5 m (21 ft 4 in) long formed by an earth-cut trench, probably originally with a wooden roof which does not survive, led, by way of some kind of creep, to a large sub-rectangular, flat-bottomed pit 9 m (29 ft 6 in) long by 3.5 m (11 ft 6 in) wide. Around the edges of the pit were the remains of 48 sawn-oak timbers which sloped inwards with traces of wattle walling in and around them. Two stout posts suggested the pit had been divided into two separate oval post-and-wattle chambers.[108] A structure of this kind is ephemeral and, in contrast to its drystone equivalent, it is unlikely to turn up by chance but only to be found during a controlled excavation.

The second major type of souterrain is on the whole less complex and is found in areas where soft rock or clay are sufficiently stable to allow tunnelling. Many examples are simply hollowed out and the spoil removed through the entrance. Usually these consist of only one or two chambers and passages, but occasionally they can be larger, as at Rathbeg, Co. Antrim, which is at least 130 m (426 ft 6 in) long with eight known chambers linked by creeps. More complicated examples are also known, particularly from west Cork, where a considerable amount of work has been done to identify different local types. Some were constructed by digging one or more large spoil-pits. The chambers and passages were then formed by tunnelling horizontally into the side of the pit, and the spoil was removed through it. When the souterrain was complete, the spoil-pits were backfilled; the only visible remains were areas of drystone blocking at the points where the passage had originally been tunnelled out of the pit. This type may be exemplified by an isolated souterrain at Keelnameela, Co. Cork (11c), consisting of four elongated chambers linked by creeps. Areas of drystone walling indicate the presence of the two spoil-pits.[109]

Many souterrains were constructed with a mixture of both the tunnelling and drystone techniques and some also used timber. At Ballycatteen, Co. Cork, a large multivallate ring-fort, three souterrains were excavated. Each consisted of three or four small rectangular chambers linked by creeps which had been dug from above straight into the soft rock. Some of the vertical facings were lined with drystone walling but for others this was unnecessary and the rock-cut surface was left exposed. In Souterrain B (11d) there were also post-holes in the corners of each chamber. These indicated the posts which had supported a timber roof structure, probably projecting above ground. This is likely to have been covered with the perforated shale tiles found nearby; only in the creeps was there any evidence for stone roof-lintels.[110]

There has been considerable debate about the function of souterrains: the two most usual suggestions have been that they were used for refuge and for storage.[111] The easiest way to test such theories is by an examination of the archaeological evidence in conjunction with the written sources. By examining the documentary references Lucas has shown[112] that souterrains were definitely used as refuges. The archaeological evidence would support this; creeps, hidden chambers and sally-ports, as well as the fact that most souterrains were invisible above ground, would all have helped to provide protection in the case of sudden attack. They could, however, turn into death-traps if the aggression was prolonged. The sources indicate that the most usual method of entry was by digging from the top but, equally, smoke or the blocking of ventilation shafts could soon lead to suffocation. It is this lack of protection against a concerted attack which has led some to doubt that they were ever intended as refuges.

Evidence for their use as store-houses is less unequivocal but there is enough to suggest that valuables may have been hidden in souterrains, at least in time of potential danger. One reference describes valuables being deposited in a souterrain by the defenders of a ring-fort and the elaborate defensive mechanisms described above would certainly have deterred the more casual pilferer. At Oldcourt, Co. Cork, an interesting discovery was made in one of the souterrain chambers where a concealed pit under the flag floor was found to contain a bell which had been carefully wrapped in moss to protect it.[113] Furthermore, since souterrains are usually found close to domestic structures and are sometimes entered from the house itself, they would seem to be a convenient place for more general storage. Lucas has suggested that, as they were fire-proof, cool, dust-free and uncontaminated by flies, they would have been ideal for the safe-keeping of dairy products, even fresh or cooked meat. There is little documentary evidence to support this and artefacts in souterrains are relatively rare. Occupation debris is more likely to have fallen down from above than to relate to activities carried out within the souterrains themselves. However, fragments of oak and willow found in the chamber of the souterrain at Balrenny, Co. Meath, have now been recognized as barrel hoops implying the presence of storage containers and the excavation of a souterrain at Shaneen Park, Ballyaghagan, Co. Antrim, revealed basin-like depressions dug into the floors of the chambers which, it was suggested, could have been designed to hold wooden, pottery or leather containers, perhaps for storing butter.[114] The idea has also been put forward that animals such as small cattle, pigs or chickens might be housed in souterrains[115] but, in view of the very confined space, this seems most unlikely.

The origins and chronology of souterrains are also problematic. Underground structures of

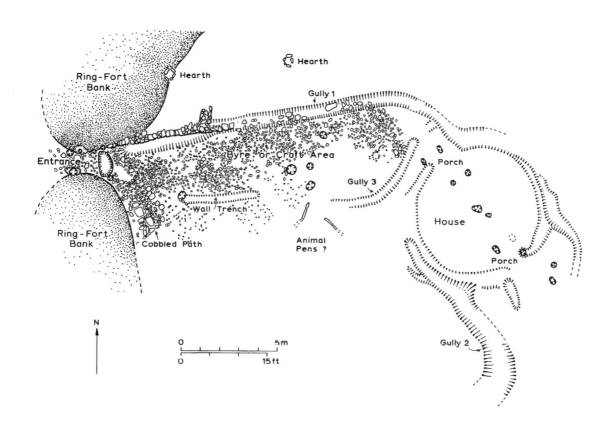

12 *Ballypalady 2, Co. Antrim; structures excavated within the ring-fort (after Waterman 1972).*

similar, though not identical type are found outside Ireland in Brittany, west Cornwall and different parts of Scotland. There has been some discussion of possible links between the different groups but their occurrence may be purely fortuitous. Irish souterrains with drystone walling may be compared with examples in Cornwall and south-east Scotland while the tunnelled variety are similar to those in Brittany. The closest parallels may perhaps be made with the passage souterrains incorporating side chambers and simple creeps found associated with wheel-houses in the Western Isles of Scotland. The Breton souterrains would seem to be Iron Age, those in Cornwall Iron Age and Roman Iron Age and those in Scotland of similar date though they may have remained in use a little longer. The association of Irish souterrains with early medieval settlements and ecclesiastical sites would suggest they are the latest in the series, and it has been argued that they were not yet current at the end of the Roman Iron Age, since they are unknown in south-west Wales which was colonized by the Irish at that time.[116] They may have come into use soon afterwards as they are associated with both round and rectangular structures, but precise dating is difficult. However Lynn has pointed out[117] that no souterrain was built until Phase 3 at Rathmullan (where it is associated with a rectangular dwelling) and that souterrains may have become more common, at least in Ulster, once the change from round to rectangular structures was complete. It is also interesting to note that there is usually only direct access to the souterrain from rectangular houses and that, where souterrains are an integral part of the ring-fort enclosure, as at Shane's Castle, they are again associated with rectangular structures. The only closely dated souterrain is Coolcran, where dendrochronological samples indicate that the timber was felled in $822 \pm 9$.[118] Is it possible that the advent of the Vikings could have increased the need for souterrains as refuges and places of safe storage for valuables? The literary evidence certainly suggests that the Vikings regarded souterrains as targets worth plundering.[119]

### Other ring-fort structures

It is very difficult to reconstruct how ring-fort interiors were used. To what extent were animals housed within the enclosure? Were there stores for fuel, grain and other crops? Where did food processing go on? Can craft areas be identified? The evidence is at best very patchy and it is often difficult to distinguish outhouses from dwellings or recognize how they were used. Some of these aspects will be discussed in more detail elsewhere (see Chs 4–5). While there must have been variations from site to site, chance discoveries are enabling us to begin to piece together a more complete picture.

At Ballypalady 2, Co. Antrim (12), the circular house was approached by a cobbled path leading from the ring-fort entrance. It augmented a drainage gully and had been constructed to prevent the area between the house and entrance from becoming boggy. Ring-forts have yet to produce evidence for the build-up of mud caused by trampling animals, but cobbled areas are relatively common within enclosures, especially round the entrance, and this would have ameliorated such a problem. In a later phase an outhouse, interpreted as a byre, though, because of the large number of artefacts, it could have been some kind of craft area, was built on the line of the cobbled path. The only surviving parts of the structure were a length of drystone walling, a parallel timber beam-slot and some post-holes. To the south of the building two narrow slots suggested light hurdles, possibly animal pens. To the north of the cobbles was a cooking area consisting of two stone-built hearths containing red dust, which may have been peat ash.[120] Such outdoor hearths have been identified on other ring-fort sites and may account for the lack of a hearth in some domestic structures since cooking outside would have lessened the danger of fire.

Other examples of outbuildings include postholes suggesting lean-to sheds set against the ring-fort bank at Seacash and Rathbeg, Co. Antrim. A large wattle-lined pit with some kind of wooden superstructure set against the inner edge of the bank at Killyliss had been used as a latrine.[121] On some sites extensive activity areas have been found. For example, at Letterkeen, Co. Mayo, an area was uncovered which may have been used for grain processing. It consisted of a possible corn-drying kiln and a rectangular burnt patch with an upper quern-stone and the burnt remains of a wicker basket. Metal-working and other crafts were also carried out, especially in the larger ring-forts. At Garryduff 1 evidence of iron-working was found within the ring-fort and Garranes Site D, situated in the shelter of the inner bank, consisted of a dense black layer with many finds demonstrating it was an area used for ornamental metal-working. A scatter of post-holes and a stone setting suggest structures of some kind.[122]

There has been surprisingly little investigation of the area immediately outside the ring-fort enclosure. This is probably a serious oversight, since a glance at air-photographs (20) suggests that adjacent enclosures and extra-mural structures may have been relatively common.[123] The only site where there has been any extensive examination of the extra-mural buildings is Carraig Aille 2. These were dug because they were clearly visible above ground prior to excavation, which duly revealed a series of rectangular houses and yards. However, hints of extra-mural activity have come to light by chance elsewhere. At Duneight, Co. Down, for example, a cursory examination of the area to the east of the outer ditch uncovered a few post-holes, several small shallow pits, patches of burning and sherds of souterrain pottery.[124]

### Ring-forts in the landscape

An indication of the landscape immediately surrounding the ring-fort at the time it was occupied can sometimes be reconstructed with the aid of pollen diagrams and other environmental evidence. At Seacash, Co. Antrim, an analysis of the ditch showed that it had been shaded by trees and bushes, ash, hazel and elderberry, and that, though tree pollen was generally low, other trees such as alder, birch, willow, holly, oak and elm also grew in the area. The ditch had become quickly overgrown with nettles and brambles, the shade attracting flowers such as primroses. Nearby were fields and waste land, suggested by cereal pollens and field weeds, particularly nettles. At Killyliss, Co. Tyrone, the pollen showed how the environment changed over the time the ring-fort was occupied. Before it was built there was considerable tree pollen indicating woods of hazel, alder and willow, perhaps with oak and holly mixed in. However, there was also some open ground suggested by grass, bracken and weeds such as plantains, docks, dandelions and thistles, which had probably been used for grazing. When the ring-fort was built the amount of tree pollen fell. The presence of hazel and alder was still indicated but oak had almost disappeared and the large amount of nettle pollen suggests a high nitrogen content to the soil. In the final phase the ditch became overgrown with brambles, hawthorn, blackthorn, ash, nettle and dock indicating that the ring-fort had been abandoned.[125]

From time to time, especially in areas which have been less exploited by modern farming methods, traces of a broader landscape still survive. Ring-forts may appear as isolated monuments but often there are several within a single townland, and two or three grouped together are not uncommon.[126] Air-photography has also hinted at surrounding field systems and enclosures[127] but more detailed survey work and excavation embracing these wider aspects has been rare. A notable exception is Cush, Co. Limerick (21b), where Ó Ríordáin investigated a large number of ring-forts together with a complex pattern of fields and enclosures.[128] However, where more than one ring-fort in a group has been excavated, it has always proved difficult to demonstrate the relationship of one site to another. In the case of Cush it was possible to trace some developments within the southern group, where it was suggested that ring-forts 2, 3, and 4 were approximately contemporary but were preceded by 1, while 5, 6 and the adjoining enclosure were all later. But no differences were detectable between the material culture of the various sites and, at the time of the excavation, the fact that there was extensive prehistoric activity in the same area made the overall chronology of the site confusing. In general, it remains difficult at present to say whether ring-forts within a given area were occupied concurrently or consecutively or how they relate to other early medieval settlement types such as open settlements or crannogs. In essence we are still dealing with isolated points in an ancient landscape rather than being able to reconstruct its gradual evolution as a whole.

### The role of ring-forts

In the past there has been some attempt to link the inhabitants of the ring-forts with the strict hierarchy of the law tracts as evidenced in *Críth Gablach*,[129] and with the *bóaire*, or well-to-do farmer, in particular.[130] Though superficially attractive, such an equation can only be speculative; indeed, because of the problematic nature of the legal texts (see p. 8), it could be misleading, especially for the latter part of the period.

All we can say is that a difference in role is indicated by the size of the site and the wealth of the artefacts. The overwhelming majority of smaller univallate ring-forts do not have a great variety of finds. Common objects include copper-alloy ringed pins, lignite bracelets, glass beads, spindle whorls, rotary querns and, in north-east Ulster, souterrain pottery. Where soil conditions are suitable, everyday iron objects, such as knives, and bone and antler artefacts, such as pins and combs, are also characteristic; occasionally waterlogged deposits preserve organic objects: wooden vessels or leather shoes. These sites were essentially mixed farms. Agricultural activity is attested by tools, the plough coulter from White Fort, Drumarood, for example (22i), or pollen; animal husbandry by the presence of bones (see Chapter 4). Limited craft activity is also sometimes found on such sites. The most common evidence is iron-rich slag suggesting simple metal-working, and the manufacture of day-to-day tools.

But many larger and better defended sites, particularly multivallate ring-forts, fulfilled a more complex role. Evidence of mixed farming is still present, but richer artefacts demonstrate the importation of luxury items and specialist craft pursuits suggest considerable wealth and higher status. At Garranes, for example, a large multivallate ring-fort with formidable defences (5c), the artefacts included imported pottery, fragments of imported glass vessels and a range of objects indicating ornamental copper-alloy working with the application of enamel, millefiori-glass inlay and possibly amber. While the identification of Garranes with *Ráth Raithleann*, the ruling seat of a branch of the Éoganacht dynasty, must remain unproven, it is certainly a site of obvious prestige where there was sufficient surplus wealth to pay for luxury goods and the services of skilled craftworkers.[131]

CHAPTER 3

# Other Settlement Types

Ring-forts are the most characteristic as well as the most numerous of early medieval Irish settlements. However, other types are also distinctive and may, perhaps, have been commoner than the surviving archaeological evidence suggests. Crannogs are related to ring-forts, but have been specially adapted to a watery environment. Promontory forts may, too, be a variation of the enclosed homestead. But there are also a variety of open settlements, round huts and rectilinear

houses, which may indicate where those who lacked the need or prestige to build a ring-fort or other enclosed homestead lived. Some of these are adapted to specialized environments, for example coastal sand-dunes; others to specific purposes, such as the temporary summer shelters for herdsmen found on the upland pastures.

## Crannogs

Crannogs (**13**, **14**) are lake-dwellings. Sometimes they are located on natural islands but often they were constructed on entirely artificial foundations. The substantial crannog make-up is kept in

**13** *Crannog, Lisleitrim, Co. Armagh. There is also a trivallate earthen ring-fort in the foreground (Crown copyright, reproduced with the permission of the Controller of Her Majesty's Stationery Office).*

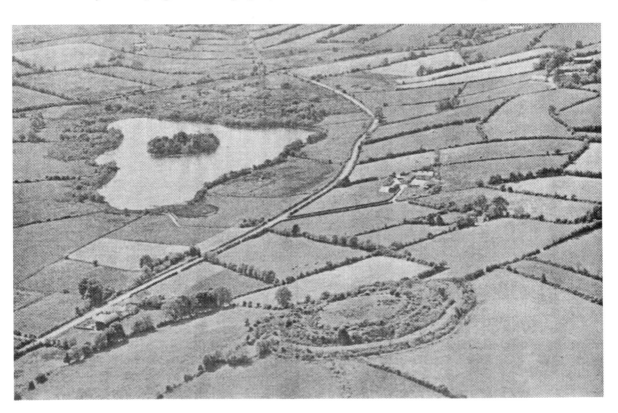

**14** *Ballinderry 2 crannog, Co. Offaly, during excavation in 1933. The post palisade may be seen in the foreground with structural piles behind. There is a dug-out boat on the right (Courtesy of the Royal Irish Academy).*

place by a ring of close-set vertical piles which form a palisade around the site. The important difference between these and nearly all other early medieval Irish settlements is that crannogs are waterlogged. This means that the whole structure of the crannog, its houses and organic artefacts, as well as a wide variety of environmental evidence, which would normally have perished, have the potential to survive. Furthermore, the frequent use of substantial oak timbers in the crannog make-up means that it is now possible, with the aid of dendrochronology, to date the construction and occupation of many of these sites with remarkable accuracy. At the moment only a handful have actually been dated in this way but the results are very interesting and have helped to fuel renewed interest in the investigation of crannog sites.

Antiquarian interest in the Irish crannogs began in the nineteenth century, partly because of the discovery of lake-dwellings in Switzerland, but mainly independently as a result of the drainage of lakes and bogs to provide improved farmland, a by-product of which was the discovery of many partially-submerged crannog sites. The most important of these, Lagore, Co. Meath, was found in 1839 by labourers digging a drainage trench across it. *The Lake Dwellings of Ireland*, a distillation

of the discoveries to date and a gazetteer of sites, was published by W.G. Wood-Martin in 1886 and must still be regarded as a seminal work. There has been little synthesis since. Instead research has centred around specific excavations: the important work at Ballinderry 1 and 2 and Lagore carried out by the Harvard expedition in the 1930s; the sampling of sites in Ulster, such as Lough Faughan and Clea Lakes during the compilation of the County Down Archaeological Survey; and, more recently, the rescue/research projects still under way at Moynagh Lough, Co. Meath, and Newtownlow, Co. Westmeath, which have arisen as a result of modern land reclamation.[1] Other sites have been recorded as a consequence of their exposure during drought and drainage which has caused lake levels to recede.

### Origins and chronology

The origin of crannogs, like ring-forts, is a controversial subject. Lake-side habitations in Ireland can be traced right back to the Mesolithic period, but the problem centres on whether prehistoric lacustrine settlements can really be described as crannogs and whether there is any continuity between these and their early medieval counterparts. The late Bronze Age phase at Ballinderry 2, Co. Offaly, was situated on a natural island at the edge of the lough. It consisted of a black occupation layer with scattered patches of brushwood and other debris associated with a timber platform 11.5 m (37 ft 9 in) square. There were no traces of extensive artificial make-up or encircling palisades and Hencken, the excavator, described it not as a crannog, but as a lake-side habitation.[2] Likewise recent re-excavation at Island MacHugh, Co. Tyrone, has suggested that the Neolithic and Bronze Age activity was centred on a small natural island, the shores of which were built up with brushwood mats, while the crannog proper was constructed at the beginning of the seventh century AD.[3] A similar definition is valid for other Bronze Age sites such as an earlier phase of Moynagh Lough, and Lough Eskragh, Co. Tyrone, and is also probably true for Rough Island, Lough Enagh, Co. Derry, Knocknalappa, Co. Clare, and Rathjordan, Co. Limerick.[4]

Evidence for the occupation of crannogs in the Iron Age is equally slight and rests principally on the interpretation of two sites: Rathtinaun (Crannog 61), on the edge of Lough Gara, Co. Sligo, and Lisnacrogher, Co. Antrim. Rathtinaun is, as yet, unpublished and therefore final judgement must await the complete report. However, the following sequence has been put forward. Phase 1 consisted of several layers of brushwood, some woven, placed on the lake bottom and anchored with birch piles. Hearths located on the surface of the brushwood suggested the presence of buildings. Artefacts, including pottery, suggested a late Bronze Age date. In Phase 2 there were more hearths but the finds included iron artefacts suggesting an early Iron Age date. After a period of desertion because of a rise in the water level, Phase 3 began with the deposition of stones encircled by wooden planks and then a further make-up of brushwood, peat and other material, on top of which was a large, circular house. Joseph Raftery describes the objects from this phase as closely resembling those from sites such as Lagore, Garranes and Ballycatteen and the only artefacts illustrated, double-sided antler combs, would certainly support this. The difficulty surrounding the interpretation of Rathtinaun is bound up with the radiocarbon dates which led Raftery to conclude that the Bronze Age continued in Ireland for two or three centuries after the mid-first millennium BC and that the Phase 3 crannog was Iron Age.[5] However, the artefacts do not seem to tally with the radiocarbon dates and, since we now know that much greater margins of error can affect radiocarbon dates, it seems unwise to place too much weight on them. A re-examination of the rest of the available evidence would suggest a sequence similar to Ballinderry 2 where a late Bronze and early Iron Age lake-side habitation was reutilized for a crannog in the early middle ages.

The sword scabbards, decorated with La Tène spirals, and other objects found at Lisnacrogher, may or may not have been associated with some kind of timber structure, but because the discovery was not recorded properly, we shall never know the nature of the association nor whether the structure was a crannog.[6] It seems possible, however, that the hoard had no connection with a habitation site, but rather made up some kind of ritual deposit similar to Llyn Cerrig Bach on Anglesey in Wales.

Overall the evidence suggests that crannogs – that is sites with a substantial artificial make-up kept in place by a ring of close-set vertical piles which form a palisade round the site – are not a Bronze Age phenomenon. Instead largely undefended lacustrine settlements were used in this period and there is little to support the idea that they continued beyond the beginning of the Iron Age. Therefore, as with ring-forts, the theory that there was continuity of crannog settlement between the late Bronze Age and early middle ages is difficult to substantiate.

Lynn has suggested[7] that the origins of both crannogs and ring-forts may lie in the fifth and sixth centuries AD and the close dating by dendrochronology for the construction of several crannogs in Ulster is an exciting development which would tend to support this. Most of the oak timbers from crannog sites were accumulated in the 1970s during research to build a tree-ring chronology for the first millennium AD. More examples were collected from Island MacHugh during trial excavations in 1985 (**Table 1**).[8] It will be seen immediately that the felling dates of the oak timbers used in the make-up of these crannogs are remarkably similar, clustering during the second half of the sixth and early seventh centuries AD. This cannot be entirely coincidental.

This implies a surge of crannog building at that time, possibly as a result of some political or social upheaval, or a sudden increase in surplus wealth, which made the construction of these well-defended homesteads a necessity for certain elements in the population. However, because the sample is so small, and confined to Ulster, it is difficult to be certain of its true significance and we shall have to wait and see whether timbers from crannogs elsewhere in Ireland reveal a similar picture.

We do not know if Irish crannogs were an indigenous development, but if their origins do lie in

**Table 1** Dendrochronology dates for timber from crannog sites

| Crannog | Felling Date of Timber |
| --- | --- |
| Island MacHugh (Tyrone) | AD 594 ± 9 |
| | AD 608 |
| | AD 616 ± 9 |
| | AD 619 |
| | AD 622 ± 9 |
| | AD 627 ± 9 |
| Midges Island (Antrim) | AD 570 ± 9 |
| Mill Lough (Fermanagh) | AD 553 ± 9 |
| Ross Lough (Fermanagh) | AD 570 ± 9 |
| Tamin (Antrim) | AD 618 ± 9 |
| Teeshan (Antrim) | AD 581 |

the fifth and sixth centuries AD, when there were close contacts with western Britain, it is worth examining the possibility that they were introduced from there.[9] In particular, the Iron Age and Roman period crannogs of south-west Scotland may provide a possible source. There has been little investigation of these in recent times, but the major excavation at Milton Loch 1, Kircudbrightshire, over 30 years ago, uncovered a definite crannog structure with encircling piles and, in the last phase, a large circular house. Two radiocarbon dates from structural timbers, one definitely re-used, may indicate that the crannog was built between the late ninth and early second centuries BC (790–190 cal. BC, 810–370 cal. BC), but the discovery of an enamelled copper-alloy loop of Roman origin suggests occupation during the first or second centuries AD.[10] A site of this kind provides a close parallel for the early medieval Irish examples and, because of the geographical proximity, an introduction from this area seems a definite possibility. In this light it is interesting to note that Warner has suggested other close cultural links between south-west Scotland and northern Ireland in the Iron Age and Roman period as well as during the fifth and sixth centuries AD.[11]

The occupation of Irish (and Scottish) crannogs is found throughout the early middle ages and continued for some centuries after. Indeed, there are sporadic examples as late as the sixteenth and seventeenth centuries when documentary sources show that they were used in Ireland as strongholds against English attack, though whether they were permanent or temporary refuges is unclear. Frequently, the archaeological evidence suggests continued occupation or reoccupation of early medieval crannog sites. For example, a section across one of the Ardakillen crannogs, Co. Roscommon, showed two distinct phases. The lower consisted of an artificial island encircled by piles and made up of clay, peat and stones with indications of several occupation levels, while the upper included a thick layer of stones with an encircling wall. Records of the site are not good but the artefactual assemblage demonstrates both early and later medieval settlement.[12]

***Siting and distribution***
Crannogs are defensive by their very location. They are situated in shallow marshy lakes, sometimes choked by vegetation, sometimes with stretches of open water, but essentially difficult of access. They may be extensions of natural islands, such as Ballinderry 2, or, like Ballinderry 1, entirely artificial structures. Occasionally, they are not real islands at all; for example, Cuilmore Lough 2, Co. Mayo, is situated on a marshy promontory defended on the landward side only by a double palisade.[13] These sites were approached by boat, causeway or wooden bridge and therefore could not have housed livestock. However large quantities of animal bones from many crannog sites and occasional discoveries of agricultural tools suggest farming activities on adjacent dry land.

Wood-Martin catalogued 220 crannog sites. The number has increased extensively over the last 100 years and may now be in the region of 1200 sites.[14] The distribution of crannogs, as might be expected, is largely confined to parts of the country with a large number of lakes and other stretches of shallow still water. The Lough Erne basin, Co. Fermanagh, a watery maze of islands and inlets, has proved ideal crannog country and a considerable number of others are to be found in the neighbouring counties of Monaghan, Cavan, Leitrim, Sligo and Roscommon. More surprisingly, a comparatively large number are known in Co. Antrim, where, though the scenery is very different, a number of small lakes, for example Lough Mourne, provided a suitable habitat.[15]

Crannogs on stretches of open water survive as small, often wooded islands, for example Lough Brickland, Co. Down, or Lisleitrim, Co. Armagh

(13). Alternatively, they may be entirely sub-merged, the water level having risen since they were occupied, or perhaps the crannog material has slowly compacted and sunk. Crannogs of this type are obviously more difficult to locate and record and have only normally come to light during drought or drainage operations such as those at Lough Gara which caused the water level to drop by more than 1 m (3 ft 3 in) exposing approximately 20 sites. In areas which have undergone drainage in the past crannogs may still be visible as tree-grown or grassy hummocks in bogland or reclaimed pasture. Prior to excavation Lough Faughan, Co. Down, had been cultivated as a garden with a treacherous swamp of reeds, willows and alders round about, while Moynagh Lough appeared as a grass-grown mound with bushes and trees rising out of the surrounding bog.[16]

### The crannog structure

It is not easy to attain a detailed understanding of crannog structures, especially those uncovered in earlier excavations, because they are very complex monuments. They may be wholly or par-tially waterlogged with large numbers of compacted timbers and other organic material which, once exposed, quickly dry out. They are liable to flooding or a high water-table level, which may require continuous pumping, and the site has sometimes been previously disturbed. The result is that the stratigraphical sequence, fre-quently involving a large number of phases, is not always clear and it has proved particularly difficult in many cases to distinguish the original crannog make-up from subsequent occupation layers and rebuilds. There has now been some attempt to reassess discoveries from earlier exca-vations, in particular Lagore and Balinderry 1.[17] But, since the evidence can no longer be examined at first hand, such exercises can only produce a very general picture, and we must await the final reports of more recent excavations in the hope of gaining more detailed information.

The term crannog comes from the Irish word *crann*,[18] meaning a tree, and though their compo-sition was dependent upon the material available, in most cases considerable amounts of timber were used. The method of construction also seems to have varied according to the depth of water and whether it was an extension of a natural island or a totally artificial one. The early medieval phase at Ballinderry 2 (14, 15) was built on a natural island in shallow water and therefore there was less need for a substantial crannog structure; the main aim was the consolidation of a marshy area. This was achieved by constructing a palisade of sturdy posts wholly or partially enclosing an area approximately 35 m (115 ft) in diameter. Post-holes were only found on the north-west side and not on the north-east and it is therefore unclear whether the circuit was originally complete. The posts were mainly oak, but poplar, ash and birch were also used. They were pointed at the lower end and would have formed a protective wall around the crannog. The area inside was stabil-ized by a large number of smaller piles set in a broad band following the inner edge of the palisade and the island was further consolidated with brushwood. The south-east quadrant was waterlogged and here the make-up was more complete. Timbers still survived on the old ground surface and, upon excavation, rushes that had been growing on the site when the crannog was built were found adhering to them. Sometimes it had proved necessary to build up more than one layer of timbers and in some places there were four layers set at right-angles to each other. At one point a dug-out boat had been incorporated into the make-up.[19]

For completely artificial islands a more substan-tial structure was necessary. At Ballinderry 1, for example, the whole crannog make-up rested upon a foundation of 19 massive split-oak timbers laid side by side. These were not tied together but had been placed on the lake bed with nothing but a few pegs and larger stakes to hold them in place. Round them was a band of small piles hammered into the lake mud and the substructure was then built up with a series of radial timbers, many of which had been reused and showed the remnants of elaborate carpentry techniques. Around and between them were layers of peat, brushwood and other organic matter. It has recently been sug-gested that a horseshoe shaped area of timbers approximately 16 m (52 ft 6 in) in diameter, origi-nally identified as House 1, may in fact be the surface of the Phase 1 crannog, which was subse-quently extended and rebuilt.[20]

At Lagore, another artificial island where ar-chaeological deposits survived up to 3 m (9 ft 10 in) deep, it has proved very difficult to distin-guish the crannog make-up from the occupation levels and Hencken's original interpretation of the stratigraphical sequence is no longer acceptable. It seems likely, however, that the lowest levels of the

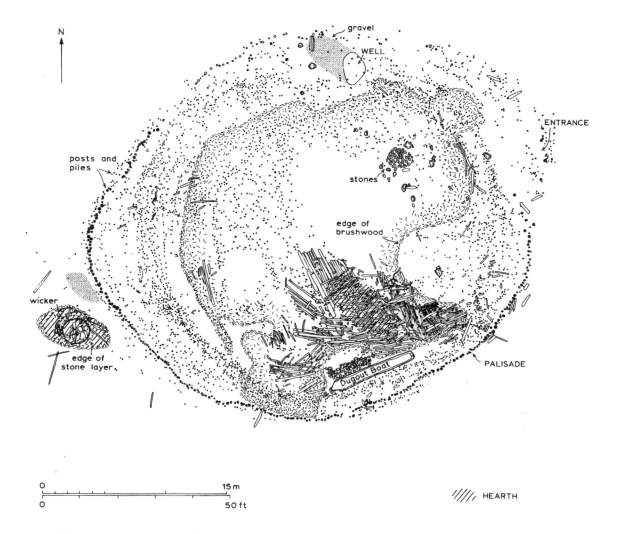

N

gravel

WELL

ENTRANCE

posts and
piles

stones

edge of
brushwood

wicker

edge of
stone layer

Dugout Boat

PALISADE

| 0 | | | | | | 15 m |
| 0 | | | | | | 50 ft |

///// HEARTH

**15**  *Ballinderry 2 crannog, Co. Offaly
(after Hencken 1942).*

crannog structure had slowly compacted and
sunken into the soft lake mud and were therefore
not investigated. For this reason what Hencken
described as a single constructional phase, Period
1a, may now be seen as a whole series of occupational levels which included fragmentary
buildings and hearths as well as piles, log platforms, brushwood, woven wattles, peat and
various kinds of vegetation. As such it seems representative of quite a number of other crannog
sites, for example, Lough Faughan.[21]

We know little of early medieval crannog construction in rockier areas of the country where
one might expect timber to be scarcer and therefore more stones to be incorporated into the

crannog make-up. However, a brief survey of Co.
Donegal crannogs suggested that they may have
been constructed entirely of stones piled up into
cairns upon the lake bed. An alternative to the
crannog structure may be exemplified by
O'Boyle's Fort, Co. Donegal, a stone-walled ring-
fort situated on a small natural island in Lough
Doon.[22]

The perimeter palisade is an important feature
of the crannog structure. It helped provide a stout
enclosing framework for the crannog make-up
and also, since it is likely to have projected above
the water to form a close-set fence around the site,
gave an additional measure of protection to the inhabitants. At Ballinderry 2 there was a single
enclosure of posts, but frequently a sequence of
palisades demonstrating different construction
techniques has been excavated. At Lagore

Hencken identified three successive palisades. The first, enclosing an area 41 m (134 ft 6 in) in diameter, consisted of wooden piles, sometimes strengthened by horizontal timbers and at one point bound together by wicker-work. A scattering of piles was also found well outside the main palisade and it is possible that these were intended to deter hostile boats in a similar manner to a *chevaux de frise*. The second palisade was presumably constructed when the first and its accompanying make-up had partially sunk and compacted making the addition of a new one essential. Made of stouter oak posts, many of which were roughly squared, it enclosed an area approximately 36 m (118 ft) in diameter. The final palisade, enclosing a slightly larger area, was, unfortunately, less well-preserved because it had been inserted into the upper strata of the site. This was a more complex structure of heavy oak posts with grooves on either side into which planks had been slotted to form a continuous wall. In addition there may have been a fourth palisade which Hencken did not recognize. It has recently been suggested that the bowed timbers at a low level on the eastern half of the site may have been an earlier palisade which had become flattened by the subsequent crannog build-up.[23] At Ballinderry 1 there is a similar sequence where a pile palisade was replaced by a plank one, but at Moynagh Lough a lighter structure of saplings with wattles interwoven between the tops of them was superseded by a palisade of squared planks set into a prepared trench. It is likely that the use of planks and saplings indicates a comparative shortage of larger oak timbers.[24]

Where crannog entrances have been traced, there seems, as with ring-forts, to have been a general preference for their orientation eastwards with slight variations to the north-east and south-east, though at Moynagh Lough it faced north. Excavations at the latter site indicated that the entrance consisted of a gap in the palisade about 1 m (3 ft 3 in) wide, with a pathway of wooden corduroy construction which led towards the interior of the crannog. Dendrochronology showed that one of the timbers, which was probaly re-used, had been felled in AD 625. We know little of the entrances themselves, though the opening through the plank palisade at Lagore seems to have been inturned, and at Cuilmore Lough 2, four substantial posts may indicate a gate-tower. Sometimes the crannog could be approached from dry land. At Cuilmore Lough 1

three pairs of large stakes to the east of the crannog suggest some kind of gangway set on stilts, while at Ballinderry 1 the entrance through the pile palisade is marked by two rows of piles 2–2.5 m (6 ft 7 in–8 ft 3 in) apart which seem to have provided cover for a brushwood roadway to the shore. Some crannogs may only have been accessible directly from the land when the water-level was low; others, however, could only be reached by boat. At Ballinderry 1 a quay constructed of unhewn timbers overlaid by layers of peat and brushwood had been added outside the pile palisade at the north-west corner of the site. Possible traces of a landing stage have also been found at Moynagh Lough and unexplained annexes of piles at Cuilmore Lough 1 and Lagore could possibly have been for berthing boats.[25]

In the past it has proved difficult to trace buildings associated with crannogs, chiefly because of the general expectation that they would be large structures. This was not the case, but, as a result of modern excavation techniques coupled with an increasing knowledge of ring-fort structures, buildings are now being found. It is also possible to reassess those recovered in previous excavations and recognize others which were not identified at the time. At Moynagh Lough a double-walled round house c.7.5 m (24 ft 7 in) in diameter has recently been excavated together with a cess-pit and two metal-working areas. In a later phase there was an unusually large round house over 11 m (36 ft) in diameter. The upper strata of the crannog were not waterlogged so it survived as a layer of compacted yellow gravelly earth with a double row of stake-holes on the south side indicating the wattle walling. Internal features included two hearths and various post-holes suggesting the presence of sleeping or sitting arrangements. There was also an occupation area to the east of the house marked out by gravel spreads and rough cobbling with hearths.[26]

Though not understood at the time, evidence for a whole sequence of waterlogged structures was uncovered at Lagore. Hencken thought that various circular huts built of flimsy wattle walling, in what he interpreted as the original crannog make-up, were temporary shelters used by the crannog builders. However, since we know that circular wattle huts are characteristic of early medieval Irish settlement sites, it makes sense to conclude that these were not temporary shelters but rather successive phases of dwellings. Equally, it has been suggested that areas of woven wattle matting may not have been part of the crannog structure, but rather hut walls, fences or hurdles which later became flattened and compacted. We also have some information about structures on the level of the plank palisade. Although these were visible in the mid-nineteenth century, they had, unfortunately, been destroyed before the site was excavated. However, antiquarian descriptions include mention of a square log-cabin style building with plank walls, the holes in which were caulked with moss. This suggests a change from round to rectangular structures similar to that already recorded for ring-forts. A similar sequence from round wattle construction in the centre to rectilinear structures round the edge of the crannog has also been suggested at Ballinderry 1.[27]

### The role of crannogs

Crannogs were defended homesteads occupied by the wealthy and prestigious in early medieval Irish society. The crannog construction would have called for the organization of a considerable labour force and, compared with most ring-forts, the artefactual assemblages are unusually rich, even after taking into account the much better preservation of organic finds.

Some crannogs were definitely royal sites. Lagore, for example, is recorded in the annals as *Loch Gabair*, the seat of the kings of Southern Brega, a branch of the Uí Néill. Their power and wealth clearly called for a well-protected home. Attacks on the site by natives and Vikings are mentioned and an unusually large number of weapons were found during the excavation (41), together with some 200 human bones, many belonging to headless bodies, presumably the victims of violence. It seems possible that two iron collars (40e) with chains and what has tentatively been identified as a leg-iron could have been used for prisoners of war. The finds also indicate the importation of exotic goods, such as Type E imported pottery, and the patronage of luxury crafts. In particular, there is good evidence for ornamental metal- and glass-working including the manufacture of glass studs and millefiori (see p. 93). While the exact status of the inhabitants of many other crannogs is unknown their wealth is clear. It has been suggested, for example, that Moynagh Lough was the home of skilled ornamental metal-workers who also practised a range of other crafts as well as farming.

### Promontory forts

It is difficult to assess the importance of coastal promontory forts in the early medieval Irish settlement pattern. This is because, although Westropp recorded large numbers at the beginning of the century, remarkably few – only eight in all – have been excavated and no distinctive pattern has emerged. They are generally regarded as originating in the Iron Age but they may have begun earlier; the first phase at Dunbeg, Co. Kerry, which may be defensive, provided a radiocarbon date spanning the end of the ninth to the late sixth centuries BC (800–530 cal. BC). However, a site such as Dubh Cathair on the largest of the Aran islands, is most readily assigned to the Iron Age because of its spectacular *chevaux de frise*. On the other hand, some promontory fort sites continued to be occupied for some centuries after the early middle ages. For example, Dooneendermotmore, Co. Cork, was refortified and inhabited as late as the seventeenth century.[28]

Three promontory forts have produced substantial evidence of early medieval occupation: Larrybane, Co. Antrim, Dalkey Island, Co. Dublin and Dunbeg (16). Others may be identified as having early medieval activity even though no excavation has taken place. Dunseverick, for example, a dramatic rocky promontory on the north Antrim coast, was of sufficient importance to attract the attention of Viking raiders. At Dunluce, also in north Antrim, the souterrain underlying the castle suggests an early medieval phase.[29]

Promontory forts, whether coastal or inland, are heavily dependent upon their location to provide an effective natural defence. Since a man-made barrier is only required across the neck of the promontory, an easily defended stronghold may be built in this way with the minimum of effort. At Larrybane there was a single rampart up to 5.18 m (17 ft) wide and 2.6 m (8 ft 6 in) high with an external ditch enclosing an area approximately 35 × 35 m (115 × 115 ft). Excavation revealed that the rampart had been built up on a low clay bank probably dug from the ditch. The core was constructed of boulders faced inside and out with huge basalt blocks and there was evidence for a secondary revetment on the inner face. The entrance may have been across the centrepoint of these defences. Inside at least four occupation layers were discovered with hearths and stone pavements indicating structures and, in the final phase, these were definitely rectangular.

At Dalkey Island the sequence was particularly

complex and difficult to interpret. The promontory had attracted occupation in the Mesolithic and some activity in the Neolithic and Bronze Age periods as well as the later middle ages. The first early medieval phase, a midden containing Type B imported pottery suggesting a fifth- or sixth-century date of occupation, predated the promontory fortification, a bank of simple dump construction with an external ditch. Evidence of a second early medieval phase within the fort after the construction of the rampart included a midden, a hearth and a possible house situated on a platform behind the bank on the eastern side of the promontory, together with Type E imported pottery, which may indicate a seventh-century date of occupation (see p. 70).

At Dunbeg (**16**) the defences are much more complicated and again the precise sequence proved difficult to recover. As already mentioned, the earliest phase may have been a large late Bronze or early Iron Age ditch accompanied by a stone wall and wattle fence. The later defences consisted of four earthen banks with a possible

**16** *Dunbeg promontory fort, Co. Kerry (after Barry 1981).*

palisade along the crest of the innermost, five ditches and an impressive stone rampart in two phases with terracing on its inner face and a well-defended entrance with guard chambers. The only dating evidence was a radiocarbon date from Ditch I which spanned the late seventh to early eleventh centuries AD (cal. AD 680–1020). The date indicates the time when the ditch, which had been recut and was much more substantial than the others, was in use rather than when it was constructed. There are further indications of early medieval activity from within the fort. A large circular *clochán* with a squared interior, approached from the entrance by a stone path, had two occupation layers, the earlier of which produced a radiocarbon date spanning the later ninth to mid-thirteenth centuries AD (cal. AD 870–1260). In addition, a souterrain had been constructed running outward from the entrance through the stone rampart with a sally-port further along the causewayed approach through the earthen defences. Thus it is possible that the stone rampart and Ditch I provided the principal defences at the time the *clochán* was in use. These could be later than the earthen banks and other ditches but there is no clear evidence of this.

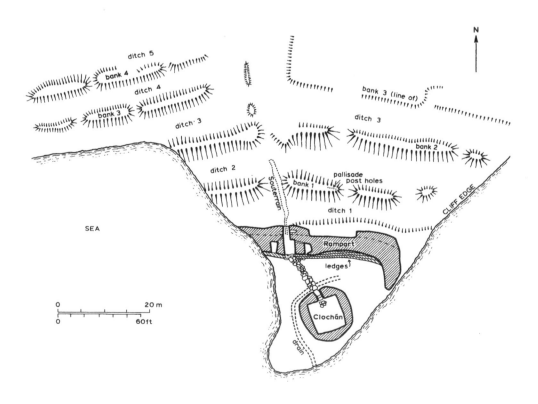

Without further excavation, the significance of these early medieval promontory forts is uncertain. Some were important and prestigious sites: Dalkey Island, with its impressive range of luxury imports, or the known royal stronghold at Dunseverick, for which Tintagel, Cornwall, recently reinterpreted in terms of a secular rather than a monastic settlement,[30] provides an interesting parallel. However others, such as Dunbeg, have proved difficult to date simply because of the almost complete lack of artefacts. In some cases, since there are few signs of internal occupation at any date, promontory forts may have acted as temporary refuges rather than sites of permanent residence.

## Knowth and Clogher

We have already noted ring-forts, crannogs and promontory forts which may be identified as royal sites from the documentary sources. Knowth, Co. Meath, first mentioned in 788 as the seat of the tribe of the Gailenga, and later associated with the kings of the Northern Brega, and Clogher, Co. Tyrone, the capital of the Airgialla, are also important royal settlements, but they do not fit into any of the categories already mentioned. Both are complex, multi-period sites where activity goes right back to the Neolithic period, and Clogher is vitally important as the only Iron Age site so far investigated which seems to demonstrate some kind of domestic occupation during the latter part of the Iron Age with possible signs of continuity into the early medieval period. Some comparison has been made between Clogher and Knowth, and, in particular, between the somewhat

**17** *Knowth, Co. Meath (after Eogan 1977).*

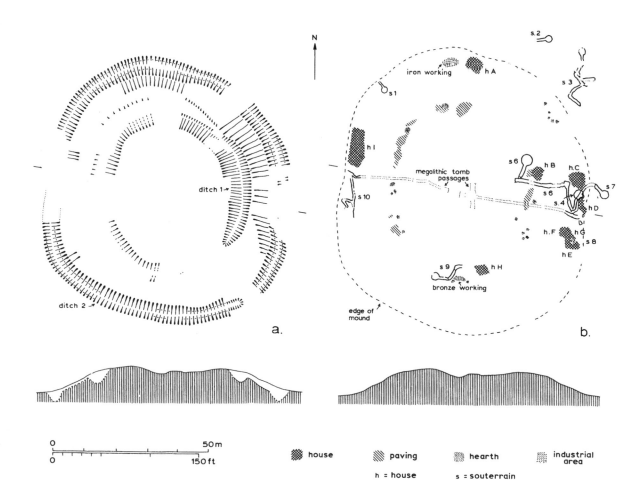

enigmatic settlement structures found on both sites at the beginning of the early medieval period.[31] Knowth is still in the process of excavation, and recent work at Clogher has yet to be finally published, but their importance merits some preliminary discussion.

Knowth[32] (17) is usually remembered, together with Newgrange and Dowth, as one of the three major Neolithic passage-grave complexes of the Boyne valley. After a brief occupation by beaker-using people, Knowth was abandoned for approximately 2,000 years and the second major phase of activity commenced with at least 36 inhumations of apparent Iron Age date (see p. 129). The early medieval occupation may be divided into two periods though it is unclear whether there is any gap between them. In the first (17a) the summit of the main passage grave was enclosed by two concentric ditches up to 6 m (19 ft 8 in) wide and 3 m (9 ft 10 in) deep, the outer dug around the base of the mound, the inner around the top which had been carefully scarped to a maximum height of 6 m (19 ft 8 in). The area enclosed was up to 40 m (131 ft 3 in) in diameter and was approached from the south-east by a causeway. Unfortunately no evidence of the interior survived because of subsequent disturbance. This structure is not dissimilar to a bivallate platform rath, the important difference being that there are no signs of any banks, though the excavator has suggested that these may have been external to the ditches. The ditches quickly silted up and it is unclear how long this phase continued. However, a sherd of E ware found near the base of the ditch suggests it was constructed and occupied at some point between the fifth and eighth centuries. There is more extensive evidence of the second phase (17b), an undefended settlement, which sprawled across both ditches, where traces of at least nine rectangular houses set on stone foundations have been located, together with a couple of souterrains which incorporated both the original east and west tomb passages. Two tenth-century Anglo-Saxon pennies from one of the souterrains suggest an approximate date for this phase coeval with its use as the seat of the kings of the Northern Brega during the ninth to eleventh centuries, and perhaps later until the Anglo-Norman conquest, when a motte was built on top of the mound. It is interesting to note that a souterrain within the mound at Dowth suggests similar early medieval activity, but at Newgrange the passage grave retained its ritual significance throughout the Iron

Age (see p. 4) and there are no traces of early medieval activity.[33]

At Clogher[34] Neolithic and probable early Bronze Age occupation was followed by the building of a drystone wall enclosing an area with large pits, probably datable to the end of the Bronze Age. During the Iron Age a hill-fort was constructed with a simple dumped earth bank and shallow external 'U'-shaped ditch dated, by a spiral finger or toe ring in its lower levels, to the first century BC or AD. The next phase consisted of a structure described by the excavator as a 'ring-ditch' which was located within the hill-fort bank. It enclosed an area approximately 50 m (164 ft) in diameter with a wide flat-bottomed ditch with a palisade on the inside, and on the outside a low, possibly timber-framed bank capped by two phases of palisading. Few internal features survived. Dating evidence for this phase was provided by a radiocarbon date for iron-working in the ditch which spanned the early fifth to the beginning of the seventh centuries AD (cal. AD 410–600) and a large quantity of Type B imported pottery which also suggested occupation during the fifth and sixth centuries. The final phase, which was built on top of the 'ring-ditch' and was separated from it by a sterile layer of yellow sand and stones, was a more conventional though large univallate ring-fort, approximately 70 m (230 ft) in internal diameter, and provisionally dated to the seventh century by E ware. The site seems to have been abandoned c.800, perhaps because of the increasing importance of the Uí Néill at the expense of the Airgialla.

Clogher and Knowth were clearly sites of prestige and wealth. Although there are no direct parallels for them, it is possible that the pattern of occupation and reoccupation over many centuries from the Neolithic onwards is mirrored in some way in ritual complexes such as Tara, Co. Meath, a site of early medieval royal inaugurations amongst the Uí Néill.

## Other settlements

It is much harder to recognize settlements with little or no sign of an enclosure because the

18 *Open and partially enclosed settlements:*
a. *Craig Hill, Co. Antrim (after Waterman 1956b);*
b. *Beginish, Co. Kerry (after O'Kelly 1956);*
c. *Ballynavenooragh, Co. Kerry (after Cuppage et al 1986);* d. *Ballywee, Co. Antrim (after Lynn 1974).*

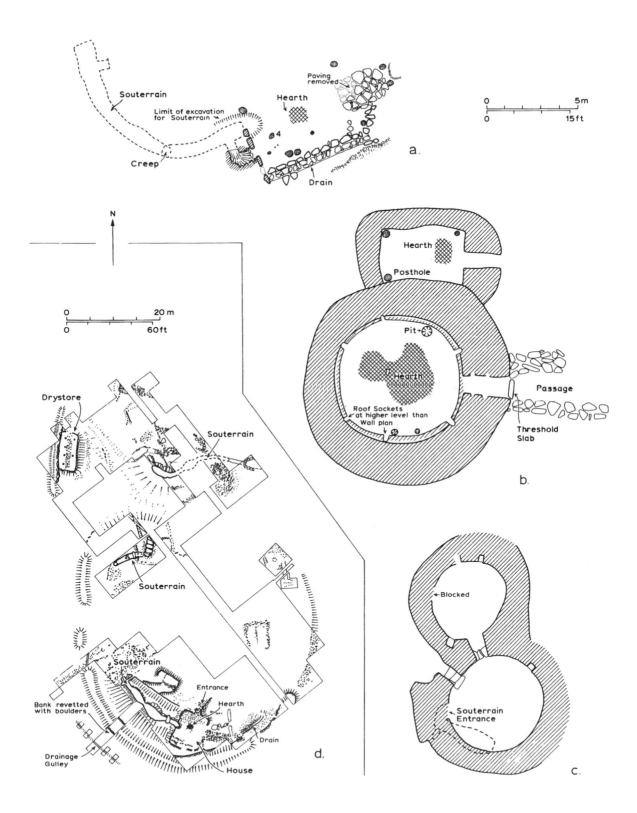

a.

Souterrain
Limit of excavation for Souterrain
Creep
Hearth
Paving removed
Drain

0   5m
0   15ft

b.

Hearth
Posthole
Pit
Hearth
Roof Sockets at higher level than Wall plan
Passage
Threshold Slab

N

0   20 m
0   60ft

d.

Drystore
Souterrain
Souterrain
Souterrain
Entrance
Hearth
Bank revetted with boulders
Drainage Gulley
Drain
House

c.

Blocked
Souterrain Entrance

remains of most early medieval domestic structures are so flimsy. Therefore archaeologists are dependent upon a variety of circumstances which facilitate their identification. Some are located through the chance discovery of a souterrain. Others survive as the result of environmental factors. In upland and other marginal areas unsuitable for modern tillage a palimpsest of past landscapes is sometimes preserved, including early medieval huts and fields. In coastal districts sea erosion and the movement of sand may reveal middens and other occupational debris with early medieval artefacts.

In some parts of Ireland isolated souterrains are found relatively frequently, usually as a result of ploughing or other agricultural activities. Unfortunately, the above-ground features have often already been destroyed or only survive as an associated occupation layer without any recognizable structures. However, from time to time buildings have been successfully located indicating open or only partially-enclosed settlements with one or more houses and outbuildings. Craig Hill, Co. Antrim, is a particularly good example of an open settlement with a single house and souterrain (18a). Situated on a terrace dug into the slope with a stone-lined drain on the uphill side, the plan of the building was delineated by post-holes indicating a timber-framed structure. The shape of the house was originally described as trapezoidal, but the position of the drain and the souterrain entrance, together with information gained from parallels excavated since, would tend to suggest a more conventional rectangular shape with post-hole 4 marking some kind of internal partition or roof support connected with the souterrain entrance rather than the line of the wall. Other features include the paved entrance porch facing east and the central hearth. The souterrain, a 12.2 m (40 ft) long passage divided into two separate chambers by a creep, had been conceived as part of the original plan and was almost certainly entered directly from the house.[35]

Two other sites from Co. Antrim have produced similar evidence. At Antiville, a marshy spot beside a tributary of the River Larne, a rectangular house and souterrain were enclosed by a shallow ditch cut through the peat with a very slight bank on the inner side. This was interpreted, not as a ring-fort enclosure, but rather as a means of draining excess water from the site. At Ballywee (18d), a rectangular house and souterrain had been built in the lee of a stretch of bank

with an external drainage gully. Traces of outbuildings were also found together with a second rectangular house and two other souterrains. At some stage a northern annexe had also been constructed containing a drystore, again in the shelter of a short stretch of bank with an outer ditch to facilitate drainage.[36]

It is interesting to note that in Co. Antrim open or partially enclosed settlements with rectangular houses and souterrains are yet to be matched by similar habitations with round houses and souterrains. However, round houses belonging to an early medieval transhumance village have been excavated at Aughnabrack, Ballyutoag at 275 m (900 ft) OD in the north-west margins of the Belfast Mountains (21a). The site, which was located from air photographs, consisted of two conjoined curvilinear enclosures delineated by low earthen banks with a group of circular hut platforms around the perimeter, a series of adjacent fields and a third, smaller enclosure to the north. On the Dingle Peninsula, Co. Kerry, stone *clocháns* have been preserved, sometimes as part of elaborate field systems, on the uncultivated slopes of Mount Brandon. Frequently they are difficult to date since their use persisted into the twentieth century, but sometimes there are clues which do suggest early medieval occupation. For example, at Ballynavenooragh (18c), there is a pair of conjoined *clocháns* with an attached souterrain entered from one of the huts. Huts and fields have also been investigated near the shores of Lough Gur, Co. Limerick. The site, known as the 'Spectacles' (21c), was situated on a rocky platform and consisted of a stone round house 4.5 m (15 ft) in diameter, two minor structures in an adjacent field and a rectangular building in the field beyond.[37]

Stretches of Ireland's coastline, including parts of Kerry, Donegal, Derry, Antrim and Down,[38] have long attracted archaeological attention because sand movement and sea erosion have from time to time exposed the remains of early medieval occupation. Unfortunately structures rarely survive and the stratification is frequently confusing because of the constant build-up and erosion of the sand which can cause material from many different periods to become hopelessly mixed. The most usual remains are old turf lines, middens and occupation layers with early medieval artefacts. Occasionally, however, more extensive evidence has been found. For example, excavations at Dooey, Co. Donegal, in a grass-covered sand-dune from which artefacts had previously been recovered, revealed a complex sequence of activity. The first phase consisted of a habitation area approximately 56 × 64 m (150 × 210 ft), the major feature of which was a series of fire pits. During Phase 2 occupation continued and the central part of the site was demarcated by a shallow ditch, which, in Phase 3, began to fill up with refuse and wind-blown sand. The finds suggested that the site had been inhabited by a community of craftworkers since there was considerable evidence for ornamental metalworking. In the final phase the area within the enclosure had been reused as a cemetery.[39] At Beginish Island, Co. Kerry, stone structures also survived. Occupation had begun before the influx of sand which later engulfed the site and prior to excavation the sand had been blown away to reveal a complex of fields with eight houses in two different phases separated by a layer of wind-blown sand. Of the structures excavated House 1, belonging to Phase 2, was the best preserved (18b). The house had been dug right into the ground, which presumably protected it from prevailing winds but at the same time made it rather damp. A circular pit had been dug 6.75 m (22 ft 2 in) in diameter and lined with drystone walling to form the inner face of the house wall. At ground level the outer face of the wall began and the inner continued with a rubble core between the two and the roof had been supported on radial rafters set into sockets near the top. The entrance was approached by a stone-lined passage roofed with lintels, one of which turned out to have been reused and had a runic inscription on it, suggesting that the house had been occupied some time after the coming of the Vikings and towards the end of the early medieval period (see p. 191). At some point a second room with a separate entrance had been appended to the house, but at ground level.[40]

Traces of early medieval occupation have also sometimes been found in caves. In Co. Antrim numerous old sea caves associated with the raised beach of north-east Ireland have been investigated. For example, at Park Cave and Potter's Cave, Ballintoy, various animal bones and shellfish remains, as well as souterrain ware, were discovered and at Portbraddon various layers indicating prehistoric activity were followed by an early medieval phase suggested by the presence of souterrain ware and a double-sided antler comb. Elsewhere caves formed in carboniferous limestone have revealed evidence of early medieval

activity at Keshkorran, Co. Sligo, Edenvale and Midleton, Co. Cork, and Kilgreany, Co. Waterford. Excavations at the last concentrated on the recovery of what is now known to be a deposit of late Pleistocene fauna mixed with material indicative of Neolithic activity, but the remains of early medieval occupation were considerable, including three possible hearths, charcoal, black earth and stones and a number of artefacts. It is difficult to assess to what extent the occupation of caves may have been temporary, but the intensive activity at Kilgreany certainly suggests more permanent habitation.[41]

Having noted the various different sorts of open and partially-enclosed settlements which have so far been recognized, we face the problem of trying to gauge their importance in the early medieval settlement pattern as a whole. The only indications we can obtain at the moment – and this must represent a great underestimate – is by plotting the various miscellaneous settlements and souterrains unassociated with ring-forts or ecclesiastical remains in a given area. The finds from such settlements are rarely rich – Dooey would seem to be a notable exception – and one gets the impression that these were usually the homes of those who lacked the prestige, wealth or need for more impressive habitations.

There has been a recurrent idea that the legal texts suggest dispersed homesteads, exemplified by ring-forts, were an expression of free status, while the servile or semi-servile lived in nucleated settlements. There has also been the notion that the *clachan*, the nucleated settlement of the small farming community which survived in parts of western Ireland into the twentieth century, may go back to the early medieval period and, indeed, beyond.[42] However, there is as yet little to support these hypotheses in the archaeological record, where, though open and partially enclosed settlements may have housed the lower echelons of society, they do not appear to have been nucleated.

## Conclusion

With modern excavation techniques our knowledge of early medieval Irish settlement is rapidly increasing. We are able to discuss some of the finer points of ring-fort and crannog construction, recover house plans, often from the frailest of archaeological evidence, and give some idea of the day-to-day activities of the occupants. However, we are still unable to answer many of the more fundamental questions.

Although a basic chronological framework has now been established, we still have a considerable way to go. The origins of early medieval Irish settlement types remain controversial and confusing. It is also almost impossible to trace changes in settlement types and patterns during the course of the period, almost 800 years: the change in house plans from round to rectangular, an interesting and potentially important discovery, is the only major development to have recognized so far. However the development of dendrochronological dating, which now offers the prospect of building up precise settlement chronologies on waterlogged sites, could prove revolutionary. Equally, judicious use of high-precision calibrated radiocarbon dating, together with a better understanding of the chronology and typology of key artefacts, such as imported pottery and copper-alloy pins, would also be of great use.

We also have surprisingly little idea of regional variations. Too often we are examining ancient settlements in isolation and it has proved difficult to relate them, either to neighbouring sites, or to begin to reconstruct the broader outlines of the early medieval landscape. We have noted more obvious differences between the rocky scenery of western Ireland, with its large numbers of stone-walled ring-forts and *clocháns*, compared with the concentrations of earthen ring-forts and the overwhelming use of timber detectable in more fertile areas. But there must be many more subtle changes which the concentration of work in certain parts of Ireland only tends to obscure further. It would be interesting to know, for example, whether the change from round to rectangular structures noted in north-east Ulster is equally true of Kerry.

There is also the problem of relating the archaeological evidence to the documentary sources. Important sites mentioned in the annals such as Lagore and Clogher have been identified and excavated, but the potential link between known historical personalities or events and the archaeological evidence remains curiously tantalizing and has sometimes proved positively misleading. The descriptions of Irish society in the legal texts and other documents are equally difficult to compare with the known types and patterns of settlement. Inevitably we know much more of the upper echelons of society from both the historical and archaeological material. Those who have little to lose leave less trace in the archaeological record.

# CHAPTER 4

# Food and Farming

## The nature of the evidence

The study of early medieval farming in Ireland has in the past largely concentrated on the historical and literary sources rather than on the archaeological evidence. The law tracts, in particular, though undoubtedly idealized and highly schematic, provide a very valuable insight into everyday farming practices which must have changed comparatively little over the generations. *Crith Gablach*, for example, describes a strict hierarchy of farmers, each listed with their possessions: agricultural tools and equipment owned personally or shared with others, crops, livestock and animal pens. The law tracts also provide more specific information on agricultural techniques such as brewing, milling, and beekeeping, the construction of fences and the value of trees.[1] Other historical sources include more incidental details. The annals, for example, frequently refer to freak weather conditions, and sometimes to bad harvests, famine or animal disease. The hagiographical literature, though mainly concerned with the life of a particular saint and his or her miracles, can also be of use. For example, in Adomnán's late seventh-century *Life of Columba* several agricultural processes are mentioned, including milking, butchering, threshing and ploughing; and in the seventh-century *Life of Brigit* by Cogitosus there is an interesting reference to the difficulties encountered in the transportation of a newly-quarried millstone to the monastery.[2] Similarly, the literary sources, though clearly open to the exaggeration and idealization inherent in all epic poetry and heroic saga, cannot be discounted, as long as their limitations are realized. For example, the theme of the most famous of the early Irish epics, *Táin Bó Cúailnge*, written in its earliest form during the eighth century but with a long oral existence before that, tells the story of an important early medieval Irish pastime, cattle raiding, with the object in this instance of carrying off a prize stud bull. At the end of the period *The Vision of MacConglinne* gives us an interesting insight into Irish culinary arts.[3]

Environmental archaeology has the potential to tell us a great deal about early medieval Irish food and farming. The first impetus to research of this kind came as a result of the excavations carried out by the Harvard expedition in the 1930s. At Cahercommaun great quantities of animal bones, a small amount of bird bones, molluscs and charcoal were collected and identified. But more interesting results were obtained from the crannog excavations at Lagore and Ballinderry 1 and 2, since waterlogging had resulted in ideal anaerobic conditions for the survival, not only of bones, but also of plant and insect remains as well as wood. In addition, at Ballinderry 2 Jessen and Mitchell were able to construct a pollen diagram, though only for the Bronze Age levels.[4] Other work on pollen followed. For example, samples from Littleton Bog, Co. Tipperary, Agha Bog, Co. Meath, Red Bog, Co. Louth and Goodland Townland, Co. Antrim, all produced diagrams indicating increased agriculture during the early medieval period.[5]

The second impetus came partly as a result of a general upsurge of interest in environmental archaeology during the 1970s but also, more particularly, as a result of the intensive excavation of areas of Viking and medieval Dublin, where waterlogged conditions again preserved a wide range of organic material. New techniques are fast developing, such as the more detailed study of the osteological material, revealing sex, age at slaughter and meat yield as well as species; the study of pollen, grain and other seeds, and of other plant remains for what they might tell us of the types and processes of crop husbandry; the study of insects and land and water molluscs to aid us with the reconstruction of the palaeoenvironment and, in the case of shellfish, as a source of food. Although some published studies[6] already indicate the importance of such research, much is still in the course of completion.

Therefore, this consideration of early medieval Irish food and farming comes at a time of change. We are still dependent upon the evidence of the historical and literary sources, and the archaeologist should continue to make use of these. But we should also be aware that the available archaeological evidence is on the brink of being superseded by much more detailed and wide-ranging research.

## Climate, soils and vegetation

Early medieval farming in Ireland must obviously have been affected by regional differences in climate, soils, and in the resulting vegetation. Such differences obviously led to varying levels of prosperity and of surplus and subsistence, as, indeed, they still do today. For example, the early medieval farming population who lived in the lush pastures of Meath would have encountered much less difficulty in producing their livelihood than their counterparts in West Donegal or Mayo, where high rainfall, low evaporation and bad drainage have caused the growth of large areas of blanket bog.

Today the most important element of the Irish climate is its rainfall. Rainbearing winds blow in predominantly from the west. Currently in most areas it rains on at least 150 days each year, though often as showers rather than continuous precipitation, and in parts of the west this rises to 200 days or more. Only very small areas of the east, mainly round Dublin, have an annual rainfall of less than 800 mm (32 in). In the central lowlands this rises to 1,000 mm (40 in) or more, and in the mountains and large areas of the west, over 1,200 mm (48 in) is the norm, but in isolated mountainous pockets it can reach double that. The dryest months are March to June; in the west the winter months are the wettest, while in the east the distribution is more even, though Dublin's annual maximum falls during August. These large amounts of rainfall and their seasonal pattern are bound to be a threat to crop production, particularly at harvest time.

On the other hand, Ireland has a mild climate, since the sea acts as an important moderating influence preventing excesses of heat and cold. Heavy snows and long frosts are rare. The mean daily air temperature in January is 3°–8°C (37°–46°F), the coldest areas in the north, the warmest in the south-west; while in July it is 14°–17°C (57°–63°F), the south being slightly warmer than the north.[7]

Though the main features of the climate must have remained relatively constant, there is a spectrum of variation which results in significant differences in temperature and rainfall over the centuries. In north-west Europe as a whole, there seems to have been some climatic deterioration during the late Bronze Age, though the situation was reversed during the early centuries AD. There appears to have been another downturn during the late sixth and seventh centuries but, from the tenth century onwards, there was a gradual rise in the mean annual temperature which peaked during the thirteenth century.[8]

In Ireland during the early medieval period unusual or adverse weather conditions were often mentioned in the annals. For example, the rainy summer of 759 was probably responsible for the famine in 760, and the long snowy winter of 764 was followed by an abnormal drought, which again led to a shortage of food in the subsequent year. In 855 there was an unusually late and heavy snowstorm on 23 April, which fell to the height of men's belts, while on the night of 2 August 783 there was a terrible thunderstorm. High winds could also be a problem. In 892 a great windstorm on the feast of St Martin (11 November) destroyed a large number of trees and blew houses and wooden churches from their foundations.[9]

Before Ireland's entry into the European Community in 1973, when substantial funds became available for land improvement, two-thirds of the country was already improved agricultural land and most of the remaining third was rough grazing. A modern map (19) of land-use capacity shows that the areas where there are no serious agricultural limitations are mainly in the south and east, where well-drained grey-brown podzolics are the major soil type. In the drumlin belt to the north, where gleys predominate, agriculture is more limited, mainly due to heavy soils and poor drainage. In parts of the central lowlands land-use is very limited owing to the growth of peat in the form of raised bog; while in the west, the growth of peat in the form of blanket bog, steep slopes and high altitudes further limit land exploitation. With the ard plough only the light well-drained soils were suitable for cultivation, but the gradual

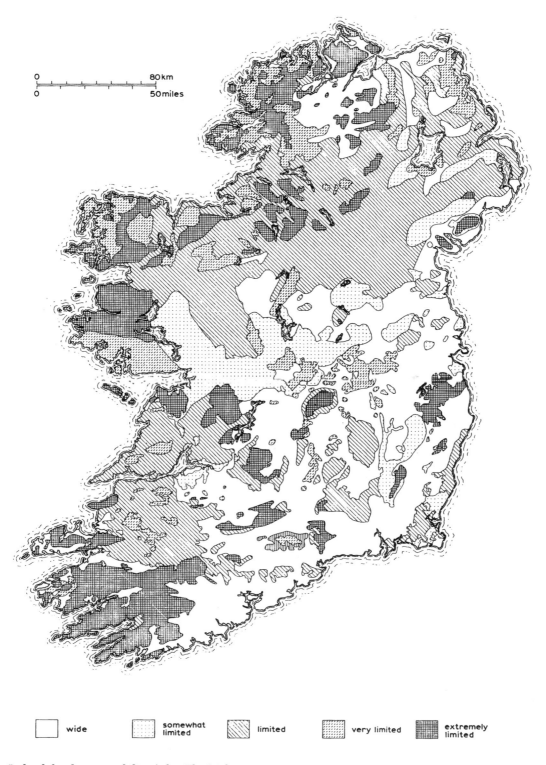

**19** *Ireland: land-use capability (after The Irish National Committee for Geography 1979).*

| | | | | |
|---|---|---|---|---|
| wide | somewhat limited | limited | very limited | extremely limited |

adoption of the more efficient coulter plough, which Mitchell has suggested was introduced from Roman Britain, coincided with an expansion of agriculture and opened the way for the exploitation of the heavier soils on the drumlins.[10]

A glance at the more fertile areas of Ireland today gives the false impression of a well-wooded landscape, but closer observation reveals that, apart from modern conifer plantations, trees usually grow in ones or twos or small clumps rather than in coppices or woods.[11] This is the culmination of a deafforestation process which continued largely without check from the early centuries AD until the mid-nineteenth century. This may be exemplified by the pollen diagram from Red Bog, Co. Louth, which shows that between the first and sixth centuries AD (cal. AD 1–600) there is a sharp fall in tree pollens, and a corresponding rise in herbaceous and cereal pollens indicating the clearance of secondary woodland for agriculture. Similarly, a radiocarbon date from Garradrean Townland, South Wexford, suggests that forest clearance took place between the fifth and eighth centuries (cal. AD 430–770) in conjunction with the establishment of a nearby ring-fort to provide suitable land for grazing and tillage.[12]

The gradual clearance of oak during the early medieval period has been particularly well charted as a result of the construction of the Belfast tree-ring chronology.[13] Problems were encountered in finding samples to extend the master chronology backwards before AD 855, though this was partially achieved with the aid of long-lived oak timbers incorporated into the structures of horizontal mills dating from the late seventh to the early tenth centuries. In other words, although long-lived oaks were available for the construction of horizontal mills until the early tenth century, they may have been scarce. They then seem to be totally lacking, as far as the dendrochronological record is concerned, until the thirteenth century. These thirteenth-century oaks had started to grow in the later ninth century, thereby demonstrating a phase of regeneration after a phase of depletion. Presumably therefore the clearance of oak woods during the early middle ages first caused a shortage of mature trees which may subsequently have become more serious. It is interesting to note that in the eighth-century legal tract *Bretha Co-maithchesa (Judgements of Neighbourhood)*[14] trees were carefully categorized according to their species, size and usefulness, and penalties exacted

accordingly for the unlawful lopping of a branch or the cutting down of a whole tree. Oak heads the list of the highest category, the 'nobles of the wood', and its size and usefulness for timber and acorns is reflected in the fine of two milch-cows for its unlawful destruction.

In the west trees are naturally less abundant. The strong, spray-laden westerly winds blowing off the sea totally prohibit their growth in some areas, such as exposed coastal sections of the Burren; in others they are bent away from the wind and their growth stunted on the windward side.

Other types of natural vegetation include sand dunes, salt marshes and heaths. Fenlands are becoming rarer because of modern agricultural improvements. However, peat bogs remain a distinctive feature of the landscape. Large areas of raised bog have formed in Counties Offaly, Westmeath, Longford and Roscommon, and blanket bog covers significant portions of the west and north where the rainfall is high, especially West Donegal, Mayo and Connemara. Peat remains a major source of fuel and was also exploited in the early middle ages, together with wood. Traces of peat ash have been recovered from the ring-fort Ballypalady 2 and the promontory fort at Larrybane, Co. Antrim.[15]

## The farming landscape

One of the Irish legal texts[16] depicts the countryside as divided into cultivable and uncultivable land of different values according to its fertility. Though highly schematic and in places difficult to interpret, it nevertheless provides an interesting insight into the types of land which would have been available to the early medieval farming community. Cultivable land was divided into three grades. At the top, land considered to be first-class had to be level, clear of undergrowth and persistent weeds such as thistles, and sufficiently fertile for a wide variety of crops to flourish without the application of manure. Less valuable grades of cultivable land were those on the uplands and those which had yet to be cleared of woodland with the aid of an axe. Uncultivable land was divided into ferny plains, heathery mountains and turf bogs. Land values may have waxed and waned, but in this text a unit of top-grade land (perhaps 13.85 hectares (34.25 acres) extent if hints of size elsewhere in the laws are correct), customarily measured in terms of cattle, was valued at a *cumal* of 24 milch cows, while a similar amount of turf bog was worth a *cumal* of only eight dry cows. (*Cumal*, originally literally a 'female slave', was usually used in the laws to denote the highest unit of value.) The value of land could be increased if it included an extra facility, such as a wood or mineral resource, the site of a mill or access to the sea. For example, the presence of a cow-track on the land leading to a cattle-pond would have increased its value by a yearling calf.

It is difficult to calculate the size of farms.[17] Between 28 and 280 hectares (70 and 700 acres) has been put forward for the various grades of free farmer listed in *Críth Gablach*, but the system is so hierarchical as to suggest that the figures may have borne little relationship to reality. Clearly those with poorer-quality land would have needed more than those with more fertile land in order to keep the same number of livestock, and land suitable for crop cultivation would have been limited to the better soils. In practice the legal texts provide a considerable amount of evidence for farming in common, and suggest that a portion of the land of the kin (*fintiu*) was held by each adult male.[18] At the beginning of the seventh century the kin was seen in terms of the *derbfine*, or four-generation family group, though by the end of the century it had become reduced to the *gelfine* or three-generation family group. Within the kin many farming processes were carried out co-operatively, for example ploughing and pasturage, though later there is some indication that the latter could be shared with a partner outside the family group. Some arable land may have consisted of a block where each man owned scattered strips. Some pasture held by individuals within the family group was fenced, but there was also lower-quality common land used for summer grazing which seems to have been utilized by the whole tribe rather than a single kin group.

The *Judgements of Neighbourhood* tell us something of fencing techniques.[19] Four fence types are listed. The first, a ditch dug with a spade where the spoil was piled up to form a bank, may have been employed on arable land, and the second, a stone-built wall, seems to have been used in the same way. The third, a stout oak fence cut with an axe, was specifically constructed to partition woodland. However, the fourth type seems to have been the most common. Constructed with a bill-hook, it was made of posts and wattles with a blackthorn crest along the top to prevent animals from jumping over it.

Using the archaeological evidence, a picture of the early medieval farming landscape is at present only very dimly perceived, and much more research needs to be done before we will know to what extent it may be possible to compare the archaeology with the documentary sources. Field systems of suspected early medieval date have been noted, usually associated with ring-forts, but very little excavation has taken place. Air-photography has proved particularly useful in their location. In lowland and more fertile regions little evidence survives, simply because the land has continued under intensive cultivation until the present day, thus erasing almost all traces of earlier field boundaries. Occasionally, however, traces can still be detected as, for example, the very small irregular fields radiating outwards from a destroyed ring-fort at Rathangan, Co. Kildare.[20] But, on more marginal land, particularly in the uplands, whole relict landscapes still survive and, though different layers of such a palimpsest are almost impossible to date without excavation or the rare survival of some documentary record, it is certain that some of these must include early medieval fields and enclosures. Stone-walled ring-forts associated with a pattern of irregular fields of different sizes have been recorded near Corrofin, Co. Clare (**20**), and more extensive work has recently been carried out in the uplands of Co. Antrim. At Ballynashee,[21] for example, on marginal land 230 m (750 ft) OD on the fringes of the Antrim plateau which is now used for sheep pasture, a complex containing two earthen ring-forts and an adjacent round hut with a curvilinear field system has been noted, together with a pair of conjoined ring-forts, a rectangular house foundation and a rectangular ditched platform nearby. The cluster of round huts set within two curvilinear enclosures with their adjacent small irregular fields at Aughnabrack, Ballyutoag (**21a**), which is probably a transhumance settlement, has already been mentioned (see p. 46). Similarly, in Co. Kerry *clocháns* associated with small irregular fields, as at Ballynavenooragh on the slopes of Mount Brandon, may suggest summer pasturing on the uplands, though the field boundaries are impossible to date without excavation. In parts of western Ireland, where considerable stretches of blanket bog have grown since the early to mid-third millennium BC, gradually enveloping the ancient landscape, there is the prospect that peat

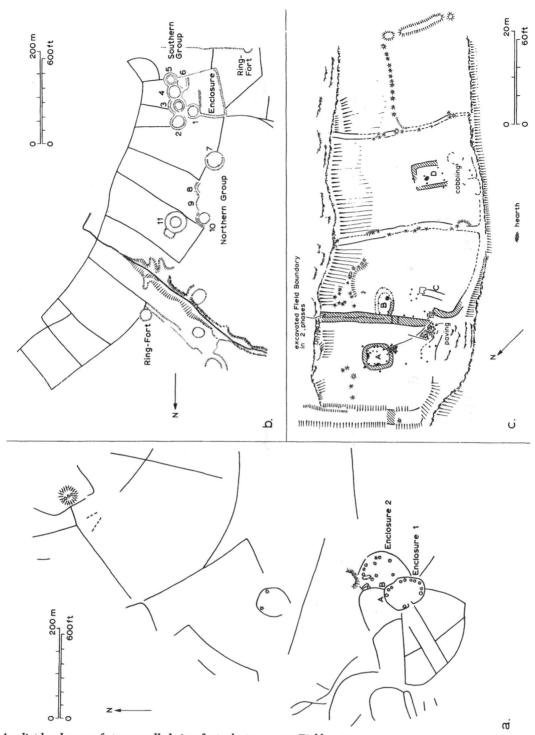

**20** *A relict landscape of stone-walled ring-forts, huts and irregular fields on a limestone hillside near Corrofin, Co. Clare (Copyright: Cambridge University Committee for Aerial Photography).*

**21** *Field systems:*
*a. Ballyutoag, Co. Antrim (after Williams 1984);*
*b. Cush, Co. Limerick (after Ó Ríordáin, S.P. 1940);*
*c. The 'Spectacles' (after Ó Ríordáin, S.P. 1949a).*

clearance will expose early field systems. Up to now research has concentrated on the Neolithic field systems of North Mayo but, since the onset of peat growth has been shown to occur at Cashel-keelty 2, Co. Kerry, as late as the thirteenth century AD (cal. AD 1190–1280), there remains the exciting possibility that one day an early medieval relict landscape may be uncovered with the fields and settlements undisturbed by modern farming.[22]

There have been no recent excavations of early medieval field systems. Indeed, the only definite early medieval field systems which have undergone any excavation at all are at Cush and the 'Spectacles', Co. Limerick, which were investigated by S.P. Ó Ríordáin in the 1930s and 1940s. At the 'Spectacles'[23] a group of huts associated with ancient fields was excavated on a terrace overlooking Lough Gur (21c). Four small rectangular fields were located on the terrace; their average area amounted to only about 0.06 hectares ($\frac{1}{7}$ acre) and they were probably used for tillage. One of the field boundaries was completely excavated and found to be a two-phase structure consisting of a double stone facing with a rubble core which had at some point been increased in width from 0.9 to 1.8 m (3 to 6 ft). The make-up of the other field boundaries was similar except for one which was simply an earthen bank. Further up the hillside there was a system of larger fields and a semi-circular enclosure and this is probably where the livestock were pastured.

At Cush Ó Ríordáin noticed that, in addition to the northern and southern groups of ring-forts, there was a line of small, approximately rectangular fields stretching along the west-facing slopes of the hillside (21b). Some of the field boundaries ran up to the ring-fort ditches, and trial excavation together with pollen analysis suggested that the fields were contemporary with at least the later stages of occupation in the ring-forts. Sections dug across these ancient field boundaries revealed that they were delineated by a 'U'-shaped ditch about 900 mm (3 ft) deep and a low bank surviving to a height of 450 mm (1 ft 6 in), which tallies remarkably well with the ditch and bank system described in the laws for the enclosure of arable land. It is also interesting to note that at Cush a block of ridge and furrow made by a heavy plough with a fixed mouldboard has been recorded running approximately east-west across part of the rectangular enclosure attached to the southern group of ring-forts. Its age has not been checked by excavation, but since it is confined to the enclosure, it could be early medieval. The closest parallel for the irregularity of these ridges, and their narrow width of 1.8–3.05 m (6–10 ft), is provided by a rectangular field of ridge and furrow at Gwithian, Cornwall, which is tenth- or eleventh-century in date.[24]

Ridge-and-furrow cultivation set in long rectangular fields approximately 0.8 hectares (2 acres) in extent has also been noted at Goodland, Co. Antrim.[25] Mitchell has suggested that these fields could be as early as *c.* AD 600, since a pollen diagram showed an increase in the weed sage (*Artemisia*), which may be associated with the introduction of the mouldboard plough, at about this time. Cairns were also located nearby with sherds of souterrain ware in them; these may have been built up by clearing the fields of stone prior to ploughing. By the fifteenth or sixteenth century, however, this field system had gone out of use, huts were built over it and the land was used for summer pasture.

Therefore our knowledge of the farming landscape from the archaeological evidence is extremely limited. It is recognized that the purpose to which fields were put and, more especially, the method of cultivation, affects their shape. For example, small square fields are associated with a light ard while elongated plots of ridge and furrow are more likely to be the product of a heavier fixed-mouldboard plough. In upland areas the size of the fields was often dictated by the need to clear stones, and these were piled up to form walls.[26] It is clear, however, that a much fuller investigation of field systems associated with early medieval settlement types is necessary, including excavation, pollen analysis and radiocarbon dating, as well as survey, both from the air and on the ground, before we can hope to reconstruct a fuller picture of the early medieval farming landscape and its evolution during the period. This must be done before modern agricultural practices completely destroy the evidence.

## Livestock and other domesticated animals

The documentary sources make it clear that cattle were one of the most important elements of the early medieval rural economy in Ireland. As we have already seen the fertility of land was graded in terms of cattle, and the status of farmers was based on the number of cattle they owned. Clients rented cattle from their lord and paid him in food render which usually included cattle, for example the pick of the yearling stock, and milk products. Cattle raiding seems to have been considered 'more like a dangerous sport than a crime'.[27]

There has been some disagreement about the number of cattle kept by individual farmers. Lucas has argued that milk yields would have been very much lower than today because of the lack of selective breeding, poor pasture and the potential shortage of winter fodder. Therefore more cattle would have to have been kept to provide the population with milk products, which were a major part of the diet during the summer months. On the other hand a study of the legal texts has shown that the highest grade of strong farmer (*mruigfer*) ideally owned only 20 cows, two bulls and four oxen in his own right and rented 24 cows from his lord. Although a lord might dispose of excess cows by renting them out to his clients, or they might be used in barter, there was a limit to how much meat and milk produce could be consumed since the means for their preservation was restricted to salting. Similarly, the number of cattle which could be over-wintered was, to a certain extent, dictated by the amount of fodder available.[28]

The mildness of the Irish climate means that cattle can be kept outside all the year round. Though in parts of the west the grass hardly ceases to grow, in the east winter pasture must have been much more limited. There is no evidence that hay was harvested, and no root crops were grown for winter feed, so cattle would have been reduced to eating what pasture there was, the stubble in the fields after harvest and perhaps holly leaves and seaweed. For this reason it was important to make the best possible use of the available grass by moving the cattle to the uplands in summer, known as booleying, and by utilizing rough pasture and temporary grazing, such as watermeadows. In this way the fields nearer the settlement could be conserved for winter food.[29] But bad weather, particularly at the end of winter, would have severely affected the availability of fodder and weakened the animals. The annals tell us, for example, that in 777 heavy rain and wind during the summer resulted in cattle murrain which persisted during 778–9 causing men to starve to death.[30]

Cattle were kept principally for their milk rather than their meat. This is made obvious by the ratio of cows to bulls and oxen given in *Críth Gablach*. All but the few male calves required for stud or draught were killed for their meat when still young, but heifers were allowed to grow to maturity. Dairy produce was largely summer food since cows gave little milk in winter. It was also a major source of protein and could be prepared in a variety of ways including skimmed and thickened milk, curds and whey, butter and both hard and soft cheeses.[31]

Cattle could not be left to wander unattended but were watched over by herdsmen who protected them from wolves or cattle raiders. When the need arose they might be herded into temporary pens – calf folds are mentioned in *Críth Gablach* – or more permanent corrals. The second ring-fort at Garryduff showed hardly any trace of occupation and may well have served as a cattle enclosure.[32]

In the past osteological samples from excavations consistently recovered a higher percentage of cattle bones compared with those of pig or sheep. Some 25 years ago Proudfoot noted that cattle bones made up 70 per cent or more of the total collected from many excavated ring-forts. Only at Boho, Co. Fermanagh, did the amount fall below 70 per cent and at Cahercommaun, Co. Clare, it was as high as 97 per cent of the total.[33] Figures such as these have sometimes led archaeologists to assume, wrongly, that the early medieval Irish population lived largely on beef and the importance of dairy products and cereals has tended to be forgotten. However, it is now recognized that the rather haphazard collecting techniques employed on earlier excavations naturally favoured the recovery of bigger bones. Since cattle are larger than sheep or pigs their bones are therefore more likely to have been collected and in acid soil cattle bones may have been preserved while those of smaller animals decayed. With more scientific sampling techniques and more detailed consideration of the evidence recovered, our perspective is changing and the importance of mixed animal husbandry is beginning to be recognized. If the percentage minimum number of individual animals (MNI) is listed rather than the total percentage of bones, though more cattle are still usually represented than sheep or pigs, they tend to form a lower percentage of the total. For example, at Moynagh Lough crannog, Co. Meath, cattle are 39 per cent of the total, pigs 36 per cent and sheep 25 per cent. Sometimes, however, the pattern is different. At Rathmullan, Co. Down, the first ring-fort excavation where it has proved possible to sample bones from different phases, the percentage MNI of pigs is consistently higher than cattle and with each phase the percentage MNI of pigs increases while that of cattle declines. However, without comparable samples from other sites it is difficult to tell to what extent Rathmullan may have been an exception.[34] With future research it would be interesting to see whether sites with a higher percentage of cattle bones are those of higher status.

Research is also beginning to be done on cattle age and slaughter patterns. Work on cattle bones from the open settlement at Knowth, Co. Meath, Moynagh Lough crannog and a settlement at Marshes Upper, Co. Louth, has shown that the majority of cattle were killed before maturity, mainly between one and two years old. Cattle bones are difficult to sex but, where this has proved possible, it has been shown that the majority of mature cattle killed were cows. This demonstrates indirectly the importance of dairy produce as evidenced in the documentary sources, since it is likely that the immature beasts slaughtered were excess male calves while the mature animals were mainly cows, possibly those past their prime.[35] Work has also been carried out on some sites to try and identify whether the cattle were being kept on site or whether joints of meat were being brought in. At Seacash ring-fort, Co. Antrim, perinatal calf bones were found suggesting the site was a primary producer rather than just a consumer, and the presence of a full range of cattle bones rather than just the meat joints indicates that entire carcasses had been cut up and utilized on site. However, cattle bones recovered from the monastic site at Armagh suggested a different picture, perhaps because it was a religious rather than a secular settlement. The bones were mainly of mature beasts, some distinctly ageing, and they were mainly good meat joints, which suggests that butchery was carried out elsewhere and the meat brought onto the site for consumption.[36]

Pigs were kept primarily for their meat though their hides and bones were also utilized. The documentary evidence indicates that the early medieval Irish were very fond of fresh and salt pork, bacon, and other culinary delicacies such as black puddings, white puddings and sausages; pork products in the form of bacon were also included as part of food render. Pigs might be fattened on corn or milk but acorns were also an important source of food, and it was frequently thought appropriate to record a good crop of oak mast in the annals: in 836, for example, acorns and nuts were reported to have been so plentiful that streams actually became blocked with them and ceased to flow![37]

Without a large sample of bones it is often difficult to tell the domestic pig from the wild boar. However, in most cases the majority of pig bones found on archaeological settlement sites were probably domestic. Pigstys are mentioned in *Crith Gablach* and there is archaeological evidence to suggest that farrowing pens must have been in the immediate vicinity of the settlement. At Marshes Upper a large number of neo-natal pig bones was found in one of the souterrains and at Killyliss, Co. Tyrone, four neo-natal pig skeletons, three probably from the same litter, were found in the ring-fort ditch, thereby suggesting that high mortality rates during farrowing may have been a problem.[38] Pigs are usually eaten young, and this is borne out by the osteological evidence. For example, at Ballinderry 2 crannog, Knockea 2 ring-fort and the ecclesiastical site at Armagh the majority of pig bones came from young animals. At Rathmullan, however, most were killed between the age of 18 and 36 months, with the majority towards the end of that period, suggesting that several beasts may have been slaughtered at one time, rather than one animal being killed at a time for the immediate needs of the ring-fort inhabitants. In some cases, as at Armagh and Seacash, the range of bones present are mainly meat joints, such as shoulder of pork, or skulls from which the offal had been extracted, suggesting that these were brought onto the site for consumption rather than the whole carcass.[39]

Sheep were mainly kept for their wool, though their meat, milk and skins would have been important by-products. In the osteological record it is difficult to distinguish sheep from goat, though it seems likely that the majority would have been sheep of similar appearance to the Soay sheep of the Northern Isles of Scotland. The percentage of sheep and goat bones from most early medieval Irish sites is less than that of cattle or pig, but there are notable exceptions where there are more sheep than pig and occasionally, as at the promontory fort of Larrybane, Co. Antrim, the percentage of cattle and sheep bones are almost the same, cattle representing 44.7 per cent of the total and sheep 43.3 per cent. The steep well-drained chalk headland at Larrybane would have been particularly favourable for grazing sheep, and the large number of sheep bones suggests the slaughter of the excess animals for their meat. At

Rathmullan only a few sheep were kept but the osteological evidence indicates that they were reared in order to optimize their wool, skin and meat yield. In Phase 1 few were killed before they reached 18–24 months, but the majority had been slaughtered by the time they were 42 months. In Phase 2 most were killed between 30 and 36 months after the first clip of wool had been taken, though up to a third, perhaps the breeding ewes, survived beyond this.[40]

Horses, or rather ponies, seem to be represented by a few bones on most sites. Horseflesh was not generally eaten though there are exceptions to this as at Ballinderry 1 and 2 crannogs, where the bones showed signs of having been split for marrow. Amongst the upper echelons of society it is clear that horses were mainly used for riding and were highly valued. Indeed, horses may have been bred specially for hunting, racing, or warfare, and in some instances they may even have been imported from Britain. On the free-standing stone crosses of the late eighth, ninth and early tenth centuries groups of horsemen are frequently depicted armed with the accoutrements of war, and in some instances horses are shown in pairs drawing light carts or chariots with a driver and passenger, perhaps an important secular or ecclesiastical dignitary, seated behind (85).[41] *Críth Gablach* suggests that some wealth was lavished on horse equipment, such as enamelled bridles, at least amongst the higher ranks, and this is borne out by the archaeological evidence. Bridle bits and occasionally spurs have been found on some of the sites of known high status, such as Lagore, Knowth and Ballinderry 1, and at Ballycatteen, Co. Cork, a copper-alloy enamelled roundel with attachments for straps has been identified as a bridle ornament. Though the curious grave from Navan, Co. Meath, is probably Viking (see p. 189), the highly decorated copper-alloy horse trappings amongst the grave goods are certainly native, and similar examples have been found in Viking graves in Norway, suggesting that both horses and their harness may have been considered worth raiding. Horses would also have been used on the farm, though not for heavy duties such as ploughing, and as pack animals; a fragmentary wooden object from Ballinderry 1 has been plausibly identified as part of a pack saddle.[42]

Irish wolf hounds were a highly-prized export to the Roman world and in *Críth Gablach* the 'leading noble' is described as owning deer-hounds while his wife might indulge a liking for lap dogs. The bones of both large and small dogs are found quite commonly on early medieval Irish sites and several different breeds are represented, though the bones of large hunting dogs are difficult to distinguish from those of wolves. At Lagore, in addition to large dog or wolf bones, species similar to modern sheep dogs, large terriers and lap dogs were identified. It has also been suggested that heavy iron collars and chains (40e) found at Lagore could have been for large dogs, though their use for humans, perhaps prisoners, hostages or slaves, seems more likely (see p. 88).[43] The bones of cats are also sometimes found, as at Seacash ring-fort where almost an entire skeleton was recovered. Useful as hunters of vermin, they also made good pets. Irish ecclesiastics seem to have held them in particular affection; a companion of scholars and artists, they are shown stalking the pages of illuminated manuscripts, such as the Book of Kells, or carved on the stone crosses (86), playing or sitting smugly with their prey in their mouths or firmly clasped between their front paws.[44]

An engaging illustration of a cockerel and his hens is also featured in the Book of Kells, but domestic fowl do not seem to have been a very important part of the farming economy, and there are few references to eggs in the documentary records. The fact that chickens are not mentioned in the earliest legal texts might suggest that they were not introduced into Ireland until the seventh century. In general bird bones are notoriously difficult to recover from archaeological deposits because of their small size and frailty, but domestic fowl bones have been found on a number of sites, suggesting that a few chickens foraging in the immediate vicinity of the settlement would have been a common sight. Bones from Lough Faughan and Lagore crannogs belonged to particularly large birds with well-developed spurs which may indicate that they had been bred for cock fighting.[45]

In one of the legal texts poultry are mentioned as being a risk to bees, possibly by eating them. Although there is no archaeological evidence for bee-keeping, the survival of the mid-seventh-century law tract (*Bechbretha*) dealing with apiculture shows it to have been important since honey was the only method of sweetening food, and was favoured as a relish, and beeswax was used for making candles. The hives, which may have been made of oat straw, were sometimes kept in or near the settlement but might also be transported some distance, perhaps to the moorlands in late summer, for example, where heather nectar would have been especially plentiful.[46]

## Crop husbandry

It has been recognized for many years that tillage played an essential role in the early medieval Irish economy and that cereals were a conspicuous part of the diet.[47] However, there has still been a tendency to underestimate the importance of crop husbandry because of the meagre nature of the evidence. A quick glance at the documentary sources gives the misleading impression that the rearing of livestock, especially cattle, was overwhelmingly important. But a longer look reveals the attention paid to agricultural tools and equipment, such as ploughs and mills, as well as mention of the crops themselves; and indicates that tillage and livestock complemented each other as part of a mixed-farming economy. The limitations of the archaeological evidence have also tended to emphasize animal rather than crop husbandry, since some animal bones survive on most sites, while querns are often the only suggestion of tillage. However, examples of structures associated with grain processing, particularly corn-drying kilns and horizontal mills, have now been excavated, and advances in environmental archaeology, including the flotation and sieving of soil samples to recover seeds, and pollen analysis, mean that we are beginning to be able to recover much more evidence about the actual crops grown and how they were prepared for consumption.

Cereals were by far the most important element of crop husbandry. One of the legal texts, *Bretha a Déin Chécht* (Judgements of Dían Cécht), gives an indication of the varieties of grain grown and their value. For example, a grain of wheat is associated with a supreme king, a bishop and a master poet, while a grain of oats is associated with the *bóaire* or strong farmer. Other types of grain mentioned include barley and rye as well as *siligo* (possibly winter wheat?) and *ruadan*, which may be a member of the buckwheat family.[48] The archaeological evidence broadly mirrors this range of cereals since oats, barley, wheat and rye have all been found in early medieval contexts. Some 22 sites have so far produced charred plant remains including cereals. The most commonly represented is barley, mainly six-row barley, but oats and rye are also frequently found, though usually

in smaller quantities. An increase in cereal growing may also be noted in the pollen record. For example, at Scragh Bog, Co. Westmeath, rye was found for the first time around the beginning of the early middle ages, while at Cashelkeelty 1, Co. Kerry, oats were first recorded between the mid-sixth and mid-ninth centuries (cal. AD 540–860). It would have been possible to grow barley, oats and rye in areas of higher rainfall, at higher altitudes and on poorer soils than it is possible to grow wheat. Indeed, wheat gives the impression of being a luxury. It is sometimes included in food render and it is interesting to note that wheat straw has been found at Lagore, a known royal site.[49]

The *Vision of MacConglinne* makes it clear that cereals were prepared in the form of porridge and bread. White porridge is described as the 'smoothest and sweetest of all food' and cakes of barley, oats, wheat and rye are mentioned, each with their own condiment and sauce. Barley was also used for making beer.[50]

The first step in the cultivation of cereals was the preparation of the ground. Once the trees and scrub had been removed, the land may have been prepared by stripping the turf, drying and burning it, and then spreading the ash as a fertilizer.[51] Other fertilizers used to maintain the soil nutrients would have included animal manure, midden material and, in coastal districts, seaweed.

The pollen record suggests that during the Iron Age there was a probable lull in, but not an absence of, agricultural activity, possibly caused by a deterioration in the climate and/or soil erosion brought about by over-cultivation, both of which resulted in the growth of blanket peat. However, it is now generally agreed that, around the beginning of the early middle ages, there was a major phase of land clearance resulting in a decline of tree pollen and a corresponding increase in grass, cereal and weed pollens denoting an expansion in agriculture which persisted throughout the period. But some regional differences are also becoming apparent; for example, as might be expected, early medieval land clearance and agricultural expansion are more pronounced in central Ireland than in the south-west.[52]

It has been suggested that the key to this increase in cultivation was improved technology. The pollen record indicates an agricultural expansion during the late Bronze Age and it is at this time that the first light wooden plough or ard may have been brought to Ireland. But a plough of this

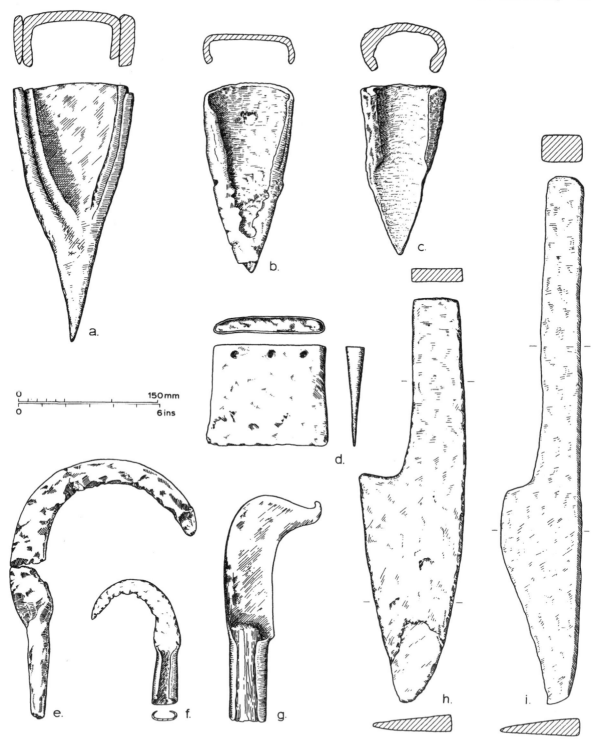

**22** *Agricultural implements:*
*ploughshares* **a.** *Lagore,* **b.** *Leacanabuaile,* **c.** *Dundrum*
*Castle;* **d.** *spade, Ballinderry 2; reaping hooks*
**e.** *Leacanabuaile,* **f.** *Lagore;* **g.** *billhook, Lagore; plough*
*coulters* **h.** *Lagore,* **i.** *Whitefort* (**a, f–h.** *after Hencken*
*1950;* **d.** *after Hencken 1942;* **b, e.** *after Ó Ríordáin,*
*S.P. and Foy 1943;* **c.** *after Archaeological Survey of*
*Northern Ireland 1966;* **i.** *after Waterman 1956a).*

kind only scratched a shallow furrow making cross-ploughing essential and its use was limited to light well-drained soils relatively free of stones. Equally, it is thought that the expansion in cultivation evident around the beginning of the early medieval period coincided with the introduction of the heavier coulter-plough, probably from Roman Britain. The original wooden plough-share was now protected by an iron shoe and an iron knife or coulter was mounted in front of it so that it might first cut a way through the ground to enable the furrow to be ploughed more efficiently. Cross-ploughing was still necessary but a much wider range of soils, including the heavier clays of the drumlin belt, could now be exploited. A further technological improvement, the introduction of the heavier fixed mould-board plough, is suggested at a slightly later date by the expansion of sage (*Artemisia*) in the pollen diagrams on several sites. This rendered cross-ploughing unnecessary since the insertion of the leading edge of the wooden mould-board into the cut made by the coulter caused the turning of the sod.[53]

The artefactual evidence for these various types of plough is rather confusing. Though fragments of wooden ploughs have occasionally survived in bogs they have yet to be studied or accurately dated, and the only parts which have been found in early medieval contexts are the iron shares and coulters. Three different types of symmetrical socketed share are represented. The comparatively light triangular share from Leacanabuaile (**22b**), Co. Kerry, may be part of an ard rather than a coulter-plough. But the heavier example (**22c**) from early medieval levels at Dundrum Castle, Co. Down, was probably used with a coulter. Both have their parallels in Roman Britain. The share from Lagore (**22a**), however, is of a more unusual kind, since it has reinforced sides and a prong on the bottom. This too was probably part of a coulter-plough and a coulter was found on the same site. Two different coulter types have been recognized. That from Lagore (**22h**) has a short handle while that from Whitefort (**22i**), Co. Down, with its much longer handle, which is similar to the Romano-British examples, implies that the plough beam was raised much higher off the ground.[54]

Ploughing took place in the spring. The legal texts suggest that only the most prosperous would have owned all the plough equipment and a complete team of oxen. The *ócaire*, for example, was expected to contribute a quarter share to

include an ox, a plough-share, a goad and a halter. Therefore the plough team in this instance would have consisted of four oxen, though two or six might also have been used. The oxen were harnessed in pairs using a wooden yoke but its precise form is unknown.[55]

Not all cultivable land was suitable for the plough and in these circumstances the iron-shod spade came into its own. The only example from an early medieval context, Ballinderry 2 crannog, is, unfortunately, fragmentary (**22d**) and not paralleled elsewhere. The position of the wooden handle on it is unknown and it is unclear whether it is a one- or two-sided implement.[56]

Harvest was an anxious time since inclement weather was a real threat and a rainy autumn could destroy the crops as they stood in the fields. Cereals were harvested with reaping hooks, the stem being cut just below the ear in order to utilize the straw for grazing. Examples of both socketed and tanged reaping hooks are known from a number of sites (**22e, f**).[57] A damp harvest made the kiln an essential piece of equipment to dry and even ripen the grain before threshing and to harden it prior to milling. Corn-drying kilns were also used in the processing of malted barley to make beer. Several likely examples have been excavated, suggesting a variety of different types. At Killederdadrum, Co. Tipperary, a pit-like feature cut into the enclosure ditch (**56a**) may have been a corn-drying kiln. The fill consisted of a layer of carbonized grain, mainly oats, but also a little barley and rye, together with charcoal, sandwiched between layers of redeposited boulder clay. A radiocarbon sample from the charred grain gave a date between the tenth and mid-twelfth centuries (cal. AD 900–1160). At Letterkeen, Co. Mayo, a rectangular stone-lined trench 1.60 × 1.50 m (5 ft 3 in × 4 ft 11 in) was excavated with a couple of lintel stones still in position. Nearby were the remains of a quern and possibly a burnt basket, which would seem to indicate that other elements of grain processing such as milling and perhaps threshing were going on in the vicinity. An hourglass-shaped structure, which may have been a kiln, recently excavated at the ecclesiastical site of Ballyman, Co. Dublin, had a radiocarbon date spanning the later fourth and early fifth centuries (cal. AD 360–430). Six-row hulled barley, wheat and oats were being processed; although in this instance the fuel was identified as hazel, peat may also have been used.[58] Peat is less likely to spark and, since the kilns had only short flues or no flues at all, fire was a definite hazard. The annals record that in 751 half the grain stored at the monastery of Clonard, Co. Meath, was burnt in the kiln. The legal texts indicate that poorer farmers shared corn-drying kilns, barns and mills while their more prosperous counterparts owned them outright. The equipment of the kiln is listed as a broom, a hide and a flail, which suggest that threshing and possibly winnowing were carried out in the immediate vicinity.[59]

We know little about how grain was stored but the documentary sources suggest barns rather than pits in the ground and this is confirmed by the archaeological evidence, since storage pits are not a feature of excavated settlement sites. The only building so far to have been identified as a possible barn or drystore is at Ballywee, Co. Antrim (18d). It was a rectangular structure 4 × 8 m (13 ft 2 in × 26 ft 3 in) built on a slight platform with a low bank and a shallow ditch on the west side, apparently designed to aid drainage. The west wall of the structure was formed by the stone kerb defining the inner face of the bank and the other three sides were delineated by boulders. A path leading from the door in the north wall

23 *Horizontal mill mechanism.*

down the centre of the building would have provided access to the goods stored on either side.[60]

Archaeological evidence for milling is, however, much more plentiful. Rotary quernstones are a common find on most sites and indicate that small amounts of grain were being ground for the immediate needs of the inhabitants. At Moynagh Lough crannog the querns also included unfinished examples, suggesting that their manufacture was actually taking place on site. Saddle querns too have occasionally been found, as at Cahercommaun and Ballinderry 2, and, although there has been some dispute as to whether they should be dated to the early medieval period rather than earlier,[61] it seems likely that they would have been retained in certain circumstances for some more specialized use where the rotary quern was not considered to be suitable.

During the early seventh century an important technological improvement, the horizontal watermill, was introduced into Ireland, possibly from France or Spain. This piece of equipment, which shows considerable carpentry and engineering skill, took much of the drudgery out of grinding larger quantites of grain and continued in use, as did the rotary quern, in some of the remoter parts of Ireland into the twentieth century. The hori-

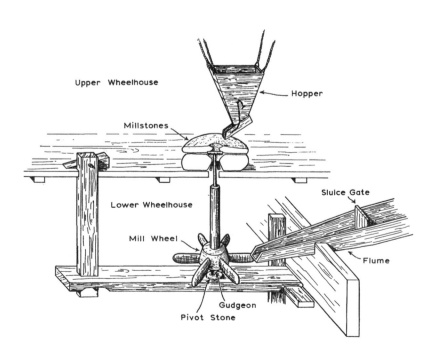

zontal mill mechanism (23) was housed in a two-storey wheelhouse which was usually constructed of wood. In the lower wheelhouse was the horizontal millwheel with its slightly dished wooden paddles. The water supply, which was usually diverted from a nearby stream, was conducted along a millrace which could be closed off with sluice gates when the mill was not in use. The water was then channelled along a wooden flume or chute and was directed onto the millwheel paddles with sufficient force to allow the wheel to turn. The stone 'gudgeon' at the base of the wheel-hub turned in a pivotstone which was mounted on a wooden beam. The turning of the wheel also turned the shaft attached to it which projected through the ceiling into the upper storey where the millstones were housed. The top of the shaft was attached to the upper millstone, which therefore turned when the millwheel turned, while the lower millstone remained stationary. The grain was ground by dropping it into a central hole in the upper millstone, possibly from a hopper, and the flour collected on the floor round the millstones.

The fragmentary structures of horizontal mills have been found fairly frequently, and sometimes excavated, but until recently it was impossible to date them since they are seldom associated with diagnostic artefacts. However, because they were built of substantial oak timbers, they were sampled and successfully used in the construction of the early medieval phase of the Belfast master tree-ring chronology. This has meant that examples from all over Ireland have now been accurately dated and currently span the period from 630 to 926 ± 9. At Ballykilleen, Co. Offaly, dated to 636 ± 9, a small stream with steep banks, one of which had been artificially heightened, was found to contain a rectangular wooden structure approximately 4.3 × 3 m (14 ft 2 in × 9 ft 10 in) consisting of two large oak timbers set at right-angles with the area between floored with nine boards. The structure, which would have been strengthened by the steep banks of the stream, has been interpreted as the lining of the mill pond at the point immediately after the mill dam. Parts of two of the mill-wheel paddles were also found but there was no evidence for the wheelhouse. At Drumard, Co. Derry, dated to 782, excavations recovered not only the flume and some of the timbers of the lower wheelhouse, but also one of the mill-wheel paddles and the lower millstone. A complete mill wheel including paddles has

recently been excavated at Cloontycarthy, near Macroom, Co. Cork.[62]

Cereals were undoubtedly the major tillage crop but other crops were also grown, although our knowledge of these is dependent upon the documentary rather than the archaeological evidence. Peas and beans are mentioned in one of the legal tracts and vegetables were also cultivated including members of the onion family, celery, some greens and possibly parsnips or carrots. Apple trees might grow nearby. Flax and dye plants were also exploited and monasteries were not complete without their herb gardens which were cultivated for the care of the sick.[63]

## Hunting, fishing and gathering

We know little of the importance of hunting in early medieval Ireland. The relevant legal texts are lost, the archaeological evidence is meagre, and therefore it is difficult to gauge to what extent it was an essential adjunct to farming and to what extent it was a sport. On the whole one gains the impression that it was an important aristocratic pastime – *Críth Gablach* tells us that ideally the king should spend every Wednesday watching his deer-hounds at the chase.[64] But for the poorer elements of society hunting may have provided a necessary and welcome addition to the diet.

In the osteological record it is important to distinguish between the systematic collection of red deer tines for antler-working, which did not involve the slaughter of the animals, and the presence of bones showing that the deer had been hunted and killed for their meat. A few red deer bones are found on many settlement sites but they seldom form more than 1 per cent or 2 per cent of the total assemblage, thereby indicating that venison cannot have played a major part in the day-to-day diet. However, the relatively frequent portrayal of deer hunting on the stone crosses may be suggestive of its popularity as a sport, though in this instance one must not forget that such scenes also have a religious connotation. On the cross at Bealin, for example, a hound is depicted catching the hind leg of a stag in its jaws while the huntsman armed with a spear pursues on horseback. On Banagher the stag is shown with its leg caught in a wooden trap. Traps of this kind have been found from time to time, as at Garvary, Co. Fermanagh, but they are very difficult to date. The legal texts also refer to the trapping of deer, either in a pit or on a spike.[65]

Evidence for the hunting of other animals is more limited. The pursuit of wild boar may well have been popular since they were driven to extinction during the twelfth century, but without a good sample their bones are difficult to distinguish from those of a domestic pig. Smaller animals were probably trapped or snared. Though the rabbit was not introduced into Ireland until the Anglo-Norman period, hare bones have occasionally been found, as at Lagore and Larrybane. Some other animals would have been caught chiefly for their pelts: at Ballinderry 2, for example, marten and otter bones are represented. In coastal districts, such as Iniskea North, Co. Mayo, seals may well have been exploited for their skins as well as their meat and seal hunting is also mentioned in Adomnán's *Life of Columba*. Whalebone has also occasionally been found on sites such as Rathmullan, Iniskea North and Lough Faughan, and while it is unlikely that whales were actually killed at sea, it is very probable that the inhabitants had taken advantage of a whale which had become stranded upon a nearby beach. Such events were sometimes considered worthy of note in the annals: in 739, for example, it is recorded that the whole of the surrounding neighbourhood turned out to see a whale which had been cast ashore at Boirche in the province of Ulster, and the legal texts indicate the value of whalebone by saying that it should be divided amongst the members of the *túath*.[66]

Where bird bones have been recovered there is some evidence for fowling. Crannog sites have produced a particularly wide range suggesting the abundance of different types of water-bird in lacustrine environments. At Lagore many types of wild goose and wild duck have been identified as well as swan, heron, moorhen, coot and grebe. In coastal districts sea-birds and their eggs may have been hunted on the cliffs. Shag, cormorant and puffin bones were found at Larrybane while cormorant, gannet and red-throated diver were noted at Beginish.[67]

There has been considerable controversy concerning the date and function of sites known as 'burnt mounds' and their associated features. Such sites are very common in Ireland, especially in Co. Cork, and are also found in Britain. In 1951 an important example was excavated by O'Kelly at Ballyvourney 1, Co. Cork (24).[68] He uncovered a wood-lined trough set into the damp peat so that it automatically filled up with water. Associated with it were two successive phases of a hearth,

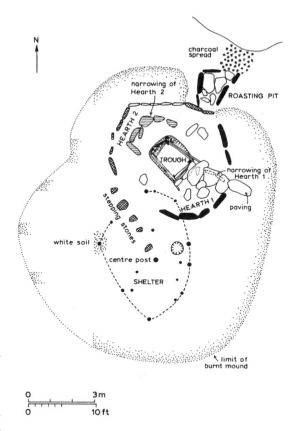

24 *Burnt mound, Ballyvourney 1, Co. Cork (after O'Kelly 1954).*

one at either end of the trough, and a large mound of burnt and broken stones; also a slab-lined pit with an adjacent charcoal spread and a group of post-holes representing a circular structure. With the aid of experimental archaeology and reference to various documentary sources, O'Kelly interpreted burnt mounds such as Ballyvourney 1, sometimes known as *fulachta fiadh* ('the cooking places of deer'), as the temporary shelters and cooking places of bands of seasonal hunters and indicated that some at least might be of early medieval date. He suggested that the wood-lined water-filled trough was for boiling meat. The water would have been brought to boiling point by dropping stones, which had previously been heated on the adjacent hearth, into the trough and after the meat had been cooked the stones would have been cleared out of the trough thereby forming the burnt mound. He interpreted the slab-lined pit as a roasting oven where the meat would have been cooked by first lighting a fire in the pit to heat it, then clearing out the embers and placing the meat in the pit surrounded by more hot stones which had been heated on the hearth. He saw the circular structure as a shelter possibly associated with the butchery of the animal carcasses.

The characteristic features of burnt mounds are their location close to water, the large number of heat-cracked stones which form the mound, hearths and a trough or basin to hold water. The function of such sites as cooking places has been questioned chiefly because of the curious lack of associated bone, though this may be partly due to acidic soil conditions; the recent excavation of Fahee South in the limestone country of Co. Clare did reveal bone. The alternatives suggested include sweat baths or saunas, a variety of industrial processes, such as brewing, textile or leather processing, and permanent settlements. As far as the Irish evidence is concerned, their interpretation as cooking places, perhaps with a secondary function for bathing, seems the most likely. The general lack of artefacts has also made the dating of such sites difficult and O'Kelly originally suggested that they might span the Bronze Age to the sixteenth century AD. More recently, however, radiocarbon sampling has shown the vast majority to be Bronze Age. But some early medieval use cannot yet be ruled out. The only Irish site with a possible early medieval radiocarbon date, Catstown, Co. Kilkenny, is problematic, since the two dates which have been given by material from the site are widely separated: one spans the end of the ninth to the early fourth centuries BC (800–390 cal. BC), the other the late seventh to late tenth centuries AD (cal. AD 680–980). However, it is interesting to note that a burnt mound from Morfa Mawr, south-west Wales, has also produced an early medieval radiocarbon date. Some early medieval use is also supported by the documentary sources. The terms *fulacht fiadh* and *fulacht fian* ('cooking place of a roving band of hunters or warriors') are first found in the law tracts and the latter is also mentioned in *Cormac's Glossary*, an early tenth-century compilation of words which were already unusual or obsolete. *Inadh fulachta* ('cooking place'), a related term, is found in a twelfth-century Irish text, *Agallamh Beg*.[69]

The importance of fishing has almost certainly been underestimated. Fish bones, because of their small size, are very difficult to retrieve without sieving, and therefore the range and proportions of fish bones reported on earlier excavations are unlikely to be truly representative. The recent sampling of a shell midden at Oughtymore on the Magilligan Peninsula, Co. Derry, recovered cod, haddock and plaice or flounder bones, as well as salmon or salmon trout and eel, suggesting the importance of both coastal and estuarine fishing. An interesting range of coastal species including cod, saithe, pollack, whiting and wrasse were also found at Larrybane. Fish were doubtless exploited in the rivers and lakes as well but, unfortunately, the major crannog excavations have produced hardly any bones to prove it. Fishing equipment has, however, sometimes been found: eel spears have been identified at Lagore and Strokestown crannogs and the marshland habitation at Larne, iron fish-hooks at the coastal sand-dune site of Dooey, stone net-sinkers at Beginish, and a double-pointed bone tool from Larrybane may have been used for making nets.[70]

The archaeological evidence is also beginning to hint at the importance of gathering a variety of fruits and nuts. Wild cherry stones were found at Ballinderry 1, blackberry seeds and sloe stones at Lisleagh ring-fort, Co. Cork, and blackberry and elderberry seeds were recovered from an eighth- or ninth-century rubbish pit in Armagh. Documentary sources suggest that strawberries, raspberries, whortleberries, cranberries and rowanberries were also eaten. Hazelnuts were particularly popular. They, or their discarded shells, are a frequent find on early medieval sites and an abundance of hazelnuts was sometimes recorded in the annals. In coastal areas edible seaweeds such as dulse were gathered and shellfish were an important addition to the diet. At Oughtymore, for example, systematic sampling of the shell midden has revealed that, while a wide variety of species was present only three, winkles, cockles and perhaps mussels, were deliberately collected; while others, such as oysters, whelks and limpets, were probably only acquired in the course of gathering the other three. Shellfish are also sometimes found on inland sites. At Rathmullan, for example, mussels are well represented with a smaller number of oysters and limpets. At Lagore both marine and fresh-water mussels have been identified.[71]

## Conclusion

At present it is only possible to reconstruct a very generalized picture of the mixed-farming economy of early medieval Ireland but the archaeological evidence is now increasing rapidly and the prospects for the future are bright. We know least about the agricultural landscape, since archaeologists have tended to deal with settlements in isolation rather than as part of a broader picture. However, survey and selective excavation of relict landscapes in upland regions or areas formerly covered by blanket bog offer the possibility of interesting discoveries to come. Further research on the osteological evidence will doubtless furnish us with a more detailed understanding of animal husbandry, while the more efficient sampling techniques now in use will soon enable us to recover a better indication of the range of crops grown and how they were processed.

But at the moment the picture is still vastly over-simplified. On the basis of the environmental evidence we can make little or no distinction between high- and low-status sites, between fertile and less fertile areas, between subsistence and surplus. With the exception of technological improvements in the plough and the introduction of the horizontal mill, we are still largely unable to recognize changes in farming methods throughout the period, or to ascertain the varying impact of these on different parts of Ireland. It is also impossible to speculate on the extent to which specialization may have existed within the more general pattern of a mixed-farming economy. Although there must have been mechanisms for trade and exchange of livestock and other agricultural produce, as the documentary sources illustrate, these remain impossible to deduce from the archaeological record.

# CHAPTER 5

# Craft, Exchange and Trade

We have archaeological evidence for many different kinds of craft activity in early medieval Ireland. The most important include small-scale pottery production; wood-working, such as lathe turning and coopering; the preparation of leather to make shoes and other articles; the spinning, weaving and dyeing of cloth; bone- and antler-working; the smelting and forging of iron; the production of ornamental copper-alloy objects and the working of glass and stone.

We do not know to what extent some of these crafts were the work of specialists. Textile production, for example, seems to have been carried out in almost every settlement since the spindle whorl is a ubiquitous find. Other crafts, however, were definitely more specialized. The excavation of sites such as Garryduff 1 and Moynagh Lough crannog, where very considerable evidence for metal-working and other crafts has been found, suggests that these were the homes of communities specifically engaged in this kind of activity in addition to farming. In other instances excavation of known royal sites, such as Lagore and perhaps Garranes, has demonstrated that the accretion of surplus wealth to the upper echelons of society resulted in the patronage of craftworkers who produced high-quality luxury goods. Craftworkers were also attracted to the larger monastic sites. There is extensive evidence of ornamental metal-, enamel- and glass-working from Armagh, for example, as well as indications of the manufacture of lignite bracelets and antler objects. Other craftworkers may have been peripatetic. The large number of settlement sites with evidence for small-scale iron-working could indicate the minor domestic production of necessary tools[1] but it might also represent the work of a visiting blacksmith, since some aspects of iron-working require very considerable skill.

In general evidence for exchange and trade remains much more difficult to reconstruct from the archaeological record. However, the import of luxury goods, such as pottery, glass and amber, is clearly recognizable in the pre-Viking period. In the tenth century the growth of the Viking towns, and the range of exotic items recovered from Dublin in particular (see p. 188), demonstrate rapid growth in the trading economy.

## Pottery

Pottery is generally one of the commonest artefacts found by archaeologists. Yet large areas of early medieval Ireland, in common with many parts of northern and western Britain, were aceramic throughout the period except for occasional luxury imports from France and the Mediterranean which reached mainly the upper strata of society during the fifth to early eighth centuries. The major exception is the production of coarse hand-made pottery, commonly known as souterrain ware, which is a characteristic find on both secular and ecclesiastical sites in north-east Ireland. There is also some indication that other types of hand-made coarse pottery may have been made on a minor scale elsewhere, as at Reask, Co. Kerry, but how common this was is unknown.

### Imported pottery

Luxury red-slipped bowls, amphorae and a range of wheel-made vessels, now commonly known as A, B and E wares, were first recognized in Ireland at Garranes nearly half a century ago but at that time it was not realized that they were exotic imports from the Mediterranean and France. Since then, however, these types of pottery, together with D ware bowls and mortaria, which are much rarer, have been identified on many sites in western Britain and Ireland and have been studied very extensively.[2] They are important for two reasons. First, they can be fairly closely dated – they span the fifth to early eighth centuries – and there is the prospect of further refinement in the future. This means that they provide valuable dating evidence for the sites on which they are found. Secondly, and perhaps more interestingly, they testify to the existence of long-distance trade routes between the British Isles and the eastern Mediterranean, North Africa and western France which may be seen as a possible continuation of Roman trade routes into the post-Roman period.

Type B amphorae form 40 per cent of the total imports in the British Isles. They may be divided into several different kinds, of which Bi, Bii and Bv have been found in Ireland, together with various sherds of amphorae as yet unidentified known as B misc(ellaneous). Bi, a large near-globular

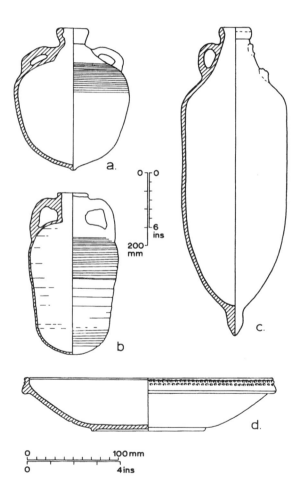

amphora (**25a**) of medium-hard pink-red, buff or orange fabric with white grit, has a short conical neck and bowed handles. The most characteristic feature is a band of combed ornament on the shoulders of the vessel. Bii (**25b**) is more cylindrical in shape and light red or reddish-buff in colour with a sprinkling of white sand in the fabric. It has thick stubby handles, a slightly narrower neck and the body is covered with tegulated ribbing. Both these types were probably wine containers, though other products may also have been carried. Bi was produced in southern Greece and Bii in the north-east Mediterranean. The Bv amphora (**25c**), however, came from the Roman province of Byzacena, now part of Tunisia, and may have carried olive oil and possibly fish products. It is large and cylindrical with a slightly collared rim, high curved handles and a stubby pointed toe. The fabric is buff to brick-red in colour covered with a paler, buff-white or greenish-white slip.

A ware bowls are much less common and may have been incidental to the cargoes of amphorae with their precious contents. Two different types have been identified. Ai or Phocean red slipware (PRS) bowls (**25d**), made of soft, orange-red or brownish-red fabric with occasional specks of yellow limestone and a darker red shiny slip, have a vertical rim incorporating a flange and a low foot ring. The rim may be decorated with rouletting and the internal base with impressed stamps such as crosses or animals. Aii or African red slipware (ARS) bowls are similar in shape, colour and decoration but the fabric contains sparse quartz grits and no limestone. The former come from Phocea in west Turkey, and therefore may have been shipped with Bi and/or Bii amphorae, while the latter were made in the Carthage area of North Africa and may thus have arrived with Bv vessels.

The importation of A and B wares from the Mediterranean, through the Straits of Gibralter along the Iberian coast and from thence to the British Isles, centres on the second half of the fifth and the sixth centuries. The majority have come to light in south-west Britain (**27a-c**), perhaps suggesting that this was their major destination; finds from elsewhere, including Ireland, might therefore be considered as secondary. We do not know how often ships carrying such cargoes may have arrived but the goods clearly found their way, not only to the upper strata of secular society, who had presumably acquired a taste for wine and

**25** *Imported pottery, A and B wares:*
*amphorae* **a.** *Bi,* **b.** *Bii,* **c.** *Bv (after Peacock and Williams 1986);* **d.** *Ai, Phocean Red Slipware bowl (after Alcock 1972).*

other exotic products, but also to some ecclesiastical sites where wine formed an essential part of the Christian liturgy. Of the three major concentrations in Ireland, and none of these exceeds a relatively small number of vessels, Clogher, Co. Tyrone, and probably Garranes, Co. Cork, are royal sites, while Dalkey Island, Co. Dublin, could possibly have been a centre where long-distance traders arrived periodically to exchange their wares. Otherwise Garryduff 1, Co. Cork, is clearly a high-status secular settlement and Inishcaltra, Co. Clare, Derrynaflan, Co. Tipperary, and Reask, Co. Kerry are ecclesiastical. Imported pottery (B misc.) has also been found at the important Iron Age complex of Navan, Co. Armagh, and the ecclesiastical site at Randalstown, Co. Meath; Bv has been located on the promontory fort of Loughshinny, Co. Dublin.[3]

E ware was made in a variety of forms, the most common of which are everted-rim jars, sometimes with lids; small carinated beakers, flared carinated

bowls and occasionally pitchers are also represented (**26**). It is likely that they functioned as a range of domestic vessels though when imported there is some evidence to suggest they contained luxury goods. These pots were thrown on a wheel, and therefore have characteristic finger corrugations on the interior surfaces, and were fired to a high temperature. E ware can prove difficult to identify since it varies greatly in colour, from dirty white with grey or yellow tones, to ochre, dull red, reddish grey or dark grey. The fabric is profusely gritted with white quartz and other materials and is pimply to the touch. Although precise parallels have yet to be found on the Continent, a source in northern or western France seems most likely on the basis of the petrological evidence.

The distributional emphasis of E ware (**27d**) is different from A and B wares, since it is largely concentrated on secular sites in Ireland and north Britain, though why this should be so is unclear. In Ireland it has now been found on nearly 30 sites. Apart from Clogher, Dalkey Island, Garryduff 1 and Lagore, no more than a few sherds have come to light in any one place, but, when compared with A and B wares, a wider range of sites is represented. One would expect royal sites, such as Knowth or Lagore, or those of clearly high status, such as Garryduff and Moynagh Lough crannog,[4] to be included; also major monasteries such as Armagh, Nendrum and Inishcaltra. However, E ware has also been found on ring-forts, Rathmullan and Langford Lodge, for example, which are less obviously wealthy, and smaller ecclesiastical sites such as Killederdadrum, Co. Tipperary, and Killucan, Co. Westmeath. Some chronological distinction between the importation of A and B wares and E ware can also be made. At Clogher it was noted that B ware was associated with the 'ring-ditch' phase (see p. 44), while E ware was associated with the later ring-fort, which was separated from the earlier levels by a layer of sterile yellow boulder clay.[5] Likewise at Dalkey Island B ware was found in the midden pre-dating the promontory fort while E ware came from layers associated with it. Although it remains difficult to say when the importation of E ware began, it is clear that it persisted into the seventh century, when the arrival of A and B wares had ceased, and perhaps as late as 700 or even afterwards.

D ware consists of a variety of mortaria, rouletted bowls and stamped plates of smooth grey fabric with traces of black slip. Pottery of this type

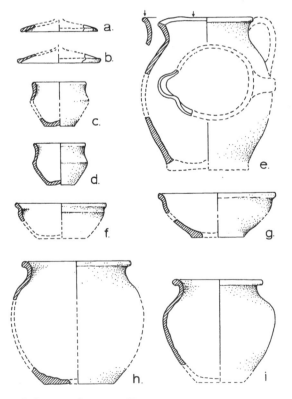

**26** *Imported pottery, E ware:*
**a**, **b**. *lids;* **c**, **d**. *beakers;* **e**. *pitcher;* **f**, **g**. *bowls;* **h**, **i**. *jars (after Thomas 1959, not to scale).*

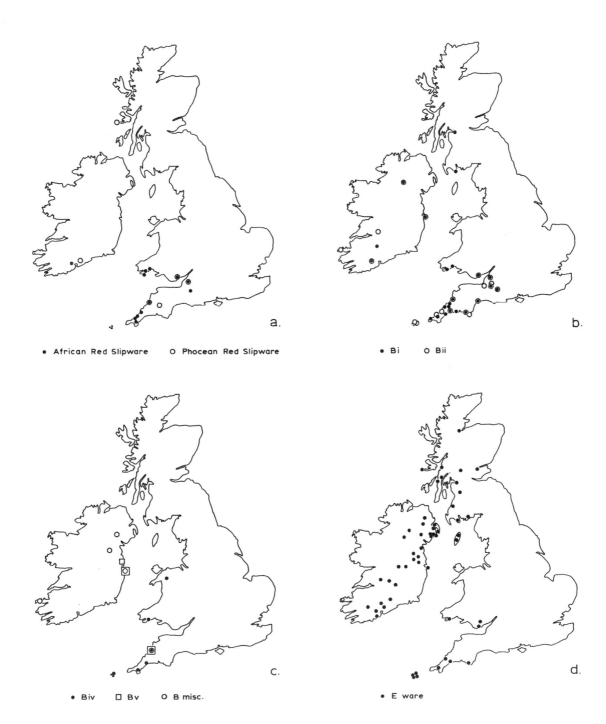

a.
● African Red Slipware    O Phocean Red Slipware

b.
● Bi    O Bii

c.
● Biv    □ Bv    O B misc.

d.
● E ware

**27** *Distribution of imported pottery in Britain and Ireland:*
**a.** *A wares;* **b, c.** *B wares;* **d.** *E ware (Ewan Campbell).*

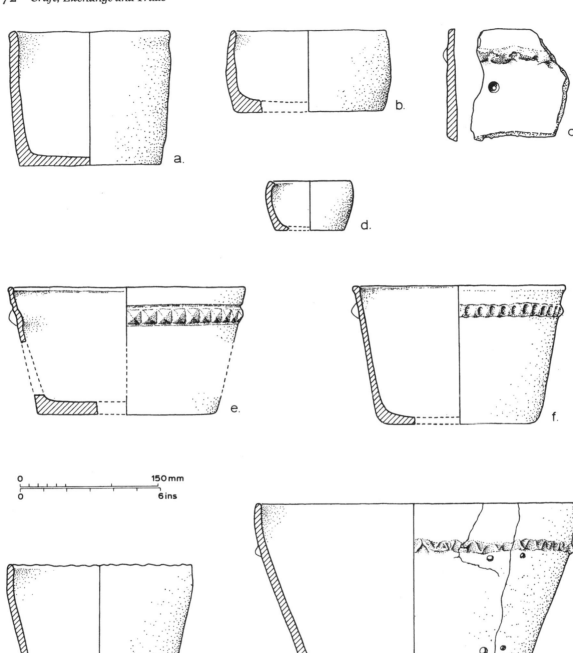

**28**  *Souterrain ware:*
**a.** *Dundrum Sandhills;* **b.** *Lough Faughan;*
**c.** *Nendrum;* **d.** *Moylarg crannog;* **e, f.** *Ballymacash;*
**g.** *Lissue;* **h.** *Hillsborough Fort (**a–c, e–g.** after*

*Archaeological Survey of Northern Ireland 1966;*
**d.** *after Ryan 1973;* **h.** *after Gaskell Brown and Brannon 1978).*

is thought to have been imported from the Bordeaux region of western France during the sixth century and possibly later. It has yet to be identified in Ireland, and its distribution in western Britain is also much more limited than other import wares.

### Native pottery

Souterrain ware has received surprisingly little scholarly attention considering its potential importance as a tool for dating sites in north-east Ireland. Equally, almost no attempt has been made to develop a detailed classification of forms, fabric or decoration to enable material from new excavations to be more easily compared with that from those already published. A major reason for this is that souterrain ware is frequently found in very small pieces, often of widely varying colour, making the reconstruction of pot profiles a difficult task: at Seacash ring-fort, for example, 2,885 sherds were recovered but it was only possible to reconstruct the forms of two vessels. In addition the forms of functional coarse pottery of this kind tend to be very conservative and, unless decorated, are seldom amenable to detailed typological study. Therefore, while it is possible to make a number of general descriptive statements and link some of these to a likely chronological development, we have as yet little idea of whether there may have been distinctive local groups or whether such pottery was produced by a household for their own use or by professional potters in workshops, and, if the latter was the case, how widely it may have been distributed.[6]

Many souterrain-ware vessels, as the carbonized material and soot adhering to their outer and occasionally their inner surfaces suggest, were used as cooking pots (**28**). They are usually flat-bottomed bucket or barrel shapes with splayed or cylindrical walls which may curve inwards or outwards towards a simple rounded or flattened rim, though sometimes it is angled, or even pointed. Perforations sometimes found below the rim (**28c**) may have been for letting out steam, assuming the vessel was covered with some sort of lid during cooking, while lugs and cordons found in a similar position may have aided lifting or suspension. Other vessels may have been used for storage and, even when pots became cracked, they may have continued in use as containers for dry goods. A pot from Hillsborough Fort (**28h**), for example, had five pairs of holes in it, each pair positioned upon either side of a crack in the

fabric. Perhaps a leather thong was threaded through the holes and tied to hold the walls of the pot together. Other forms, including shallow dishes and small cups, were probably used as tableware. Overall the size range is large: diameters have been recorded varying from 60–100 mm ($2\frac{3}{8}$–4 in) up to 350–400 mm ($13\frac{3}{4}$–$15\frac{3}{4}$ in) and heights from 35 mm ($1\frac{3}{8}$ in) up to 300 mm ($11\frac{7}{8}$ in).[7]

These pots were constructed entirely by hand using the coil-building technique. Traces of this are sometimes detectable as irregularities in the profile of the pot and at Larrybane it was thought that a clay slurry smoothed with a spatula, brush or coarse cloth might have been used on some pots to improve the surface.[8] The impressions of cut grass, and sometimes other organic matter such as straw, chaff, seeds or hazel leaves, are a characteristic feature of souterrain ware, found chiefly on the bases of the pots but also on the outside wall and occasionally on the inside or even incorporated into the fabric. It used to be thought that these were caused by leaving the pot to dry to green hard on a bed of grass cuttings to prevent it sticking; the grass was then burnt out in the subsequent firing. However, recent experiments have shown that grass cuttings or other organic matter were probably laid on a surface to prevent adhesion and facilitate rotation during the construction process itself. This would account for the impressions found on parts of the pot other than the base.[9]

The fabric is coarse with considerable quantities of grit added as temper. The use of vegetable temper has occasionally been commented upon though this may have been grass accidentally incorporated into the fabric during the manufacturing process. Very little research has been carried out to identify the sources of the clays and the tempers used, but where this has been done, as at Carnalbanagh East, Moira, Co. Down, they were local. Petrological analysis is potentially useful since it might be able to establish to what extent the production of souterrain ware was a domestic craft or a workshop industry with a distributional network.[10]

The colour of souterrain ware has been noted as varying very considerably, from pale greys and buffs, through reddish browns to black. Sometimes a wide range of colours may be recorded on a single pot and in some instances the core is one colour, grey, and the surfaces another, brick red. Equally, many pots are hard and well-fired, though some are so hard as to be brittle, while the fabric of others is very soft. Such diversity is presumably caused by primitive firing techniques using a clamp or bonfire kiln which usually leaves little trace in the archaeological record. The report of a possible kiln excavated outside a cave at Ballintoy, Co. Antrim, is doubtful.[11]

Many pots are completely unornamented. The most common addition is a cordon placed a little way below the rim. This is usually an applied clay strip, but sometimes it is pinched out from the surface of the pot itself. Often the cordon is plain but it may also be decorated in a variety of ways, frequently with finger-tipping, sometimes with incised lines or impressed shapes. The rims may be scalloped or incised and the bases ringed with finger-tipping. Occasionally there is some decoration on the body of the pot such as applied vertical strips, dotting or intermittent combing with a two-pronged instrument.

The vast majority of souterrain ware has been found on sites in Co. Down and Co. Antrim (**29**). This distribution may be slightly misleading since a disproportionate number of excavations have been carried out in this part of Ulster. A few sites with souterrain ware are known in Counties Louth, Armagh and Derry and there are recent isolated finds further west from Killyliss, Co. Tyrone, and possibly from Lisdoo, Co. Fermanagh. It seems likely that with further excavations more sites will be added in these counties but souterrain ware does seem to be concentrated in north-east Ireland and its distribution may be related to the confederation of the Ulaid which (in addition to Dalriada) was based in the area to the east of the River Bann and Lough Neagh, with outposts in eastern Derry, south Down and Louth. Indeed, souterrain ware has recently been recognized in Dalriada on the monastic site of Iona; some was locally made but the rest had been imported. The outlier from Killegar, Co. Wicklow, is not readily explicable, but the finds from late eleventh- and early twelfth-century levels in Viking Dublin suggest trade, though whether for the pottery or its contents is unclear.[12]

The origins of souterrain ware are obscure. A link with late Bronze Age pottery has been suggested but this may now be discounted in view of the long gap between the two. The date when souterrain ware came into use is also difficult to determine, though on present evidence some time during the seventh or eighth centuries seems likely. It is interesting to note that, although E

**29** *Distribution of souterrain ware (after Ryan 1973 with additions).*

ware is sometimes found in the same layers as souterrain ware as at Ballyfounder and Langford Lodge, in other cases, notably the well-stratified sites of Rathmullan and Gransha, they are clearly separated, E ware being found in the early layers, souterrain ware in the later. At Drumard, Co. Derry, a sherd of plain souterrain ware was found under one of the timbers of the horizontal mill dated by dendrochronology to AD 782. Unfortunately it is unclear whether the sherd was sealed by the timber, indicating that souterrain ware had come into use by that date, or whether it reached that position during the subsequent decades when the mill was in use. In the light of this it should be noted that, although stylistic links have been suggested between souterrain ware and the grass-marked pottery of Cornwall, it seems unwise to regard the former as giving rise to the latter – both pottery types are very simple – or, unless further independent evidence can be found, to suggest that the link signals Irish emigration to Cornwall from north-east Ulster. Grass-marked pottery, like souterrain ware, may have begun as late as the eighth century, long after the period of the Irish migrations.[13]

It was noted during excavations at Lissue that souterrain ware from the earlier ring-fort ditch was almost all undecorated apart from plain applied cordons. However, the rims, bases and cordons of the pottery from the later ring-fort tended to be decorated. There is now sufficient evidence from a number of other sites to suggest the gradual evolution from plain vessels, through pots with plain cordons, to those decorated with incised ornament and finger-tipping. Though it is unknown when these changes took place and how universal they may have been, this realization is potentially important for the dating of sites in north-east Ireland, and it has been persuasively suggested that those with decorated souterrain ware may have been occupied towards the end of the early medieval period. Precisely when souterrain ware gave way to its successor, the everted-rim cooking pot, is unclear. The latter is clearly a native response to Anglo-Norman cooking-pot forms in use at the end of the twelfth century. However, souterrain ware is sometimes found in the same contexts as both everted-rim cooking pots and Anglo-Norman glazed wares, as at Doonbought, Co. Antrim. It may be residual but it is also possible that souterrain ware continued into the thirteenth century and may have been used for a period side by side with everted-rim cooking pots.[14]

Apart from a single sherd of coarse black pottery of unknown type from Lagore and some sherds of a similar kind from Moynagh Lough, the only other hand-made coarse wares so far to have been recognized come from early occupation levels on the ecclesiastical site at Reask, Co. Kerry (see p. 117).[15] Two different types were noted. The first, a light porous grass-tempered ware, varying from brown to light brown to buff, but frequently with blackened surfaces, may have been cooking pottery, since the possible remains of carbonized food were found adhering to some of the sherds. The second, a heavier, more compact coarseware with large sandy grits, was mainly grey or brown, though sometimes orange, on the outside and blackened on the inside. It was impossible to reconstruct any profiles of either kind of pottery and at present no parallels have been located. However it appears to be early since a radiocarbon date from a hearth in the same area spans the late third to mid-seventh centuries (cal. AD 260-650)

and Bii imported pottery (*c.* 450-600) was found overlying it.

## Wood

Wood was clearly a material of vital importance to the early medieval Irish. As we have seen most buildings and other structures were of wood, as were very many day-to-day artefacts; in a society which was largely aceramic wooden vessels must have been of special importance. Some luxury items were also made of wood and occasional examples of highly decorated objects have been found. Wooden structures and artefacts are however only preserved in waterlogged conditions, and therefore the bulk of the evidence is limited to crannog sites with rare occurrences in other contexts such as ring-fort ditches. On the vast majority of sites the only evidence of wood is in the form of post-holes, stake-holes and charcoal, with the resulting tendency to underestimate its almost ubiquitous use.

Carpentry tools have been found on quite a number of sites. There is a particularly good collection from Lagore which includes an adze, at least one possible hand-saw, a draw-knife and a variety of chisels and gouges as well as several awls. There are also two very good examples of bow-saws (**40d**) from Garryduff 1 and a socketed gouge with its bone handle still in place from the Clea Lakes crannog.[16] Tools such as these demonstrate carpentry skills even on sites where no wooden artefacts survive. Hints of sophisticated carpentry techniques are also seen in the structures of horizontal mills and in pieces of worked wood found in crannogs, though the original uses of such timbers can now seldom be recovered. From Lough Faughan, for example, there were a number of squared and dressed timbers with mortice holes which included parts of what may have been a large wooden cart. From Lagore and Ballinderry 1 there were worked timbers with a complexity of grooves and mortice-and-tenon joints, as well as wooden pegs and dowels, or iron nails, still in place, which were perhaps once part of buildings or furniture.[17]

*Críth Gablach* describes the prosperous farmer as owning a wide variety of domestic utensils including a vat for boiling, a washing-trough, a bath, various tubs, trays and mugs. These were almost certainly made of wood and some of the most common wooden artefacts from archaeological sites are whole or fragmentary wooden vessels.

Some were stave-built but others were turned on a lathe or simply hollowed out.

The construction of stave-built vessels is a highly skilled craft first demonstrable in the British Isles during the Iron Age but which remained of very considerable importance until recent times. Only mature trees could be used since the length of the staves, cut like the slices of a cake, was determined by the radius of the trunk. It was only by cutting them in this way that warping was prevented and the tight fit between the staves, necessary to produce watertight containers, might be achieved. In early medieval Ireland a variety of woods were used, but oak, and more especially yew, seem to have been the most common. Once the roughed-out staves had seasoned they were shaped – 15 unfinished examples have been found at Moynagh Lough – and the vessel was then ready for assembly. This was done by raising a circle of moistened staves into a vertical position within a hoop, heating them over a small fire, and then shaping the vessel by driving successively smaller hoops over the staves to achieve exact joins. Once this had been done the staves were trimmed top and bottom and a groove cut around the interior to receive the base of the vessel and, if necessary, a lid. The hoops used during construction were then replaced with permanent ones.[18]

The variety of staves, hoops and bases which have been found on waterlogged sites demonstrates the diversity of stave-built vessels in use ranging from large tubs, buckets and barrels to small drinking tankards and containers. It is rare for complete vessels to survive but from Ballinderry 1 there is a yew bucket (30a), the handle of which is now missing, made up of 19 staves held in place by two hoops, each made of a branch split lengthwise, the flat side of which lay against the wall of the tub. Each hoop was joined by overlapping the ends, the one underneath being much thinner than the one above, and was held in place by an iron clamp supplemented by wooden pegs. Further pegs hammered into the side of the bucket served to keep the hoops in position. At Lissue an oak butter churn (30b) was found. Its circular base was made up of three parts joined with wooden pegs, and the walls were made of 19 carefully smoothed staves skilfully shaped so that the top of the vessel was oval rather than round. These were held in place by two wooden hoops fastened by iron clamps, the grip of the upper being further strengthened by iron nails hammered into the staves. The vessel was completed with an iron rim mount with an everted lip to facilitate pouring held in place with iron nails, and an iron hoop fixed to the body of the vessel with iron cramps with two rings through which a rope could be passed to swing the churn. Occasionally stave-built vessels were highly decorated. A number of ornamented buckets, which may have been manufactured in Ireland or perhaps Scotland or Northumbria, have come to light in Scandinavian contexts. These include the Hopperstad pail, the walls of which are covered with copper-alloy sheets held in place by rivets and decorated with engraved spirals, and the Oseberg bucket with its handle escutcheons in the form of seated figures decorated with enamel and millefiori glass.[19]

Small wide-mouthed bowls, narrower beakers and shallow platters for use in the preparation and consumption of food might be turned using a simple pole lathe operated by a treadle. A variety of woods, usually used green, as they were then moist and easier to shape, might be employed including alder, yew, hazel, poplar, birch and willow. Examples of oak have also been identified but this was not very satisfactory unless seasoned. The felled trees were cut into logs of a suitable length, then quartered or halved according to their girth, and the rough-outs cut and shaped, usually with the bases facing towards the outer sapwood to prevent warping or splitting. Three roughed-out bowls have been found at Lagore. The rough-out was then placed on the lathe secured at either end by rods or mandrels set into holes which had been drilled in the vessel. The bowl could then be turned on the lathe leaving the hands free to work the cutting tools which would have consisted of gouges, chisels and hook-ended irons. The outside of the vessel would have been turned first, the interior hollowed out second; the central core of waste could then be removed and the vessel finished. Lathe waste including cores and thin discs with a hole in the centre, which represent the wood cut away from the base in the finishing process, have been found at Lagore, Lissue (30d, e) and Moynagh Lough.

A number of finished bowls have also been recovered from Lagore. These are of varying depth, with or without foot rings and other surfaces are ornamented with grooves. Other decorative features include plain raised cordons on a bowl from Lissue (30c) and lines burnt into the rim of a vessel from Ballinderry 2. It has been suggested on the basis of evidence from Lagore that earlier

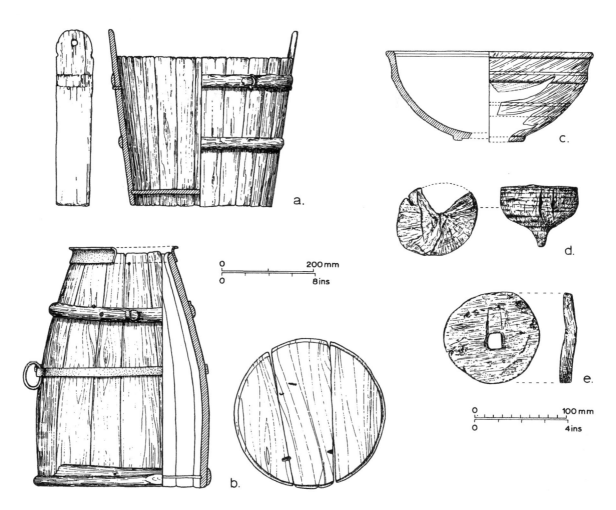

**30** *Wooden vessels:*
**a.** *stave-built bucket, Ballinderry 1;* **b.** *stave-built butter churn, Lissue;* **c.** *lathe-turned bowl, Lissue;* **d, e.** *lathe-turning waste, Lissue (**a.** after Hencken 1936;* **b–e.** *after Bersu 1947).*

bowls may be shallower than later examples, but this needs to be checked if a sufficient quantity comes to light in future excavations elsewhere. Their forms have also been compared with pottery bowls, but bearing in mind the general lack of ceramics from Ireland in this period, such parallels seem unnecessary; their shape and ornament were probably influenced more by the limitations of the lathe technique. Lathes were also used to manufacture other wooden objects such as the wheel-hub from Lough Faughan (**31d**).[20]

Alternatively, vessels might be hollowed out without the aid of a lathe. Fragments of a large willow bowl with a separate base and a decorated rim were found on Ballinderry 1 and parts of two troughs on Ballinderrry 2. A small hollowed yew bucket bound with three copper-alloy bands decorated with openwork ornament was found in the River Glyde, near Annagassan, Co. Louth.[21]

A glance at the finds from crannog excavations shows a wide range of wooden artefacts and it is impossible to discuss them all in detail here. They include mallets and pounders, scoops (**31c**), ladles and spatulas, lids and boxes, hollowed handles for knives and other tools, pins, pegs and wedges as well as other items which are not so readily identifiable. However, there are some more unusual objects which deserve mention. Particularly famous is the gaming board from Ballinderry 1 (**32**). Made of yew, the board is pierced by seven

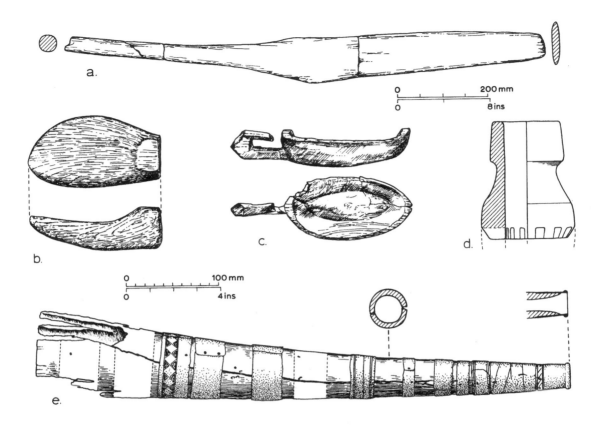

0 ⎯⎯⎯⎯⎯ 200 mm
0 ⎯⎯⎯⎯⎯ 8 ins

0 ⎯⎯⎯⎯⎯ 100 mm
0 ⎯⎯⎯⎯⎯ 4 ins

31  *Wooden objects:*
**a.** *oar, Ballinderry 2 (after Hencken 1942);*
**b.** *shoe last,* **c.** *scoop, Lagore (after Hencken 1950);*
**d.** *wheel-hub, Lough Faughan (after Collins 1955);*
**e.** *musical horn, River Erne (after Waterman 1969).*

rows of seven holes, the one in the centre and those at the corners being demarcated by compass-drawn lines. It may have been used to play a game with wooden pegs akin to 'fox and geese'. The frame of the board is decorated with interlace and fret patterns and at either end are 'handles' in the form of a man and a beast. The ornament, which includes a Viking Borre-style ring-chain motif, suggests a tenth-century date. A board of similar type, but now lost, was found at Knockanboy, Derrykeighan, Co. Antrim during the nineteenth century. Objects such as these are interesting because, with the exception of a range of artefacts from waterlogged levels in Viking Dublin (see p. 186), the survival of carved wood is surprisingly rare, though hints in the documentary sources suggest that it must have been relatively common. Also worthy of note is a wind instrument from the River Erne (31e). A hollow yew horn with its copper-alloy mouth piece was bound with narrow copper-alloy sheets, one of which was decorated with an engraved fret pattern. Instruments such as this may have been used in both warfare and entertainment and are sometimes depicted in manuscripts and on sculpture.[22] Dug-out boats are a relatively common discovery. Almost complete examples were found on Lagore and Ballinderry 2 (14, 15) crannogs and a small fragment on Ballinderry 1. In all upwards of 170 dug-out boats have been recorded from Ireland but many do not now survive and, in the absence of modern research, the remaining examples are difficult to classify. Although their use in Ireland may span the Bronze Age until relatively modern times, dendrochronology does offer the potential for close dating. An unfinished example brought ashore at Oxford Island, Lough Neagh, Co. Armagh, has been dated to AD 524 ± 9.[23]

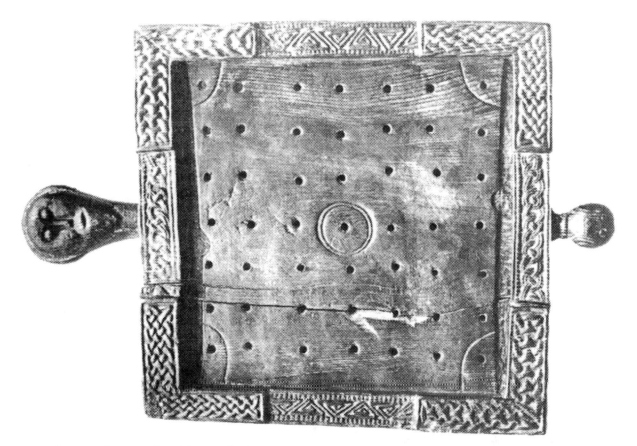

32 *Yew-wood gaming board from Ballinderry 1 crannog, Co. Westmeath (Copyright: National Museum of Ireland).*

## Leather

Leather was an important by-product of animal husbandry. Oxhides and calfskins in particular were utilized; also horse hides and the skins of sheep and goats, as well as those of wild animals, such as red deer and seals. Little is known directly of the preparation of the hides or the tanning of the leather since no examples of early medieval Irish tanning pits have been recognized. Equally, when artefacts have been recovered, it has proved difficult to say how the leather was originally processed since it only survives in a waterlogged environment and long submersion has destroyed the evidence. However, until relatively recently the most common method of preserving hides and skins was by tanning them in a solution of water and oak bark. The hides and skins would probably have been soaked in an alkaline solution in order to soften them so that the hair and sub-cutaneous

fat could be scraped away with the aid of a draw-knife. Then they would have been submerged in a succession of tanks filled with a progressively stronger solution of oak bark until the tanning process was completed. Finally the leather would have been dressed by rubbing oil, perhaps in the form of sheep tallow, into it and polishing it with stones called slickers to keep it supple and prevent it from cracking. Evidence of leather-working in the form of offcuts is sometimes found on water-logged sites. Elsewhere tools such as awls and punches may indicate leather-working and a pronged-and-socketed instrument (40c), the purpose of which has caused some debate, may have been used for scoring leather; a wooden shoe last was found at Lagore (31b).[24]

Shoes are the most common leather artefacts found and must have been worn at least amongst the upper classes. They usually survive in a fragmentary state, since presumably they were only discarded when they were no longer usable, but sufficient have now been discovered to enable the reconstruction of a number of different types. There are two major kinds. The first was made of a

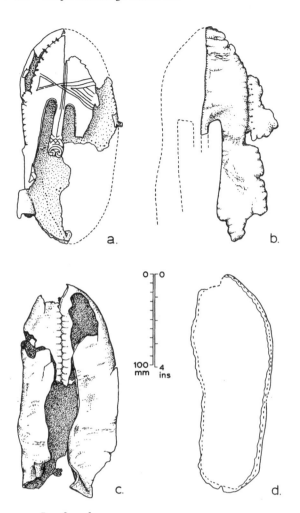

**33** *Leather shoes:*
**a, b.** *Ballinderry 2 (after Hencken 1942);*
**c.** *Lagore (after Hencken 1950);* **d.** *Killyliss*
*(after Ivens 1984a).*

single piece of leather which was carefully cut, folded and stitched and then turned inside out. These single-piece shoes varied greatly in complexity. Skilfully modelled slippers, such as that from Ballinderry 2, with its scored ornament and decorated tongue (**33a**), are sometimes paralleled in the footwear of figures in illuminated manuscripts. Others, with a central seam running the length of the upper or vamp, might be shaped and sewn in a similar fashion (**33b**), but some were much rougher and simply laced up the front (**33c**). It is interesting to note that single-piece rawhide shoes of this kind known as *pampooties* continued in use on the Aran Islands into the twentieth century, but they were not strong, and needed to

be replaced as often as once a month. The second major type would have been stronger since each shoe consisted of a separate thick leather sole and a thinner upper, which might itself have been made of more than one piece, and was sometimes further strengthened with an insole and a thin band of leather to protect the sewn seams. Evidence of simple multiple-piece shoes, which were sewn and then turned inside out, has recently been found at Killyliss ring-fort (**33d**) and other, more complex examples with pronounced tongues on the instep and heel were recovered from the enclosure ditch of the monastery at Iona in western Scotland.[25]

Though rarely found, other leather objects include knife sheaths, such as those from Moynagh Lough, straps, bags and other containers. Documentary sources, such as the ninth-century *Navigatio Brendani* (*Voyage of Brendan*), suggest the importance of hide boats. Though no early medieval examples have been found, the *currach*, which is still used in some parts of western Ireland, demonstrates the survival of hide boats up until the present.[26] There are also hints of very considerable skill in leather decoration. In particular, three leather book satchels known as *budgets* have survived. These may be exemplified by the *Breac Maodhóg* budget which was made of oak-tanned cattlehide shaved down to about 3 mm ($\frac{1}{8}$ in) in thickness, cut out, dampened and then decorated with impressed interlace ornament, probably made with a blunt bone or wooden scriber, before being sewn together. The date of these budgets is problematic, and indeed the ornament suggests that they may be slightly later than 1200. Nevertheless, they demonstrate the kind of techniques which would have been available to decorate, not only book satchels, but also book bindings and other objects at an earlier date. Another highly skilled task was the preparation of very young calf or occasionally sheepskins to make the vellum on which manuscripts were written. The tanned skins were split into thin sheets and then dressed to make them pale and translucent; because of the great number of skins required for a single manuscript, little waste could be afforded and even imperfect skins were used.[27]

### Textiles and dress

Textiles are rarely found on excavations, even in waterlogged conditions, and the only major collection to have been recovered so far from a native

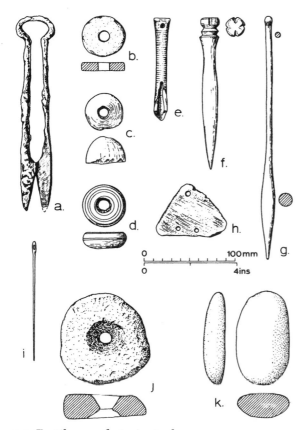

**34** *Textile manufacturing tools:*
**a.** *iron shears, Garryduff 1; spindle whorls* **b.** *stone,*
**c.** *ox femora,* **d.** *lathe-turned bone, Cahercommaun;*
**e.** *bone weft beater, Lagore;* **f.** *wooden distaff, Lough*
*Faughan;* **g.** *wooden spindle, Ballinderry 2;* **h.** *bone*
*?tablet weaving plaque, Lagore;* **i.** *copper-alloy needle,*
*Lagore;* **j.** *stone loom weight, Cush;* **k.** *stone linen*
*smoother, Ballyaghagan* (**a.** *after O'Kelly 1963;*
**b–d.** *after Hencken 1938;* **e, h, i.** *after Hencken*
*1950;* **f.** *after Collins 1955;* **g.** *after Hencken 1942;*
**j.** *after Ó Ríordáin, S.P. 1940;* **k.** *after Proudfoot*
*1958).*

Irish site is from Lagore.[28] Because of this we are
forced to depend very largely upon other forms of
evidence: examples of the equipment used in the
processing of cloth (**34**), representations on sculpture and in manuscripts, and occasional hints in
the documentary sources can all help to give us
an indication of the various stages in the manufacture of textiles and of the clothes worn by the
men and women of the period.

There were two different types of cloth. The first
was made of wool which was clipped from the
backs of sheep using iron shears (**34a**). However,

there are also some indications that hair, probably
from goats, was used, and some of the textile fragments from Lagore are made from a mixture of
wool and hair. The fineness of this kind of cloth
and the quality of the thread depended upon the
careful preparation of the wool or hair prior to
spinning. The dirt would need to be removed but it
was not always thought necessary to arrange the
fibres in a single direction by the process known as
carding. One example from Lagore shows the
thread in the course of being spun straight from a
fragment of uncarded wool.

The second type of cloth was linen. This was
manufactured from flax which was sown in
March or April and harvested five or six months
later before the seeds were fully ripe, then soaked,
dried, beaten, and combed to separate the fibrous
stems from the rest of the plant and make them
ready for spinning. Flax fibres rarely survive in the
archaeological record, but carbonized flax seeds
have been identified at Carraig Aille 2 which
suggests that flax was grown in the vicinity of the
site.[29]

Spinning the thread by hand must have been a
long and laborious task and evidence for spinning
is found on almost every settlement site in the
form of spindle whorls (**34b–d**). These were
usually made of stone (soft sandstones, shales and
chlorite were the most suitable) or bone (the
rounded heads of ox femora were preferred) but
also occasionally of antler and possibly of wood.
Evidence for the manufacture of stone spindle
whorls has been found on several sites including
Knowth and Cahercommaun, usually in the form
of unfinished examples and those which had been
broken during the drilling of the central hole.
They may be disc, hemispherical or cylindrical in
shape and are sometimes ornamented with simple
incised lines. Bone and antler spindle whorls are of
similar shapes but may also be turned on a lathe,
producing a characteristic bowl shape which is
often decorated with incised lines and occasionally with ring-and-dot ornament. The spindles
themselves are much rarer since they are made of
wood (**34g**). The spinster is also likely to have used
a wooden distaff (**34f**) (which was held in the
hand rather than under the arm or tucked into
the belt) onto which the roughly rolled wool was
wound before spinning.[30]

Stone loom weights with an hourglass-shaped
hole in the centre (**34j**) have sometimes been
identified suggesting the use of vertical warp-
weighted looms. Small gouge-shaped tools (**34e**)

thought to be for beating up the weft on this type of loom are also known and a wooden weaving sword carved with Insular fret patterns was found in Littleton Bog, Co. Tipperary. It is also possible that narrow vertical-framed looms were used. Almost all the textile fragments from Lagore were of a simple tabby weave and might easily have been produced on a vertical warp-weighted loom. The largest piece was only 343 mm (13½ in) wide and 432 mm (17 in) long with a rough warp fringe surviving at one end. Most of the variety in the finished tabby-woven cloth seems to have been achieved by variation in the texture, using different types and thicknesses of thread or a finer weft than warp. However one fragment of finely-woven cloth from Lagore, which may have been dyed with madder, has a diagonal weave, and for this reason it could be of Viking manufacture. There is also evidence of tablet weaving to make narrow decorative braids. A square bone tablet with well-worn holes in the corners through which the warp threads would have passed was found on Rathtinaun crannog, Co. Sligo and a

35 *Dye manufacturing workshop, Inishkea North, Co. Mayo (after Henry 1952).*

possible triangular example (34h) has been identified from Lagore. Two fragments of braid were also found at Lagore, one fringed, the other with a raised chevron pattern woven into it.

If the cloth were wool it needed to be finished after weaving by fulling. It was steeped in cold water with detergent in the form of vegetable ash or stale human urine and trampled to release the natural grease or lanolin. This process also caused the cloth to shrink. If it were linen it needed to be finished by smoothing with a polished stone. Possible examples of these have been excavated at Ballyaghagan ring-fort (34k) and Clea Lakes crannog.[31]

Wool was dyed prior to spinning, while flax was dyed in the hank. Of particular interest is the use in early medieval Ireland of a species of shellfish, the dog whelk, which contains a transparent liquid which, when exposed to the sun, turns first green, then bluish-purple and then purplish-red. This dye, which was highly valued in the Ancient World, is tedious to extract but the wide variety and the richness of the colours obtained doubtless made it worthwhile. Indications of dye extraction from the dog whelk have come to light on a number of sites along the west coast of Ireland

and on the island of Inishkea North, Co. Mayo, a dye workshop (35) has been excavated. The structure was approximately oval, 7.3 m (24 ft) in diameter, with an entrance at the eastern end and was probably made of wattle walls set on stone footings. On the west side of the hut was an annexe defined by upright stone slabs in which there was a pit and nearby a large pile of dog-whelk shells. In the centre of the hut was a large hearth and outside it to the north-west a large stone-lined pit. The dog-whelk shells were gathered from rocks on the shore and the dye was then extracted by crushing the live shellfish, possibly in the pit in the annexe. Next it was steeped with salt, perhaps in the pit outside the hut which may have been lined with wood or leather to prevent leakage. The final stage was to boil it for a long time to reduce greatly the amount of liquid. This was done with pot boilers, many of which were found on the site, heated on the hearth. The excavator suggested that the major use of the dye obtained was as a manuscript pigment. However, since chlorite spindle-whorls were also manufactured on the site, it seems far more likely that it was primarily used for the dyeing of yarn.[32]

There are also hints of other dyes being used. At Boho ring-fort five madder seeds were identified but it was unclear whether they came from native wild or imported cultivated plants. Analysis of the residues in some E ware pots, from Teeshan crannog, for example, has shown that they contained cultivated madder which was presumably specially imported from France as a red dye. Woad pods have recently been found on the raised rath at Deer Park Farms.[33] Other natural native substances may also have been used such as blackberries and lichens.

We know little of sewing, though the written sources indicate that aristocratic ladies were expert embroiderers. A finely-worked hem and decorative stitching survives on one fragment of tabby-woven cloth from Lagore and a skilful darn can just be traced on another. Usually, however, needles (34i) made of copper alloy or iron for finer work, or sometimes bone, are the only evidence for sewing which survives.[34]

Representations in illuminated manuscripts and on the stone crosses give an indication of how at least the upper classes dressed. The early tenth-century West Cross at Clonmacnois (36), for example, shows two figures, possibly Abbot Colmán and King Flann mac Máel Sechnaill,

planting a staff in the ground with two onlookers depicted on the panel above. The men on the upper panel (36 left) are typically dressed in an ankle-length robe or *léine*, which was usually of linen gathered at the waist with a belt, and a woollen cloak or *brat* fastened at the shoulder with a brooch. The secular figure on the lower panel (36 right) wears a shorter knee-length tunic while the ecclesiastic wears an ankle-length robe and an upper garment. The hems of the tunics and robes are decorated, probably with tablet-woven borders. Women would also have worn long tunics and cloaks, as, for example, in the depiction of the Virgin in the Book of Kells. Some of the ornamental figures in this manuscript and others on the crosses suggest that short, tight, knee-length trews may sometimes have been worn by men. Indeed, for the Vikings trousers were the most usual form of male dress.[35]

## Bone, antler and horn

Objects made of skeletal materials in the form of bone and antler were very common in the early middle ages.[36] Items of textile equipment made of bone, such as spindle whorls and needles, have already been mentioned, but there was also a wide variety of other everyday artefacts including antler combs, bone pins and antler and bone knife handles. In contrast evidence of horn-working is rare, since it is much more prone to decay, but there are some indications of objects such as drinking horns.

Bone, like leather, is a by-product of animal husbandry and was therefore readily available. Antler tines, on the other hand, were collected in the woods in the late winter and early spring when the red deer shed their antlers. Bone- and antler-working are frequently evidenced on the same site and are therefore likely to have been carried out in conjunction with each other. At Dooey, Co. Donegal, for example, a considerable quantity of antler waste was found in the form of cut, sawn and partly worked tines, and bone-working was indicated by incomplete lathe-turned spindle whorls and pins at various stages of manufacture: the partially-shaped bones from which the pins were cut, roughed-out pins and pins which had yet to be finally polished.[37] Tools for bone- and antler-working are yet to be specifically recognized but, like those used in wood-working, they would have included saws and axes for cutting and shaping, knives for more intricate

36 *The West Cross, Clonmacnois, Co. Offaly,*
*details of east face showing figures in contemporary*
*clothing (Photographs: author).*

whittling and for executing much of the decoration, draw-knives, lathes and drills, and abrasives
for polishing. Bone and antler would probably
have been softened prior to working by immersion
in water. Some objects, such as pig-fibula pins,
could have been manufactured with relatively
little skill, but others, such as antler combs and
decorated pins, were the work of professionals.[38]

The most characteristic antler objects are
combs. Though bone was sometimes used, antler
was definitely preferred since it is tougher, more
pliable and has a better capacity to absorb shocks.
However, combs are still delicate objects and
seldom survive other than in a fragmentary condition. The types available in pre-Viking Ireland
may therefore best be demonstrated by examining
the fine collection from Lagore where a considerable number have survived more or less intact.
Firstly, there is a single example of a small one-
piece, single-sided comb with a rounded back and
simple ring-and-dot ornament (37a). Though
superficially similar to combs in Germanic Europe
during the Roman Iron Age, it is probably closer
to one-piece single-sided combs found in Roman

Iron Age and early medieval contexts in Scotland.
It is possible that this is the earliest type represented at Lagore.

Much more common are single- and double-
sided composite combs. Each comb is made up of a
series of tooth-plates cut with the grain of the
antler and placed side by side between two carefully shaped and polished side-plates, the various
components being held together with iron, bone
or occasionally copper-alloy rivets. The teeth were
then cut with the aid of a saw, polished and sharp-
ened to give them their characteristic shape. Two
principal forms of pre-Viking composite comb are
represented at Lagore. The first (37b) is short and
single-sided with the tooth-plates projecting well
above and beyond the short side-plates to form a
decorative crest which may be ornamented with
zoomorphic and/or openwork designs. This high-
backed type, the zoomorphic elements of which
have been compared with late Roman metalwork,
is characteristic of Ireland and Scotland. The
second type (37c), a double-sided comb of short or
sometimes medium length, is more numerous. It
has short, deep, flat side-plates, frequently decorated with ring-and-dot motifs but sometimes
with complex fret, spiral or interlace designs, and
the projecting end-plates are often curved.
Though double-sided composite combs are char-

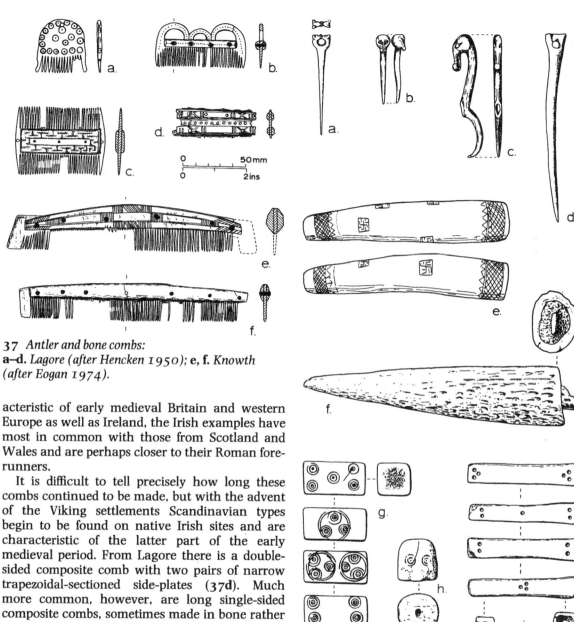

37 *Antler and bone combs:*
**a–d.** *Lagore (after Hencken 1950);* **e, f.** *Knowth*
*(after Eogan 1974).*

acteristic of early medieval Britain and western
Europe as well as Ireland, the Irish examples have
most in common with those from Scotland and
Wales and are perhaps closer to their Roman forerunners.

It is difficult to tell precisely how long these
combs continued to be made, but with the advent
of the Viking settlements Scandinavian types
begin to be found on native Irish sites and are
characteristic of the latter part of the early
medieval period. From Lagore there is a double-
sided composite comb with two pairs of narrow
trapezoidal-sectioned side-plates (**37d**). Much
more common, however, are long single-sided
composite combs, sometimes made in bone rather
than antler. These are poorly represented at
Lagore but several have been found at Knowth.
Here two principal forms may be noted. The first
(**37e**) has curved, trapezoidal-sectioned side-
plates, freqently decorated with longitudinal
grooves; the second (**37f**) has narrow, highly
polished D-sectioned side-plates and is rarely ornamented. Both are also characteristic of Viking
levels in Dublin as well as other areas of Viking
settlement.[39]

Combs were essential toilet articles, since the
hair was worn long by both men and women and

38 *Bone and antler objects:*
**a, b, d.** *pins, Lagore;* **c.** *toilet implement, Lagore;*
*knife handles* **e.** *Armagh,* **f.** *Lagore; dice* **g.** *Lagore,*
**i.** *Ballinderry 2;* **h.** *gaming piece, Ballinderry 2*
*(**a–d, f, g.** after Hencken 1950;* **h, i.** *after Hencken*
*1942;* **e.** *after Gaskell Brown and Harper 1984).*

the men also had long beards or drooping moustaches; only clerics had short hair and were clean-
shaven (36). The hair might be elaborately dressed
or even bleached, and it is likely that some of the
short single-sided combs and possibly some of the
bone pins may have been worn as hair ornaments.[40]

The most characteristic bone artefacts are pins.
The most common type is the simple pig-fibula pin
(38d), often with a perforation in the head, presumably to hold a retaining string which might
then be wound round the shank to keep the pin in
place. However, a wide variety of carefully shaped
and polished pins with ornamented heads and occasionally decorated shanks have also been found.
Many of the types are identical to copper-alloy
pins. Indeed, in some instances bone originals
may have been used in the manufacture of clay
moulds for casting copper-alloy pins. The large
number of bone pins from Lagore gives an indication of some of the types: simple spherical-headed
pins, nail-headed pins, segmented-headed pins
and smaller disc-headed pins; more complex pins
include zoomorphic- and anthropomorphic-
headed examples (38a, b), a fragmentary ringed
pin from Ballinderry 2 and a cruciform-headed pin
from Co. Roscommon. There is also a series of
bone pins with hipped shanks and sometimes
elaborately carved heads (38c). These are usually
regarded as toilet articles and have their origins in
the Roman world.[41]

Many tanged knives and similar implements
had cylindrical handles of bone or antler (38e, f).
On Cathedral Hill, Armagh, evidence for the production of antler knife handles has been found:
two were only partially smoothed; others were
smoothed and undecorated and some were ornamented with cross-hatching or ring-and-dot
motifs. Other more unusual bone artefacts include
dice, both the long Iron Age type from Ballinderry
2 (38i) and the shorter, rectangular Roman-
influenced form from Lagore (38g), a possible dice
box from Lagore and gaming pieces, including a
plano-convex example from Ballinderry 2 (38h)
and a square disc from Armagh both decorated
with ring-and-dot ornament. Beads are also sometimes found. There are bone barrel- and disc-
shaped beads from Carraig Aille 2, the former
turned on a lathe, and cylindrical antler beads
from Cahercommaun.[42]

Horn-working is rarely evidenced but the partially cut and broken tip of a sheep or goat horn
has been found at Knowth. Though objects are
occasionally found, such as the Insular drinking
horn from the Viking grave at Voll, Nord
Trøndelag in Norway, more usually it is the attachments which were once affixed to the horn
objects which survive. For example, the metal rim
mounts and, more frequently, the zoomorphic terminals on the drinking horns are sometimes
found. The fact that these are often highly decorated suggests they were prestige items. No
examples of blast horns have been found but they
are sometimes depicted in manuscripts. Other
objects also occasionally come to light. From
Lagore there is a curious piece of horn or tooth set
with an amber stud which might be an amulet,
and from Ballinderry 2 there is a unique bracelet
made from three jointed pieces of boar's tusk.[43]

## Metal-working

### Iron-working

The study of primitive iron technology and iron
artefacts is highly specialized and, although a considerable amount of research is under way, much
has yet to be published. For the early medieval
period in Ireland we are still largely dependent
upon accounts of iron-working in earlier excavation reports and the original interpretations of
what was found may be misleading. For example,
it can be difficult to tell smelting furnaces from
smithing hearths and, on many earlier excavations, slag was not systematically collected; nor
has it been analyzed for what it might reveal
about the technological processes being carried
out.

The documentary sources demonstrate that the
early medieval Irish blacksmith was held in high
regard and the forge was an important focus in
the community. On the other hand the archaeological evidence, mainly slag but sometimes
smelting furnaces or smithing hearths and other
debris, shows that some iron-working was carried
out on almost every occupation site, both secular
and ecclesiastical.[44] It is therefore possible that,
while basic tools could have been made by the less
skilled, more specialized iron-working, such as the
manufacture of weapons, was left to the professional.

There are several sources of iron available in
Ireland but we know little of how they were exploited in the early middle ages. The only clues are
provided by occasional finds of unprocessed iron
ore as, for example, at Lough Faughan crannog
and Oldcourt ring-fort, and a possible fragment of

bog ore from Cush. There is also little evidence of how the ore was prepared prior to smelting, but cleaning and roasting would have greatly increased the iron yield and there are some indications of ore roasting at Oldcourt and Reask.[45]

The majority of archaeological evidence for iron-working so far recovered has been interpreted as connected with the smelting process. It has been suggested that the smelting furnaces were of a simple 'bowl' type. But it is difficult to reconstruct their original form or determine their superstructure because they are seldom well-preserved since, after firing, they would have been dismantled to remove the iron bloom and slag. It is also likely that in the past some smithing hearths, which are generally smaller than smelting furnaces and produce less slag, have been wrongly interpreted as for smelting. The evidence may be further complicated by the fact that dismantled smelting furnaces might later be used for smithing or copper-alloy melting.[46] Often the only indications of the former presence of likely smelting furnaces are shallow hollows in the ground; burning; the slag which had sunk to form the distinctive 'furnace bottom', which was then frequently broken up when the furnace was dismantled; other slag which had once adhered to the iron bloom, but which had been hammered away prior to forging; and fragments of clay *tuyères* into which the nozzle of the bellows had fitted to funnel the air into the furnace to increase the heat to the $1,100$-$1,200°C$ required for smelting to take place. The bloom itself is rarely found because it was subsequently forged, though a fragment was identified at Lough Faughan.[47]

The best-preserved smelting furnace so far to have been excavated comes from Garryduff 1. It was located in the lee of the bank at the northern end of the ring-fort interior. It consisted of a small, circular hollow 100 mm (4 in) deep and 300 mm ($11\frac{3}{4}$ in) in diameter built up with a wall of clay and small stones which survived up to 175 mm ($6\frac{7}{8}$ in) in height and was 230–300 mm (9–$11\frac{3}{4}$ in) thick making the whole structure not more than 1.2m (3 ft $11\frac{1}{2}$ in) in overall diameter. The interior was also lined with clay and the whole furnace was burnt red and partially vitrified. Nearby was a dump of clean yellow clay which may have been used for purposes such as sealing the *tuyère* into position. At Reask a series of five small 'bowl' furnaces were set into the floor of a disused *clochán* (Structure D) and outside more evidence was found (**54b**), including traces of a possible

peat stack which may have been burnt nearby to provide charcoal for smelting. At Ballyvourney, Co. Cork, the interior of an abandoned stone round house was again used for iron smelting. No furnace or furnace base was found intact, but there were a number of hollows in the floor 300–600 mm ($11\frac{3}{4}$–1 ft $11\frac{5}{8}$ in) in diameter, indications of intense burning, 57 complete dish-shaped furnace bottoms, mostly 130–150 mm ($5\frac{1}{8}$–$5\frac{7}{8}$ in) in diameter and approximately 70 mm ($2\frac{3}{4}$ in) thick, and many other fragments. At the time the excavator thought that he had also found evidence of the clay furnace covers, but these are now known to be *tuyère* fragments. *Tuyères* usually only survive in very small pieces. The inner part becomes vitrified and coated with slag while the outer part crumbles away when the furnace is dismantled. Such circular disc-shaped fragments have been identified at Ballyvourney and Reask. Originally the *tuyère* would have been funnel-shaped and more complete examples were found at Ballyvollen, Co. Antrim (**39a**). Although only limited rescue excavations were carried out on this site a total of 170 kg (375 lbs) of slag was recovered.[48]

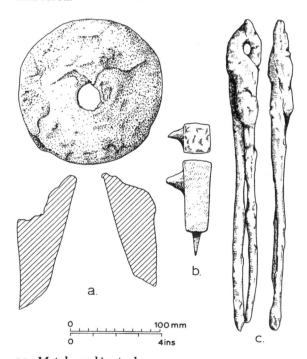

**39** *Metal–working tools:*
**a.** *tuyère, Ballyvollen (after Williams 1985b);*
**b.** *anvil, Garryduff 1 (after O'Kelly 1963);* **c.** *tongs, Garranes (after Ó Ríordáin, S.P. 1942).*

The next stage is to forge the bloom by heating it red hot and hammering it on an anvil to remove impurities and consolidate the iron prior to shaping. An eighth-century law text, while giving details of compensation for accidents which might happen during forging, also presents a picture of those engaged in the work: the smith, those who wielded the heavy hammers, the man who blew the bellows and the apprentices. Less archaeological evidence has been identified for smithing than for smelting but that from Clogher, though not as yet fully published, is particularly interesting. Iron-working was carried out in the ditch of the earlier 'ring-ditch' phase. Two 'bowl' furnaces were found and a stone-built, clay-lined smithing hearth. Beside this, and surrounded by debris including hammer scale, was a large rectangular block of limestone with a smooth flat top which had been used as an anvil. This iron-working site has been radiocarbon-dated to between the early fifth and the beginning of the seventh centuries (cal. AD 410–600). No other anvils have been found except for a small iron example from Garryduff 1 (**39b**). This would have been mounted on a large wooden block and used for fine work. Iron metal-working tongs are also sometimes found and may be exemplified by a pair from Garranes(**39c**).[49]

Iron objects are frequently severely corroded and, in the past, without the aid of modern X-ray techniques, it was often difficult to identify their precise size, shape or use; details of their construction and decoration were usually totally lost. However, a glance at the iron artefacts recovered from Garryduff 1 gives an indication of the importance of iron technology to the early medieval Irish for the manufacture of a wide range of everyday tools and equipment, as well as a number of more specialized items. Objects include a variety of knives, some with curved backs and straight cutting edges, others with straight backs and curved cutting edges; shears (**34a**) and awls; saws (**40d**) and chisels; keys and barrel padlocks; shallow ladles (**40a**); ringed and spiral-headed pins and cosmetic implements. The purpose of some of the tools found at Garryduff and elsewhere is disputed. For example, it has been suggested that the slotted-and-pointed object (**40b**) could have been a strike-a-light, a punch or auger, or an instrument for weaving rush matting. The pronged-and-socketed tool (**40c**) may have been used in weaving or carding wool or for scoring leather or harder surfaces.[50] Some iron objects are clearly of high technical achievement. The recent study of a possible dog or more probably a slave collar from Lagore (**40e**) has shown that the outside was decorated with applied iron strips, which had been twisted into a herring-bone pattern, and that, unusually, the attached chain was of figure-of-eight links which gradually decreased in size from the collar

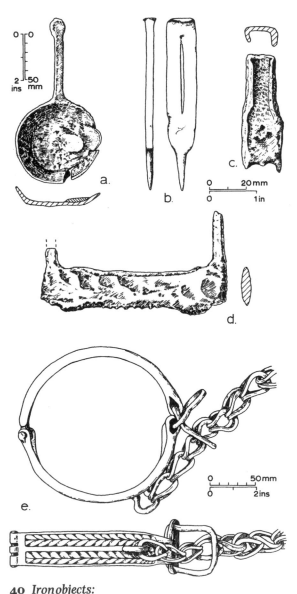

**40** *Iron objects:*
**a.** *ladle, Garryduff 1;* **b.** *slotted-and-pointed object, Lagore;* **c.** *pronged-and-socketed tool,* **d.** *bow-saw, Garryduff 1;* **e.** *slave or dog collar, Lagore* (**a, c, d.** *after O'Kelly 1963;* **b, e.** *after Hencken 1950*).

outwards. The closest parallels for these details are to be found in Roman and, more especially, Anglo-Saxon iron-working techniques.[51]

We know little in detail of early medieval Irish warfare. The main evidence comes in the form of iron weapons, swords and spears, but also iron shield bosses. There are occasional indications from other sources: for example, horsemen with swords and shields and footsoldiers with spears and shields are depicted on the Market Cross, Kells, Co. Meath. Swords are not very common finds, but the surprisingly large number from the royal site at Lagore confirms the view that they are aristocratic weapons. Studies of sword typology suggest that when the Irish came into military contact with the Romans they abandoned their very short La Tène swords in favour of small versions of the Roman *spatha*, a slashing sword, though some of them are closer in their proportions to the shorter Roman *gladius*, which may have been used for both thrusting and slashing. The Irish examples (**41a**) are characterized by straight shoulders, an almost parallel-sided blade with a central ridge, and a round tang, which was roughened to receive an organic hilt, and sometimes capped by a small bronze knob. More distinctively Irish variations are also known with flat or heavy rod-shaped tangs and blades which expand towards their points (**41b**). The extra weight near the point of the blade would have increased the efficiency of the sword as a slashing weapon. The Irish may also have been influenced by swords in use in the Germanic world. Three from Lagore have a shallow groove down the centre of the blade (**41c**) and a further example has recently been identified from the ring-fort at Killyliss. Large single-edged iron knives or scramasaxes of Continental type have also been identified at Lagore (**41d**). The coming of the Vikings, however, brought great changes, since the small Irish weapons were no match for the larger and heavier slashing swords of the enemy, and Viking types (**91**) were swiftly adopted.[52]

Iron spearheads, and sometimes butts and ferrules, are found on a wider variety of sites. Spears were more universal weapons than swords, but it is difficult to distinguish their purpose, since they were employed in hunting as well as warfare. Two types of spearhead may be

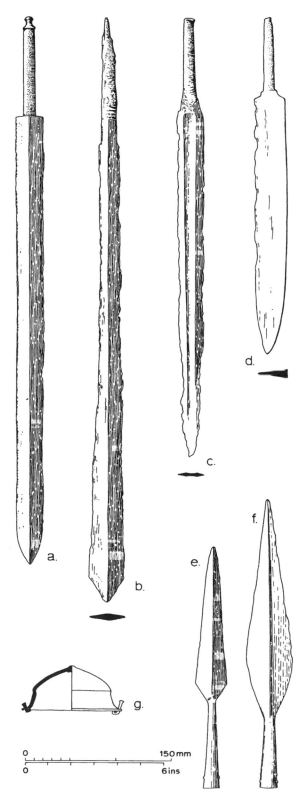

**41** *Iron swords, spear-heads and shield boss:*
**a, b, d–g.** *Lagore,* **c.** *no locality (after Hencken 1950).*

identified at Lagore: the leaf-shaped (41e), which was used both in the Iron Age and by the Romans, and the shouldered (41f), which was current in the post-Roman Germanic world and may have been introduced into Ireland by the Vikings. Some of the examples at Lagore are definitely of Viking type. The length of the spearhead may give some indication as to how it was used. Small spearheads may have been for throwing spears or javelins while larger, longer examples may have been for hand-held cavalry lances or infantry pikes. The soldiers protected themselves with small round shields, of which only the tiny dome-shaped iron bosses now survive (41g).[53]

## Copper and copper-alloy working

Although a wide variety of early medieval objects were made of copper alloy, as yet almost no metallurgical analysis has been carried out in Ireland. However, copper alloy in this period was usually in the form of either bronze or gunmetal, an alloy of copper and tin with lead added to improve the casting qualities. Copper-alloy objects included many items of personal adornment, mainly pins and brooches, but also buckles, strap-ends, rings and studs, as well as larger objects such as bowls, wooden buckets covered in copper-alloy sheets, or complex shrines for Christian relics. Many of these were highly decorated and for this reason they will be discussed in connection with ornamental metal-working in Chapter 7. Here some aspects of the technology will be considered.

Copper would have been smelted in much the same way as iron. Evidence is scarce, though two pieces of copper ore were found at Lagore which suggest that smelting was taking place. The next stage was to purify the copper by melting it in a clay crucible and stirring it with green sticks. The smelted tin could also be added at this stage to form bronze. The metal was then ready to be cast in stone or, more frequently, clay moulds. Evidence for these processes has come to light on several sites, both secular and ecclesiastical. At Garranes, for example, copper-alloy working took place up against the bank on the south side of the ring-fort interior. A black layer was excavated which contained small lumps of tin, crucibles (some whole, but many fragmentary), moulds of clay and stone, unfinished copper-alloy objects and the waste left over from the casting process, as well as evidence of glass-working. At Armagh excavation of part of the ditch which had probably enclosed the summit of Cathedral Hill revealed what was almost certainly a monastic workshop with its attendant metal- and glass-working debris. The area just within the ditch had been burnt twice; the upper layer contained finds such as crucibles and slate motif pieces, and the lower clay floor had evidence for glass- and enamel-working. The waste, including clay moulds and crucibles, had been tipped into the adjacent ditch.[54] Other important evidence has come from Lagore, Garryduff 1, Movilla Abbey, Moynagh Lough crannog, where large numbers of crucibles and clay moulds have been found, and Clogher, where the impressions on the clay moulds demonstrate the existence of a workshop manufacturing penannular brooches.[55]

Several different types of crucible may be identified. The most common are small with triangular mouths and are usually termed pyramidal (42a). They show signs of intense heat over the entire surface including vitrifaction which has coloured them a combination of red, green and grey. This indicates that they were actually placed in the metal-working hearths. In most instances crucibles of this kind seem to have been used for copper or copper-alloy melting as in some cases fragments have actually been found in them. Occasionally they are fitted with permanent lids with a knob on top to facilitate handling with tongs while hot (42b). The second type is similar but deeper and more bag-shaped. One example from Armagh (42c) had corroded copper alloy still clinging to its broken surfaces. There is some evidence at Lagore that the bag-shaped crucibles are later than the pyramidal ones, and it is interesting to note that there are none of the former at Garranes. Shallow, round flat-bottomed crucibles (42d) of varying size form another major type. These were usually made of clay but, uniquely, at Garranes, of sandstone (42e). They were not heated in metal-working hearths but instead from the top with the aid of clay blowpipes. This left accretions round the mouths of the crucibles and in their interiors but not on their sides. Some had been relined with clay (42d) indicating that they had been used more than once. At Lagore they seem to have been used for copper and copper-alloy working, but there are indications from Garranes, Moynagh Lough and Knowth that they were also employed as heating trays for use in enamelling.[56]

Simple objects might be manufactured in 'open' stone moulds. An example from Garranes (42h) was used for casting ingots of different sizes and a

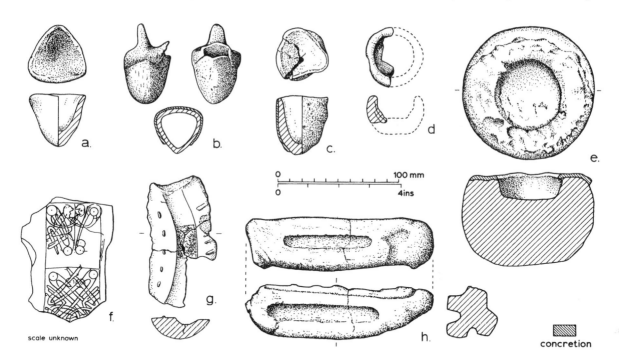

0

100 mm

0

4ins

scale unknown

concretion

42 *Crucibles, moulds and motif piece:*
*clay crucibles* **a.** *Garranes,* **b, d.** *Garryduff 1,*
**c.** *Armagh;* **e.** *sandstone crucible, Garranes;* **f.** *stone*
*motif piece, Garryduff 1;* **g.** *clay two-piece mould,*
*Armagh;* **h.** *stone ingot mould, Garranes* (**a, e, h.** *after*
*Ó Ríordáin, S.P. 1942;* **b, d, f.** *after O'Kelly 1963;*
**c, g.** *after Gaskell Brown and Harper 1984).*

copper-alloy ingot found there actually fitted into one of the moulds. Ingots such as these could be hammered out on an anvil to form metal sheets or later melted down for casting. Two-piece clay moulds (**42g**) were used for making highly-decorated objects, and were a considerable advance upon the Iron Age technique of lost-wax casting since they allow for multiple copies of one die. A very interesting collection has come to light in Armagh, though most are fragmentary, since the mould was usually broken in order to extract the casting. In addition to the shape of the object to be cast, some mould fragments show the remains of projections or depressions called 'keys' which would have helped to unite the two halves of the mould; on others the mouth or gate, through which the molten metal would have been poured, is still intact. Experiment has shown that two-piece clay moulds were made in several stages. First, the back was formed by pressing the die into a carefully-shaped pad of soft clay. At the

simplest level the die might be a finished object; in other cases a model of lead, bone, wood or wax. A former was then placed in order to shape the gate and the keys made with the tip of a knife blade. The clay pad was then left to dry for several hours. The front of the mould was then made by pressing a second pad of clay over the first and leaving it to dry. Later the two halves of the mould could be separated and the die and former removed. The mould was then reassembled and a strip of clay placed along the join to ensure the two halves were firmly united. Finally the mould needed to be thoroughly dried before the melted copper-alloy was poured in. Once cast, objects were removed from the mould and finished by filing away their rough edges and polishing. They would then be ready for assembly and for any further decoration such as enamel, millefiori, or the insertion of glass or amber studs.[57]

A word should be said about motif pieces (**42f**) which have often been found, as at Armagh, in metal-working areas. These are pieces of stone, antler and bone, or sometimes wood, which have designs or motifs scratched or carved upon them. They vary greatly in accomplishment: some are mere doodles; others the products of highly-skilled craftworkers. There has been considerable discussion as to their purpose. It has generally been agreed that they were used to try out patterns prior to reproducing them in metalwork or some other medium; they may also have been made by apprentices in the course of their training. But it has also been suggested that they could have been used in the metal-working process itself, either in the manufacture of dies for two-piece moulds or as moulds for stamping designs on thin metal foils. Recent detailed research has, however, cast doubt on this since no indisputable evidence for their use in metal-working has been found.[58]

### Gold and silver

The early medieval Irish also made use of gold and silver for ornamental metal-working, as is clearly indicated by some of the surviving objects, such as the 'Tara' brooch and the Ardagh chalice (see Chapter 7). Native sources of gold may have been exploited and objects would also have been melted down and the gold reused. However, gold can never have been common as it is used sparingly throughout the period in the form of leaf, gilding, filigree and granulation. Almost no evidence of gold-working survives on archaeological sites simply because the metal was too precious to be wasted or lost. Tiny fragments of gold-filigree wire have been found at Moynagh Lough crannog and Movilla Abbey, but that is all.

No evidence of silver-working has come to light, though surviving objects show that it was becoming more common during the course of the eighth century and was used in a wide variety of ways for casting, the raising of silver vessels, wire-drawing, silvering and silver foil. With the coming of the Vikings there was a great influx of imported silver (see p. 174), and silver objects became more common, but sources of silver in the pre-Viking period are less well understood. Native silver ores may have been exploited, though this has yet to be proved. Other sources included the recycling of Romano-British silver pillaged by Irish raiding parties in the late fourth and early fifth centuries (see p. 4) and possibly the importation of silver from Continental Europe.[59]

### Enamel and glass

Enamel and glass were used for decorating metalwork, usually copper alloy but occasionally iron. In the early part of the period red enamel and/or millefiori glass ornamented the terminals of penannular brooches, hand-pins and latchets (63, 69a). During the eighth century more complex pieces were produced, such as the Moylough belt shrine (66), where red and yellow enamel and blue and white millefiori, frequently set in rectangular and 'L'-shaped cells, were used together with decorative glass studs. These techniques died out in the course of the ninth century but were revived towards the end of the period on objects such as St Manchan's shrine (75). In addition glass was used for manufacturing beads and bangles. Glass vessels were not produced but there is some evidence to suggest that these were imported as luxury items from England or the Continent.

Enamel- and glass-working were carried out in the same areas as copper and copper-alloy working – much of the equipment, such as hearths, crucibles and tongs, is the same – and it seems likely that the same craftworkers would often have been involved in both activities. There is as yet no evidence for the manufacture of enamel or glass from their raw materials in early medieval Ireland, though there is no technical reason why this could not have been done. There is, however, considerable evidence for the recycling of glass. Scrap glass or cullet has been found on several glass-working sites, for example Garranes and Lagore. The pieces are very small but on closer inspection they have turned out to be fragments of vessels, such as beakers and palm-cups, originally manufactured somewhere in Anglo-Saxon England, northern France, Belgium or the Rhineland. It has been suggested that the glass may have reached sites in western Britain and Ireland as cullet. But it seems far more likely that it arrived in the form of the vessels themselves, imported for use by those who also owned imported pottery; the two are frequently found on the same high-status sites. Fragility meant the life-span of such glass vessels was inevitably limited; when they broke the glass was simply recycled. So far the only vessel to have been found intact is a small pale yellow flask decorated with a raised opaque-white spiral trail which was discovered in a souterrain at Mullaroe, Co. Sligo. The type is unusual but it may have been imported towards the end of the early medieval period.[60]

During the Iron Age enamel circulated in the form of lumps and rods. This also seems to have been true during the early medieval period. Several pieces of decayed enamel were found at Garranes and a stick of opaque-yellow enamel was found in Armagh. The enamel was prepared by grinding it into a fine powder with the aid of a pestle and mortar. The powder was then placed on

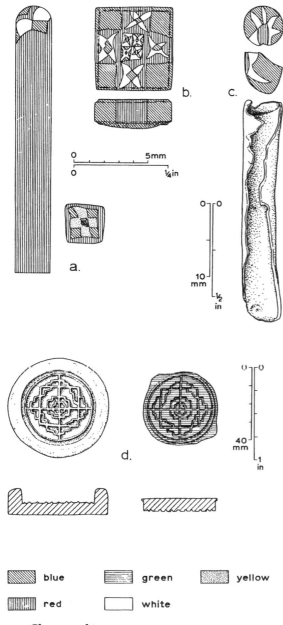

| blue | green | yellow |
| red | white | |

**43** *Glass-working:*
**a.** *millefiori rod,* **b.** *end of millefiori rod,* **c.** *end of millefiori rod in copper-alloy holder, Garranes (after Ó Ríordáin, S.P. 1942);* **d.** *clay mould and glass stud, Lagore (after Hencken 1950).*

cool, the enamel was finished by polishing with an abrasive.[61]

Millefiori-glass working is related to enamelling. Originally a Roman invention, millefiori is made by fusing several different coloured glass rods together to form a pattern, and then, while still hot and pliable, rolling and drawing them out into a single long thin rod which preserves the pattern throughout its length in the manner of a stick of rock. A millefiori inset is then made by cutting a thin slice off the end of the rod and, either fusing it directly to the metal object in the manner of enamelling, or laying it in a bed of enamel which, when fused to the metal, will hold it in position. At Lagore two fragments of blue glass cane may indicate the manufacture of millefiori rods or they could have been used for glass insets or for ornamenting beads. However, the decoration of metalwork with millefiori was certainly taking place, as is demonstrated by a short length of millefiori rod with a blue and white chequer-board pattern.[62] Similar millefiori rods were found at Garranes (**43a, b**) together with a short length decorated with a red, white and blue flower pattern which was set in a copper-alloy tube (**43c**) in order to hold the glass securely while slices were cut off.

At Lagore evidence for the manufacture of highly-ornamented glass studs has also come to light. Eight small clay moulds were found, one with a green glass stud still in it (**43d**). More complex multi-coloured glass studs were made by placing a metal grille upside-down in the clay mould. Enamel was then inserted into some of the compartments and fused before filling the rest of the mould with glass of a contrasting colour.[63]

The skill of the early medieval Irish glass worker is also demonstrated by the manufacture of beads and bangles. Beads, usually plain, but sometimes highly decorated, are a relatively common find on sites of the period. However, surprisingly little work has been done on them despite their potential as a tool for dating. Some interesting preliminary experiments have been carried out in order to try and date beads by non-destructive chemical analysis. These suggested a rising antimony content as the period proceeds. But a more detailed understanding of the visual typology is still required as well as the recovery of beads from more closely-datable excavated contexts. It is clear that some are long-lived types with their origins in the Iron Age and Roman Iron Age periods. Others may eventually be datable to within a couple of centuries. There are also hints

the parts of the metal object to be enamelled, which was in turn placed in a shallow clay crucible or heating tray. A flame was then directed onto the surface of the object to effect adhesion between the metal and enamel. Once

that the manufacture of beads may have reached its height during the seventh and eighth centuries, but this needs to be checked by further work.[64]

There is as yet no definite evidence of bead-making workshops, but at Movilla Abbey two fragments of twisted green glass rod, which may be the waste from a bead made by winding a glass rod round a metal one, were found, together with a twisted blue and white glass cane of a type frequently used for ornamenting beads and bangles with decorative cables. A small glass blob

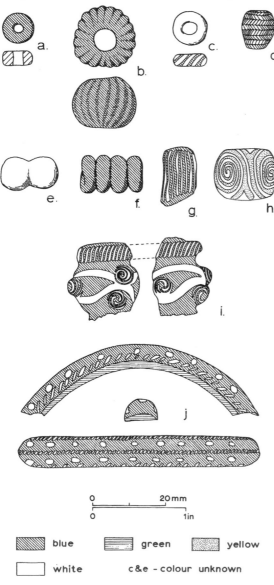

44 *Glass beads and bangle, Lagore (after Hencken 1950).*

with what may have been a partial perforation may also indicate bead making at Garryduff I.[65]

The major types of bead available in early medieval Ireland may best be reviewed by examining a selection of the very considerable collection from Lagore.[66] To begin with there is a variety of plain beads. Small dark blue beads (44a) are particularly common, but there are also similar light blue, white and yellow examples. Larger ones include blue melon beads (44b), a continuation of the well-known Iron Age and Roman type, but less well made; large green and khaki-coloured beads; and green tubular beads, which are common in Anglo-Saxon contexts and may therefore be imports. Blue segmented beads (44f) are also found together with what is known as a dumb-bell type (44e), which is distinctively Irish and may not necessarily be perforated, in which case it is technically a toggle rather than a bead. There are also many different kinds of polychrome beads. A large number are characteristically decorated with twisted cables of different coloured glass threads which were either smoothed flat round the body of the bead or left in relief. Beads may be ornamented with a single cable (44c), or many cables alternating in different directions to create a herring-bone effect (44d). Alternatively, single threads may be smoothed into the surface of the bead to form spirals, stripes and other patterns (44g, h). Some are decorated with a combination of cables wound round the ends of the bead and single threads which form spiralled knobs and waves on the body (44i). Other more unusual techniques include a bead with millefiori insets and a black bead with haphazard red, yellow and white spots.

The cabled decoration and other ornament found on beads is also characteristic of the glass bangles (44j). Though they are known as bangles, this may be a misnomer since the diameters of many are too small for them to have been worn by anyone other than a small child; for this reason some at least may have been pendants. The bangles have a 'D'-shaped section. The core is usually of dark blue glass, though examples of light blue, grey and green have also been found. The ornament consists of blue and white cables and white spots, either fused directly onto the core, or onto a band of dark blue glass which is then fused to the core. The decoration has usually been carefully smoothed and therefore seldom stands out in relief. Though not common finds, there are several fragments from Lagore and one or two other examples from other sites, such as Knowth and Cahercommaun. Glass bangles are first found on the Continent during the Iron Age, are known in native contexts in Scotland and Wales in the first and second centuries AD, and re-emerge in Ireland in the early middle ages. A few are also known from Anglo-Saxon contexts. At the moment there are no clear signs of continuity, though the Irish examples have a certain resemblance to the Type 2 bangles identified in Scotland.[67]

**45** *Stone objects:*

*whetstones* **a–c.** *Cahercommaun (after Hencken 1938);* **d.** *grindstone, Lagore (after Hencken 1950);* **e.** *stone lamp,* **f.** *gaming board, Garryduff 1 (after O'Kelly 1963).*

## Stone and related materials

As we have already seen techniques of drystone building were commonly used in Ireland, particularly in the west. From the late seventh century onwards simple masonry churches were also built (see p. 124), carved stone crosses erected, and later tall stone round towers came to dominate the monastic landscape. During the twelfth century Romanesque influences may be detected in church architecture in such features as the decorated round arches and carved stone doorways.

But stone was also employed to make a wide range of everyday tools and artefacts. Many of those used for specialist purposes, such as querns and millstones, spindle whorls and loom weights, have already been discussed, but some stone tools were used much more widely. Particularly important are a variety of hones and whetstones used for sharpening. These are very common finds, and at Cahercommaun over 500 examples were recovered. They vary greatly in size: some are long

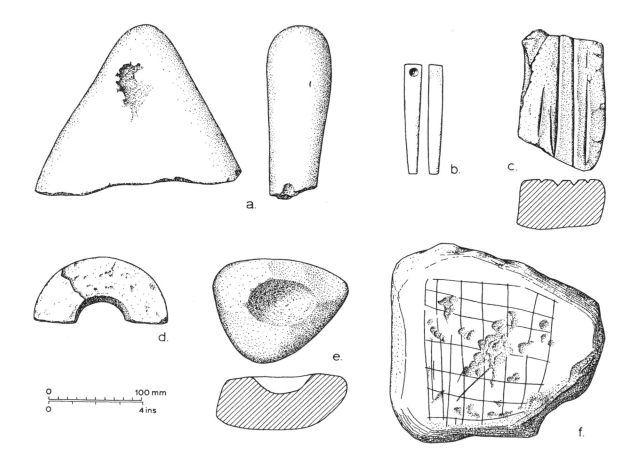

narrow pebbles or flat stones, hardly worked, but smoothed through use (45a); some are formed into a rough rectangle; others are small with a rectangular section, very carefully shaped, with a perforation at the top to take a copper-alloy ring for suspension at the waist (45b). Sometimes the surface is marked with grooves for sharpening objects such as pins. At Lagore possible grind-stones (45d), which are circular with holes in the middle for rotating on a wooden axle, have also been identified; these may have been used for sharpening weapons. In addition pounding and rubbing stones are common, as are small round discs, the purpose of which is unknown. Other objects include roughly-incised gaming boards (45f) and stone lamps (45e).[68]

The frequent occurrence of small assemblages of worked flint on many early medieval sites has caused considerable discussion. Sometimes these have been interpreted as prehistoric artefacts, either in a residual context, or reused during the early medieval period. However, their very ubiquity has argued against this and it is now generally agreed that flints were worked on early medieval sites. There is actual evidence of this at Ballyutoag where a multi-platformed core, indica-tive of flint knapping, was found. The range of flint artefacts is not great and the crudity of the work-manship has been commented on as distinguish-ing them from their prehistoric counterparts. Tools include different kinds of scrapers and small blades; strike-a-lights are common, though quartz examples are also sometimes found.[69]

Jet, lignite and shale were used for the produc-tion of bracelets, pendants and rings. Bracelets of this kind were manufactured as far back as the Bronze Age, as indicated by the finds from Ballin-derry 2. Early medieval examples can often be distinguished by their 'D'-shaped sections (46a). Although commonly found on early medieval sites, they have been little studied. There are many examples from Lagore together with lignite beads (46f) and a small truncated cone, perhaps a gaming piece (46e). One bracelet is possibly only partly finished which may indicate their manufac-ture on the site. This is certainly true at Oldcourt ring-fort, where a disc-shaped core, the waste left over from making a lignite bracelet, was found. This shows that bracelets of this kind were made by splitting slabs of the requisite thickness and trimming them into discs. The interior was removed by cutting a 'V'-shaped groove with a narrow chisel on either side of the disc. The

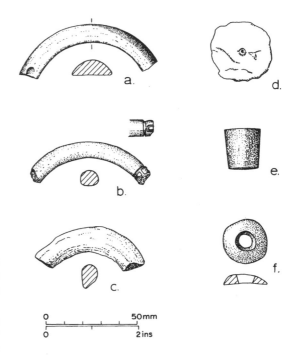

46  *Lignite objects:*
*bracelets* **a.** *Lagore,* **b.** *Armagh;* **c.** *unfinished bracelet,*
**d.** *central waste core from lathe-turned bracelet,*
*Armagh;* **e.** *gaming piece,* **f.** *bead, Lagore (**a, e, f.** after*
*Hencken 1950;* **b–d.** *after Gaskell Brown and Harper*
*1984).*

bracelet was then finished by smoothing and polishing. Some bracelets were definitely manu-factured on a lathe. In Armagh unfinished lignite bracelets and waste discs with perforations where they were held on the lathe have been found (46c, d). There are also unique examples of a jet bracelet decorated with rectilinear ornament (46b) and two small pieces of a lathe-turned lignite bowl dec-orated with a spiral pattern.[70]

## Exchange and trade

As we have seen the archaeological evidence suggests a wide range of craft activity: the manu-facture of both everyday artefacts and luxury goods. We have also glimpsed, in imported pottery and glass, the products of long-distance trade. However, what the archaeology cannot tell us at present is how these goods, both native and exotic, changed hands. For this we have to resort to the written sources.

It has been shown that gift-giving, reciprocity and the redistribution of goods were important mechanisms of exchange in early medieval Ireland which existed alongside a growing market economy.[71] In a society where hierarchy, status and kin were extremely important these helped to bind the people together. Clients gave food render to their lords; the lords rented cattle to their clients. Those with surplus wealth might seek to transform it into luxury goods, either through trade, or by the patronage of skilled craftworkers who made objects such as brooches and other ornamental metalwork for display. Such luxury goods, as well as swords, horses, female slaves and drinking horns, for example, might then be redistributed to those who gave service. Surplus goods might also be donated to the Church.

In the early part of the period trade and exchange, as well as ceremonial gift-giving and religious activities, took place at the tribal *óenach* or fair which was held on the border of the territory. Some of these sites have been identified, but the date of any archaeological remains is difficult to ascertain since no excavation has taken place and some survived as gathering places until relatively recent times. At Teltown, Co. Meath, for example, there is a variety of earthworks including ring-forts; an enclosure partly surrounding a large cairn or tumulus; another enclosure, which formerly had a ditch and external bank thereby suggesting some kind of sanctuary area; and, not far away, an unusual monument of unknown function consisting of two parallel earthen banks with a ditch between them.[72] But, with the rise of Christianity, these sites lost their role as pagan religious centres, and it appears that some of the larger monasteries also began to act as gathering-places where an *óenach* might be held. The earliest evidence of a monastic *óenach* is at Lusk, Co. Dublin, in 800. These fairs sprang up in response to the need for local exchange and trade, and it is likely that craftworkers were attracted to work in the environs of the major monasteries, at least partly for this reason. The variety of crafts evidenced in the excavations at Armagh would certainly suggest this. In the course of the ninth and tenth centuries these monastic fairs gradually developed into proper markets with fixed market places indicated by crosses, examples of which are known at Armagh and Kells.[73]

The similarity of the material culture in Ireland and northern and western Britain in the early middle ages is well-known. Indeed, the Irish settlements in western Scotland, Wales and south-west England at the end of the Roman period, as well as

the possible emigration of Britons to Ireland, must have helped to bring this about. The influence of Roman technology and artefact types is clearly demonstrable and documentary references show continuing contacts throughout the period. However, because of the very similarity of the artefactual assemblages on either side of the Irish Sea, it is as yet almost impossible to recognize the objects of trade and exchange in the archaeological record. A rare example, the hanging-bowl escutcheon from the River Bann, is almost certainly from Scotland,[74] but contacts between north-east Ireland and western Scotland are much better shown using historical, linguistic and place-name evidence.

Evidence of trade and exchange between Ireland and the kingdoms of Anglo-Saxon England before the Vikings is, more surprisingly, equally difficult to trace in the archaeological record, even though there are more differences in the artefactual assemblages. It is possible to suggest the importation of Anglo-Saxon glass vessels and beads into Ireland and hint at the influence of Anglo-Saxon technology, as, for example, in iron and decorative metal-working, but at present that is all. In the other direction it may be possible to trace the influence of Celtic ornamental metal-working techniques at Sutton Hoo, for example, though these are not necessarily specifically Irish; indisputably Irish artefacts in Anglo-Saxon contexts, if they exist, have yet to be identified.

The trade of items from further afield is more easily identified simply because they are distinguishable in the archaeological record. There may have been direct or indirect trade contacts with other parts of northern Europe, though at present the fragmentary glass vessels imported possibly from northern France, Belgium or the Rhineland provide the only archaeological evidence. The importation of E ware demonstrates contacts with western France, and documentary references show that the ports of Nantes on the Loire and perhaps Bordeaux on the Garonne may have been particularly important. It is difficult to say what goods other than E ware and perhaps dye may have been imported into Ireland from western France. Wine is certainly suggested by the written sources, but, since it would have been transported in wooden casks, it has left no identifiable archaeological evidence. Equally, we know little of the goods the Irish may have supplied in return. The ninth-century *Life of St Filibert* describes Irish ships arriving at the island of Noirmoutier at the mouth of the Loire with shoes and clothes, and, in the late twelfth century, Gerald of Wales mentions the importation of wine from Poitou in return for hides and skins.[75]

Christian contacts between Ireland and Rome are well-known, though the extent of trade is unclear. Relics were brought back to Ireland by pilgrims: the porphyry fragments dating from towards the end of the period which have been found on some ecclesiastical sites, were probably pilgrims' souvenirs. Christian contacts with Spain are also evidenced and boats from the Mediterranean, carrying such items as A and B wares, would certainly have called at Iberian ports where the cargoes may have been transferred to other boats before the long voyage north.[76]

During the ninth century the arrival of the Vikings resulted in the spread of Insular goods to Scandinavia and some of these at least, such as those found in the emporium at Kaupang, Norway, could have been trade items. However, in Ireland the real trade expansion came during the tenth century with the growth of Viking towns (see Chapter 8), particularly Dublin, which attracted specialized craftworkers and long-distance traders, as well as an exchange of goods with the surrounding countryside. This in turn led to an expansion of monastic markets. Before this foreign traders may have brought their boats to special ports of trade where exchange took place at certain times of the year. It has been suggested that Dalkey Island, situated on the southern end of Dublin Bay, may have been one of these 'gateway communities' because of the discovery of a comparatively large quantity of exotic goods, both pottery and glass.[77]

# CHAPTER 6

# The Church

## The historical background

It is important to give a brief outline of the history of the early medieval Irish Church in order to illuminate the archaeological evidence. It may also serve to highlight some of the questions which archaeology should try to answer. The written sources are of great variety. They include the moving testimony of Patrick himself; ascetic rules and penitentials for early monks and converts; ecclesiastical legislation which helped to secure the position of the Church in early Irish society; early lives of saints written to enhance their growing cults; hymns, prayers and poetry; and the terse documentation of events recorded in the annals.[1] Other forms of evidence may also be used, such as the study of place-names or Latin Christian loan-words in Old Irish.

As we have already seen, the introduction of Christianity was a lasting aspect of the Roman impact on Ireland. There were probably already Christians in Ireland during the fourth century: perhaps traders and settlers from Roman Britain, slaves captured by Irish raiding parties, and native mercenaries who had returned from service in the Roman army. At any rate, by 431 the number was sufficient for Palladius to be sent from Gaul at the behest of Pope Celestine as bishop 'to the Irish believing in Christ'. The outcome of his ministry is unknown, though there is some evidence to suggest that it may have centred on the east coast.[2] The life of Patrick, and his mission, which was apparently concentrated in the north, are equally obscure and have been the subjects of intense debate. Many of the problems have arisen because of the elaboration of Patrick's life by later biographers and the frequently puzzling nature of his own short works, the *Confession*, which was written in reply to criticisms made of him, and the *Letter* to the soldiers of Coroticus, complaining about the enslavement of newly-baptized Christians. Patrick, whenever he may have lived during the fifth century, came from a well-to-do Romano-British Christian background. When he was 16 he was captured by Irish raiders and taken to Ireland where, during the course of six years in slavery, he came to believe in God. Finally he escaped and may have sailed to Gaul before returning to Britain. Some time later he went back to Ireland with the object of converting the Irish and at that point or subsequently was made a bishop. The *Confession* makes it clear that Patrick's mission was lonely, arduous and frequently dangerous; though he won some converts he was clearly anxious about what would happen after his death.[3]

It is therefore possible to show that there were early Christian contacts with both Britain and Gaul. However, it is important to emphasize that Ireland was not swiftly converted. Indeed, it has been convincingly demonstrated that during the sixth century Christianity was 'still struggling against a pagan environment'[4] and that some aspects of paganism, such as sacred trees and wells, were ultimately incorporated into a Christian context.[5] It may eventually be possible to trace this interesting intermediate period in the archaeological record.

During the second half of the sixth century we can chart the rapid spread of monasticism in Ireland, and it is in this period that many important monasteries, such as Durrow and Clonmacnois, Co. Offaly, and Bangor, Co. Down, were founded. Irish missionaries also began to seek exile abroad: in 563 Columba founded Iona in the kingdom of Dalriada and Columbanus (d. 615) travelled extensively on the Continent, setting up several important houses including Luxeuil and Bobbio. With the growth of the monasteries, Ireland swiftly became a Christian country and during the seventh and eighth centuries it is possible to trace in the secular and ecclesiastical legislation the gradual assimilation of the Church into early Irish society. Some monasteries became wealthy and began to vie with each other for power and patronage. Armagh, for example, built up the cult of Patrick, and claimed ecclesiastical suzerainty over other monasteries and churches. Occasionally even inter-monastery battles were fought as, for example, between Clonmacnois and Durrow in 764. At the end of the century the recognition of abuses such as these resulted in a growing spiritual revival known as the *Céli dé* (servants of God) or Culdee movement which led to the foundation of new monasteries such as Castledermot, Co. Kildare, and the establishment of more ascetic communities in or near many of the established houses.[6]

At this point something should be said about the organization of the early Irish Church, since this has been the subject of considerable debate, and certain aspects will assume particular relevance when we come to consider the status of many ecclesiastical sites which survive on the ground. It used to be thought that Patrick and Palladius set up a territorial diocesan church led by bishops, the organization of which mirrored that found throughout the Roman Christian world. However, because Ireland had never been part of the Roman Empire and had no towns to act as diocesan centres, this system was difficult to maintain and, with the rise of monasticism, the power of the bishops was sapped by the increasing strength of the abbots. It was at one time suggested that the territorial dioceses were replaced by monastic confederations (*paruchiae*) of major mother and dependent daughter houses and that bishops were subsumed into these and became subservient to abbots. A similar organizational structure was assumed to have evolved, with or without direct Irish influence, in other Celtic countries and this, together with idiosyncracies, such as an old-fashioned method of calculating the date of Easter and the wearing of an unusual form of tonsure, led to the coining of the misleading term, the 'Celtic Church', sometimes with the added implication that this was somehow independent of Rome.[7]

It is now thought that this picture is greatly over-simplified. Though there were undoubted similarities between the early Churches of Britain and Ireland, there is no evidence for a pan-Celtic Church or for its independence from Rome. As far as Ireland is concerned, it is now realized that we know almost nothing of the organization of the Church before the seventh century, and that it may have grown up on a much more *ad hoc* basis

than was previously thought. More importantly, it can be shown that during the seventh century, with the exception of the Columban *familia*, territorial episcopal dioceses were not replaced by monastic confederations; instead the two existed side by side. During the eighth century bishops did not lose their powers to abbots, though subsequently it does appear that abbots, and later coarbs, did control the more temporal aspects of the Church. Overall the diversity of the early Irish Church has not been sufficiently stressed. Not all churches were necessarily monastic: some were major churches founded by bishops, others were regional churches with clergy administering to a lay population group. As well as the major monasteries and their daughter houses, there were also hermitages and small independent foundations attached to family estates.[8]

The impact of the Vikings on the Irish Church will be considered elsewhere (see p. 173), but it appears that, despite repeated raiding with the resultant decline of many smaller foundations, important monasteries, such as Armagh and Clonmacnois, had sufficient resources to be able to recuperate with relative speed. Indeed, their power grew, though they became increasingly dependent on royal patronage. The evidence for such alliances is sometimes still detectable. For example, in 908 it is recorded in the annals that a stone church was built at Clonmacnois by Abbot Colmán under the patronage of the Uí Néill highking, Flann Sinna. It is his name and that of Colmán which are inscribed on the nearby West Cross together with a panel depicting the unity of Church and state, showing two figures, almost certainly Colmán and Flann, planting a ceremonial stake in the ground (36 right).[9]

From the tenth century onwards the larger monasteries were becoming proto-urban complexes with considerable populations, not only of monks, but also of lay men and women including estate workers, craftworkers and those who had sought sanctuary within the monastic enclosure. The monasteries were divided into different areas with streets, houses and public buildings in the form of churches. Outside the enclosures markets were springing up to take advantage of the opportunity for trade and exchange.[10]

Ireland was also coming into increasing contact with the Church in England and on the Continent. The foundation of new Irish houses in Germany, the growing popularity of pilgrimage to Rome and the links between the sees of Canterbury and

Dublin helped to create an awareness amongst some Irish kings and clergy of the needs for ecclesiastical reform. The first reforming synod was held at Cashel in 1101. This was primarily concerned with matters of Christian discipline, including the regulation of ecclesiastical appointments and marriage. The next synod at *Ráith Bresail* in 1111 concentrated on Church organization and set about the establishment of territorial dioceses; this process culminated in 1152 with the arrival of a papal legate carrying *pallia* for four Irish archbishops at Armagh, Cashel, Dublin and Tuam. Monasteries also underwent change and new orders were introduced into Ireland. Many existing monasteries came under the Augustinian rule, and the first Irish Cistercian house was founded by St Malachy at Mellifont, Co. Louth, in 1142. The coming of the Anglo-Normans gave further impetus to organizational reform, including the setting up of parishes. Such changes are also reflected in the archaeological evidence, as, for example, in the introduction of Romanesque church architecture exemplified by Cormac's Chapel at Cashel, Co. Tipperary.[11]

## The nature of the evidence

During the nineteenth century there was an increasing interest in early medieval ecclesiastical antiquities. This was one aspect of a growing sense of Irish cultural identity which drew as much on the past as it did on the present. Amongst the most important figures of this revival was George Petrie who, together with a small group of associates, laid the foundations for the study of the early Irish Church. In the 1830s he was involved in the Ordnance Survey and organized the recording and illustrating of many church sites for the first time. He wrote extensively, including an important book on the ecclesiastical architecture and round towers of Ireland. He was also responsible for arranging the antiquities belonging to the Royal Irish Academy (later the core of the National Museum collection) and acquired several spectacular examples of early medieval ecclesiastical metalwork, such as the Cross of Cong and the Ardagh chalice.[12] Activities such as these greatly increased public awareness of the archaeological remains of the early Irish Church. In addition the disestablishment of the Church of Ireland in 1869 resulted in many important early ecclesiastical sites being taken into state care.

The first extensive excavation of a large ecclesiastical site was carried out by H.C. Lawlor at Nendrum, Co. Down, in 1922-4 (50). By modern standards the excavation techniques left much to be desired, but Nendrum remains of crucial importance because it is still the only major monastic site to have undergone large-scale excavations which have been subsequently published.[13] Likewise the work of H.G. Leask on early Irish church architecture and R.A.S. Macalister on inscriptions, though both now in need of major revision, have yet to be superseded.[14] Françoise Henry is best remembered for her research on early medieval Irish art, much of it religious. But she also took considerable interest in ecclesiastical remains, as exemplified by her archaeological survey of the Iveragh peninsula, Co. Kerry, published in 1957, which described and illustrated many characteristic small church sites.[15] One of these, Church Island (54c), was excavated by M.J. O'Kelly in 1956–7.[16]

Over the past 25 years our knowledge of early medieval church archaeology has greatly increased as a result of both survey and excavation. Systematic surveys of Co. Down and, more recently, Co. Donegal and the Dingle peninsula, Co. Kerry, have provided up-to-date plans and descriptions of a wide range of ecclesiastical monuments.[17] Equally, aerial photography has played a particularly important role in the recognition of ecclesiastical sites since it was customary to surround them with curvilinear (or occasionally rectilinear) enclosures. Though often difficult to trace on the ground, these have been preserved in modern street layouts or as hedge lines and crop marks, all easily visible from the air (49).[18] Our knowledge of early Irish church architecture has also been refined.[19] However, excavation of major ecclesiastical sites is still rare, though interesting results have been obtained from small rescue excavations at sites such as Armagh and Movilla Abbey, Co. Down.[20] Many more small church sites and cemeteries have been investigated, some as research projects, but most as the result of rescue excavations.

Inevitably, the archaeological evidence is at present very patchy and there has been an understandable tendency towards survey rather than excavation. Large numbers of early medieval ecclesiastical sites have remained in continuous or intermittent use over the centuries, though only a few ancient churches are still active places of worship; most have fallen into ruin while the adjacent graveyard often continues or has continued until very recent times as a place of burial. In some cases, though the buildings are ruinous, and the occupants of the cemetery have been long forgotten, the site is still a place of Christian devotion with occasional visitors to the holy well, perhaps, or the tomb associated with the founding saint; until recently some were the focus of a pilgrimage or pattern to celebrate the saint's feast-day. Others have, however, been almost completely forgotten and may only be recognized as a pile of rubble marked by an ancient cross-slab, or remembered in a field-name, or because they were re-used in times gone by for the burial of unbaptized children. Some are no longer distinguishable from early medieval secular settlements since, like ring-

forts, they are surrounded by curvilinear enclosures.

The continued use of a large number of ecclesiastical sites presents a further problem for the archaeologist, one of chronology. The origin and date of some features may now be impossible to determine; the context of others, which are clearly early medieval, may have been lost or subtly changed.

Many ecclesiastical objects have also survived: manuscripts, such as Gospel Books and psalters, and ornamental metalwork in the form of church plate, shrines and reliquaries (see Chapter 7). Some, the Lough Kinale book shrine and the Ardagh chalice for example, had been lost or carefully hidden in antiquity and were subsequently recovered by accident. Others, however, did not need to be rediscovered. After the dissolution of the monasteries many objects, such as the Book of Durrow and the Cross of Cong, survived in the hands of hereditary keepers for generations before they were acquired by collectors or presented to

**47** *Oghams:*
**a.** *distribution of ogham inscriptions in Ireland (after Macalister 1945);* **b.** *ogham alphabet (after Thomas 1971);* **c.** *ogham-inscribed stone, Ballineesteenig, Co. Kerry (after Cuppage et al 1986).*

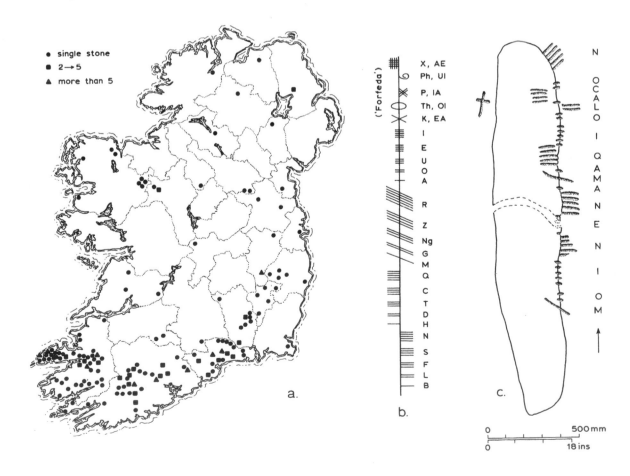

libraries and museums. A few, such as St Manchan's shrine (75), now housed in the Catholic church near Lemanaghan, Co. Offaly, remain near their place of origin. Other shrines and manuscripts were taken overseas as the loot of Viking raiders or as gifts to Irish foundations abroad, but, because their original contexts have been lost, it is now almost impossible to provide that they are of Irish manufacture.

## Ogham stones

An important aspect of Roman influence on Ireland was the introduction of literacy. Irish was written down for the first time using the ogham script (47b), an alphabet of 20 letters made up of groups of strokes set at different angles against or across a vertical base-line. Later other symbols, technically known as the *forfeda*, were added. The ogham alphabet is thought to be based on the Latin alphabet of the later Roman Empire, and the formation of the script may have been influenced by the use of notched tally-sticks. The majority of the ogham inscriptions which survive today are carved on pillar stones or boulders. The edge of the stone is usually used as the base-line and the inscription, depending on length, usually reads up one side and, if necessary, across the top and down the other. The inscriptions consist of simple set formulae. The most common is '(The stone of) X son of Y' as, for example, in the inscription from Ballineesteenig, Co. Kerry (47c), which says MOINENA MAQI OLACON meaning '(The stone of) Moinena son of Olacon'. The expression of kinship is clearly important and a variation of this is '(The stone of) X son of the tribe of Y' as in an inscription from Drumlohan, Co. Waterford, which says BIR MAQI MUCOI ROTTAIS meaning '(The stone of) Bir son of the tribe of Rottais'. Another common formula begins with ANM, which literally means 'soul', but may have a secondary meaning implying 'the remains or relics of'. Such inscriptions are likely to be Christian and may be exemplified by one from Keenrath, Co. Cork, which says ANM CASONI [MAQ]I RODAGNI meaning 'The soul of (or the remains of) Casoni son of Rodagni'.[21]

These inscriptions are commemorative and ogham stones are therefore commemorative monuments. However, it is not known whether they were simply memorials or whether they also acted as grave markers. Very few survive *in situ* and no ogham stone has yet been found in direct associ-ation with a grave. The law tracts also suggest that they acted as boundary markers, the inscription showing whose kin owned the land. This is not incompatible with their likely use as grave markers since there are hints that cemeteries were also located on land boundaries.[22]

Over 300 ogham stones have been recorded from Ireland (47a), mainly in the south-west in the counties of Kerry, Cork, and Waterford, though a few have also been found in Kilkenny, Carlow, Wicklow, and Kildare and there are other isolated examples elsewhere. The significance of this distribution is unclear since the ogham script was presumably known throughout Ireland. Outside Ireland ogham stones are also found in areas colonized by the Irish at the end of the Roman period: south-west Wales and Dumnonia and to a lesser extent north Wales, the Isle of Man and Dalriada.[23]

Individual inscriptions are often difficult to date since they differ little epigraphically and some of the linguistic forms may be consciously archaic. However the use of ogham may have begun during the fourth century, it was certainly at its most popular during the fifth and sixth and con-tinued during the seventh and into the eighth. The dating of ogham stones raises an important issue: are they pagan or Christian monuments? This problem has given rise to considerable debate. Some of them are certainly Christian. Some 14 per cent have inscribed crosses, though in certain instances these seem to have been added, thereby suggesting the possible Christianiz-ing of a pagan monument. A few refer specifically to Christian office as, for example, a seventh-century stone from Arraglen, Co. Kerry, which commemorates 'Ronán the priest son of Comgán'. Over 34 per cent are associated with known eccle-siastical sites. However, it has also been suggested that the preoccupation with kin in the inscriptions and, more particularly, the mention on some of tribal ancestors, perhaps pagan gods, means that at least some were pagan. It has also been pointed out that some of the inscriptions naming tribal ancestors appear to have been deliberately defaced. Clearly more research is needed on this interesting question, though it should be noted that the expression of kinship is not necessarily un-Christian; it simply mirrors the general stress on kinship in early Irish society. All that can be said at present is that ogham stones span the period of conversion to Christianity and that those with Christian associations are the earliest identifiable evidence of Christianity in Ireland in the archaeological record. Indeed, these stones may provide the key to the identification of the earliest Christian sites in Ireland.[24]

## Large ecclesiastical sites

The monastic site of Clonmacnois, Co. Offaly (48), was traditionally founded by St Ciarán in the mid-sixth century. The stone-walled enclosure is modern, but a keen eye will spot a low bank above the river which may mark the line of the original monastic enclosure. The surviving buildings are mainly of the eleventh or twelfth centuries and later. There are eight churches, including the cathedral, which, though much altered, may have its origins in the great stone church erected by Abbot Colmán and King Flann in 908; the diminutive Temple Kieran, which may once have housed the relics of the saint; and Temple Finghin, a Romanesque church with a small round tower built as an integral part of the structure. Other monuments include the round tower struck by lightning in 1135, several stone shafts and

*48 The monastic ruins at Clonmacnois, Co. Offaly, with the River Shannon beyond (Courtesy of the Commissioners of Public Works, Ireland).*

crosses, which together span the late eighth to twelfth centuries, and the largest collection of carved grave-slabs anywhere in Ireland. A little way to the north-east, along a possibly ancient causeway, and beyond the monastic enclosure, is the Nuns' Church, completed in 1167. To the west lie an early thirteenth-century Anglo-Norman castle and St Ciarán's well.[25]

But why did sites such as Clonmacnois develop and how did they change over the centuries? What can history and archaeology tell us about these large ecclesiastical sites, their structures and layout, and the various activities which went on within them?

### Location

Important ecclesiastical sites like Clonmacnois were not shut away from the world. To develop the way they did, and to attract wealth and prestige, they needed easy access to good communications. For this reason the majority of great church sites seem to have been located in eastern or central Ireland, and not in the poorer, less accessible parts of the west. Recent work in Co. Kerry, for instance, has failed to reveal any large ecclesiastical enclosures, though Kilmalkedar on the Dingle peninsula may be a rare example of a major foundation. Many important sites were situated, like Kilmalkedar, on or near the coast.

From Bangor, for example, at the mouth of Belfast Lough, it was only a short trip to Galloway in south-west Scotland, and the voyage from Derry, at the mouth of the River Foyle, to her sister Columban house on Iona off the coast of Mull, was only a little more arduous. Similarly, sites in the south, such as Ardmore, Co. Waterford, which overlooks the sea at Ram Head, and Lismore, a few miles up the navigable River Blackwater, would have had easy access to western Britain and France. Other important sites on navigable rivers include St Mullins on the Barrow and Slane on the Boyne; and monasteries, such as Inishcaltra, located on an island in Lough Derg, Co. Clare, would have been equally accessible. Land routes were also important. Durrow, Co. Offaly, for example, grew up beside the great east-west route, *Slighe Mhór*, and Roscrea, Co. Tipperary, was situated further south on the other major east-west road, *Slighe Dhála*. Some sites were located at a focus of both land and water routes. Clonmacnois may be approached from the River Shannon or along *Slighe Mhór* and Killaloe, Co. Clare, is at the point where *Slighe Dhála* crosses the River Shannon as it issues from Lough Derg. It is interesting to note that foundations situated in out-of-the-way places might need to change their locations in order to develop. The original hermitage at Glendalough, for example, seems to have been founded on an isolated lakeside in the Wicklow mountains. Later a second focus grew up half a mile to the east on a larger and more accessible site which was less liable to flooding. It is here that the great monastery with its cathedral, round tower and market-place developed.[26]

It has been shown that many churches, both large and small, were founded on the borders of kingdoms. This was probably because such areas, by their very position, were more accessible. Royal dwellings and assembly places were also located on borders and it is likely that pagan religious sanctuaries were too. Some important churches were undoubtedly founded in places which had formerly been of pagan significance, and in certain cases pagan rites seem to have continued in a Christianized context. At Seirkieran, Co. Offaly, for example, which was situated on the traditional boundary between the northern and southern halves of the island, there was said to have been a fire which had never been extinguished. Fires of this kind seem to have played an important part in pagan ritual and another example is recorded at Kildare as late as 1220;

Brigit, who is credited with the foundation of the site, may in fact be a pagan goddess rather than a Christian saint. Armagh (51, 52) is situated only 3 km (2 miles) from the major royal site and ritual complex at Navan (*Emain Macha*) and the name, *Ard Macha* ('the Height of Macha'), also incorporates the name of the pagan goddess, Macha.[27] Archaeology takes the history of Armagh back to a very early period, but whether the Christian site was preceded by pagan activity remains unproven. Although the earliest enclosure round the top of the hill seems to have had an *inner* ditch and an *outer* bank in the manner of pagan ritual complexes, such as Navan, the radiocarbon date which spans the late second to mid-sixth centuries (cal. AD 180–560) for twigs from near the bottom of the ditch does not necessarily indicate pre-Christian activity and there is no evidence that the enclosure was used for a ritual purpose. Equally, stone sculptures of bears and human figures now in the old Cathedral may be pagan, but it is uncertain whether they come from Armagh itself or the surrounding countryside. Ancient place-names recorded within Armagh, *fidnemed* and *Teampull na ferta*, may have pagan connotations. *Nemed* is associated with a sacred grove and *ferta* with pagan burial mounds and/or ditches. Excavations in the area of *Teampull na ferta* (Scotch Street) near the bottom of the hill have revealed parts of an early, apparently Christian, cemetery (one grave had a radiocarbon date of cal. AD 430–640), and there were also signs of earlier activity. There is a possibility that either there were earlier pagan burials in the vicinity, or that some of the Christian burials may originally have been marked by mounds and/or ditches in the pagan manner.[28]

Armagh, as the place-name indicates, is situated on a prominent hill, and other major ecclesiastical sites, such as Downpatrick, Co. Down, and Cashel, Co. Tipperary, were similarly located. Others were situated on promontories or on islands in lakes, rivers, or bogs. Many have topographical elements in their names, such as *Cluain*, meaning 'meadow', as in Clonmacnois, or *Cell-dara* (Kildare) meaning 'the church of the oak-wood'. Place-names incorporating trees may, again, have pagan connotations: Movilla, Co. Down, for example, is derived from *Magh Bile*, meaning 'the plain of the sacred tree'.[29]

### Layout

It has been suggested[30] that by the seventh century the full Christianization of Ireland, the expansion of monasticism, and the growing cult of relics led to a need for the organization of important ecclesiastical sites in order to protect their sanctity and prevent the violation of graves. We have no evidence as to the appearance of such sites before this, but it seems that, from the seventh century onwards, when the concept of areas of sanctuary is first attested, enclosures or *valla* were constructed round ecclesiastical sites and their interiors and environs were increasingly organized to encompass the varying needs of a growing population of monks and clerics, and sometimes nuns, lay people and pilgrims.

To the archaeologist many of the enclosures surrounding early ecclesiastical sites appear com-

**49** *Duleek, Co. Meath, from the north. The original line of the oval ecclesiastical enclosure is defined by the modern street pattern and a hedged lane in the bottom right of the photograph. The main ecclesiastical complex, with St Cianan's Church still partly outlined by an inner curvilinear enclosure, may be seen towards the centre. The fragmentary remains of St Patrick's Church are located in the light-coloured field to the east (Courtesy of Leo Swan).*

parable with those encompassing secular ringforts. They are composed of banks usually with accompanying ditches or stone walls, and the size of the enclosure would seem to state something about the size and status of the community. As we have seen secular enclosures provided an element of defence which was combined with the need to display wealth and status. But in addition, ecclesiastical enclosures seem to have been invested with the spiritual properties of sanctuary and divine protection. In this way the enclosures of the major church sites were not only similar to their secular counterparts, but also mirrored the Old Testament cities of refuge, and the concept of a 'holy of holies' in the centre, with churches and a cemetery, and surrounding areas of sanctuary which decreased in importance the further they were from the centre, came into being. One difference between secular and ecclesiastical enclosures was that the latter might be marked by the erection of crosses in wood or stone on the boundary or *termon* of an area of sanctuary or at the gateway to the enclosure. These were the Christian symbols of sanctuary and protection, 'a pious cloister behind a circle of crosses'. In the

past it was suggested that the colophon illustration in the Book of Mulling, which depicts two compass-drawn concentric circles with crosses dedicated to Christ, the evangelists and the prophets, was an actual plan of the monastery of St Mullins with its enclosure and crosses, but this may now be rejected. It is instead a more abstract, visual evocation asking for the protection of the monastery by representing the symbols of that protection.[31]

The *valla* surrounding major ecclesiastical sites frequently enclose very large areas. They are usually curvilinear and two, or occasionally three, widely-spaced concentric enclosures are not uncommon. Churches are either located in the central enclosure or are dotted around the site in small separate enclosures. There are also some examples of rectilinear enclosures, but the significance of this shape and whether it denotes any difference in date or function is unknown, though comparisons with Roman forts and fortified Middle Eastern monasteries have been suggested.[32]

Some enclosures are still clearly visible on the ground. At Seirkieran impressive earthworks surround an approximately circular area of 12 hectares (30 acres) or more and there are also traces of possible interior divisions. At Rahan, Co. Offaly, the surviving earthworks are smaller, but the two Romanesque churches which stand at opposite ends of the enclosure give a clear impression of its original size. At Clonmacnois earthworks are still clearly visible beside the river and on the ridge to the south and east of the ruins. Many enclosures are, however, only really visible from the air. The enclosure at Duleek, Co. Meath (49), with the remains of two churches in the centre, which may once have stood in separate enclosures, has left clear traces on the modern street pattern, though the actual earthworks have been lost. At Lorrha, Co. Tipperary, the remains of an inner enclosure may be detected in the area where the nucleus of the monastery still stands and the line of the outer enclosure survives partly as a modern field boundary and partly as a levelled bank.[33]

Very few ecclesiastical enclosures have been surveyed in detail and almost none have been excavated. Though extensive excavations were carried out at Nendrum in the 1920s, the results are now almost impossible to interpret and the amount of subsequent restoration is unclear. A new survey in 1954, together with minor excavations carried out with the object of clarifying earlier work, did little to help. The site (50) is surrounded by three concentric walls made up of mainly small stones with a few large boulders at the base. The inner enclosure with a wall 1.85–2.15 m (6–7 ft) thick, surrounds an area approximately 76 m (250 ft) in diameter containing the stone church, a fragmentary round tower and the cemetery. Excavation of the middle enclosure, which is 122 m (400 ft) or more in diameter, was concentrated on the western side and it is here that the precise stratigraphical sequence has proved so difficult to interpret. Lawlor claimed to have uncovered the evidence for two major phases. He suggested that the interior of the middle enclosure had been occupied for some considerable time, so that the stone wall had fallen into disrepair, and that it had subsequently been filled up on the inner side with midden material to form a terrace on which a group of structures had been built. Traces of earlier structures were also visible underneath these, but were only partially investigated. He further suggested that the pre-terrace phase might belong to a prehistoric secular occupation of the site while the terrace could be linked with the early Christian monastery. However, there is no evidence to prove the existence of either prehistoric or secular activity and the sequence seems better interpreted as prolonged early medieval occupation, probably of an ecclesiastical nature throughout. It also seems likely that the stone wall gradually fell into disrepair and midden material, together with several successive phases of structures, slowly built up against it until a point was reached when a terrace was either formed naturally or formally constructed. A small excavation in 1954 outside the present line of the enclosure revealed foundations of a further drystone wall. This seems to be the original line of the enclosure at this point; the present line is probably entirely a modern reconstruction. The outermost enclosure, which surrounds an oval area up to 183 m (600 ft) in diameter, was not extensively investigated. Overall the enclosures lack precise dating evidence and their chronology and relationship to each other are unknown. The only clues to the sequence are a single sherd of E ware from the site, a considerable amount of souterrain ware, some of which is from the build-up on the inner side of the middle enclosure before the formation of the terrace, and a Viking coin dated by Lawlor to c.930, which was found on the terrace.[34]

Less excavation has taken place in Armagh, but

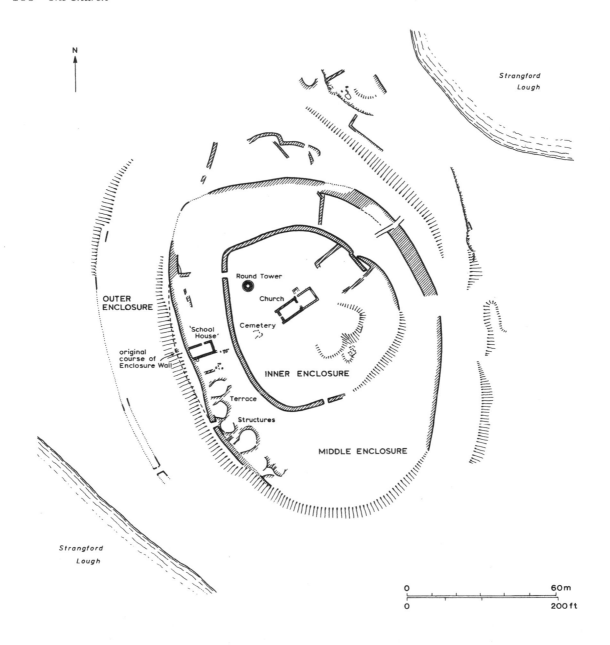

N

Strangford
Lough

OUTER
ENCLOSURE

Round Tower

Church

Cemetery

'School
House'

original
course of
Enclosure Wall

INNER ENCLOSURE

Terrace

Structures

MIDDLE ENCLOSURE

Strangford
Lough

0                                              60m

0                                              200 ft

**50** *Nendrum, Co. Down (after Archaeological Survey of Northern Ireland 1966).*

an interesting picture of the enclosures and layout of the monastery can be built up using a number of different types of evidence. Particularly useful is a very early seventeenth-century map of Armagh by Richard Bartlett (**51**), which provides a bird's-eye view over the ruins of the town which at that time lay almost completely derelict. Many of the features shown on the map can be identified and

some of them related to those mentioned in the annals during the eleventh and twelfth centuries. The top of the hill, known as the *Ráth* in the annals, is surrounded by the remains of an enclosure within which stands the medieval cathedral, with the ruinous church of the Culdees to the south. Further south again, and just outside the enclosure, is a tiny roofless church for nuns, Templebrede. The main eastern entrance to the *Ráth* is marked by a cross, the remains of which are datable to the late ninth or tenth centuries and are

51 *Early seventeenth-century map of Armagh by Richard Bartlett showing the ecclesiastical remains at that time (Dublin, National Library of Ireland MS 2656, III; courtesy of National Library of Ireland).*

now housed in the cathedral. It is known from the annals that, by the beginning of the eleventh century, the settlement round the cathedral was divided into three districts or thirds, and Bartlett's map gives some clues as to their whereabouts. It has been suggested that the area to the left of the main street is *Trian Mór* and the church set within its own separate enclosure is *Teampall na ferta*, which probably formed the nucleus of the ecclesiastical site in its very early phases and was later the focus·of a nunnery; to the right of the street may be *Trian Masain*, and further to the right again *Trian Saxan* (Saxon), with the ruins of the church of SS Peter and Paul. The ruin beyond the cathedral is the abbot's house and on the left-hand edge of the map is the Franciscan friary. The annals indicate that in the eleventh and twelfth centuries there was a great stone church, the predecessor of the cathedral, and a round tower within the *Ráth*, and other churches and crosses,

**52** *Armagh, where the modern street-plan hints at the lines of earlier monastic enclosures. The open space to the east of the cathedral is Market Street and part of Scotch Street may be seen in the bottom right-hand corner of the photograph (Copyright: Cambridge University Committee for Aerial Photography).*

which had already completely disappeared by the time Bartlett's map was drawn.[35]

Today Armagh is again a built-up area, but the modern street plan as seen from the air hints at the lines of the original monastic enclosures (**52**). The likely line of the inner enclosure, which surrounds an area approximately 200 m (656 ft) in diameter round the summit of the hill, is particularly well-preserved, and excavations within this on the south-east side revealed a substantial ditch, 6.4 m (21 ft) wide by between 2.28 m (7 ft 6 in) and 3 m (9 ft 10 in) deep, between the street and the modern graveyard wall. The line of the ditch suggested that it may originally have encompassed

the hill-top, possibly enclosing an area *c.*50 m (164 ft) in diameter. As previously noted the ditch, the first phase of which may be dated by radiocarbon to between the late second and mid-sixth centuries (cal. AD 180–560) appeared to be inside the bank. Radiocarbon dating also revealed that at some point between the fifth and eighth centuries (cal. AD 430–770) the ditch had been filled in with material from the outer bank and that the area was then used as a tip for metal-working debris. Though no trace appears on Bartlett's map, the street plan also suggests the line of an outer enclosure surrounding an oval area approximately 480 m (1,575 ft) north/south by 360 m (1,181 ft) east/west. On the north-east side the line includes part of Upper English Street, the name of which still echoes that of the Saxon Third of the original monastery. The main street shown on Bartlett's map is now Market Street and Scotch Street and the probable line of this enclosure crosses at the point where the two join. As already

**53** *Iona, Argyll, western Scotland. A rectangular vallum encloses the later medieval abbey complex; St Oran's Chapel and Reilig Odhráin may be seen to the south-west (Copyright: Cambridge University Committee for Aerial Photography).*

mentioned excavations on the south side of Scotch Street have uncovered part of an early cemetery in the vicinity of *Teampall na ferta*.[36] Overall the evidence hints at the gradual evolution of the site over many centuries with the likelihood that there were several different phases of enclosure, particularly round the summit of the hill.

Enclosures are also a feature of ecclesiastical sites outside Ireland, both in Britain and France.

The important monastery at Iona in Argyll is especially worthy of note in this context because, as part of the Columban *familia*, the foundation maintained close links with Ireland. It is therefore possible that evidence from Iona may be able to shed light on similar sites in Ireland, especially as so few of the latter have been excavated. We know something of the appearance of the monastery by the end of the seventh century, since many features are mentioned in Adomnán's *Life of Columba*: a *vallum*, for example, was already in existence in Adomnán's day and possibly in Columba's.[37] In addition recent detailed ground and air survey, together with small excavations, have revealed a complex series of enclosures which almost certainly represent several different phases. Major earthworks (53), enclosing a rectangular area of 8 hectares (20 acres) or more, are visible to the north, west and south of the later abbey, and a second smaller sub-rectangular enclosure may be detected within the first on the northern part of the site. The cemetery, *Reilig Odhráin*, together with St Oran's chapel, seems to have been enclosed in an adjoining annexe to the south-west. A small section across the west side of the main enclosure revealed an inner bank approximately 4.5m (14 ft 9 in) wide and surviving to a height of 1.5 m (5 ft), a rock-cut ditch 4.2 m (13 ft 9 in) wide, which was not excavated due to waterlogging, and an outer rubble and earth bank approximately 4 m (13 ft 2 in) wide and 1.2 m (4 ft) high. The inner bank was built up on a layer of turf and consisted of loosely-packed rubble and clay with larger stones towards the centre. It contained two turf lines which suggest that the bank had been heightened or refurbished at least once. A ditch section was excavated on the probable south side of the main enclosure adjacent to the entrance causeway to *Reilig Odhráin*. The ditch, which cut an earlier one, was 'V'-shaped, 6 m (19 ft 8 in) wide and approximately 2.9 m (9 ft 6 in) deep with a trench in the bottom into which brushwood had been packed, perhaps to act as a filter since the ditch apparently always contained water. The adjacent causeway was cut by a transverse drainage slot and a sample of peat at the bottom of this gave a radiocarbon date spanning the late sixth to later eighth centuries (cal. AD 580–770). The causeway was later widened, the drainage slot filled in and the ditch gradually silted up. Holly leaves found in the ditch may indicate that the enclosure was marked at this point by a holly hedge, possibly cultivated to provide ink.[38]

We know almost nothing about the entrances into these large ecclesiastical sites except that sometimes, as at Armagh, they were marked by a cross. No excavations have taken place and it is therefore impossible to speculate upon their form or complexity or to compare them with entrances to secular ring-forts. The only upstanding gateway to have survived is at Glendalough. This is a square stone structure with projecting *antae* and a round-arched doorway at either end. It originally had a tower and the floor surface is paved. There has been no discussion of its date, but it is probably twelfth-century.[39]

### Structures

Much more excavation is needed on a variety of sites in order to produce well-dated stratified sequences. Only then can we begin to understand the gradual development of ecclesiastical enclosures and see what, if any, patterns may emerge. This is even truer of the structures within them, since almost none have been excavated, and we are largely dependent upon hints provided by the written sources and the evidence of standing buildings and their relationship to each other.

Multiple churches are a feature of these large ecclesiastical sites. They may be concentrated within the inner enclosure and/or set within small separate enclosures. It is clear that they carried out different functions: a major church for big congregations, smaller churches to house relics or to cater for particular groups. It is interesting to note that churches for nuns are often located slightly apart from the main ecclesiastical complex, either outside the inner enclosure, as at Armagh, or outside the main enclosure, as at Clonmacnois. There may have been restrictions on laymen and all women entering the core of the monastery and there may also have been some segregation for worship and burial.[40] We must suppose that in the early part of the period the churches were of wood, but during the eighth to tenth centuries a few stone churches are recorded on important sites and these become much more common in the eleventh and twelfth (see below). Another feature of the mid-tenth century onwards are tall stone round towers which were primarily used as belfries (see below). At Clonmacnois and Glendalough these are situated to the north-west of the principal church and a similar location is suggested on some other sites. The *platea* or *plateola*, which is an early feature first mentioned by Adomnán at Iona, may also have been to the west of the principal church.[41] This seems to have been a courtyard, possibly paved, and may have been an area for monks to walk or a place for assembly. Crosses might be set up there, and the West Cross, Clonmacnois (36) may be an example of this. There was probably also a cemetery near the principal church – the key to the general location is often the survival of carved grave-slabs – but they are very seldom *in situ*. There may also have been other burial grounds, perhaps for specific groups of people, adjacent to other churches (see below).

Other buildings were usually of wood. At the end of the seventh century Adomnán mentions that Iona had a *magna domus* or 'great house', a large, communal building made of substantial timbers, very probably circular in shape, since a similar round structure is described at Durrow. Other buildings noted are the guest-house, which was constructed of wattles, and St Columba's hut for writing. No library or refectory are remarked upon – it is possible that the *magna domus* may have fulfilled these functions – and judging by the evidence of secular sites, cooking may have been carried out in the open. However, both a refectory and a kitchen, and also an abbot's house, are noted on some of the larger ecclesiastical sites before 800. At Iona we know little of the sleeping quarters of either the abbot or the monks. Senior monks may have slept in separate cells, small round wattle huts perhaps, while ordinary monks may have shared a large dormitory or smaller huts.[42]

There have been several excavations on Iona in areas to the north-west, west and south-west of the later abbey as well as in its immediate vicinity. Early medieval levels have been uncovered, together with evidence for timber structures including two possible circular buildings and part of a rectilinear structure made of vertical planks set into a trench, but so far it has proved impossible to recover complete building plans or to identify their function.[43]

By the twelfth century large ecclesiastical sites, such as Armagh and Clonmacnois, contained streets with large numbers of timber buildings which probably housed not just monks, students and visiting pilgrims, but also a considerable lay population of craftworkers, estate workers and their families. The annals tell us that in 1020 the library at Armagh was the only building within the *Ráth* to escape a fire and that many houses in the Thirds were burnt. Indeed, conflagrations,

which burnt considerable areas of the larger monasteries, were a relatively frequent occurrence. In 1179 fire destroyed 105 houses at Clonmacnois. The exact nature of these structures is unknown but they are likely to have been similar to those on secular sites. Round wattle huts may have been characteristic of the early part of the period, but perhaps during the eighth and ninth centuries these may have been replaced by rectilinear wooden houses, sometimes set on stone foundations (see p. 26). Souterrains are also sometimes a feature as at Monasterboice, Co. Louth.[44]

The only two large ecclesiastical sites where considerable structural evidence has been excavated are Inishcaltra and Nendrum. Little can be said about the former since the excavation is unpublished, though large round buildings of possibly seventh- or eighth-century date, 10 m (33 ft) or more in diameter and delineated by slots containing post pits, together with smaller round huts of earth and wood have been reported.[45] At Nendrum (50) traces of stone foundations for several phases of what are almost certainly round huts were partially excavated on the west side of the middle enclosure below the terrace. On the terrace itself a path and at least four curvilinear stone platforms *c.*10 m (33 ft) in diameter were uncovered on which it was suggested wattle huts had been built. A rectangular stone building measuring internally 14.3 m × 11.25 m (47 ft × 37 ft) with walls surviving to between 0.3 m (1 ft) and 0.6 m (2 ft) in height was also excavated. It was clear that this structure had been destroyed by fire since charred wood and thatch, as well as iron nails, were found. The finds included motif pieces, some with traces of lettering, styli, knives, and stone discs and this led Lawlor to suggest the structure was a 'school house'. Certainly craft activities and writing seem to have been carried out in the building and the other huts were probably also used as workshops; one definitely had evidence for bronze-working, and indications of bone-working were also recovered.[46]

Indeed, archaeological evidence for craft activity has proved more plentiful than evidence for any other aspect of life within the large monasteries. Stone carvers fashioned grave-slabs and crosses. Ornamental metalworkers were employed to produce reliquaries and church plate. Some craftworkers may have manufactured objects primarily for the use of the community, but others may have made goods for a wider clientele including pilgrims and visitors to the markets which grew up outside the larger sites. In Armagh, for example, a workshop area with a clay floor has been excavated just inside the ditch round the top of the hill. The artefacts indicate enamel-, glass- and ornamental metal-working as well as the manufacture of objects in antler and lignite. The cemetery in the vicinity of *Teampall na ferta* was later used as a dump for craft-working debris denoting the manufacture of amber, glass and lignite objects nearby. Other sites where extensive evidence of craft activity has been found include Movilla Abbey and Iona.[47]

### Estates

Important ecclesiastical sites had large landholdings. These were acquired as gifts and bequests or sometimes by purchase, or even by the subjugation of a less powerful ecclesiastical neighbour. In the seventh century Adomnán makes it clear that the farmland around Iona sustained the community. The monks are glimpsed labouring in the fields on the western plain of the island, harvesting and building stone field walls. A barn is reported to be filled with enough grain to last the community for a year and pollen evidence suggests that cereal was grown just outside the enclosure. Early ninth-century additions to the *Book of Armagh* mention the vegetable garden within the monastic enclosure at Armagh and the estate beyond, which consisted of woodland, arable land, permanent pasture and pasture by the river. Water-mills are also sometimes noted. With the increasing size of ecclesiastical landholdings the monks were no longer responsible for all the agricultural labour and lay estate workers, known as *manaig*, did much of the work. They may have lived with their families in the outer parts of the enclosed area or beyond its walls. Ecclesiastical estates would often have included land at a considerable distance from the site. This was also worked by *manaig* who, like secular clients, may have lived in ring-forts and other settlements and paid their dues in the form of food render.[48]

### Small ecclesiastical sites and hermitages

A large number of small ecclesiastical sites may still be identified on the ground though few are recorded in the written sources. Some were minor monasteries; others were small church sites with priests who served a lay community; some may have been a mixture of both. There were also her-

mitages for monks who wished to retire from the world. The difficulty is that it is usually impossible to identify the precise function of the site from the archaeological evidence. Indeed, recent excavation of some sites has shown that they can be remarkably similar to their secular counterparts, and in some cases sites may have begun as secular settlements and only later been handed over to the Church. Some hermitages can, however, be definitely identified: because they are mentioned in the written sources, because of their extremely isolated location, or because they have *dísert* place-names. *Dísert*, meaning 'a place apart', is often coupled with a personal name and in the early part of the period means a hermitage, though during the eighth and ninth centuries it may develop a more specialized connotation, since it is often connected with the more ascetic foundations of the *Céli Dé*.[49]

Until recently the majority of the work on small ecclesiastical sites and hermitages, principally survey but also some excavation, has been concentrated in western Ireland, particularly on the Dingle and Iveragh peninsulas of Co. Kerry. This is because the enclosures, churches, and other structures were built of stone rather than wood and therefore more substantial above-ground evidence has survived. It also seems that in the less Anglicized parts of Ireland a memory of the ancient church sites remained longer and they were thus preserved from destruction; indeed, some continued as sites of pilgrimage and many were used as burial grounds for unbaptized children as late as the nineteenth century. Small ecclesiastical sites of this kind may be exemplified by Killabuonia (54a) on the Iveragh peninsula. The site is located on a hillside overlooking the sea and on a clear day the Skellig rocks can just be seen in the distance. The site consists of three terraces, the edges of which are revetted with drystone walling, but, in this instance, there is no proper surviving enclosure. On the uppermost terrace are the remains of a small ruined church, a crude stone cross, a special tent-shaped stone shrine, a small rectangular enclosure, which may mark another grave, and a cross-marked pillar. In the nineteenth century nine corbelled-stone huts or *clocháns* were recorded together with a larger

54 *Small ecclesiastical sites:*
a. *Killabuonia, Co. Kerry (after Henry 1957);*
b. *Reask, Co. Kerry (after Fanning 1981a);*
c. *Church Island, Co. Kerry (after O'Kelly 1958).*

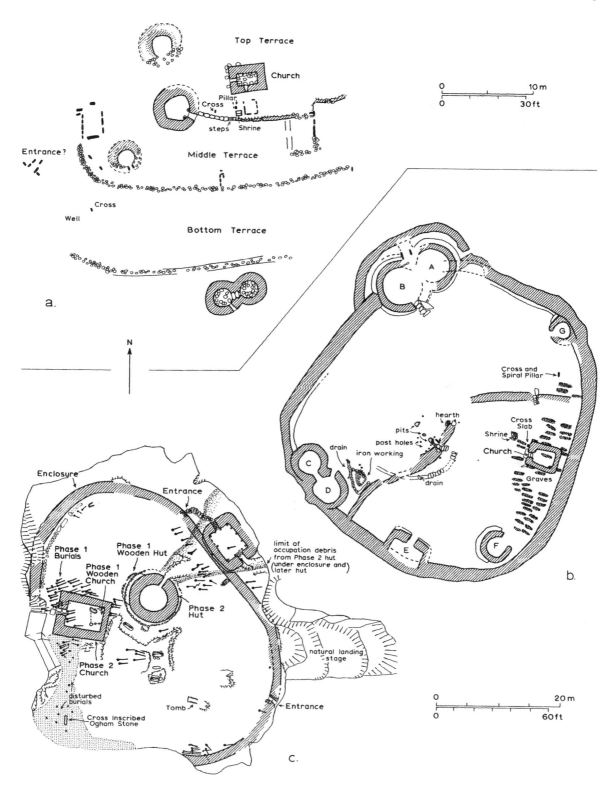

Top Terrace

Church

Pillar

Cross

steps    Shrine

Middle Terrace

Entrance?

Cross

Well

Bottom Terrace

a.

N

0        10 m

0        30 ft

A

B

G

Cross and
Spiral Pillar

hearth

pits

post holes

Cross
Slab

Shrine

Church

Graves

drain

iron working

C

drain

D

E

F

b.

Enclosure

Entrance

Phase 1
Burials

Phase 1
Wooden Hut

Phase 1
Wooden
Church

Phase 2
Hut

limit of
occupation debris
from Phase 2 hut
(under enclosure and
later hut)

Phase 2
Church

natural landing
stage

disturbed
burials

Tomb

Entrance

Cross Inscribed
Ogham Stone

c.

0        20 m

0        60 ft

ruinous structure, but today the remains of only three *clocháns*, one on the uppermost and two on the middle terrace, and two rectangular buildings, both on the middle terrace, can be detected. On the lowest terrace is a cross and the holy well, which is still frequented, and there is a further double *clochán* in a field to the south.[50] Without excavation it is of course extremely difficult to date the various features or to trace the development of a site of this kind; it is only possible to suggest that the core of the site is of early medieval date.

A recent study of ecclesiastical sites in southwest Ireland has shown that, in fact, very few, with the exception of hermitages like Skellig Michael or places of pilgrimage like Mount Brandon, are located in remote places. Indeed, they are often in areas of dense secular settlement suggested by the presence of ring-forts and *clocháns*. They are usually located on good agricultural land, either in river valleys or on the coast. Most are found between 30.5 m (100 ft) and 122 m (400 ft) above sea level, but some, like Killabuonia, are situated as high as 183 m (600 ft). Hermitages indicated by *dísert* names may be located in wet river valleys below 30.5 m (100 ft) and away from secular settlements. There is also a group of sites located almost on the shore just above sea level. Favoured positions include the shoulder of a low hill or ridge, hillsides, coastal headlands, offshore islands and islands in lakes.[51]

On many of the ecclesiastical sites of the Dingle and Iveragh peninsulas at least part of a curvilinear or occasionally sub-rectangular drystone enclosure, usually 30–50 m (100–160 ft) across, is still visible. There is a good example at Currauly near Mount Brandon. But in some instances, as at Reask before excavation, later field boundaries have obscured the line of the original enclosure, and terraced sites like Killabuonia may never have been completely enclosed. Sometimes, as at Gallarus, the cemetery and church are separated from the rest of the site by an internal wall which, like the multiple enclosures of the larger ecclesiastical sites, may have divided the most holy area from the rest. A small drystone church is characteristic, and more than one is also sometimes found, as at Illauntanig, a likely hermitage located on the largest of the Magharee islands. Excavation has shown that these small stone churches sometimes replaced earlier wooden examples. A variety of features are often visible within the cemetery area, some of which may be associated with later re-use of the site for child burial, and their dating is frequently difficult to establish without excavation. Some of the most common features are cross-marked pillars and grave markers. There are also occasional ogham stones, sometimes marked with a cross, as at Ballynamoreragh overlooking Dingle harbour. There are sometimes tent-shaped shrines (see below) and rectilinear stone grave enclosures as at Killabuonia. *Leachts*, small rectangular stone mounds often faced with drystone-walling and sometimes marked by a cross-slab, as at Inishvickillane on the southernmost of the Blasket islands, are another feature which may be associated with the demarcation of special graves. However, they may also have been open-air altars, and their antiquity is in any case disputed, since they have frequently been renovated in modern times to serve as penitential stations. Hollowed stone basins or *ballauns* are also often found on both large and small ecclesiastical sites, but rarely on their secular counterparts. Their function is unknown but they may have been used with a mortar for grinding grain or pounding herbs. The domestic structures are usually situated slightly apart from the religious core. They consist of round and sometimes quadrangular drystone huts and sometimes souterrains. Excavation has shown that there are earlier wooden huts on some sites. Holy wells are also commonly found a little distance from the main complex. They sometimes have a stone superstructure, frequently of no great antiquity, and they are often marked by a carved stone pillar or cross-slab.[52]

Two sites have been excavated in west Kerry: Church Island and Reask. The evidence recovered tells us a considerable amount about the sites concerned but, since the sample is so small, it is difficult to know how far they are typical of the group as a whole. Church Island (54c) is a small tidal islet off Beginish Island on the north side of Valencia Island.[53] Excavation revealed two major phases of early medieval occupation. The first consisted of at least 33 burials on the western side of the island which were on the same alignment as a small wooden structure approximately 3 × 2 m (9 ft 10 in × 6 ft 7 in) indicated by five post-holes. This was almost certainly a tiny church. To the east the fragmentary remains of a small circular wooden hut were also uncovered. This is probably contemporary with the church though they are not stratigraphically related. The structure consisted of an arc of small stone slabs set on edge, two post-holes and an occupation layer which included extensive remains of iron-working. Later these wooden buildings were replaced in stone. The wooden church had a larger corbelled-stone church 8.6 m × 6.5 m (28 ft 3 in × 21 ft 4 in) similar to that at Gallarus (57) built over it on a slightly different orientation, and suitable slate was specially imported from Valencia for the purpose. A further eight burials are aligned on this structure. At about the same time, though this cannot be proved stratigraphically, the wooden round hut was replaced by one of rough local stone. A low wall or *annulus* round the exterior indicates that turf had been stacked against the wall to provide better insulation. The hut had a timber-framed roof demonstrated by a ring of post-holes round the interior. Traces of organic material, which was probably burnt thatch, were also found on the floor. Underneath a hearth, a drain and an occupation layer were excavated, and the quarry which had provided much of the stone was located just to the south of the hut. Some time later a second rectangular stone hut with a timber-framed roof was built in the north-east corner of the island. Later again a stone-walled enclosure was constructed and it is interesting to note that this was built so late in the sequence as a whole. There were many other burials found within the enclosure, some of which are early medieval, though many are likely to be later, and a special stone-lined tomb may originally have looked similar to that at Killabuonia. The different phases of the site are difficult to date. The only evidence is provided by a cross-decorated ogham stone, unfortunately not found *in situ*, which may date between the mid-seventh and mid-eighth centuries. It was originally suggested that the Gallarus-type church was perhaps mid-eighth-century, but more recent research has shown (see below) that it could be as late as the twelfth. The excavator also suggested that it was the site of an eremitical monastery, which may also have served the early medieval settlement on Beginish. In fact there is no evidence to prove that the site was monastic. It may merely have housed a priest serving the local people, and the fact that a female grave was included amongst the Phase 1 burials suggests it was a community cemetery.

Reask (54b) is located on the northern side of the Dingle peninsula overlooking Smerwick Harbour. Excavation[54] provided evidence of prolonged early medieval occupation and subsequent activity including re-use of the site for child burial. The earliest datable activity consisted of a sub-stantial occupation layer in the centre of the site which covered a roughly circular area approximately 10 m (33 ft) in diameter, several post holes possibly indicating a circular structure, a stone-covered drain, a yellow clay spread, a hearth and three pits which may have been associated with iron-working. Artefacts from the area included two types of hand-made coarse pottery so far unique to Reask (see p. 75). A radiocarbon date from the hearth suggested occupation at some time between the late third and mid-seventh centuries (cal. AD 260–650) and sherds of Bii imported amphora from a slightly higher level suggested activity during the second half of the fifth and the sixth centuries. The stone-walled enclosure, which is approximately 45 m (148 ft) in diameter, and the cemetery, which consists mainly of cist-and-lintel but also some dug graves, may also belong to this phase. The graves clearly respect the curve of the enclosure. A rectilinear slab-lined structure 900 × 850 mm (2 ft 11½ in × 2 ft 9½ in), which may be interpreted as a shrine, was located at the same level as the graves on the western edge of the cemetery. The fill contained an abraded sherd of Bii pottery. There is also an extensive collection of carved stone grave-markers from the site and a cross-and-spiral carved pillar (83c) of likely sixth- or seventh-century date. This appears to be *in situ* and may have marked the northern edge of the cemetery. It is unclear whether there was a church in this phase. Two post-holes were excavated to the south of the slab-lined structure, which might indicate a wooden church, but the evidence is certainly insufficient to be sure. Two *clocháns*, F and G, may also belong to this phase. F, which had an incomplete *annulus*, may have been built and in use at the same time as the enclosure, and the erection of G, from where there is extensive evidence of iron-working, may be contemporary with the enclosure or slightly earlier than it.

The second major phase may have been preceded by the building of two conjoined *clocháns*, C and D. Excavation suggested that these had been erected later than the enclosure and probably at a time when it had been partially rebuilt or repaired. Again, there was extensive evidence of iron-working both from structure D and its environs. Structure E was also set into or against the enclosure wall but is otherwise undatable. The second major phase began with considerable reorganization of the site. A drystone church 3.5 × 2.7 m (11 ft 6 in × 8 ft 10 in) was constructed partly overlying the cemetery, which may have continued in use. The roof of the church was probably corbelled but the building is different from the larger boat-shaped churches of Gallarus type. A wall was also built across the enclosure and over the Phase I occupation in the central area to divide the church and cemetery from the rest of the site. The partial survival of a paved area outside the church and the paved entrance through the dividing wall suggest that their construction was probably approximately contemporary. The excavator suggested that the larger pair of conjoined *clocháns*, A and B, which are similar to the stone round hut on Church Island, also belong to this phase. These were built over the line of the enclosure, which had either fallen into disrepair or been demolished prior to their construction. An extension of the wall was then added so as to incorporate them into the enclosure.

The earliest occupation at Reask may be dated to between the late third and mid-seventh centuries, but it is unclear whether it was secular or ecclesiastical or whether it predated the use of the site as a cemetery. The precise religious role of the site and whether it was initially established as a monastery or continued as such are also unclear. It is impossible to tell whether the cemetery was lay or monastic because no bone has survived, though the possible presence of two child burials may suggest the former. The artefacts simply suggest a largely self-sufficient community. The impressive collection of sculpture, which includes Mediterranean motifs such as peacocks, and the presence of Bii imported pottery, certainly suggest that Reask may have been an important ecclesiastical site at an early date, but it is unclear whether there were any direct contacts with Mediterranean Christianity. The erection of the stone church and the dividing wall could be as early as the eighth century, and might therefore mirror the reorganization of major ecclesiastical sites around this time, but the recent later dating of corbelled stone churches like Gallarus (see below) suggests that it could be as late as the twelfth.

Hermitage sites are characteristic of many of the remoter islands off the west coast. Skellig Michael and Inishmurray are two of the more interesting examples. Skellig Michael (**56c**) is named several times in the documentary sources from the eighth to eleventh centuries and it may have had connections with the *Céli Dé* movement. The monastic remains are located on the larger of the Skelligs, two dramatic rocks which project from

the sea some 13 km (8 miles) west of Bolus Head, Co. Kerry. The main ruins perch on two terraces between 168 m (550 ft) and 183 m (600 ft) up and are reached by long flights of rock-cut steps. On the upper terrace are six *clocháns*, a corbelled church (1) and a church (3) of twelfth-century date or later. The *clocháns* appear to be of two phases, beginning with a nucleus of four small cells (B, C, D, F), which are quadrangular internally and circular externally, to which two larger quadrangular cells with stone projections (A, E), which were possibly to support turf insulation, were later added. There are several carved cross-slabs and a second corbelled church (2) is located on the edge of the cliff to the north. The lower terrace is enclosed by a stone wall and may have included a small area suitable for cultivation. To the south-west the rock rises precipitously to 217.6 m (714 ft) above the sea and on this peak there are three other terraces including one with a tiny church, cross-slab and *leacht*.[55] Life on Skellig Michael must have been extremely hard and the monks would have largely existed on a diet of fish, shellfish, seabirds and their eggs. Other items, such as grain, may have been brought from the mainland but it is unclear to what extent the survival of the monks was dependent upon constant outside support.

Inishmurray, which is also mentioned in the documentary sources, is a low-lying island 1.6 km (1 mile) long and 0.8 km (half a mile) wide situated about 7.2 km (4½ miles) off the coast of Co. Sligo. The ecclesiastical remains are of exceptional interest but no excavation has taken place and most of the features are extremely difficult to date. This is partly due to the badly-recorded restoration in the late nineteenth century and partly because of continued worship and burial on the site until the final evacuation of the islanders in 1948. The core of the site (**56b**) is contained within an imposing enclosure up to 53 m (175 ft) in diameter. Before restoration its drystone walls survived up to 3.95 m (13 ft) high and 4.55 m (15 ft) thick. Several flights of stone steps give access to the top of the wall and a number of chambers are incorporated into its thickness. There is a likely original entrance on the east and two other curious openings on the north which drop to a lower level in the manner of souterrains. It has been suggested that the enclosure is Iron Age, though such an early date for enclosures of this kind is difficult to substantiate (see p. 17), and only excavation would provide the opportu-

55 *Clocha Breca ('the speckled stones'),
Inishmurray, Co. Sligo. This curious structure
known as a* leacht *may be an open-air altar.
In the centre on the left is a hollowed stone carved
with crosses and other carved water-worn boulders
may be seen on top of the monument (Courtesy of the
Commissioners of Public Works, Ireland).*

nity to explore the possibility that the enclosure
pre-dates the ecclesiastical buildings within. Low
stone walls divide the interior into four. The
largest area on the east side contains the principal
church, a building with *antae*, and the smaller
stone-roofed *Teach Molaise* (Molaise's House),
where the relics of the founding saint may have
been kept. In addition there are a number of early
medieval carved pillars and grave-slabs and three
*leachts*, which may be open-air altars, possibly
covering special graves. The most interesting of
these is called *Clocha Breaca* ('the speckled stones')
(55). It is a quadrangular drystone structure
about 2.15 m (7 ft) square and 0.9 m (3 ft) high on
top of which are a considerable number of large
waterworn boulders. These include examples decorated with carved crosses and other ornament of

likely early medieval date and it has been suggested that the stones may have been turned
during the course of devotions. A curious carved
and partially hollowed stone with a stone stopper
is also stuck into the top of the *leacht*. The purpose
of this is unknown, though it has been suggested
that it might have served as a reliquary. On the
western side of the enclosure is a large circular
*clochán*, a rectangular structure of probable late
medieval date and a souterrain. It is interesting to
note another possible example of the exclusion of
women from the main monastic enclosure: in
modern times only the men were buried within
the cashel; the women were interred outside in
the cemetery of another largely late medieval
church dedicated to the Virgin which is located to
the south-east. Twelve other *leachts* of less careful
construction with cross-slabs stuck into them are
found in the vicinity of this church and at other
points around the island.[56]

The remains of small ecclesiastical sites in other
parts of Ireland, where early medieval structures
were predominantly of wood, are not nearly as obvious. From the air it may be possible to trace the
line of a curvilinear enclosure; internal divisions

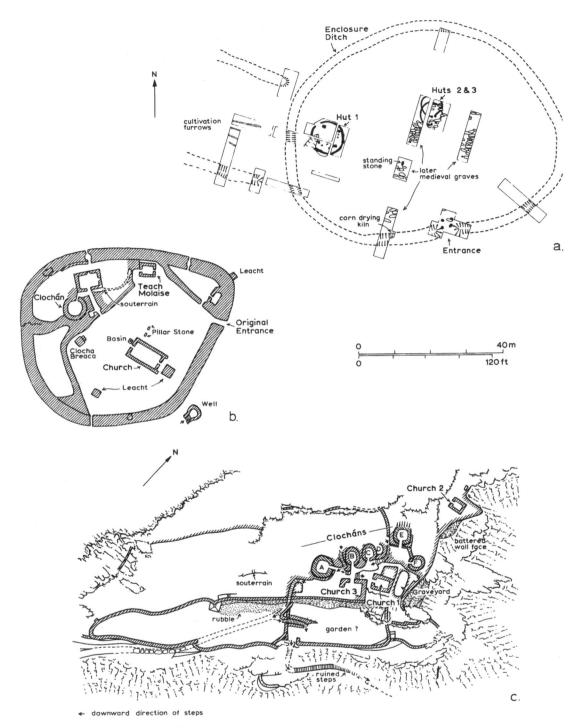

**56** *Small ecclesiastical sites and hermitages:*
**a.** *Killederdadrum, Co. Tipperary*
*(after Manning 1984);* **b.** *Inishmurray, Co. Sligo*
*(after Wakeman 1893);* **c.** *Skellig Michael, Co. Kerry*
*(after de Paor 1955).*

may be visible, and there are occasionally indications of structures. On the ground the core of the site may be marked by a later ruined church and graveyard. Cross-slabs and other early medieval sculpture, together with features such as *ballauns* and hōly wells, may be the only clues to the antiquity of the site. Hermitages may occasionally be recognized as, for example, at Mona Incha, Co. Tipperary, which is mentioned several times in the documentary sources as a *Celí Dé* establishment which had links with the major monastery at Roscrea nearby. In antiquity the hermitage was situated on two islands in Lough Cré, and at the end of the twelfth century the church of St Hilaire is recorded on one island and the chapel of St Colum on the other. Today, the draining of the lough has greatly changed the appearance of the site, but the surrounding marsh still gives some feeling of its original remoteness. One of the islands is preserved and the remains of a curvilinear earthen enclosure may still be detected. On the eastern side of this is a raised area with the twelfth-century Romanesque church of St Hilaire, an eighth- or ninth-century cross-base, and a twelfth-century cross-head.[57]

There has been little excavation of these small ecclesiastical sites outside the west and the evidence which has emerged is often ambiguous. At Killederdadrum, Co. Tipperary (**56a**), limited excavation of an oval enclosure up to 70 m (230 ft) in diameter, which was delineated by a 'V'-sectioned ditch 2.8 m (9 ft 2 in) wide at the top and up to 1.8 m (5 ft 11 in) deep, showed that a post-medieval cemetery had been preceded by early medieval occupation. This consisted of a circular house indicated by a trench with packing stones on the western side of the enclosure and two similar huts, one overlying the other, towards the centre. A rectangular annexe had been appended to the western side of the enclosure. The finds suggested a mixed-farming economy with a range of craft activities including iron-working, antler-working and textile production. Occupation may have continued for some centuries: a sherd of E ware from the rectangular annexe suggests activity during the sixth or seventh centuries, while a radiocarbon date from a probable corn-drying kiln set into the ditch gave a later date spanning the tenth to mid-twelfth centuries (cal. AD 900–1160). The problem is that there is no evidence to identify the early medieval occupation as ecclesiastical rather than secular. The enclosure was only partially excavated so traces of

an early medieval church or burials may have been missed. But the parish of Killederdadrum is not recorded until the beginning of the fourteenth century and there is no proof of its ecclesiastical use before this.

Similar problems have been encountered as a result of excavations at Kilpatrick, Co. Westmeath, and Doras, Co. Tyrone. However, at Fennor, Co. Louth, it was possible to establish an ecclesiastical context for the early medieval occupation debris because the site is mentioned in the annals. A partial rescue excavation at Millockstown, Co. Meath, suggested that the site began as a secular settlement which was later handed over to the Church. The earliest phase consisted of several spreads of habitation refuse enclosed by a narrow ditch. A radiocarbon date suggested occupation between the mid-third and mid-seventh centuries (cal. AD 260–660). This was superseded by a ring-fort, but in Phase 3 the status of the site appears to have changed. A much larger curvilinear enclosure 40 by 100 m (131 ft 4 in × 328 ft) was constructed with a bank *c.*3 m (10 ft) wide and an external ditch 2.8 m (9 ft 2 in) wide and 1.5 m (4 ft 11 in) deep with a stepped section on the inner face. Charcoal from the bottom of the ditch gave a radiocarbon date suggesting its construction between the later sixth and early eleventh centuries (cal. AD 570–1020). Within the enclosure was a cist-and-lintel grave cemetery, which mainly dates to this phase but which may have been established during Phase 2, and remains of occupation including two souterrains and various pits.[58]

All in all, much more extensive excavation of a range of small ecclesiastical sites is required before it will be possible to demonstrate to what extent those so far excavated are characteristic. In particular, much more dating evidence is needed to allow the establishment of possible general phases of development and to sort out the early medieval features from those of the twelfth century or later. It is only then that we may be able to say more about the role of individual sites and to suggest how they may have interacted with other early medieval sites in their vicinity.

## Church architecture

As we have seen it was customary for large ecclesiastical sites to have several churches of different sizes which were located either within the main enclosure or in their own small enclosures on

other parts of the site. Even the smaller ecclesiastical sites and hermitages sometimes had more than
one church. This practice of building multiple
churches was not confined to Ireland; it is also
found in Anglo-Saxon England and Merovingian
France.[59] The different churches were required to
fulfil different roles and cater for different groups
within the congregation. It has been suggested,
for example, that in the documentary sources the
term *basilica* is restricted to churches which
housed major relics, and in the eighth century
two churches are mentioned at Armagh: the
southern basilica served the monks and clergy
while the northern church served virgins, peni-
tents and 'those serving the church in legitimate
matrimony'.[60]

By examination of the written sources it has
become increasingly clear that in the earlier part
of the period wooden churches were the norm and
remained common on many sites until the
eleventh or twelfth century. But, unfortunately,
none have survived as standing buildings, so we
are largely dependent upon documentary descriptions for an indication of how they may have
looked. Traces of several possible wooden
churches have been uncovered by excavation in
the form of post-holes and beam-slots, but up to
now these have only provided a very general idea
of the above-ground structures. There has also
been considerable controversy concerning the
origins, dating and chronology of early medieval
stone churches in Ireland because of their architectural simplicity. It is only in the second quarter
of the twelfth century, with the advent of the
Hiberno-Romanesque architectural style, that we
can begin to isolate features which are more
closely datable.

*Dairthech* is the most usual word for a church in
the early medieval Irish documentary sources. Literally it means 'oak house' and therefore indicates
that churches were commonly made of wood. References in the saints' lives also mention churches
of smooth planks, wattles and occasionally mud,
clay or earth, and a stylized illustration in the
Book of Kells (79) appears to represent the Temple
in Jerusalem in the form of an ornate wooden
church with a shingle roof and carved gable
finials.[61] Two more detailed descriptions of
wooden churches have come down to us. The
first, in an obscure seventh-century work called
the *Hisperica Famina*, appears to describe a square
oratory fashioned out of massive beams with a
door at the west end, a western porch, a central

altar, an ornamented roof and 'four steeples'.[62]
The second is in Cogitosus' seventh-century *Life of
St Brigit* of Kildare and, though the building
material is not specifically mentioned, there is
little doubt that it was wood. The description,
though well-known, is worth quoting in full, since
it gives a remarkably detailed picture of the
internal organization and decoration of a large
church in this period.

'There (at Kildare) repose the glorious bodies
of both Archbishop Conled and the noble
virgin Brigit in their sarcophagi, the one to
the right and the other to the left of the
beautifully adorned altar. These sarcophagi
are richly decorated with gold, silver and
multicoloured precious stones; they have
also pictorial representations in relief and in
colours, and are surmounted by crowns of
gold and silver. The church, however, is not
the original one: a new church has been
erected in the place of the old one, in order to
hold the increased numbers of the faithful.
Its ground-plan is large, and it rises to a dizzy
height. It is adorned with painted tablets.
The interior contains three large oratories,
divided from one another by walls of timber,
but all under one roof. One wall covered with
linen curtains and decorated with paintings,
traverses the eastern part of the church from
one side to the other. There are doors in it at
either end. The one door gives access to the
sanctuary and the altar, where the bishop,
with his school of clerics and those who are
called to the celebration of the holy myster-
ies, offers the divine sacrifice to the Lord. By
the other door of the dividing wall, the
abbess enters with her virgins and with pious
widows in order to participate in the Supper
of Jesus Christ, which is His flesh and blood.
The remainder of the building is divided
lengthwise into two equal parts by another
wall, which runs from the western side to the
transverse wall. The church has many
windows. Priests and lay persons of the male
sex enter by an ornamented door on the
right-hand side; matrons and virgins enter
by another door on the left-hand side. In this
way the one basilica is sufficient for a huge
crowd, separated by walls according to state,
grade and sex, but united in Spirit, to pray to
the almighty Lord.'[63]

The most impressive remains of what may have

The Church 123

been a wooden church have been excavated at Inishcaltra. The rectangular building, which measured approximately 8 × 5 m (26 ft 3 in × 16 ft 5 in) and was orientated east/west, consisted of three phases. In Phases 1 and 2 the walls were constructed of three parallel rows of wattles with a covering of earth and the position of the altar may be indicated by a stain at the east end of the structure. The excavator suggested that the building might be early in the sequence on the site. On White Island, Co. Fermanagh, traces of two or possibly three phases of a wooden church were uncovered in the form of sleeper-beam trenches under and on a similar alignment to the twelfth-century stone church. At Derry, Co. Down, an early structure of drystone walling reinforced by timber uprights, possibly in two phases, was excavated under the south church, a simple stone building with *antae*. Remains of another timber building have been recovered under St Mel's

Church, Ardagh, Co. Longford, and the small timber structure at Church Island has already been mentioned. Post-holes under the late medieval church of St Vogue, Carnsore, Co. Wexford, have also been tentatively reconstructed as a similar tiny structure only 2.25 × 1.5 m (7 ft 5 in × x 4 ft 11 in) and a radiocarbon sample from these provided a date spanning the early seventh to mid-tenth centuries (cal. AD 610–940). But unfortunately at present there is insufficient detail to attempt a reconstruction of any of these buildings, and in many cases the ground-plan is incomplete or disputed. However, the archaeological evidence is enough to confirm the impression given by the documentary sources that wooden churches of different sizes and built using a variety of construction techniques were common. It is interesting to note that wooden churches superseded by stone have also been excavated outside Ireland in Anglo-Saxon England and on Ardwall Isle in Scotland and Burryholms in Wales.[64]

It used to be thought that the origins of stone

57 *Gallarus 'Oratory', Co. Kerry (Courtesy of the Commissioners of Public Works, Ireland).*

churches in Ireland could be traced back to a group of small corbelled boat-shaped structures found on the west coast mainly in Co. Kerry. The group may be exemplified by the only complete survivor, Gallarus 'Oratory', on the Dingle peninsula (57). The walls of this building, which is orientated east/west and measures 6.7 × 5.5 m (22 ft × 18 ft) externally, curve into a corbelled-stone roof and there are some traces of mortar on the interior. The only other major features are the inclined west doorway and the round-headed window. The gables may once have been crowned by carved stone finials. In the past simple stone churches like Gallarus were dated to the seventh to ninth centuries or even earlier. They were assumed to have evolved from corbelled *clocháns* independent of external influences and to have given rise to more complex churches with upright walls and stone roofs.[65]

However, a study of the references to stone churches in the written sources indicates that few were known at such an early date. It is also most unlikely that the evolution of stone churches would have taken place in a comparatively remote part of Ireland in apparent isolation from developments in ecclesiastical architecture in Britain and on the Continent. The first references to a stone church are to Duleek, Co. Meath, mentioned in Tírechán's *Life of St Patrick* written in the second half of the seventh century and in the *Annals of Ulster* in 724. The place-name, Duleek, is derived from the Old-Irish word for a stone church, *damliac*, and the site may have acquired this name either because at that time stone churches were unusual or this example was unique. Duleek is situated near the east coast of Ireland and may thus have been influenced by developments in the architecture of stone churches taking place in Anglo-Saxon England at this time. No other examples are known until 789 when a stone church is mentioned in Armagh, and during the ninth century references remain rare and are confined to the major sites of Armagh and Kells, Co. Meath. During the tenth century some stone churches are mentioned on lesser sites such as Tuamgraney, Co. Clare, but it is only during the eleventh and twelfth centuries that references become more frequent.[66]

Pre-twelfth-century stone churches have proved remarkably difficult to identify or date because of their architectural simplicity, and almost no detailed survey or fabric recording, which might make possible a clearer understanding of the various types and their chronology, has taken place. It has been suggested that simple rectangular structures with projections known as *antae* (possibly skeuomorphic of wooden features) on the corners of the east and/or west wall faces, which supported the timbering of the roof with its thatch or shingle covering, were being built by the tenth century. The first phase of the cathedral at Glendalough and the western end of the church at Tuamgraney may be of this date. However, simple rectangular churches with *antae* and stone roofs, such as the church on St MacDara's Island, Co. Galway, are likely to be twelfth-century or later. Simple rectangular churches with thatched or shingle roofs and without *antae* are almost impossible to date but, since they are mainly found in the west, they may be late. Similar structures with stone roofs, such as St Columcille's, Kells, probably also belong to the twelfth century. Many churches with a rectangular nave and smaller rectangular chancel are definitely twelfth-century on account of their Hiberno-Romanesque ornament.[67] In this light the early dating of corbelled churches such as Gallarus seems unlikely. Though the corbelled technique is ancient – it was first used in prehistoric times – the stone roof and inclined doorway would fit much better into a twelfth-century context and it is possible that the stone-roofed Hiberno-Romanesque cathedral nearby at Kilmalkedar (59a) could have served as a model.[68]

As we have seen Ireland came into increasing contact with Britain and the Continent during the eleventh and twelfth centuries. Churchmen would have seen elaborate ecclesiastical stone architecture on their travels abroad, and this is almost certain to have had some bearing on the construction of early stone churches in Ireland, though they show little sign of external stylistic influence. It certainly resulted in the introduction of the Romanesque style of architecture in the second quarter of the twelfth century. But Irish church builders did not adopt it without change; instead they adapted it and moulded it to Irish tradition and taste.

The only church which may be described as fully Romanesque is Cormac's Chapel, Cashel (58, 59b). This was begun in 1127 and consecrated in 1134 and is now considered to be the initiator of the style in Ireland. The small scale of the building, together with the steeply-pitched stone roof, are characteristic of native churches, but other architectural features, and the wide range of

**58** *Cormac's Chapel, Cashel, Co. Tipperary,*
*from the south (Courtesy of the Commissioners of*
*Public Works, Ireland).*

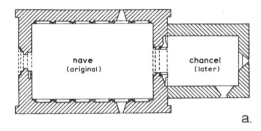

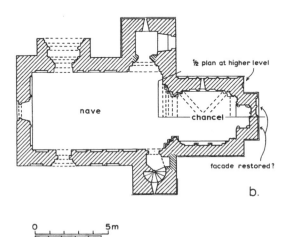

0 — 5 m
0 — 15 ft

**59** *Hiberno-Romanesque church plans:*
**a.** *Kilmalkedar, Co. Kerry (after Cuppage et al 1986);*
**b.** *Cormac's Chapel, Cashel, Co. Tipperary (after Leask 1955).*

carved ornament, are undoubtedly exotic, showing clear links with south-west Britain and less direct contacts with western France and Germany. The chapel consists of a nave and chancel with internal dimensions of 9 m × 5.4 m (29 ft 6 in × 17 ft 9 in) and 4.15 × 3.3 m (13 ft 6½ in × 10 ft 10½ in) respectively. The east end of the nave is flanked by two tall square towers, originally with pyramidal stone roofs, which may be inspired by German examples. On the north side is the main entrance with its imposing round-arched doorway, the tympanum carved with a lion and a centaur, and above a steeply-pitched pediment ornamented with zig-zag chevrons and rosettes. The south doorway is less impressive but the whole elevation is characterized by blind arcading. In addition to the ubiquitous chevron other architectural ornament includes capitals with carved scallops and human face-masks.[69]

**60** *Hiberno-Romanesque doorway, Clonfert Cathedral, Co. Galway (Courtesy of the Commissioners of Public Works, Ireland).*

Other Hiberno-Romanesque churches, while adopting many of the exotic features found in Cormac's Chapel and some new ones, retain many more native characteristics, particularly their small scale and architectural simplicity. Indeed, when St Malachy began to build a more complex church at Bangor in 1140 along the lines he had witnessed on the Continent, there seems to have been considerable opposition. The Romanesque ornament is concentrated on the round-arched doorways, sometimes with the addition of a carved pediment or tympanum, and chancel arches, though it is also found on some windows and occasionally spreads onto the walls in the form of blind arcading. Few of these churches can be dated with any precision but a study of the ornament does demonstrate some progression. An earlier group of churches, mainly concentrated in Munster, may be seen as directly influenced by Cormac's Chapel, though only one, St Cronan's, Roscrea, shows English West Country features in their pure form. The group also includes Kilmalkedar Cathedral, Co. Kerry, a church with a simple rectangular nave with a corbelled stone roof and *antae* and a slightly later chancel which was rebuilt to replace the original altar recess (59a). The tympanum over the west door and the blind arcading in the nave may be compared with Cormac's Chapel as well as many of the ornamental features, such as the simple chevrons on the west doorway and chancel arches. A slightly later group is found mainly in the Midlands and may be exemplified by Clonfert Cathedral, Co. Galway, where the spectacular west doorway with its triangular pediment (60) is decorated with a riot of pattern, much of it native-inspired or Viking-influenced, blended with more developed forms of Romanesque ornament.[70]

The introduction of new monastic orders, particularly the Cistercians, brought more lasting architectural change. On the Continent Cistercian monasteries were set out according to uniform guide-lines and the Irish houses followed suit. St Malachy founded the first Irish Cistercian monastery, a daughter house of Clairvaux in Burgundy, at Mellifont in 1142 and a French monk, Robert, helped with the building operations. The result in Irish terms was revolutionary. The church was comparatively large with an aisled nave, square presbytery and transepts with side chapels (61). To the south was an almost square cloister garth with the sacristy, chapter house, parlour and 'day room', with the monks' dormitory above, on the east side; the warming room, refectory and kitchen on the south and on the west store-rooms and the lay brothers' accommodation. It is difficult to judge the extent of the Burgundian architectural influence at Mellifont since the earliest phase only survives at foundation level, but the plan and Burgundian characteristics found in other twelfth-century Irish Cistercian houses suggest that it was profound.[71]

## Round towers

One of the most characteristic features of early medieval Irish ecclesiastical architecture is the round tower. Some 65 are still extant but comparatively few survive to their original height, many have been extensively restored, and others have completely disappeared and can only be traced in documentary sources. In some cases, such as Antrim (62), the round tower is now the only clue to a once-important ecclesiastical site, but in others it is situated amidst more extensive remains and there is evidence from several sites, including Clonmacnois (48), that it was located to the north-west or south-west of the principal church with the doorway of the tower facing the doorway of the church.

Many round towers survive to a height of 20 m (65 ft) or more and one, Kilmacduagh, Co. Galway, though the conical cap has been restored, reaches a height of approximately 34 m (112 ft). For their height they appear very slender, only 5–6 m (16 ft 5 in–19 ft 9 in) in diameter at the bottom and their foundations are also surprisingly slight, consisting only of a projecting stepped base set into a circular trench. Many are of rubble construction though some are of finer ashlar masonry. The towers gradually taper as they rise to a conical stone cap. They may be divided into between three and eight storeys. The positions of the wooden floors, which would have been reached by wooden ladders, are indicated by pro-

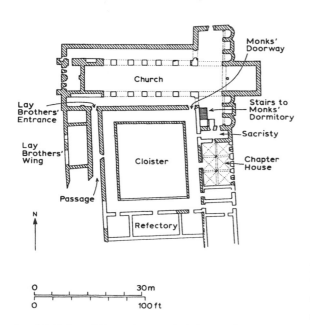

61 *Mellifont Abbey, Co. Louth (after Stalley 1987).*

**62** *Antrim round tower (Crown copyright, reproduced with the permission of the Controller of Her Majesty's Stationery Office).*

jecting stones or ledges and sometimes by the holes for wooden joists. Other clues to the construction of the towers may include exterior putlog holes which show the scaffolding system. Each storey is usually lit by a quadrangular, round-arched or angular-headed aperture and the top floor is pierced by four, or sometimes as many as eight, windows. The door, which may have a plain flat lintel or a round arch, sometimes decorated with Romanesque carved ornament, is positioned several feet above ground at first-floor level.

The Irish word *cloicthech*, meaning bell house, indicates the primary function of these impressive structures. The bells were not hung in the towers; a hand-bell would have been rung out of the windows at the top. However a glance at the annals reveals that they were also used as sacristies to house relics, books and other valuables and in time of danger they became places of refuge; hence the need for a doorway at above-ground level. They may also have served as watchtowers and landmarks visible from some distance.

There has been considerable controversy over the dating of round towers. It has been suggested, most recently by Barrow,[72] that they could be as early as the sixth or seventh century, but there is nothing to support this. We have already noted that there is no documentary evidence for stone churches before the late seventh century and that it is only during the eleventh and twelfth centuries that references become relatively common. Similarly, the first mention of a round tower is not until 950 when that at Slane, Co. Meath, was burnt by the Vikings together with the valuables and ecclesiastics inside. The annals also record that round towers were still being built as late as 1238 when Annaghdown, Co. Galway, was constructed. A twelfth-century date for quite a few others is confirmed by Romanesque architectural and ornamental features and at this time round towers were also sometimes incorporated into churches as, for example, at St Kevin's, Glendalough, and Temple Finghin, Clonmacnois. There has also been some speculation as to whether wooden belfries of some kind may have existed before the advent of the stone towers, but this is almost impossible to verify.[73]

Round towers are almost certainly the products of architectural influences reaching Ireland from the Carolingian Continent though their precise origins are obscure. It has been suggested that detached *campanili*, exemplified by those in Ravenna, northern Italy, could have served as models; alternatively churches in the Rhineland with staircase turrets or the round towers at the west end of the church at St Gall in Switzerland. However, round towers are essentially Irish. The only examples outside Ireland, Abernethy and Brechin in Scotland and Peel in the Isle of Man, are the products of Irish architectural influence.

## Burial

As we have seen the Irish were not converted to Christianity quickly. Many pagan practices lingered on and it was not until the seventh century that the Church began to be fully assimilated into early Irish society. Indeed, a recent study of the documentary evidence suggests that in the seventh century 'Burial in formal Christian cemeteries was not yet the norm, and in many instances pagan burial practices were still known and even tolerated to a certain extent.'[74] More light would be shed on this fascinating period of conversion if it were possible to identify pagan and Christian graves in the archaeological evidence by differing burial customs, but unfortunately this is not the case. We understand very little indeed about the graves and cemeteries of the early centuries AD and the various burial rites which have been identified are not closely datable. Artefacts found within the grave can sometimes provide an indication of date but most burials are not accompanied by grave-goods and therefore, where bone or charcoal survive, we are dependent upon radiocarbon dating. However, very few burials attributed to this period have been dated in this way and the method is sometimes insufficiently precise to be of any real use.

Remarkably few early Iron Age burials have been identified. What evidence we have suggests that they were cremations associated with earthen monuments: ring-barrows (mounds surrounded by a ditch and outer bank), mounds with or without an enclosing ditch, or embanked enclosures without mounds. They are usually accompanied by grave-goods. During the early centuries AD inhumations gradually replaced cremations. Some are accompanied by grave-goods but only a few are associated with earthen monuments, including some secondary inhumations in earlier burial mounds. It has been suggested that the rite of crouched inhumation was introduced into Ireland in the first century AD, perhaps as a result of contacts with the native British population. This was followed by the introduction of what appear to be Roman burial customs: extended, often findless inhumations, isolated or in groups, often orientated approximately east/west with the head at the western end, sometimes in simple dug graves, sometimes in graves lined with slabs known as long-cists, which may or may not be topped by lintels. It would be tempting to regard such graves as Christian but this is not necessarily the case: the earliest known examples of

long-cist burials from Bray Head, Co. Wicklow, are dated to the second century because of the presence of Roman coins. Regrettably we must come to the conclusion that burials cannot be identified as Christian solely on the grounds of burial rite. There must be other supporting evidence such as their location on a known ecclesiastical site. Indeed, there are strong hints from the documentary sources that conversion to Christianity did not necessarily mean subsequent interment in a Christian cemetery according to specifically Christian burial customs; pagan and Christian might be buried side by side in a tribal cemetery.[75] The cemetery at Knowth, Co. Meath, which is datable on artefactual evidence to the early centuries AD, may be of this type and it is interesting to note that it is located on the same site as the Neolithic passage grave suggesting an element of continuity in the choice of burial site. The cemetery so far consists of 36 inhumations. Men, women and children are all represented. The majority are in simple dug graves. The earlier burials appear to be those with bodies in crouched or flexed positions. These have no fixed orientation but do contain grave-goods. A likely later group, which are all findless, appear to be those orientated approximately east/west with heads at the west and bodies in an extended position. Four of these are in long-cists. Other cemeteries which may belong to this period include Bettystown, Co. Meath and Circle J, Lough Gur, Co. Limerick.[76]

During the seventh century the increasing power and influence of the Church and the rising popularity of the cult of relics provided the impetus for burial in cemeteries attached to the major monasteries and other ecclesiastical sites. The bones of the founding saints were translated and enshrined as, for example, Brigit and Conled at Kildare, and became a pious focus for the patronage of the faithful. These saintly relics were believed to impart grace not only to the living but also to the dead who were buried within the adjacent cemetery. Indeed, by the late seventh century the Irish word for a Christian cemetery was *reilic*, borrowed from the Latin *reliquiae* meaning 'the relics of the saints'.[77]

The documentary sources suggest that cemeteries at major monastic sites were either internally divided to cater for different groups of people, or that different groups of people may have been buried in different cemeteries on different parts of the site. For example, the royal graveyard at Armagh is mentioned in the annals in 935 and the name of Reefert Church at Glendalough implies the presence of a royal cemetery. As we have seen there is evidence that women sometimes worshipped in a separate church outside the main monastic complex and they may also have been buried apart.[78] The large numbers of cross-marked stones, recumbent slabs and other carved grave-markers from some sites, such as Clonmac-nois (**83d-f**), also suggest the careful organization of cemeteries but, apart from rare examples at Glendalough and Inishcaltra, very few survive *in situ.*

Not surprisingly, there has been little archaeological excavation of the cemeteries at large ecclesiastical sites because of their continued use for burial. Excavations at Gallen Priory, Co. Offaly, in the 1930s uncovered over 200 east/west dug graves mainly located to the south of a stone church with thirteenth-century architectural details. Burials below the church were on a slightly different alignment. Many early medieval grave-slabs were found but none *in situ* and the impression given was that the early medieval graves had been disturbed by later interments. More recently excavations in the area of *Teampull na ferta,* Armagh, uncovered a small cemetery which is potentially of great interest because of its early date. About 60 east/west dug graves have been excavated so far, some with traces of wooden coffins and one, which was marked out by wooden posts, contained disarticulated remains suggesting the reinterment of a body in a specially marked grave. A radiocarbon determination from one grave gave a date spanning the mid-fifth to mid-seventh centuries (cal. AD 430–640).[79]

A larger number of cemeteries connected with smaller ecclesiastical sites have been sampled. For example, at St John's Point, Co. Down, excavations inside and outside the north wall of the church (which is single cell with *antae*) uncovered long-cists, at least one of which pre-dated the church. At Kilnasaggart, Co. Armagh, a group of mixed dug and long-cist graves was excavated near a probably early eighth-century inscribed stone which records the donation of the site to the Church. Other cemeteries, although unconnected with known ecclesiastical sites, are associated with other early medieval structures. At Boolies Little, Co. Meath, 18 long-cists were uncovered, some of which pre-dated a souterrain. At Millockstown, Co. Louth, an enclosed cemetery with cist-and-lintel graves was partially excavated. Men, women and children were all represented. The cemetery was of the same period as two souterrains and there were two earlier phases of activity including a ring-fort. Excavations at Dunmisk Fort, Co. Tyrone, have up to now uncovered over 400 graves mainly in the south-east quadrant of the enclosure. There was a particular concentration in the area of a fragmentary timber building, probably a church. Most of the burials were extended in simple dug graves orientated approximately east/west, but a few were orientated north/south and three may have been flexed. There was a small group of long-cists and several graves were covered with quartz pebbles. Other activity on the site included early medieval metal- and glass-working. Another possibly early Christian cemetery is the unique site at Knockea, Co. Limerick. This consisted of a sub-square enclosure 18 × 18 m (59 × 59 ft) with the entrance to the west surrounded by a bank and ditch with a row of large post-holes along the top of the bank. It contained 65 extended inhumations, mainly orientated approximately east/west, and one crouched one. When the ditch had silted up a house was built in it and this was associated with early medieval artefacts.[80]

The importance of the corporeal relics of the saints has already been mentioned. Sometimes their bodies were exhumed and the disarticulated bones placed in shrines inside the church. A unique surviving example is the wooden tent-shaped shrine of St Manchan (**75**) decorated with copper-alloy plates datable to the twelfth century. Otherwise important graves might be specially marked in some way, or the bones translated into an above-ground shrine within the cemetery in order to facilitate veneration. At least two different kinds of structure have been recorded but, unfortunately, many of the examples are very difficult to date. Of particular interest are stone slab-shrines of similar shape to St Manchan's shrine. They are sufficiently large to contain a disarticulated skeleton and that at Killabuonia has a small hole in the gable end to enable visiting pilgrims to touch the enshrined bones. Some are placed within a small rectangular enclosure or associated with cross-marked pillars (**54a**). There are at least five known from Co. Kerry, but there are also two very fine examples at Teampull Chronain, Co. Clare, two on the Aran islands and an isolated example at Slane, Co. Meath. Thomas has suggested that slab-shrines are the Irish equivalents of eastern Mediterranean martyrial graves such as those of fifth-century date at Salonae in Yugoslavia. If so they could be seventh-century or even earlier. However, it should be remembered that none of these slab-shrines has been dated and that their counterparts in Ulster seem to be considerably later. The stone mortuary house at Banagher, Co. Derry, is located to the south-east of the church. This small house-shaped building measuring externally 3.3 × 1.45 m (10 ft  8½ in × 4 ft  9½ in) and 2.2 m (7 ft  3 in) high is reputedly the tomb of the founder St Muiredach O'Heney. The style of the ecclesiastical figure carved on the west face of the structure suggests that it is of similar date to the early thirteenth-century chancel of the adjacent church. There are other mortuary houses at Saul, Co. Down, Cooley, Co. Donegal, and Bovevagh and Tamlaght, Co. Derry. A small opening in the east wall of the Bovevagh example must have given access to the relics. At Clones, Co. Monaghan, there is a stone sarcophagus with a solid gabled roof and carved finials. It is unclear whether this was originally intended to stand in the cemetery or within a church.[81]

## Conclusion

The visible remains of the early Irish Church are impressive, but we should not allow them to lure us into creating an oversimplified and static image which takes little account of the variety of church sites which existed and how they changed over the centuries. Further archaeological investigation will help us to build up a clearer picture, but chronology remains a real problem. We know almost nothing about the period of conversion. A better understanding of burial practices and more dated examples, together with a more detailed archaeological and linguistic study of the ogham stones,[82] may shed some light. However, we also need to know about the early stages in the foundation of ecclesiastical sites. To what extent were secular settlements handed over to the Church? To what extent did pagan religious sites become Christian ones? Did cemeteries become church sites or, as seems more likely on the available evidence, did church sites attract Christian burial? What did the ecclesiastical sites of the conversion period look like?

During the seventh and eighth centuries we can trace the growth of the major monasteries in the documentary sources and on some sites, such as Armagh and Iona, we can also glimpse their growing importance from the archaeological evidence: the construction of enclosures and the activities of craftworkers, for example. But we still know very little of the churches and living quarters of the monks and nuns in this period because they were made of wood, and the kind of work which has recently revealed so much of the ephemeral structures on secular sites (see p. 23) needs to be attempted on their ecclesiastical counterparts. Where excavation has taken place smaller church sites are beginning to reveal a range of structures, but close dating and a real understanding of the role of individual sites remain difficult.

From the eighth century onwards the documentary sources suggest that churches on some major sites such as Duleek and Armagh were built in stone. Some visible remains, such as freestanding stone crosses, may date to this period but the stone churches and round towers which survive are tenth-century or later. Closer scrutiny of these standing buildings is necessary to date them more precisely, and further excavation is needed to build up a fuller picture of other structures, which were usually of wood, and of the activities which went on in them. Further investigation of cemeteries is also needed to understand their organization and growth. Well-preserved bones have the potential to say something about the early medieval population and the diseases they suffered from. It is only when considerably more excavation has taken place that we will be able to amplify and refine our understanding of the physical remains of the early Irish Church.

# CHAPTER 7

# Art

The art of early medieval Britain and Ireland has attracted considerable attention. This is not only because of the wealth of ornamental metalwork, illuminated manuscripts and stone sculpture which has come down to us but also because Insular art has been described as the only art form indigenous to Britain and Ireland which is of world significance.[1] Indeed, the art of the early medieval period in these islands has continued to engage the interest of artists and craftsmen to the present day.

## Problems

The majority of art which survives from early medieval Ireland is religious and this creates a distorted picture of the range of material which may once have existed. The skills of the ornamental metalworker were lavished on the production of shrines and altar plate; scribes illuminated luxury Gospel Books and sculptors carved intricately patterned stone crosses. These objects were considered sacred: the shrines housed precious relics, some of the manuscripts came to be regarded as relics, and the crosses continued to act as foci for prayers and devotion.[2] Though artistic fashions changed, the reverence with which these objects were regarded helped to ensure their survival, often in the hands of hereditary keepers. Though shrines may have required repair, this often involved additions to or remodelling of the original rather than complete replacement.

The survival rate of secular art objects is much lower since they were not cherished by successive generations. Excess wealth might be translated into personal adornment, ornamented brooches and pins, for example, or other items such as decorated horse harness. But these were subject to changing fashions and might be melted down and recast to suit more modern taste. In times of hardship they might easily be converted into bullion. Therefore, apart from some items buried in Viking graves mainly in Norway, most of the secular objects which have come down to us are those found on excavated sites or chance finds, casual losses which were insufficiently valued to merit a prolonged search. The lack of identifiably secular metalwork has sometimes led to the supposition that almost all objects were for religious use. This seems unlikely, especially since ornamental metal-working is evidenced on many of the higher status secular sites such as Lagore, together with a range of brooches, pins and personal trinkets.

In general it should be remembered that, despite the considerable quantity of metalwork, manuscripts and sculpture which has survived, it is impossible to gauge what has perished. When studying the development of art in this period there is always the temptation to ignore the losses and make comparisons between the remaining pieces. This may be misleading, but it is now impossible to reconstruct a fuller picture. There is also the tendency to forget that some art forms are almost completely lost to us: wood-carving, with the exception of the recently excavated examples from Viking Dublin (see p. 186), and embroidery, for example.

The second major problem is establishing where many of the surviving objects were made. Sculpture presents little difficulty since it was almost always carved of local stone or occasionally better quality stone was moved longer distances by boat.[3] But ornamental metalwork and manuscripts are easily portable. Churchmen travelled and brought back souvenirs. Manuscripts were given to other ecclesiastical libraries. Ornamental metalwork was attractive to Viking raiders and shrines with their precious contents might even be captured on the battlefield, since they frequently accompanied Irish armies into war.[4] Therefore very few manuscripts or pieces of metalwork can be connected with a specific scriptorium or workshop.

This difficulty is compounded by the fact that it is often impossible to say by examining an object whether it was made in Ireland or northern or western Britain since the same art style was current on either side of the Irish Sea for much of the period. This style is sometimes called Hiberno-Saxon but Insular is, perhaps, a better term because it also allows for the possibility of manufacture either in Pictland and Dalriada or the British kingdoms, as well as Ireland or Anglo-Saxon England. This problem of provenance has led to sometimes heated and occasionally vitriolic debate.

Insular style is essentially a blending of Celtic, Classical and later Germanic art motifs to make formal patterns of spirals, interlace, frets, steps, lacertine beasts and sometimes plant ornament. Naturalistic animals and birds or human figures are also decorated with these patterns and may become so stylized as to appear almost abstract. Although we know that the Insular art style was evolving during the fifth, sixth and seventh centuries, reached its zenith during the eighth and, with an influx of Viking influence, continued in Ireland into the twelfth, it is exceedingly difficult to date individual items closely, especially in the earlier part of the period. A *terminus ante quem* is provided for some metalwork discovered in mainly ninth-century Viking graves in Norway. A few manuscripts, such as the Lindisfarne Gospels and the Book of Armagh, may be dated by colophon inscriptions naming the scribe but some other examples of these are forged. Some of the later metalwork, the Cross of Cong, for example, is also datable by inscription as are some of the stone crosses. However the vast majority of material can only be dated by direct or indirect art-historical comparison with dated objects and in this way a rather precarious relative chronology can be constructed. However, there is still considerable disagreement over the dating of many objects and in some cases, such as the Fahan Mura cross-slab, Co. Donegal, the suggestions which have been put forward span several centuries.[5]

## Ornamental metalwork

The origins of Insular metalwork are complex and it would be a mistake to examine Ireland in isolation from contemporary developments in Britain. Indeed, Insular metalwork is essentially a product of the continuing cross-fertilization of ideas brought about by the movement of people back and forth across the Irish Sea, particularly at the end of the Roman occupation with the establishment of major Irish settlements in western Britain.

Our knowledge of the development of Irish ornamental metalwork in the early centuries AD is limited. Recent research[6] on La Tène metalwork in Ireland has done much to establish a better understanding of the range of material and the relationship of particular pieces to each other, but chronology remains an important problem since we are almost completely dependent upon art-historical criteria such as motif analysis. What does emerge are increasing links between Britain and Ireland as the Iron Age progressed. In particular several writers[7] have remarked upon the apparent close contacts between the Irish and the native tribes inhabiting the Military Zone of northern Britain between Hadrian's Wall and the Antonine Wall during the Roman occupation. It has been suggested that certain artefacts, which were developed in this area around the third century AD, or more probably the fourth, were the product of Irish artistic influences on provincial Roman artefact types[8] and that the knowledge of many of these objects was passed back to Ireland at the end of the Roman period, perhaps through Irish raids, where they became part of the Irish metal-working repertoire and may be recognized as the first evidence of Insular Irish ornamental metalwork.

The objects concerned are small items of personal adornment cast in copper alloy or sometimes silver: penannular brooches and pins. Penannular brooches have a separate pin which swivels on the hoop. This pin, which was worn pointing upwards, is passed through the cloth and the gap between the terminals of the hoop which is then moved round behind the pin to keep it in place. Several different attempts have been made to work out a classification for penannular brooches. Fowler's relatively simple system based on the major different types of terminal is used here. The brooch evolves during the Iron Age and Roman periods and continues into the early middle ages. The main post-Roman types are F, G and H. Type F brooches (**63a**), which are characterized by zoomorphic-headed terminals, appear to evolve during the fourth century in northern Britain and probably reached Ireland through Irish raiding. Kilbride-Jones put forward a much

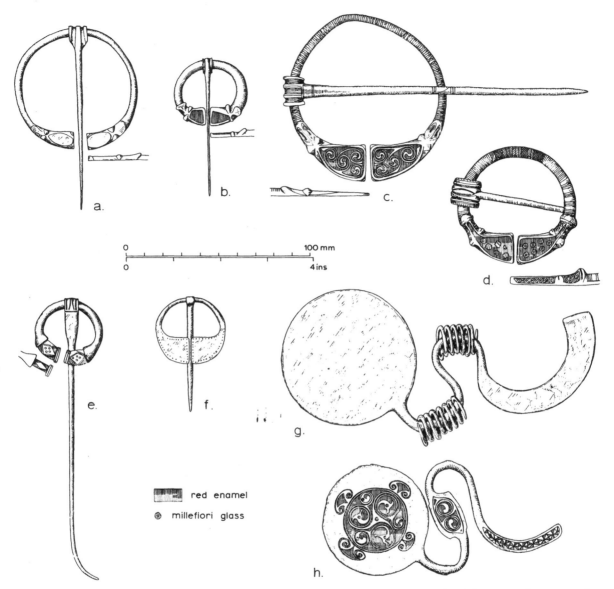

red enamel

millefiori glass

**63** *Penannular brooches and latchets:*
*penannular brooches* **a.** *Type F, Ardagh, Co. Longford;*
**b.** *Type F1, Ireland, unprovenanced;* **c.** *Type F2,*
*River Shannon, near Athlone, Co. Westmeath;*
**d.** *Type F2, Ballintore, Co. Kildare;* **e.** *Type G, Ireland,*
*unprovenanced;* **f.** *Type H, Lagore, Co. Meath;*
*latchets* **g.** *River Shannon, Athlone, Co. Westmeath;*
**h.** *Ireland, unprovenanced (***a, b, f.** *after Fowler, E.*
*1963;* **c, d.** *after Kilbride–Jones 1980b;* **e.** *after*
*Dickinson, T.M. 1982;* **g, h.** *after Smith 1917–8).*

earlier date at the end of the second century for
their development but this has found little accept-
ance. The terminal may be ornamented with red
enamel (Type F1) (**63b**) or further elaborated with
enamel, millefiori and spiral designs (Type F2)
(**63c, d**). Types F1 and F2 are both common in
Ireland (**64a**) and the distribution of the latter is
almost entirely Irish, suggesting that it is a specifically Irish type. Kilbride-Jones has made a more
detailed typological study of Type F brooches and,
as a result of this, has suggested that some specific
sub-groups may have been manufactured in particular parts of Ireland. Especially interesting is the
penannular brooch workshop identified at

64 *Distribution of penannular brooches:*
a. *Type F (after Kilbride-Jones 1980b);* b. *Type G (after Dickinson, T.M. 1982);* c, d. *Type H (after Longley 1975).*

Clogher, Co. Tyrone. Manufacturing debris and penannular brooches have been found on this site and brooches of the same type from elsewhere may be ascribed to the same workshop. Dating is difficult but F2 brooches would seem to span the sixth and seventh centuries before the emergence of more complex brooches during the eighth. In contrast the smaller Type G penannular brooch with its faceted terminals and lozenge ornament (63e) is virtually absent from Ireland except for a few seventh- to ninth-century examples (64b). Type H brooches, which may have evolved in Scotland at the end of the Roman period, are characterized by flattened and expanded terminals and a few examples are known from Ireland (63f, 64c, d). Variations include brooches with enamel or millefiori decoration (H1), brooches with expanded disc terminals (H2) and brooches with expanded disc terminals decorated with red enamel (H3). Type H3 and the composite H/F are mainly Irish types.[9]

Similarly, a variety of pins seem to have evolved in northern Britain and found their way to Ireland during the fourth and fifth centuries. The types include the hand-pin (69a), characterized by three to five 'digits' set above a flat semi-circular disc often ornamented with red enamel and spiral designs, and its possible forerunner, the smaller proto-hand pin (69b), which has a flat ring head, the upper half of which is sometimes beaded. The latchet (63g, h) is another form of dress fastener, but it is a specifically Irish type. It has a disc-shaped head, sometimes decorated with red enamel or spiral ornament, and an extended 'S'-shaped body which was attached to the cloth by means of two wire coils.[10]

Hanging bowls made of copper alloy or occasionally silver are derived from Roman types. They have three handles with escutcheons decorated with openwork patterns, spirals, interlace, animal ornament, enamel and occasionally millefiori through which rings passed to enable the bowls to be suspended in some way. They may also have decorated basal mounts and plaques applied to the body. The function of these bowls is unclear. They may have been used for water or possibly wine, or even as oil lamps, and some, because of their context or decoration, suggest a Christian association. The majority of examples, either complete bowls or more often fragmentary escutcheons, have been found in Anglo-Saxon areas, often in pagan graves, though a few are known from northern Britain, including a mould fragment from Craig Phadrig near Inverness. Not a single bowl has been identified from Ireland and only two escutcheons have been found; one, from the River Bann, is almost certainly an import from Scotland. Most seem to be datable on stylistic grounds to the fifth to seventh centuries, though there are also some eighth- and possibly ninth-century examples, mainly from Viking graves in Norway.

There has been considerable controversy as to whether hanging bowls were manufactured in Ireland. Henry has suggested that, although no bowls have been found in Ireland, the similarities between those with enamelled ornament and enamelled brooches and pins in Ireland are sufficient to indicate that these bowls were of Irish manufacture. The reason why they had failed to turn up in Ireland was because burials were not accompanied by grave-goods. But in the light of the contacts between Ireland and northern Britain outlined above and the similarities between the ornamental repertoire on both sides of the Irish Sea in this period there seems little to support Henry's theory. Although it is possible that a few hanging bowls were made in Ireland, especially some of the late examples from Viking graves in Norway, the distribution suggests that the majority were probably made by Celtic craftsmen in Anglo-Saxon England, the British kingdoms or Pictland.[11]

We have already traced the growing power and wealth of the Irish Church during the seventh and eighth centuries (see p. 99). The seventh century saw the establishment of Irish monasteries in Britain and on the Continent and these increased contacts, particularly those with Anglo-Saxon England brought about by the foundation of houses such as Lindisfarne in Northumbria and Burgh Castle in East Anglia, were crucial to the development of the techniques and motifs of Insular art. In addition to enamelwork and millefiori we see, for example, the introduction of cast chip-carving, gilding and filigree wire and the ornamental repertoire is enriched with interlace, frets and zoomorphic patterns. This is also the period which witnessed the rapid spread of the cult of relics in Ireland, the translation of the bodies of the saints, the enshrinement of their possessions, and the importation of *palliola* and *brandea*. These were small pieces of cloth which had touched the tombs of the saints in far-away places, such as Rome, and so, it was believed, become imbued with their grace and holiness.[12] Such treasures needed to be displayed in containers worthy of them and the Insular metalwork which survives from the period spanning approximately the late seventh to early ninth centuries, mainly reliquaries and other ecclesiastical objects, is of particularly high quality and demonstrates the assimilation and elaboration of the techniques and ideas experimented with earlier. Though much less secular metalwork has come down to us, the religious material must reflect the growing wealth of at least the upper echelons of society since it was they who provided much of the patronage which enabled these beautiful objects to be made.

Surprisingly few pieces of metalwork with the exception of the Moylough belt-shrine (66), the Ardagh chalice and more recently the Derrynaflan hoard (67, 69) have undergone detailed study to determine exactly how they were constructed and the techniques of ornament used. Research has tended to concentrate on art-historical comparison with other metalwork, manuscripts and sculpture. It should be stressed that it is impossible to recognize specific workshops in this period or to say whether many of the surviving objects were

manufactured in Ireland; those found in Viking graves in Norway may have come from any of the Insular areas. But whether they are Irish or not, they do reflect the range of material available in Ireland at this time. Similarly, no close dating is possible and there have been criticisms of the tendency to date so many objects to the eighth century.[13] However, many of the motifs visible on the metalwork are also found in the Lindisfarne Gospels, a manuscript of definite late seventh- or early eighth-century date and this is almost the only fixed chronological point we have.[14] But at the same time it should be remembered that there must have been some regional variation and that some workshops or craftworkers may have been more conservative than others.

The range of objects, techniques and ornamental motifs which were available between the late seventh and early ninth centuries may best be examined by describing a few examples in detail.

**65** *The Emly shrine (Courtesy of the Museum of Fine Arts, Boston, Theodora Wilbour Fund in memory of Charlotte Beebe Wilbour).*

First, nine small house-shaped shrines for carrying portable relics, probably *palliola* and *brandea*, are known: the Emly, Shannon and Lough Erne shrines from Ireland, the Monymusk reliquary from Scotland, the Copenhagen, Melhus and Setnes shrines from Norway and the S. Salvatore and Bologna shrines from Italy. Though each is different in detail the group may be exemplified by the Emly shrine (65) from Co. Limerick which may belong early in the series. The small hollowed yew-wood box 105 mm (4½ in) long, 41 mm (1⅞ in) wide and 92 mm (3¾ in) high would have had a carrying strap or chain attached to hinged mounts on the narrow sides to enable the shrine to be hung round the neck. The mouldings which frame the wood are of gilded copper alloy and the ridge-pole is typically decorated with enamelled dragon finials and a tiny house-shaped mount in the centre. Only the front is ornamented since only this was visible when the shrine was being carried. The three circular mounts are characteristic, though rectilinear ones are also found, but the green and yellow enamel cells are unusual, as in the background of step patterns outlined by hammering lead-tin alloy into the yew-wood surface; most of the other shrines are covered with decorated metal sheets bound and riveted to the wooden surface. However, the overall effect of dark and light, gold, silver and polychrome enamel is typical of Insular metalwork in this period.[15]

The survival of other types of reliquary is rare.

66 *The Moylough belt shrine*
*(Copyright: National Museum of Ireland).*

Cogitosus' seventh-century *Life of Brigit* describes the bodies of Archbishop Conled and St Brigit as lying in richly-decorated sarcophagi (see p. 122). The only objects which might be identified as coming from shrines of this type are three almost identical 'D'-shaped cast copper-alloy plaques decorated with openwork spirals and high-relief bosses, snakes and dragons, two in the Musé des Antiquities Nationales, St Germain-en-Laye, outside Paris, and one from Gausel in Norway, which may have formed the roof finials of a large tent- or house-shaped reliquary.[16] Examples of reliquaries which were made to contain objects include the recently discovered Lough Kinale book-shrine and the Moylough belt-shrine (66). The latter, which was discovered in a peat bog in Co. Sligo, is made up of a leather belt, the reputed possession of some saint, which has been cut into four pieces, each of which is entirely encased in tinned copper-alloy plates held in place by copper or copper-alloy binding strips attached with rivets. The segments are joined by hinges with a skeuomorphic buckle at the front. The ornament is centred on the buckle and the hinges with the addition of four cruciform mounts, one on each section of the belt. It consists of cast copper-alloy mounts set with red and yellow enamel in rectilinear 'L', 'T' and 'S'-shaped recesses and blue and white millefiori glass framing stamped silver-foil plaques stiffened by copper backing plates and decorated with spiral designs. The buckle is also ornamented with dragon and bird heads and blue and red glass studs with sheet-silver grids or wires embedded in their surfaces. Again the effect is rich and colourful and the combination of techniques

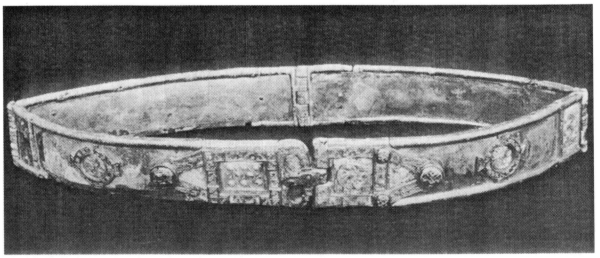

67 *The Derrynaflan paten and stand*
*(Copyright: National Museum of Ireland).*

used might suggest an early eighth-century date. The shrine shows considerable signs of wear, presumably the result of handling by those seeking to benefit from the relic, and has been repaired subsequently with much less skill.[17]

In addition to reliquaries some altar plate has survived. Particularly well-known is the silver chalice which was found in 1868, together with four brooches and a plain copper-alloy chalice, while digging potatoes in Ardagh, Co. Limerick.[18] The recently discovered silver paten (67) from the Derrynaflan hoard, Co. Tipperary, which also contained a chalice and wine strainer, displays many of the same complex range of materials and techniques as the Ardagh silver chalice and the two pieces, which are of the highest craftsmanship, may be considered approximately contemporary. They have a more sophisticated appearance than

the Moylough belt-shrine with less emphasis on polychrome enamel and no millefiori glass, and for this reason they may be later in date. A preliminary examination[19] of the Derrynaflan paten has shown that it consists of a raised sheet-silver lathe-polished plate approximately 360 mm (1 ft 2 in) in diameter with a low silvered copper-alloy hoop or foot riveted onto it. A hoop-shaped stand of silvered copper alloy, which had once been attached to the paten, was also found in the hoard. The ornament on the paten is concentrated in bands round the rim of the plate and on the side of the foot. The bands are bordered by knitted bindings of silver and copper wire, a technique known as trichinopoly. The decoration on the rim consists of 12 curved gilt copper-alloy frames decorated with cast chip-carved spirals and interlace. The rim is marked with the engraved letters a–m, presumably to enable a literate craftsman to assemble the ornamental plates correctly. Each frame contains two foil panels, many cut away to form openwork designs, decorated with a variety of gold filigree. The filigree motifs include interlaced beasts, snakes and men; also abstract spiral and interlace patterns. Set between the panels are 24 circular polychrome-glass studs placed in cast copper-alloy settings ornamented with filigree or trichonopoly. The outer face of the foot is decorated with 12 silver-gilt panels stamped with interlace and spiral designs interspersed with rectangular polychrome-glass studs, and the bottom with round and rectilinear silver panels also stamped with spirals and interlace.

A range of other ecclesiastical metalwork from this period is also known. There is a fragmentary copper-alloy altar or processional cross decorated with red and yellow enamel and blue and white millefiori glass from Co. Antrim, and a wooden processional cross covered with gilded copper-alloy panels with amber settings has recently come to light. The openwork copper-alloy plaque depicting the Crucifixion from near Athlone, Co. Westmeath, may have been attached to a book.[20] A dragon-headed finial cast in high relief with

chip-carving and polychrome enamelwork from Ëkero in Sweden may be the head of a crozier and an engraved copper-alloy spherical object from Vinjum in Norway could be a thurible or censer.[21] Over 60 quadrangular hand-bells are known and, though difficult to date since very few are ornamented, some at least are likely to have been made in this period. Some were cut from sheet iron and then bent and fastened together with rivets and coated with copper alloy, while others were cast in solid copper alloy. The recently discovered Donore hoard from Co. Meath probably originally came from an ecclesiastical context and includes a highly ornamented door-pull which may once have been attached to the door of a church.[22] It is difficult to say whether some objects are ecclesiastical or secular. For example, many of the copper-alloy bowls with enamel and millefiori ornamented escutcheons and wooden buckets covered with engraved copper-alloy sheets which have been found in Viking graves in Norway could have been either.[23]

Most of the rest of the ornamental metalwork known from this period consists of objects of personal adornment, mainly brooches and pins. Penannulars remain the most common brooch

**68** *The 'Tara' brooch*
*(Copyright: National Museum of Ireland).*

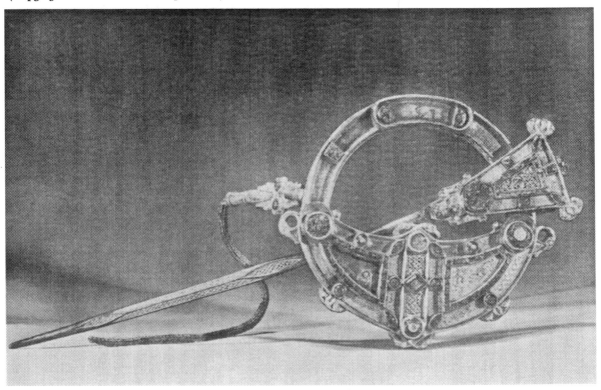

type in Scotland and Ireland and during the seventh century they gradually became larger, heavier and more highly ornamented. The hoop is flattened and widened to enable increased decoration. The pin is lengthened and increasingly elaborated at its junction with the hoop. The flattened terminals of Type H brooches become larger, thereby producing a greater area for adornment, and the increasing emphasis on the decoration of the terminals, perhaps coupled with their greater weight, finally results in a form common in Ireland where the terminals are joined together by one or more bars or sometimes completely fused. These are not penannulars in the true sense, since the pin cannot pass between the terminals of the hoop, and they are therefore termed pseudo-penannular brooches. Instead the pin-head may have been attached to the hoop by means of a removable bolt, or the brooch could be secured in position with a cord.[24]

A number of highly decorated pseudo-penannular brooches are known but few have been studied in detail. They may be exemplified by the 'Tara' brooch (68) which was found c. 1850 at Bettystown, Co. Meath. It is the most elaborate of the group and the range of ornament is similar to that on the Ardagh chalice and the Derrynaflan paten, suggesting that it is of a similar date. The brooch is relatively small, 90 mm ($3\frac{1}{2}$ in) in diameter, with a disproportionally long pin. It is cast in silver and decorated on both faces. It would have been secured in position by winding the gilded serpent with glass eyes and trichinopoly body attached to the edge of the hoop round the pin. The flat terminals are completely fused together and the edge of the hoop is ornamented with dragons and birds cast in high relief and gilded. The whole of the front of the brooch and the head of the pin are divided symmetrically into panels decorated with complex gold-filigree ornament, spirals, interlace, snakes and other zoomorphic motifs, soldered onto gold foil backing plates interspersed with amber insets and amber and blue and red glass studs, sometimes further decorated with filigree. The back of the brooch is much flatter since it would have lain against the garment and, though it would have been invisible, it is elaborately ornamented with gilded panels of cast chip-carved spirals, panels of silver and gold decorated with engraved spirals and polychrome-glass studs. The 'Tara' brooch may be compared with other highly ornamented examples outside Ireland, such as the Hunterston brooch, which

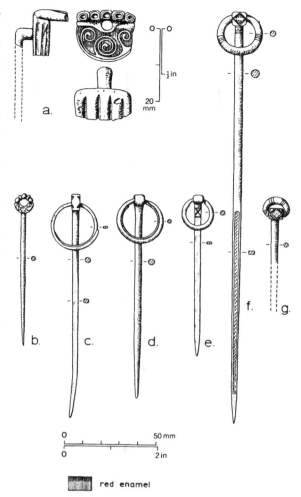

red enamel

69 Pins:
a. hand-pin, Ballycatteen, Co. Cork (after Ó Ríordáin, S.P. and Hartnett 1943); b. proto hand-pin, Ireland, unprovenanced (after Fowler, E. 1963); ringed pins c. Roosky, Co. Roscommon; d. Co. Westmeath; e. near Athlone, Co. Westmeath; f, g. Clonmacnois, Co. Offaly (after Fanning 1974–5).

was found in Ayrshire, south-west Scotland.[25]

Most penannular brooches were of course much less elaborate, but for the majority of the population pins would probably have been the usual dress-fastener. In seventh- and eighth-century Ireland the commonest type of pin was the ringed pin, which is usually of copper alloy, though iron examples are also known. These are made up of two elements, a pin with a looped or perforated head through which a loose swivel ring was inserted. There is evidence that like pseudo-penannular brooches some pins were secured with a cord tied to the ring and wound round the pin. Recent work[26] on the typology of ringed pins suggests that they may have evolved during the fifth and sixth centuries. The earliest type is probably the spiral ringed pin where the ring, a piece of spiralled wire, is inserted through a baluster pin-head (**69c**) or occasionally a looped pin-head (**69d**). Simple ornament is concentrated on the pin-head and sometimes the ring. This was gradually replaced by the plain ringed pin where the ring is inserted through a looped pin-head (**69e**) or sometimes a polyhedral (**69f**) or baluster pin-head. This type continued into the ninth

century and was adopted by the Vikings. During the eighth and early ninth centuries another dress fastener known from Ireland was the ring brooch. This is a cross between a pseudo-penannular brooch and a ringed pin. In general remarkably little research[27] has been done on the great variety of copper-alloy pins from early medieval Ireland, and few are highly decorated. It is therefore difficult to trace their typological development or date them with any accuracy.

During the course of the ninth century the style of ornamental metalwork changed. The Viking raids must have had an impact on the production of luxury goods especially during the 830s and 840s (see p. 172). These unsettled times would have made it extremely difficult to manufacture objects of the quality witnessed earlier, and there would have been less wealth available to lavish on artistic patronage. Consequently, the ornamental

**70** *The Derrynaflan chalice*
*(Copyright: National Museum of Ireland).*

metalwork becomes coarser and less accomplished and is gradually replaced by a plainer style. Cast chip-carved ornament and gold filigree first degenerate and then die out. Enamel, millefiori glass and polychrome-glass studs also go out of fashion though for a time amber appears to become more popular. Motifs also change. Spirals and step patterns gradually disappear from the ornamental repertoire and interlace knotwork is reduced for the most part to simple plaitwork patterns. Animal ornament remains popular, though the motifs gradually evolve and by the end of the ninth century the influence of Anglo-Saxon Trewhiddle style is clearly detectable. Continental vegetal ornament in the form of acanthus is also introduced about this time, probably as a result of contacts with Anglo-Saxon England.[28]

Although in this period it is easier to recognize objects of Irish manufacture, no workshops can be identified and only relative dating of individual items is possible. However, from the objects which survive it is clear that some ecclesiastical metalwork continued to be made. The changing style may be demonstrated by examining two objects: the Derrynaflan chalice and the 'Kells' crozier.

The Derrynaflan chalice (70), which may be dated approximately to the first half of the ninth century, is very similar in design to the Ardagh chalice. It consists of a large beaten-silver lathe-polished bowl with a separate foot joined by a cast copper-alloy stem. It has two handles with decorated escutcheons, and the rest of the ornament is concentrated in bands below the rim of the bowl, round the stem, round the flange of the foot and underneath at the point where the foot joins the stem. The decoration is, however, different from the Ardagh chalice and the range of techniques and motifs is much more limited. The gold filigree is coarser and the animals portrayed are semi-naturalistic and do not interlace with each other. Instead of polychrome-glass studs the filigree panels are interspersed with both round and rectilinear amber studs, some decorated with filigree. The chip-carved interlace on the handles and the stem has lost much of its sharpness and is relatively simple and repetitive.[29]

More than 15 crozier shrines[30] have now been identified as dating to the ninth and tenth centuries. These consist of wooden staffs, possibly the possessions of holy men and saints, enshrined in decorated metal casings which came to be regarded as elaborate symbols of office used by the leading clerics of the day. Though each is different

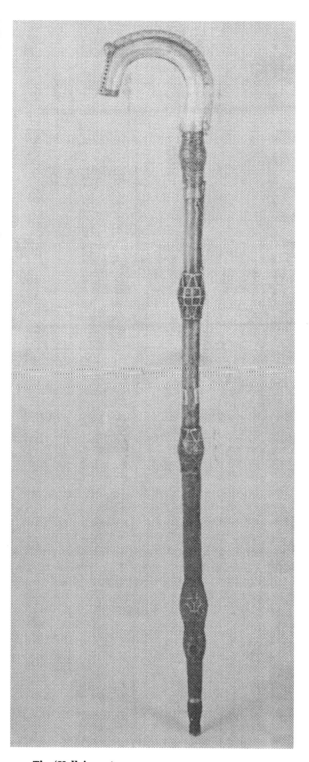

71 *The 'Kells' crozier*
*(Copyright: the Trustees of the British Museum).*

*72 The Ballyspellan brooch*
*(Copyright: National Museum of Ireland).*

in detail, they may be exemplified by the 'Kells' crozier[31] (71) which came to light in a solicitor's office in London in 1850. The crozier, which is 1.32 m (4 ft 4 in) long, may be identified as Irish both by its decoration and by the names on an undated inscription attached to the crook. It consists of a yew-wood staff covered in a composite metal casing. Two major phases of ornament may be identified, and it is the first which concerns us here. In the late ninth or early tenth century the crook and shaft were covered in copper-alloy sheets held in position with cast knops, the lower three of which now survive, and binding strips. There are some traces of ornament on the crook but most of the decoration is concentrated on the binding strips and knops. The latter, which were originally covered in silver foil, are bi-conical in section and divided into a large number

of small decorated panels of different shapes, outlined by raised bands which give a faceted appearance. Many of the panels are ornamented with animals contorted and intertwined to fit the shape of individual panels. These animals have their origins in earlier zoomorphic ornament but some are clearly influenced by Anglo-Saxon Trewhiddle style. Other decoration includes simple interlace, a few degenerate spiral patterns, and a single panel of acanthus foliage on one of the binding strips. The second phase of ornament belongs to the eleventh century, when the copper-alloy casing was covered in sheet silver, of which only the topmost knop and the crook, with its openwork crest and the drop or tip modelled to enclose a relic, now survive.

Many of the changes which can be detected in ninth-century ecclesiastical metalwork are also found on brooches. The ornate style of the eighth-century pseudo-penannulars such as the 'Tara' brooch was gradually simplified and there was considerable variety and experiment with both form and ornament. Pseudo-penannular forms remained in use but the true penannular was also re-introduced from Pictland. There was a gradual decrease in the use of filigree, gilding and settings, and brooches were increasingly made of plain silver, possibly because of the influx of Viking silver at this time. The most characteristic decorations are marginal animals round the edges of the brooch terminals and a variety of bosses sometimes patterned with criss-crossed brambled ornament reminiscent of studs decorated with filigree or granulation. The most common form of bossed penannular brooch, a type current during the second half of the ninth and possibly the early tenth century, may be exemplified by a silver brooch (diameter 120 mm ($4\frac{1}{2}$ in)) from Ballyspellan, Co. Kilkenny (72). It is characterized by a cylindrical pin-head, plano-convex hoop section, and flat sub-triangular terminals ornamented with dome-headed bosses linked by billeted lines (another feature adopted as a result of influence from Anglo-Saxon Trewhiddle style), the intervening panels being decorated with zoomorphic ornament.[32] Another penannular brooch type, the silver thistle brooch which has solid globular brambled terminals, also evolved in Ireland during this period and represents the final development of the penannular brooch form. But unlike bossed penannular brooches, which, with the exception of one type, were not adopted by the Vikings, thistle brooches evolved into a variety of different types with plain and decorated ball terminals which were popular in the Viking Irish Sea area during the tenth century.[33]

Ringed pins also remained fashionable during this period and were used by native and Viking alike. During the tenth century plain ringed pins with polyhedral heads (69f) with simple ornament concentrated on the head and shank were the most common type. However, gradually the pin-head increased in size with the result that the ring was reduced to a close-fitting kidney-shaped cap fixed by means of tiny projections set into small sockets in the head (69g). Like penannular brooches many of the pin-heads were decorated with brambled ornament. Kite brooches were a new form of dress fastener which came into use at this time and became popular amongst the Vikings. These are made of silver and are really long pins with large kite-shaped pendant heads, often richly ornamented, which have a cord attached like a tail to wind round the shank to hold the brooch in position.[34]

Remarkably little research has been done on Irish ecclesiastical metalwork of the eleventh and twelfth centuries, considering its quantity, quality and variety. This is all the more notable when it is realized that it is only in this period that we can begin to construct an agreed chronological framework and provide a date range for at least some of the objects; others can then be grouped around these because of the similarity of their techniques and ornament. The establishment of a chronological framework is possible because some objects have inscriptions giving the names of secular or ecclesiastical patrons and craftworkers and, although no dates are recorded, the same names are sometimes mentioned in the annals thereby giving an approximate date for individual pieces of metalwork. These inscriptions also help us to begin to identify regional groupings of metalwork, families of craftsmen, and the location of their workshops and it is clear that ecclesiastical metalwork in this period was being made in the major monasteries.

The range of material consists almost entirely of reliquaries including bell-shrines, book-shrines, and croziers as well as shrines for corporeal relics. This supports the evidence of the annals that the enshrining of relics reached a peak during the twelfth century. The datable pieces may be listed as follows: the Soiscél Molaise (book-shrine) 1026–33; the Cumdach of the Stowe Missal (book-shrine) made at Clonmacnois between 1045 and 1052; the Cumdach of the Cathach (book-shrine) made at Kells between c.1062 and 1098; the shrine of St Patrick's bell 1094–1105; the Lismore crozier 1090–1113; the shrine of St Lachtin's arm 1118–21; and the Cross of Cong 1123–36, which may have been made at Roscommon. Chronological and regional groupings based on this frame work were originally put forward by Henry and have recently been revised by Ó Floinn.[35]

The difficulty with Irish eleventh- and twelfth-century ecclesiastical metalwork lies in attempting to analyze the eclectic nature of its changing style and ornament. To what extent are we witnessing the continuous evolution of native art, and to what extent was there a conscious revival of older motifs and techniques which had originally reached their zenith during the eighth century? Equally, to what extent were ecclesiastical craftsmen subject to outside stylistic influences, particularly from Anglo-Saxon England and Scandinavia, which were filtering into Ireland via

73  *Detail of Hiberno-Ringerike ornament on the side of the Cumdach of the Cathach book-shrine (after Henry 1970).*

Dublin at this time, and to what extent did they mix these with Insular elements to create something new? As far as the metalwork is concerned these problems, which have given rise to considerable debate, can only be approached by detailed technical and stylistic analysis of individual pieces. However, our understanding of the general development of art styles in Ircland at this time has recently taken a major step forward as a result of the discovery of a large number of carved wooden objects from tenth- and eleventh-century stratified contexts in Dublin (see p. 186) and, although it is frequently difficult to compare the changing fashions seen in everyday artefacts with the much more conservative style of ecclesiastical metalwork, the study of these has done much to define and date the various motifs and influences available.[36]

We can catch a glimpse of the range of techniques and the changing style of ecclesiastical metalwork during the eleventh and twelfth centuries by examining three objects in more detail: first the Cumdach of the Cathach, which may be grouped with several other objects including the Misach, St Mura's bell-shrine and the second phase of the 'Kells' crozier. The Cumdach of the Cathach is a book-shrine consisting of a wooden box 250 mm (9¾ in) long, 190 mm (7½ in) wide and 70 mm (2¾ in) thick covered in copper-alloy plates. The top is fourteenth-century but the majority of the rest may be dated to the second half of the eleventh century. The back is decorated with openwork step patterns, silver-foil-covered copper alloy against gold foil or gilt copper alloy,

74  *The shrine of St Lachtin's arm (Copyright: National Museum of Ireland).*

without doubt a conscious revival of an eighth-century motif. However, the surviving ornament in the centre of the sides of the box (73), which consists of cast gilt copper-alloy panels decorated in silver and niello (a black paste of sulphur fused with silver or copper) inlays, shows a predominance of interlace and foliage designs, whose symmetrical organization betrays distinctive Insular traits. But the zoomorphic forms with their foliage tendrils demonstrate the influence of Scandinavian Ringerike style, though not in its pure form. This was almost certainly reaching the workshop at Kells via Dublin.

The shrine of St Lachtin's arm (1118–21 (74) from Donaghmore, Co. Cork, which is 400 mm (1 ft 3¾ in) high, is made up of a wooden core covered with copper-alloy panels held in place by a cast openwork ring and binding strips. The hand

75 *St Manchan's shrine*
*(Copyright: the Trustees of the British Museum).*

is decorated with cast interlace and foliage designs while the panels on the arm are ornamented with a fine mesh of zoomorphic interlace in silver inlay outlined with niello. These creatures, with their loosely looping bodies, demonstrate some traits of Scandinavian Urnes style, but their organization and almost abstract quality are essentially Insular.

St Manchan's shrine from Lemanaghan, Co. Offaly, (75) is of a similar date, but has different technical and stylistic details and may be grouped with the Cross of Cong (1123–36) and other objects including the shrine of the Book of Dimma and possibly the earlier phase of the shrine of St Patrick's tooth. All these come from the central Shannon area and may have been produced at the monastery of Roscommon. St Manchan's shrine is a tent-shaped yew-wood box 600 mm (2 ft) long, 400 mm (1 ft 4 in) wide and 480 mm (1 ft 7 in) high. It stands on small feet, each with a large copper-alloy ring through which poles might be

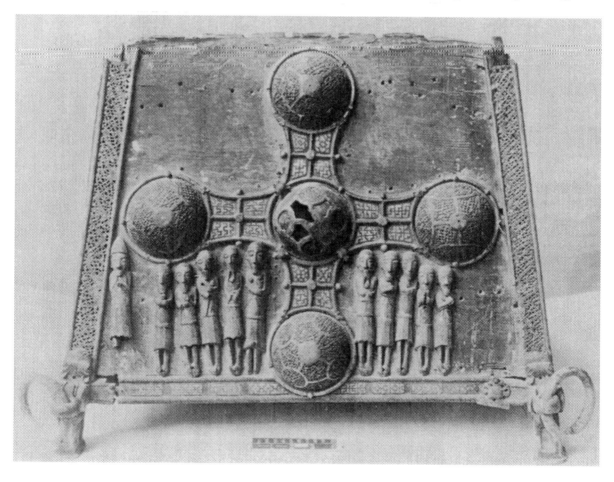

inserted to enable the shrine to be carried around. The main faces were originally covered with silver foil, almost all of which has now disappeared, and the whole surface may originally have been covered with ornament. The principal decoration which now survives on the major faces is based on a cross motif, and this is characteristic of the whole group. The ornament on the cross arms, red and yellow enamels set in step patterns, is clearly a revival of eighth-century techniques. The cast copper-alloy bosses may also recall earlier metalwork, but the zoomorphic ornament which decorates them shows a mixture of Insular and Scandinavian Urnes traits. There are similar zoomorphic patterns and enamelwork on the binding strips and the gabled ends of the shrine. In addition small cast copper-alloy figures, probably saints and apostles, but modelled on representations of Christ Crucified, are attached to the main faces of the shrine. Only ten of the originals now survive. The details of the figures are Irish but their form shows the influence of Continental Romanesque metalwork. They could be part of the original scheme of decoration for the shrine, but it seems more likely that they were added at a slightly later date since the feet of one of the figures have been cut off to fit it into the available space.[37]

In contrast little secular metalwork seems to have survived from the eleventh and twelfth centuries. Penannular brooches went out of fashion and pins were the main dress-fasteners. Ringed pins, however, were gradually replaced by stick pins which, though current throughout the early middle ages in Ireland, became the characteristic pin type in this period. But, with the exception of some examples from dated, stratified contexts in Dublin, little attempt has been made at constructing a typology or dating specific forms.[38]

## Illuminated manuscripts

The advent of Christianity in Ireland brought with it both Latin and literacy. Ecclesiastics needed to learn Latin to read the Bible and the liturgy and early Irish churchmen were much preoccupied with writing Latin grammars for Irish-speaking clergy. The growth of the Church meant that there was a constant need to copy religious books, and some of the major monasteries became important centres of learning which attracted students from as far away as Anglo-Saxon England and Merovingian Gaul. Monastic libraries were built

up and scriptoria established. Irish ecclesiastical scholars had a wide range of interests. Though much of their energy went into Biblical exegesis and study of the Church Fathers, they also showed some knowledge of Classical authors. They wrote hymns, prayers, poetry and penitentials, Easter tables, annals and martyrologies, ecclesiastical law and hagiography. But they also maintained an interest in secular learning in Irish and were responsible for committing many stories and sagas to writing.[39]

The production of vellum manuscripts was expensive and therefore scriptoria were confined to the wealthy monasteries. However, waxed wooden tablets inscribed with a stylus were for more everyday use. Very few examples have survived, but an interesting 'book' of waxed wooden tablets was found near Springmount bog, Co. Antrim, in 1914. It is made up of six leaves of yew-wood each 210 mm (8¼ in) long, 75 mm (3 in) broad and approximately 4 mm (¼ in) thick, which were pierced and tied together with a leather thong and then bound with leather straps. It was also provided with a leather carrying strap. Each leaf, with the exception of the external faces of the two outer ones, had been hollowed out slightly on both sides leaving a margin round the edge and then waxed. The waxed surfaces were covered in writing which turned out to be Psalms 30, 31 and probably 32 and the script suggests that the tablets may date to the seventh century. Two other wooden writing tablets have recently come to light in Dublin, and iron or copper-alloy styli are also occasionally found as, for example, at Gransha and Armagh.[40]

Bibles and other religious books would have been brought to Ireland from Britain and the Continent by the earliest Christian missionaries and converts and were subsequently copied by Irish scribes. The earliest Insular manuscripts to have come down to us may be dated palaeographically to the late sixth and early seventh centuries. Some were written in Ireland but others are connected with Bobbio, an Irish foundation in northern Italy. The fragmentary Gospel Book, the Codex Usserianus Primus, is perhaps the oldest and the surviving decoration, which fills the bottom of the page between the end of St Luke's and the beginning of St Mark's Gospels, consists of a framed

*76 The Cathach of St Columba*
*(Dublin, Royal Irish Academy MS s.n., f. 40r;*
*courtesy of the Royal Irish Academy).*

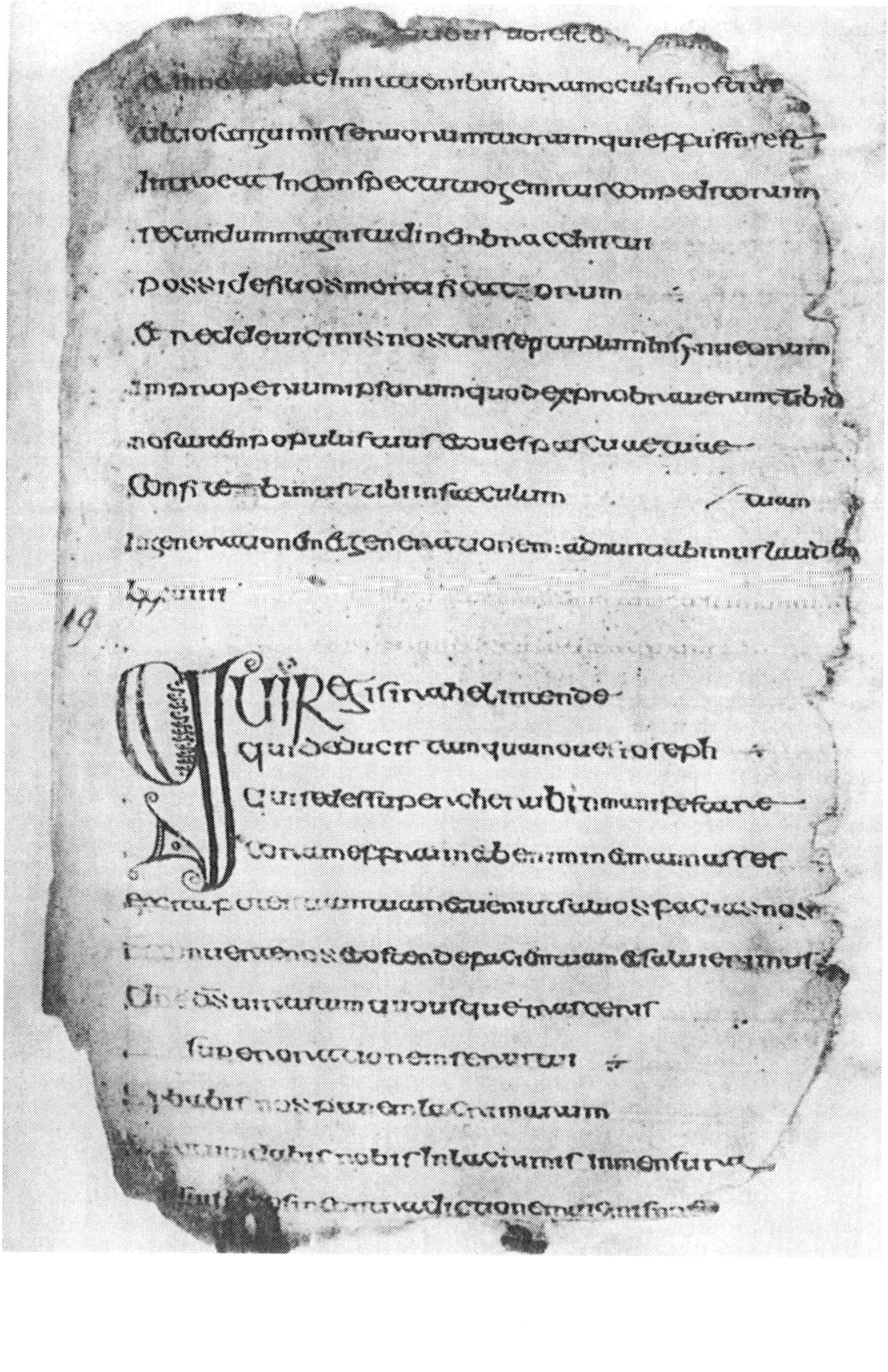

...uber...

de im... tuo ... anc oculis nostris

salus animarum nostrarum quiesppsit est

Introeat in conspectu tuo gemitum compeditorum

secundum magnitudinem brachii tui

posside filios mortificatorum

Et redde uicinis nostris septuplum in sinu eorum

improperium ipsorum quod exprobrauerunt tibi

nostram populus tuus Et oues pascuae tuae

Confitebimur tibi in saeculum · tuam

In generatione et generationem: adnuntiabimur laudem

tuam

19

**QVI** Regis israhel intende

qui deducis tamquam ouem ioseph

Qui sedes super cherubin manifestare

coram effraim beniamin et manasse

Excita potentiam tuam et ueni ut saluos facias nos

[deus] conuerte nos et ostende faciem tuam et salui erimus

[domine] deus uirtutum quousque irasceris

super orationem serui tui

[ci]babis nos pane lacrimarum

[et po]tum dabis nobis in lacrimis in mensura

[posu]isti nos in contradictionem uicinis nostris

cross with a chi-rho hook denoting the first two letters of Christ's name in Greek and the Greek letters alpha and omega. The character of the ornament is essentially Late Antique and shows no sign of Insular influence.

In contrast, the Cathach of St Columba, which is probably slightly later and more certainly written in Ireland, has distinctly Insular ornamental traits. The Cathach, which literally means the 'Battler', was carried in its precious Cumdach (see p. 146) at the head of the O'Donnell army as late as the fifteenth century. Its name also suggests a direct connection with St Columba, and while it is unlikely, though not impossible, that he wrote it, it has a definite link with the Columban monasteries. The Cathach is a psalter and the decoration consists of illuminated initials in black ink often outlined with orange dots at the beginning of each psalm (76). The initials have a much more fluid appearance than those in Late Antique manuscripts and, as well as Late Antique stylistic features such as crosses and dolphins, they are ornamented with Insular spirals, either used as terminals or forming parts of the letters themselves. The decoration has a tendency to break up the form of the initial and it is notable that the first letters of each psalm gradually become smaller until the size of the main script is reached. These features are both typical of later Insular manuscripts.[41]

The finest of the Insular illuminated manuscripts are approximately datable to the second half of the seventh, eighth and early ninth centuries, but only a handful may be dated with any precision and linked with specific scriptoria: for example, the Lindisfarne Gospels were written at Lindisfarne in the late seventh or early eighth centuries; the Book of Armagh was written at Armagh *c.*807; and the Gospels of Macregol were written at Birr, Co. Offaly, in the early ninth century.[42] Other manuscripts are fitted into a relative chronology around these on the basis of their layout, ornament, palaeography and Biblical text, as well as art-historical comparisons with ornamental metalwork and sculpture. Such a process is inevitably unsatisfactory and has led to considerable disagreement about the dating of specific manuscripts. Equally, the expansion of the Irish Church abroad in the second half of the sixth and the first half of the seventh centuries, and the development of the Insular art style on both sides of the Irish Sea make it impossible to connect most manuscripts with a particular scriptorium, or

even to say with any confidence whether they come from Ireland, Scotland or Northumbria. Some scholars, such as Henry, have tended to see many of the manuscripts as Irish or Ionan while others, such as E. Masai and T.J. Brown, have suggested that most were produced in Northumbria. These problems are intractable but the illuminated manuscripts which survive, mainly luxury Gospel Books and smaller pocket Gospel Books for everyday use, suggest the type of material available in Ireland during this period.

The fragmentary luxury Gospel Book Durham Cathedral Library MS A.II.10 is probably mid-seventh-century and is likely to have been written at Lindisfarne.[43] The ornament comprises a colophon at the end of St Matthew's Gospel consisting of three 'D' shapes reminiscent of architectural arches and columns decorated with simple interlace painted yellow and patterned with red dots and filled with red lettering, and, at the beginning of St Mark's Gospel, decorative initials with spirals and animals. It provides an important link between earlier manuscripts, such as the Codex Usserianus Primus and the Cathach, and the fully developed Insular manuscript style which is first witnessed in the Book of Durrow.[44] The Book of Durrow was at Durrow, Co. Offaly, a major monastery in the Columban federation, by the late eleventh or twelfth century, and the colophon also suggests a connection with a Columban foundation. It is a small luxury Gospel Book and, in contrast with the Codex Usserianus Primus and to a lesser extent Durham A.II.10, the ornament is mainly concentrated at the beginning of each Gospel. It consists of framed canon tables at the beginning of the manuscript, 'carpet pages', Evangelist-symbol pages, and illuminated initials. The major stylistic features, many of which appear to be experimental, may be illustrated by examining the carpet page (f.1ᵛ) at the beginning of the manuscript (77). Carpet pages, which may have their origins in Eastern Mediterranean exemplars, are so-called because they are patterned all over in the manner of an oriental carpet, and the most important element in the majority of examples is the cross symbol. Folio 1ᵛ is dominated by a double cross, and a closer look at the background of step-patterns and interlace indicates many other smaller crosses. In fact the page

77 *The Book of Durrow, cross-carpet page* (*Dublin, Trinity College Lib., A. 4. 5 (57), f.1ᵛ; courtesy of the Board of Trinity College Dublin*).

might be interpreted as a visual meditation on the cross symbol.[45] The page, and indeed the whole manuscript, are painted in brownish-black ink, red lead, yellow orpiment and green verdigris. The yellow double cross is set against a red, green and blackish-brown background and the frame is decorated with a wide variety of broad-band interlace. The effect of these colours, together with details of the design, is immediately to recall the techniques and motifs of ornamental metalworking, particularly enamelling and millefiori. But on the carpet page preceding St John's Gospel it is Anglo-Saxon, rather than Celtic metalworking motifs and techniques, which are most clearly evidenced since it is covered in processions of Germanic beasts reminiscent of those on the Sutton Hoo purse and shoulder clasps. Features of the Evangelist symbols, which have their ultimate origins in the Mediterranean, are also influenced by metal-working colours and techniques, and comparisons may also be made with the animals on the Pictish symbol stones.

The Book of Durrow was illuminated at a time when Insular artists were absorbing Germanic animal ornament into their repertoire of spirals, interlace, steps and frets, but the two were not yet integrated. At the same time, though Mediterranean models were available and incorporated into the manuscript, they were totally transformed by their contact with Insular motifs. Most scholars are agreed that the Book of Durrow was produced around 675, and a recently suggested alternative date early in the seventh century based on comparisons with motifs in Germanic metalwork[46] has received little support. However, there is no consensus about where the book was written. Those who emphasize the Anglo-Saxon elements in the manuscript have suggested it is Northumbrian and that Lindisfarne is the likely scriptorium, but the influence of enamelling and millefiori, as well as the Pictish comparisons, make Iona, which maintained close contacts with Lindisfarne, perhaps more likely. Equally, Columban foundations in Ireland, such as Derry and Durrow, cannot be ruled out assuming they had access to Anglo-Saxon designs and motifs.

The next generation of luxury Insular Gospel Books shows a greater complexity, and, where animal ornament is used, it is fully integrated with the abstract patterns. The manuscripts include the Lindisfarne Gospels, the Durham Gospels, the Echternach Gospels, and two fragments of the same manuscript: Cambridge Corpus Christi College MS

197B and London British Library Cotton MS Otho C.V.[47] These demonstrate considerable stylistic variety, though the illumination of Echternach and the two Gospel fragments is very similar. The late seventh- or early eighth-century date and the scriptorium of the Lindisfarne Gospels indicated by the colophon inscription added in the mid-tenth century are not in dispute, but the relationship of the other manuscripts to the Lindisfarne Gospels and to each other and the location of where they were written have caused very considerable controversy. The problems may be clearly illustrated by examining the Echternach Gospels, which show clear parallels with the Book of Durrow. The ornament consists of framed canon tables, Evangelist-symbol pages and illuminated initials. The St John Evangelist symbol (78), for example, is highly stylized. The delicately-drawn eagle is shown in profile with an identifying inscription above and below. The bird is outlined in orange with red and yellow spotted feathers and yellow highlights on its eye, beak, feet and tail. The curves of its body have been constructed with the aid of a compass or templates, while the rest of the page is filled with a simple framework of ruled lines outlined in scarlet. This manuscript comes from the monastery of Echternach in modern Luxembourg which was founded in 698 by the Anglo-Saxon missionary St Willibrord. It is possible, therefore, that the book was written there, but it may have been written before 698 in which case it could have come from Ireland since Willibrord's mission set out from there. Willibrord had previously lived in Ireland for 12 years, and it has recently been suggested that the Echternach Gospels could have been produced in the Hiberno-Saxon monastery of *Rath Melsigi*. On the other hand it has also been argued that, though they are visually very different, the Echternach Gospels and the Durham Gospels are by the same hand and that, since the latter is later glossed by the same hand that glossed the Lindisfarne Gospels, it is likely to have been produced at Lindisfarne and therefore the Echternach Gospels were written there too.[48] Such problems as these seem insuperable.

The Book of Kells[49] is the most complex of the

**78** *The Echternach Gospels, St John Evangelist-symbol page (Paris, Bibl. Nat., lat. 9389, f. 176ᵛ; copyright: Bibliothèque Nationale, Paris).*

Insular luxury Gospel Books. It is the work of several hands and the illumination is unfinished. The canon tables, which indicate where the same story is found in different gospels, are particularly intricately decorated and their format is changed more than once. However, the main ornamental emphasis is on their architectural layout, combining arches and columns with the constant repetition of winged Evangelist symbols shown in different combinations and poses and occasionally with mixed features: one example of the eagle of St John has the legs of the lion of St Mark which is not otherwise depicted on that page. The four-winged Evangelist symbols grouped round a cross are also found at the beginning of Matthew, Mark and John. Other decorated pages include a single carpet page; portraits of Christ and the Virgin and Child and a probable portrait of St Matthew; and two other miniatures, one of which depicts the arrest of Christ. In addition to the decoration of the letters at the beginning of each Gospel to such an extent that the opening words are barely detectable for ornament, much of the rest of the text is also illuminated: important passages are highlighted; naturalistic animals and birds, even human figures, creep between the lines; words terminate in delicate fronds of vegetation and initial letters are enlarged and twisted to form the bodies of lions and dragons.

The virtuosity of the illuminators of the Book of Kells may be illustrated with reference to the miniature on folio 202ᵛ (**79**). It is painted with a subtle palette of purple, red, yellow, orange, brown, green, turquoise, blue and black, though the colours of some of the decorated pages are much brighter and some are so vibrant they suggest the influence of metal-working. The page is framed with a quasi-architectural border. The columns are filled with delicate, thread-like interlace, and flying angels with books and chalices filled with trailing vines inhabit the upper corners. The miniature depicts a young bearded and haloed half-figure with a pair of flying angels above his head. He has a scroll in his left hand and to the right is a small black creature with wings. To the left is a group of figures and below is a structure with dragon finials reminiscent of a house-shaped shrine or wooden church. This has an opening in

which there is a second half-figure holding two flower-headed wands, and underneath are two groups of people shown in profile facing each other. At one level the most plausible explanation for this scene is that its upper half depicts Christ being tempted by the Devil to throw Himself from the top of the Temple in Jerusalem by saying that the angels will save Him and the lower half may show the Last Judgement. However, it has recently been suggested that the scene is more symbolic than narrative and that the upper half represents not only the Temptation but also the newly-baptized Christ full of the Holy Spirit reading Isaiah in the pulpit of the synagogue to an assembled congregation, the episode immediately after the Temptation. Indeed, recent research on the Book of Kells has tended to emphasize the symbolism of the decoration used: for example, the vines represent the Eucharist, while the peacocks and the snakes draw attention to the concepts of eternity and resurrection.[50]

The Book of Kells clearly demonstrates the next stage in the development of Insular illumination after manuscripts such as the Lindisfarne, Durham and Echternach Gospels. The range of decorated pages is broader, and we see the introduction of new types of ornament such as vine-scroll and anthropomorphic interlace. However, the date and provenance of the Book of Kells have provoked much debate. Brown has argued[51] for a mid-eighth-century date mainly on the basis of the palaeography, and for a Northumbrian or possibly Pictish provenance because of comparisons with the Lindisfarne Gospels and elements in Pictish art. However, it seems much more likely that the manuscript was illuminated in Iona because of close ornamental and iconographic parallels between the Book of Kells and the Ionan stone crosses. The manuscript was probably at Kells by the early eleventh century and was definitely there during the twelfth, and it has been persuasively suggested[52] that the book was begun at Iona in the late eighth century but never completed because of the disruption of the Viking raids with the resulting transfer of monks and possibly the manuscript to Kells in 807. Alternatively, some have argued[53] for a late eighth- or early ninth-century date because of the possible influence of Carolingian manuscript illumination but this connection remains unproven. Such a date implies the additional possibilities that either the manuscript was begun on Iona and continued in Kells or was written entirely at Kells. A late

eighth- or early ninth-century date is also suggested[54] by the close comparisons which may be made between the Evangelist symbols in the Book of Kells and those in the Book of Armagh.

Other luxury Gospel Books of likely Irish origin survived in the libraries of Irish foundations on the Continent. For example, St Gall Stiftsbibliothek Cod. 51 was at the library of St Gall in Switzerland by the thirteenth century. The ornament comprises Evangelist portraits, some accompanied by their symbols, and illuminated initial pages at the beginnings of the Gospels; a carpet page; the highlighting of the text of the genealogy of Christ; and two miniatures, the Crucifixion and the Last Judgement. Such a range is paralleled in the Book of Kells, but the execution is much simpler and the manuscript may therefore be earlier, perhaps dating from the second half of the eighth century. The fragmentary remains of the Turin Gospels, which were once at Bobbio, are also impressive. They consist of two carpet pages and two miniatures depicting the Ascension and the Second Coming and the manuscript is also known to have had decorative initials. The surviving ornament has a complexity comparable with the Book of Kells, though it is not so accomplished, and it is likely to be of a similar date.[55]

Probably the latest luxury Gospel Book to have come down to us from this period is the Gospels of Macregol.[56] This has received surprisingly little scholarly attention when it is realized that the colophon naming the scribe, Macregol, may be identified with the abbot of Birr who died in 822, thereby providing an approximate date and provenance for the manuscript. The decoration is made up of an Evangelist page and an initial page at the beginning of each Gospel. The St Mark Evangelist page (80) gives an indication of the ornament. It consists of an Evangelist portrait with the accompanying symbol of the lion flying above his head. St Mark, haloed and holding a book, is shown face on and seated, though the chair has been reduced to a few suggestive lines, and the striped drapery of his robe is also highly abstract. The portrait and symbol are flanked by vertical panels of ornament and surrounded by a heavy frame decorated with interlace, steps, frets and zoomorphic patterns. The decoration is very solid; it has none of the sophistication or complexity of the Book of Kells.

*80 The Gospels of Macregol, St Mark Evangelist page (Oxford, Bodl. Lib., MS. Auct. D. 2. 19, f. 51ᵛ; courtesy of the Bodleian Library, Oxford).*

Nevertheless the illumination is competently carried out and the simple colour scheme of orange, yellow, green, black and pinkish brown, together with their thick application, is reminiscent of enamelling.

At the same time as this series of luxury Gospel Books was being produced, other smaller, less impressive manuscripts were illuminated. For example, several pocket Gospel Books have been identified as Irish and may date to the second half of the eighth century. They include the Book of Mulling, which was probably written at St Mullins, Co. Carlow, and the Book of Dimma, which is associated with Roscrea, Co. Tipperary. The decoration usually consists of an Evangelist portrait and/or symbol page and illuminated text at the beginning of each gospel. In addition the Book of Armagh, which was written at Armagh *c.*807, is particularly interesting, not only because it can be both dated and provenanced by its colophon inscription, but also because it demonstrates a different style of illumination. The book is made up of various documents relating to St Patrick; a New Testament, which is decorated; and a Life of St Martin of Tours. The ornament of the New Testament is mainly in the form of elegant line drawings in black ink rather than paintings. It consists of winged Evangelist-symbol pages and a page with all four symbols, as well as illuminated initials, some of which are coloured. Other religious books may be exemplified by the Stowe Missal (a sacramentary) which contains small decorative initials. It has been dated to the late eighth century and was probably produced in the Irish Midlands, possibly at Lorrha or Terryglass, Co. Tipperary.[57]

Few Insular Irish illuminated manuscripts may be ascribed to the second half of the ninth, tenth or early eleventh centuries. The style of those which do survive appears to change little but is much less ambitious or accomplished. Indeed, no luxury illuminated manuscripts have come down to us from this period and it may be that there were insufficient resources to produce them. The impact of the Viking incursions on the native economy would have made the acquisition of large amounts of vellum much more difficult, and therefore the resources available would naturally have been concentrated on the production of books for everyday use. It is interesting to note that after the early tenth century the deaths of masters of scriptoria are rarely recorded in the annals and instead the obits of lectors or men of learning are noted. Furthermore, only the major monasteries of Clonmacnois and Armagh continue to record the obits of both scribes and lectors until the end of the century. This emphasis suggests a move away from transcription and illumination in all but the richest and most powerful monasteries.[58]

The Book of Macdurnan[59] demonstrates the continuing production of small illuminated Gospel Books. An inscription in the manuscript suggests that it was in the possession of Maelbrigte Macdurnan who became abbot of Armagh *c.*888 and died in 927. It was later given by the Anglo-Saxon King Athelstan (924-39) to Christ Church, Canterbury. Aspects of both the palaeography and the decoration suggest links with the Book of Armagh, and it is possible that it was produced in the Armagh scriptorium in the second half of the ninth century. The decoration is comparatively simple but surprisingly elegant. Colour – pinky-red, orange, yellow and green – with the addition of black and white, though applied thickly, is used sparingly and in some cases the emphasis is on drawn rather than painted ornament. The decoration opens with the four winged Evangelist symbols grouped round a cross which may be compared with representations in both the Book of Kells and the Book of Armagh. There are also four Evangelist portrait pages, though only St Mark appears to be accompanied by an Evangelist symbol, and decorative initials at the beginning of each Gospel. The ornament is separated into small panels of rather bulky interlace, zoomorphic patterns and delicately-drawn frets but there are no step patterns and few spirals. Such changes may be compared with ornamental metalwork of the late ninth and tenth centuries.

No early psalters of Irish origin have survived apart from the Cathach. However, it is possible to trace the development of Insular psalter illumination during the eighth century in the Durham Cassiodorus[60] which was written in Northumbria. The psalter is divided into three equal sections and a full-page miniature of David probably originally opened each. The two extant miniatures depict David playing the lyre and David the victor.

The same pattern of illumination is found in two later psalters of Irish origin. The British Library MS Cotton Vitellius F. XI was unfortunately severely damaged by fire. However, the remains of two miniatures and two pages with decorated borders and initials survive at the beginning of the sections and there are also

decorated initials at the beginning of each psalm. The two highly-stylized miniatures show David and the fallen Goliath and David playing the lyre surrounded by panelled borders of simple fret and interlace patterns. The former may be compared with a similar scene on the South Cross, Monasterboice (**86**) and the latter with a panel on the West Cross, Clonmacnois. These crosses may be dated by inscription to the late ninth and early tenth centuries and the manuscript, the lost colophon of which named an Irish scribe, may be of a similar date.

The Southampton Psalter, which is glossed in Irish, is rather later, and has been dated palaeographically to the second half of the tenth or early eleventh century. The layout of the ornament is very similar to that of the Cotton Psalter and there are three surviving miniatures at the beginning of the sections: David fighting the lion; the Crucifix-

81 *The Southampton Psalter, David and the fallen Goliath (Cambridge, St John's College, C. 9 (59), f. 51ᵛ; courtesy of the Master and Fellows of St John's College, Cambridge).*

ion; and David and the fallen Goliath. The last (**81**) is comparable with that in the Cotton Psalter and is painted in pinkish-purple, brown and yellow. The figures are extremely simple and stylized. David is on the left holding an animal-headed staff. On the right is the fallen Goliath shown upside-down with his hand held up to his eye to indicate that he has been hit by the stone. The figures are framed by small panels of frets and interlace. Similar borders with frets, interlace and animal ornament comparable with that on the 'Kells' crozier and the Soiscél Molaise are also found with decorative initials at the beginning of each section. Again, the absence of spirals and step patterns is notable. Some of the decorative initials in the text are made up of painted interlaced animals (**82a**), whilst others are finely executed in black ink with interlace knots and animal-headed terminals filled in or surrounded by paint (**82b**). Henry has termed these 'ribbon animal' and 'knotted wire' initials.[61]

Many more illuminated manuscripts have come down to us from the second half of the eleventh and twelfth centuries, but their decoration has received comparatively little attention.[62] The range of manuscripts is wider than in earlier periods, reflecting the broad interests of Irish ecclesiastical scholars of the day. Though religious books, such as small Gospel Books, psalters, missals and hymn books, are still in the majority, books for teaching and compilations in Latin, and increasingly Irish, are also found, including chronicles, annals, genealogies, sagas, and poetry. Some of these manuscripts may be dated and provenanced either by their colophons or by other pieces of information contained within them. The Chronicle of Marianus of Mainz was written by an Irish scribe at Mainz in 1072–3 and another manuscript of the Epistles of St Paul, which has some echoes of Irish ornament, was written in Regensburg in 1079. The Book of the Dun Cow (*Lebor na hUidre*), a compilation by several hands, is of late eleventh- or early twelfth-century date and is associated with Clonmacnois. The Gospel Book, British Library Harley MS 1802, was written in

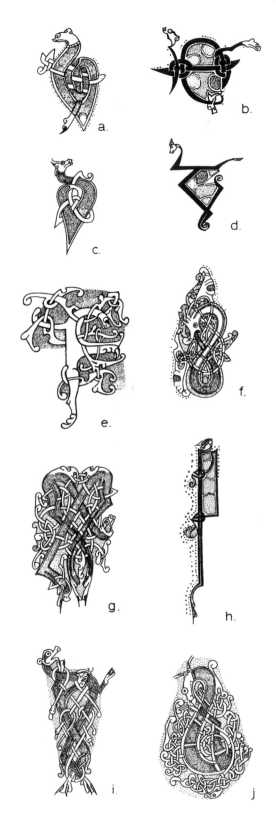

**82** *Decorated initials from Irish illuminated manuscripts, late tenth to twelfth centuries:* **a, b.** *Southampton Psalter;* **c, d.** *Book of the Dun Cow;* **e.** *Chronicle of Marianus of Mainz;* **f.** *Liber Hymnorum;* **g, h.** *London, British Library Harley MS 1802;* **i.** *Corpus Missal;* **j.** *Corpus Gospels (not to scale).*

Armagh in 1138 and The Book of Leinster was compiled c.1151–61 at Terryglass. These manuscripts provide a chronological framework to which others may be related.

These manuscripts are seldom lavishly decorated, though the ornament is usually competently executed and, where the vivid colours preserve their brightness, some of the original impact is still evident. Much of the ornament, mainly initials decorated with interlace, zoomorphic, and even spiral patterns, and occasionally full-page illustrations in the form of Evangelist-symbol pages in the Gospel Books, demonstrate the survival, and in some cases the revival of traditional Insular manuscript illumination. However, in some manuscripts, like the ornamental metalwork, it is also possible to trace the influence of Scandinavian art styles, Ringerike and Urnes, though the motifs are not in a pure form but have become mixed with Insular ornament and adapted to native taste. Occasionally Continental influences are also detectable. These may have reached Ireland from Irish foundations in Germany and Cistercian houses in France, or as a result of more general ecclesiastical contacts between Ireland, England and the Continent.

A brief examination of some of the decorative initials will enable us to trace the main developments in Insular Irish manuscript illumination during the second half of the eleventh and twelfth centuries. As we have already seen in the Southampton Psalter, two different types of decorative initial were in use during the tenth and early eleventh centuries. These have their origins in earlier Insular manuscripts and remain a characteristic feature. To begin with there is a group of late eleventh- and early twelfth-century manuscripts where the decoration is very conservative and shows no sign of outside influence. Several of these manuscripts were produced in major Irish monasteries, such as Clonmacnois, Glendalough and Armagh, and this suggests that their scriptoria were steeped in tradition. For example, in the Book of the Dun Cow, which was written at Clonmacnois in the late eleventh or early twelfth century, the ornament mainly consists of decorative initials; the majority are of knotted-wire type (82d) but ribbon-animal examples are also represented (82c). Another manuscript, a small incomplete Gospel Book, British Library Harley MS 1023, which may be of early twelfth-century date and was almost certainly written at Armagh, seems to be a conscious revival of an earlier style

of illumination. Both the knotted-wire initials and the two surviving Evangelist-symbol pages demonstrate clear analogies with the elegant drawings of the Book of Armagh, and the artist may have drawn upon these as his model.

However, at the same time, and perhaps in the same scriptoria, some illuminators were beginning to be influenced by Scandinavian Ringerike patterns filtering in via Dublin. The earliest datable manuscript to show such traits is the Chronicle of Marianus of Mainz written in Germany by an Irish scribe in 1072–3. The initials are almost all of ribbon-animal type, and the animals portrayed are essentially Insular, but they are enmeshed in foliate tendrils and their head lappets and tails sprout foliate terminals (82e). This foliage shows clear signs of Scandinavian Ringerike influence which has been adapted to native taste. Other Irish manuscripts of probable late eleventh- or early twelfth-century date demonstrate similar features. For example, the Liber Hymnorum, a hymn book now in Trinity College Dublin, which may be dated palaeographically to the second half of the eleventh century, is ornamented with decorative initials in once-brilliant colours: red, yellow, green and purple. Most of the initials are of ribbon-animal type and again a mixture of native animal ornament and Ringerike-influenced foliage is evident (82f).

The small Gospel Book, British Library Harley MS 1802, is particularly interesting, not only because it can be closely dated and provenanced – it was written in Armagh in 1138 – but also because it shows a mixture of the very traditional with Ringerike-inspired foliate elements. The knotted-wire initials (82h) are highly conservative while the ribbon-animal initials incorporate a mass of interlacing foliate strands (82g). The two surviving Evangelist-symbol pages, though rather crudely executed, would not look out of place in a much earlier period but for the fact that the tail of the lion of St Mark terminates in a foliate flourish.

The influence of Scandinavian Urnes ornament may also be detected in some manuscripts. The decoration of the Corpus Missal consists of elaborate, brightly coloured initials incorporating Scandinavian Urnes style beast-and-snake motifs but again the patterns have been moulded to native taste (82i). They are much more symmetrical than their Scandinavian counterparts and diagonals are an essential part of the composition. The beasts are less elongated and retain many of their Insular characteristics.[63] The designs in the

Corpus Missal have been compared with those in metalwork, for example the Cross of Cong (1123–36) and St Manchan's shrine (75), and it is possible that manuscript illuminators were influenced by developments in ornamental metalworking. The date and provenance of the Corpus Missal are problematic. Henry and Marsh-Micheli have suggested that it may have a similar date and provenance to the Cross of Cong: but a study of details in the text led Gwynn to suggest it was written in Armagh, though his late twelfth-century dating of the manuscript cannot be accepted on the basis of the ornament.[64] In the Corpus Gospels we can again recognize a curious mixture of highly traditional ornament, for example a chi-rho initial decorated with interlace and spirals reminiscent of seventh- and eighth-century manuscripts, and Urnes-inspired initials (82j) which have become so stylized that they have lost almost every characteristic of their original models. However, Continental influence is also recognizable in the script and canon tables. There are indications that the manuscript was perhaps written in the mid-twelfth century at Bangor, Co. Down, where St Malachy was bishop from 1137 to 1148 and where therefore the advent of such Continental influence is to be expected.

## Stone sculpture

The early medieval crosses (often known as high crosses) are well-known, but a wide variety of other stone sculpture is also found on early ecclesiastical sites all over Ireland. It includes decorated ogham stones, carved stone pillars, cross-inscribed grave markers, and recumbent graveslabs, but remarkably little architectural sculpture before the twelfth century. However, this is probably only a small fraction of the sculpture produced. Though almost none is extant, there are hints that wood-carving was popular (see pp. 77, 186) and, indeed, wood is much easier to fashion. A rare surviving example is an interlace-decorated boss which came to light in Dublin. Analogies with stone sculpture suggest that this may originally have been a boss attached to a wooden cross.[65]

The origins of Christian sculpture in Ireland may be traced back to the ogham stones (see p. 103). Some of these are merely rough pillars and boulders reminiscent of prehistoric standing stones, whilst others are more carefully-shaped, suggesting the influence of Roman milestones or tombstones. Some 14 per cent are decorated with one or more incised crosses in a variety of forms, inspired by crosses on portable objects such as manuscripts or A ware imported pottery. The cross symbol remains the most important feature of Irish stone sculpture throughout the early middle ages.[66]

A variety of other cross-carved stones and pillars are also early monuments but they have received comparatively little attention.[67] They are concentrated along the western seaboard of Ireland from Donegal to Kerry and are often found on otherwise obscure ecclesiastical sites. It is unclear why there are so few further east, although it is possible that in these areas similar monuments could have been fashioned from wood. These stones and pillars served a number of different functions. Some are grave markers but others may have been set up within or around an ecclesiastical site to act as a focus for worship or to mark out an area of sanctuary. Inscriptions indicate that some are dedicated to apostles or saints; others may have been set up to commemorate events. But some have no apparent connection with ecclesiastical sites; they may have been set up beside routeways or on boundaries, but their precise function is obscure.

Perhaps the main reason why such monuments have been so little studied is because they are very difficult to date. Occasionally inscriptions provide a key, as on the pillar at Kilnasaggart, Co. Armagh, which may be dated to c.700.[68] But in most cases the ornament and the typology of the cross symbol are the only clues to dating. These can provide an indication and suggest that some stones are early, perhaps spanning the sixth to eighth centuries, but at present insufficient research has been carried out to attempt the reconstruction of a relative chronology. Furthermore, much of the decoration is simple and there is a tendency to equate simple with early, but this may be misleading. Similarly, on some sites, such as Reask, a group of monuments may have been executed over a fairly short space of time but on others, such as Inishmurray, they may span several centuries. It should also be remembered that freestanding crosses are found in western Ireland only towards the end of the period, and therefore simpler cross-carved stones and pillars may have fulfilled the functions of a cross in areas where the stone was unsuitable, or where resources were insufficient for more major sculptural projects.

Studies of groups of cross-carved stones and pillars from specific sites or regions together with research on particular motifs has revealed that, while many of the same designs occur in widely-separated areas along the western seaboard, there are distinctive local variations. Models for cross symbols and associated Christian motifs were probably introduced into Ireland on portable objects from Britain, the Continent and the Mediterranean, and these were sometimes mixed with native ornament such as spirals. Some early stones are decorated with a form of the chi-rho symbol representing the first two letters of Christ's name in Greek combined with a cross. These are known as 'monogram' chi-rhos. For example, the stone at Drumaqueran, Co. Antrim, which is not associated with any known ecclesiastical site, is

83 *Cross-carved stones, pillars and recumbent graveslabs:*
**a.** *Drumaqueran, Co. Antrim (after Hamlin 1972);*
**b.** *Loher, Co. Kerry (not to scale);* **c.** *Reask, Co. Kerry (after Fanning 1981a);* **d–f.** *grave-slabs, Clonmacnois, Co. Offaly (after Macalister 1909).*

decorated on both sides with a 'monogram' chi-rho (**83a**), but one is a mirror image, suggesting that the sculptor may not have entirely understood his model, which could perhaps have been in the form of engraved glass or a signet ring which might be viewed in more than one direction. A small metalwork cross with pendant alpha and omega symbols may be the ultimate model for the design on the pillar from Loher, Co. Kerry (**83b**). At Reask (**83c**) a large slab, which appears to mark the edge of the cemetery, is carved with an encircled Maltese cross of arcs with a stem reminiscent of a *flabellum* or liturgical fan. The interstices between the cross arms and the stem are ornamented with simple spiral patterns. The decoration, together with the inscription DNE (DOMINE), an invocation to God, suggest a sixth- or seventh-century date.[69]

Large freestanding stone crosses evolved in Britain and Ireland during the course of the eighth century, but their origins are obscure. There are no known parallels elsewhere in Europe and the superficial resemblance of carvings of fifth- to seventh-century date in Armenia and Georgia[70] is

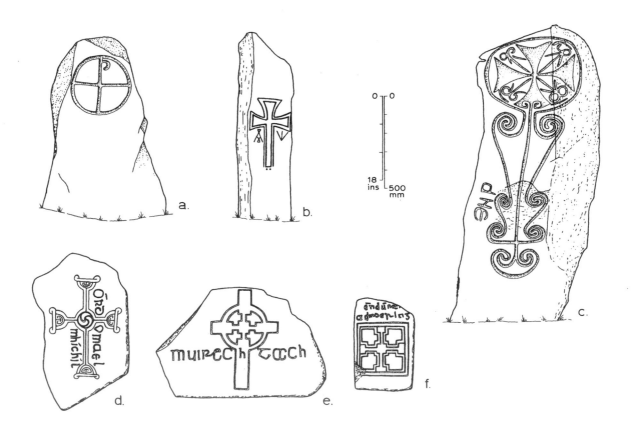

probably purely fortuitous. Henry suggested[71] that in Ireland the antecedents of the cross may be traced back to a series of upright slabs and pillars of increasing monumentality and elaborateness which she dated to the late seventh and early eighth centuries. However, though they are linked by their slab or pillar shape and incised or low-relief ornament, they do not form a coherent group. Indeed, many are from the north-west, where the freestanding crosses are few and late, and therefore they may be the contemporary equivalents of freestanding crosses rather than their forerunners. For example, that at Carndonagh, Co. Donegal, a simple freestanding slab cross carved with a Crucifixion scene, has now been re-dated to the ninth or tenth centuries and, though some would continue to date the cross slab at Fahan Mura, Co. Donegal, to the late seventh or eighth centuries, others would regard it as contemporary with Carndonagh. In this light the origins of Irish crosses become more difficult to ascertain because of the apparent lack of antecedents in the areas where they are found.[72]

Instead the origins of the freestanding cross in Ireland must be sought in a variety of other factors which combined to produce the final monumental result. First, it is worth emphasizing the importance of the cross symbol in every aspect of Insular Christian art and ecclesiastical writing. It was a sign of victory and a sign of protection. The importance of the cross symbol in Britain and Ireland stemmed from the growing cult of the cross in the Middle East. The pilgrim Arculf, who visited the Holy Land and Constantinople in the 680s, and was later shipwrecked on Iona where he described what he had seen to Adomnán, provides vital evidence of this cult, mentioning, for instance, a tall wooden cross set up over the place where Christ was baptized and a silver cross on the site of Christ's Crucifixion at Golgotha. Tales of crosses such as these together with portable representations may have provided the inspiration for the production of both wooden and metal crosses in Britain and Ireland. For example, in his *Life of Columba* written c.688–92 Adomnán describes a cross set up in a millstone at Iona which was still extant in his own day. The small hole in the centre of a millstone could only have supported a slender wooden cross. It is also interesting to note that the freestanding stone crosses at Iona, which may be dated to the second half of the eighth century, demonstrate the influence of carpentry techniques. The manufacture of metalwork

crosses in Ireland has already been mentioned, and the influence of metal-working techniques on crosses such as those at Ahenny, Co. Tipperary, is indisputable (see below).

It has been suggested[73] that the evolution of the freestanding stone cross in Ireland and Northumbria was a parallel development. But, as we have seen, in Ireland the sculptural antecedents of the freestanding stone cross are unclear and ecclesiastical stone architecture was still a novelty (see p. 124). Therefore, from where did the Irish gain the knowledge necessary to carve these monumental blocks of stone? The answer may lie in the established links between the Irish Church and those in Dalriada, Pictland and Northumbria. Bede tells us that Benedict Biscop sought the assistance of Gaulish masons to build the monastery at Monkwearmouth in 674 and it is from this period that the Northumbrian stone sculpture stems. The skills of Northumbrian stone masons were requested by King Nechtan of the Picts c.710. The monastery at Iona maintained close contacts with both Ireland and Northumbria and the stone crosses there appear experimental in both form and ornament as well as showing some close Northumbrian parallels. It should also be noted that the decoration on the early Northumbrian crosses, mainly Scriptural iconography and vine-scroll, is not primarily Insular but imported. In contrast the ornament on the early crosses and related sculpture in Scotland and Ireland demonstrates the adaptation of essentially Insular ornament to a new medium. The knowledge of how to fashion large blocks of stone which was available in Northumbria combined with the innovative ornamental repertoire would therefore suggest that Northumbria may have been the initiator of the freestanding cross series, and Scotland and Ireland the receivers.[74]

Once established, the cross remained the most important form of stone sculpture in Ireland until the mid-twelfth century, but it has proved surprisingly difficult to establish an agreed chronology for these monuments despite the fact that a small number can be reliably dated by inscription. Henry suggested[75] on the basis of art-historical comparison combined with dating by inscription where available that the earliest Irish crosses are of eighth-century date. These are dominated by Insular ornament rather than figural representation. However, during the course of the ninth century panels depicting episodes from the Bible, probably inspired by Carolingian models, become increasingly important at the expense of the Insular patterns, culminating in the early tenth-century crosses which are dominated by complex cycles of Scriptural iconography. Finally, there is a revival of interest in the freestanding cross form at the end of the eleventh and the first half of the twelfth centuries, when the decoration is mainly characterized by high-relief figures and Urnes-influenced ornament. While most crosses remain difficult to date precisely and there continues to be considerable disagreement about some monuments, most scholars would agree with the main framework of Henry's chronology and this has recently been backed up by further work on the inscriptions.[76]

However, Harbison has espoused the theory that Irish crosses are much more heavily indebted to Carolingian influence and because of this suggested that both the figural and ornamental monuments are largely datable to the second quarter of the ninth century.[77] But, though the influence of Carolingian iconography on some of the figural scenes is not in doubt, it seems unlikely that crosses with such widely differing ornament could have been carved in such a short space of time and occasionally on the same site. Harbison has suggested that the stone crosses may be seen as a response to Viking raids because they were less easily destroyed. However, the production of monuments on this scale would have required considerable time and resources and the evolution of the freestanding cross is far more likely to have taken place in the comparatively settled environment of the eighth century than in the second quarter of the ninth when Viking raids were rapidly reaching a crescendo. Harbison's dating of the crosses with Insular ornament to this period has also necessitated his redating of Insular metalwork, such as the Ardagh chalice, normally ascribed to the eighth century, to the early ninth. In the light of our increasing understanding of the changing style of Irish metalwork during the ninth century (see p. 142), this seems unlikely.

The functions of the Irish crosses may have been complex[78] and they are only partially understood. In one sense they were visible signs of the glory of God, but they were also much more than this. They were set up within and around the ecclesiastical enclosure, particularly at gateways and in the courtyard to the west of the principal church, as a symbol of power and protection, and were used to demarcate the *termon* or area of sanctuary. They demonstrate not only the strength of the Church but also, through some of the inscriptions, the combined power and patronage of Church and state. They even came to act as a focus for the markets held in the vicinity of the larger monasteries. However, these crosses were also objects of devotion and meditation, confession and penitence and it is becoming increasingly clear that they played their part in the liturgy; they may have acted as stations for processions or possibly as a place where Mass was said.

The crosses range in height from approximately 2.5–7m (8–23ft). In the majority the crosshead and shaft are carved from a single block of stone. The crosshead is often topped by a capstone in a variety of designs: conical, roof-shaped or resembling a house-shaped shrine or church. The crosses are characterized by a ring encircling the head. This is almost certainly ultimately derived from the chi-rho symbol surrounded by a wreath but it also has a structural function. The heads of the Irish crosses are much larger than their Northumbrian counterparts and the ring would have given vital stability to the monument. At Iona there is evidence that St John's Cross was originally erected without a ring which was only added after an early fall.[79] There is often a step at the bottom of the shaft and, if the cross has an inscription, it is usually placed here. The base is almost always the shape of a truncated pyramid, sometimes stepped, but a couple of examples are round.

Two early groups of crosses and related sculpture from the Irish Midlands may be dated on art-historical grounds to the second half of the eighth and early ninth centuries. One cross, at Bealin, Co. Westmeath, which may originally have come from Clonmacnois, may be approximately datable by inscription. The inscription in Irish asks passers-by to pray for Tuathgal who set up the cross. The obit of an abbot of Clonmacnois named Tuathgal, not a common name, is recorded in the annals in 811.[80] This cross may be grouped with a number of other shafts concentrated on Clonmacnois. There is a second group of crosses, mainly from Ahenny, Co. Tipperary, and Kilkieran, Co. Kilkenny, in the southern part of the kingdom of Ossory, but also with outliers further north. It is interesting to note that at this stage a variety of monument types are represented, suggesting some experimentation, not only crosses but shafts of various sizes and at Gallen Priory, Co. Offaly, there is a slab reminiscent of those in Pictland. The decorative emphasis with all these monu-

also found but they play a subordinate role. The comparisons with manuscript illumination are particularly clear amongst the Clonmacnois monuments; those with metalwork amongst the Ossory crosses. Important parallels may also be made with sculpture in Pictland and Dalriada but, interestingly, comparisons with Anglo-Saxon sculpture are few.[81]

These early crosses may be exemplified by that at Ahenny North (84) which is extremely well-preserved. The style of the ornament may be understood immediately if it is realized that this is essentially a metalwork cross translated into stone. The original model was probably a wooden cross covered with metal sheets. The cabled mouldings resemble metalwork bindings and the bosses glass or enamelled studs which, in the model, would have hidden the rivets which attached the metal sheets to the wooden core. The sharp-cut spiral, interlace and fret patterns emulate cast chip-carved ornament. Originally it may even have been painted to give the impression of a great golden cross studded with glass and enamel insets. In contrast the figural panels depicting Biblical scenes and ecclesiastical processions are confined to the base and are carved in low relief. That on the west face probably shows Christ's mission to the Apostles and may be compared with similar scenes on Late Antique sarcophagi.

A number of crosses may be identified as stylistically transitional between those decorated with Insular patterns and those where Scriptural iconography predominates. During the first half of the ninth century we can trace the beginnings of this transition in the Midlands on the two closely-related crosses at Kilree and Killamery, Co. Kilkenny, and on the South Cross, Clonmacnois,[82] where the decoration is still predominantly Insular ornament, but where small figural scenes in very low relief are depicted on the crosshead and at the top of the shaft. These changes may in part reflect developments further north in the Boyne Valley where crosses with a larger number of figural representations were beginning to be produced. The South Cross, Kells[83] is of key importance in this transitory phase. In the centre of the crosshead on the west face (85) is Christ in Majesty surrounded by the four Evangelist symbols, with Matthew holding up the Lamb of God enclosed in a circle representing a wreath. Below is the Crucifixion. Its position at the top of the shaft is paralleled on examples at Killamery and Clonmacnois South but this scene is more

**84** *The North Cross, Ahenny, Co. Tipperary, west face (Photograph: author).*

ments is overwhelmingly on Insular ornament: interlace, spirals, frets, step-patterns, zoomorphic, and anthropomorphic motifs. Depictions of fantastic beasts, hunting scenes, ecclesiastical processions and some Scriptural iconography are

**85** *The South Cross, Kells, Co. Meath, west face (Courtesy of the Commissioners of Public Works, Ireland).*

usually found on the crosshead and it is likely that these crosses were produced at a time before the position of the Crucifixion became fixed. Christ, young and beardless, is clad in a knee-length tunic. Below His arms are the spear and sponge bearers, the latter holding up a cup as is usual in Insular representations rather than a sponge. The figures above possibly represent the sun and moon, details which may have been adopted from some Carolingian model, perhaps a manuscript or ivory. The appearance of the Crucifixion on the Irish crosses probably reflects the growing interest in Christ's Passion and Crucifixion on the Carolingian Continent from the early ninth century onwards. On the base is a procession of two horsemen, a dog, and a chariot, but the cross arms and bottom of the shaft are decorated with Insular patterns. The bossed spirals on the cross arms are paralleled on sculpture in Pictland and Dalriada, a link to be expected in the light of the close contacts between Kells and Iona. At the bottom of the shaft are bands of interlace and fret patterns with anthropomorphic interlace set between them. The other faces show a similar mixture of figural iconography and Insular patterns – there is even a rare example of inhabited vine-scroll comparable with representations on Anglo-Saxon sculpture and in the Book of Kells – but the cross shows little of the careful organization witnessed on the crosses where Scriptural scenes predominate. On the Market Cross, Kells, the Crucifixion, which shows the Carolingian type of Christ in a loincloth rather than a tunic, is placed on the west side of the crosshead, the iconographic episodes on the shaft are divided into separate panels and the Insular ornament is confined to insignificant parts of the monument.

Other local groups of crosses appear to reflect these slightly later developments. For example, the more simply-carved granite crosses of the Barrow Valley, such as those at Castledermot North and South, display many of the same iconographic episodes as the South and Market Crosses, Kells. The Crucifixions are placed on the crossheads and the shafts are characteristically divided into panels. The granite cross at Moone, Co. Kildare, is more difficult to place but, since the iconography again shows the influence of the Kells crosses, it is not as early as the late eighth-century date suggested by Henry.[84] In the Midlands crosses at Kinnitty and Tihilly, Co. Offaly, make considerable use of Insular ornament found on other stylistically earlier crosses in the locality but at the same time incorporate new ideas, in all likelihood emanating from Kells, in the form of figural iconography including the Carolingian Crucifixion type placed on the crosshead. Inscriptions on the cross at Kinnitty have recently been read for the first time and provide important dating evidence. They ask us to pray for King Máelsechnaill son of Maelrúanaid and for Colmán 'who made this cross for the King of Ireland'. Though Colmán might be the sculptor, the name is more likely to refer to the abbot of Kinnitty. Máelsechnaill was king of the Southern Uí Néill from 846 to 862 and therefore the cross must have been carved during this period.[85]

By the beginning of the tenth century crosses with predominantly figural iconography had become the norm and the range of Scriptural scenes was becoming more complex. Crosses which belong to this phase include those at Monasterboice South, Co. Louth, the fragmentary Market Cross at Armagh, Clonmacnois West, and Durrow. One, and very possibly two, of these may be dated by inscription. Recent meticulous work has resulted in the recovery of reliable readings of the fragmentary inscriptions on Clonmacnois West.[86] They ask for prayers for King Flann and Colmán who made the cross for him. The Flann concerned, who was king of the Southern Uí Néill from 879 to 916, was the son of the Máelsechnaill commemorated on the cross at Kinnitty. Colmán may probably be identified with the abbot of Clonmacnois c.904–21. If this is so, the cross may be dated c.904–16. As we have seen, the annals record that Abbot Colmán and King Flann erected a great stone church at Clonmacnois in 908. The carving of the cross could have been part of the same building programme and the two figures at the shaft base (36 right) on the east face may well represent King Flann and Abbot Colmán planting a rod in the ground, thereby symbolizing a pact between Church and state.[86] The inscription on Monasterboice South asks for a prayer for Muiredach. The lack of patronym or title means that the identification cannot be proven but, if the dating of Clonmacnois West is taken into account, the most likely candidate is Muiredach the abbot of Monasterboice who died in 924. He was also vice-abbot of Armagh and chief steward of the Southern Uí Néill, and was therefore important in both secular and ecclesiastical society.[87]

A glance at the example of Monasterboice South[88] gives an indication of the complexity of the iconography. The detail of the figures is well-preserved and they have a vivacious quality not generally paralleled elsewhere. The crosshead on the east face (86) is dominated by a complicated representation of the Last Judgement. Christ is in the centre. Above His head is a bird possibly repre-

86 *The South Cross, Monasterboice, Co. Louth, east face (Courtesy of the Commissioners of Public Works, Ireland).*

senting the Holy Spirit and the figure flanked by angels above that may be God the Father; this scene may therefore be a representation of the Trinity. To the left of Christ is David playing the lyre. The bird perched on top of the lyre symbolizes the inspiration of God helping him to compose the psalms. Below him there is possibly an accompanying dancer and to the right of Christ an accompanying musician plays the pipes. Below Christ's feet is St Michael weighing a soul on a balance and underneath a little devil is attempting to interfere with it. On the right cross arm a second devil with a pitchfork follows the damned off to Hell while on the left an angel blows a trumpet. Behind him are the massed ranks of the saved. The panels on the shaft show from top to bottom: the adoration of the Magi; Moses striking the rock; King Saul and David with his staff and sling, then the dead Goliath and the victorious David; Eve offering Adam the fruit of the Tree of Knowledge and Cain killing Abel with the jawbone of a camel; finally a lively depiction of two cats playing. The carvings on the base consist of signs of the zodiac and interlace.

The details of many of the figures carved on this cross are essentially Irish. For example, in the arrest scene on the west face Christ wears a penannular brooch while the soldiers sport Celtic moustaches and are armed with Viking swords. But the sculptor undoubtedly used outside models which he adapted to native taste. Precise parallels are often difficult to locate but many of the scenes, for example those from the Passion Cycle, were probably inspired by Carolingian iconography perhaps on ivories or in manuscripts. Other episodes, such as the murder of Abel, are found in Late Antique art. It is interesting to note that there are no surviving examples of the depiction of the Last Judgement outside the Insular milieu before the Romanesque period. However, it is clear from a study of the literature that Irish churchmen had an interest in the Day of Judgement. For example, a vision in the late eleventh- or early twelfth-century Book of the Dun Cow describes Heaven and Hell, the rewards of the righteous and the torments of the damned. The Last Judgement on Monasterboice South has a patchwork appearance and it could have been put together from a number of different sources. The robed Christ may be compared with the figure of Christ in Majesty on the South Cross, Kells. The David iconography was probably culled from psalters while the little devils are reminiscent of the figure on the Temptation page (79) in the Book of Kells. The crowds of the saved and the damned may be compared with related scenes in other Insular manuscripts, such as the Turin Gospels.[89]

Recent research is beginning to make us more aware of both the Scriptural iconography and the Insular patterns, not merely in terms of their identification and comparison, but also in terms of their liturgical symbolism and the relationship this may have had to the overall layout of the crosses. Flower realized long ago that grouped sculptural representations of episodes such as Adam and Eve, the Sacrifice of Isaac, and Daniel in the Lions' Den, which he identified as the 'Help of God' cycle, recalled verses in prayers said for the dying and these were also used when calling upon God for protection against evil. But the liturgical symbolism of the crosses may be much more complex and individual scenes may have a variety of different meanings. Indeed, Ó Carragáin has suggested that they are monuments of considerable theological sophistication. For example, the iconography indicates a deep interest in the liturgy of the Mass and the Passion, and there is a preoccupation with Scriptural history and the relationship of Old and New Testament episodes. On the South Cross, Kells, for instance, there are sufficient iconographic allusions to the Eucharist for Ó Carragáin to suggest that Mass may have been said in front of the west face of the cross.[90]

It is possible to trace a further development on some of the figural crosses of the Boyne Valley and Ulster. Crosses such as Monasterboice West, Arboe, Co. Tyrone, and the fragmentary West Cross, Kells are taller and more slender. Where the crosshead survives it is carved from a separate block of stone. The shaft panels increase to as many as six and there is a junction or ornamental collar at or near the top of the shaft. The iconography may be compared with Monasterboice South but the scenes are frequently much abbreviated. There are also several other crosses with figural iconography in Ulster but they have received comparatively little attention probably because of their rather fragmentary state which makes their carvings sometimes difficult to identify.[91]

It is unknown for how long the carving of these figural crosses continued. Indeed, few crosses have been associated with the eleventh century[92] and on present evidence it seems possible that the practice of erecting stone crosses died out altogether for a time, though why this may have happened is unclear. Alternatively, it may have been transferred to and kept alive in the west, for it is here that we find a major revival in cross-carving datable to the end of the eleventh and the first half of the twelfth centuries.[93] Though a few crosses were erected in the Midlands during this period, and there is also one at Glendalough, the majority are found in Clare, Galway and Aran. Where inscriptions survive it is again possible to trace the patronage of both kings and important clerics. At Inishcaltra, Co. Clare, the inscription asks for a prayer for Cathasach, chief senior of Ireland. This is thought to refer to an ecclesiastic from Armagh who died in 1111. At Tuam, Co. Galway, the carving of two crosses may be linked with King Turlough O'Connor of Connacht (1106–56) and the abbot of Tuam, Aed O'Oissín (1128–56). The crosses may therefore be dated to between 1128 and 1156 and are both likely to have been carved before 1152 when Aed O'Oissín became Archbishop since this title is not mentioned in the inscriptions. The carving of the crosses at Tuam is connected with a larger building programme patronized by Turlough O'Connor, including the remodelling of the ecclesiastical enclosure in 1127 and the replacement of the native monastery with an Augustinian priory in 1140. Indeed, the crosses are evidence of the ambitions which Turlough O'Connor and Aed O'Oissín had for Tuam in the twelfth-century ecclesiastical reform. These were realized in the Synod of Kells in 1152 when Tuam became an archbishopric. Other crosses carved during this period also hint at the ambitions of particular ecclesiastical foundations to become bishoprics. A third crosshead fragment from Tuam and crosses at Kilfenora and Dysert O Dea, Co. Clare, Cashel and probably Roscrea, Co. Tipperary, all have figures of bishops carved upon them.

Some of the major stylistic elements on these monuments may be seen on the cross at Dysert O Dea (87) which has now been re-erected on an additional rectangular base. Some of the crosses in this period retain a ring but on Dysert O Dea the small size of the crosshead makes a ring unnecessary. The beading round the perimeter may recall a metalwork model. The west face of the crosshead is dominated by a Crucifixion figure in high relief. In this period the Carolingian model of Christ Crucified has been abandoned and replaced either, as at Dysert O Dea, with a figure in a long belted robe comparable with the Lucca Crucifix in northern Italy or, as on the third cross fragment at Tuam and at Glendalough, with a crowned figure in a loincloth, His head is tilted, comparable with those on Irish twelfth-century metal crucifixes.[94] The bishop below has some features in common with the figures on St Manchan's shrine (75). His mitre is of a type which was coming into use during the twelfth century and his crozier with its

87 *The cross at Dysert O Dea Co. Clare, west face (Courtesy of the Commissioners of Public Works, Ireland).*

spiralled crook is of a Continental type. Both features demonstrate the influence of the ecclesiastical reform movement. The hole where his right hand should be indicates that a carved hand, presumably in the act of benediction, was attached by means of a mortice-and-tenon joint. Such attachments are relatively common on crosses in this period and enabled the addition of extra figures and other features carved in the round to the cross form. The ornament on the west face of the base is interlace of a traditional type but some of the other patterns such as the foliage are similar to those found on Hiberno-Romanesque architecture. Scenes on the other faces of the base include Adam and Eve, Daniel in the Lions' Den, and a foundation scene showing two figures planting a staff in the ground similar to those on Clonmacnois West. The lions in the Daniel scene are, however, entwined with snakes showing the influence of Scandinavian Urnes style. Such ornament is much more widely used on some of the other crosses: the Market Cross at Tuam, Glendalough, Roscrea and Mona Incha, for example. These motifs may also be compared with patterns on the Cross of Cong and St Manchan's shrine.

But in addition to these new themes there are also indications of a conscious revival of a much more conservative sculptural style. A small shaft or ringless cross from Clonmacnois[95] is decorated with interlace indistinguishable from patterns on the late eighth- and early ninth-century monuments on the same site, but the fourth side is carved with a pair of confronted interlaced lion-like beasts. Their species and pose are also comparable with beasts on earlier sculpture but the details of the carving have much in common with Hiberno-Romanesque architectural carving of a fairly mature phase suggesting a date in the third quarter of the twelfth century.

Other forms of sculpture are contemporary with the stone crosses. In the west a variety of slabs and pillars were produced instead of freestanding crosses. Sundials, such as those at Clogher, Co. Tyrone, and Nendrum, Co. Down, are also occasionally found. They are not part of the church fabric as in Anglo-Saxon England but freestanding pillars. Altar slabs carved with five consecration crosses have also been recognized on some sites.[96] Very little architectural stone carving has been identified before the Hiberno-Romanesque sculpture of the twelfth century (see p. 126) and it is mainly confined to door lintels decorated with simple crosses or carved gable finials. However, the White Island figures from Co. Fermanagh may indicate that occasionally much more ambitious projects were undertaken. Six figures of varying heights up to 1.05 m (3 ft 6 in), including an eccle-

siastic with bell and crozier and a representation of David, have been found. Sockets in the tops of their heads indicate an architectural function and it has been suggested that they could have supported the steps of a pulpit. The details of the figures are highly stylized and contrast sharply with figural representations on the crosses with the exception of Moone, Co. Kildare. Indeed, there seems to have been a local tradition of stone carving in the Lough Erne area of Co. Fermanagh in both the Iron Age and the early medieval periods. Because of this the date of the White Island figures has caused considerable controversy but their attributes, for example the form of the crozier, would seem to suggest they were made during the ninth to eleventh centuries.[97]

Another very common form of stone sculpture is the recumbent graveslab.[98] Almost 700 are known from Clonmacnois alone and they are also found on many other sites in the Midlands but are less common elsewhere. Recumbent graveslabs are essentially grave markers. They were laid flat over the grave and, though it has been suggested that some of the smaller examples could have been contained in the grave fill, this seems unlikely since, if they were invisible, they could not have fulfilled their function. The origin of recumbent graveslabs is unclear. They could have been sparked off by the name-stones found on sites such as Lindisfarne and Hartlepool in Northumbria which have been dated between the mid-seventh and mid-eighth centuries. In addition the reputedly Anglo-Saxon foundation of Tullylease, Co. Cork, has a series of larger slabs, one possibly datable by inscription to c.700, which could also have been influential. However, they may equally have been an independent development. The recumbent graveslabs have a mass-produced appearance and individual sites favour particular types of ornament. At Clonmacnois, for example, the slabs are only very roughly shaped and sometimes the surface is very uneven. They are dominated by the cross symbol in a variety of forms. Some may be compared with manuscript carpet pages (83f), others with the freestanding crosses (83e), and the expansional crosses (83d) are similar to designs on some of the later metalwork. The ornament is simple and repetitive, mainly frets, spirals and interlace, and there are almost no zoomorphic patterns or figural representations. A large number of the slabs have inscriptions in Irish. Some merely give the name of the deceased but others use the formula OR[oit]

DO, or a variation of it, meaning 'Pray for' followed by the name. In the past many of the slabs have been dated by comparing the name on the slab with obits in the annals. This practice can be misleading, since many of the names are very common, but it does remain of possible value in some instances where a patronym or title is supplied. Reappraisal of the value of the inscriptions, together with art-historical comparison, may eventually allow a greater understanding of the chronology of these monuments which may have begun as early as the seventh or eighth centuries and continued well into the twelfth. Other forms of grave marker may also be recognized. They range from rough cross-inscribed boulders, slabs and pillars to the unique twelfth-century sarcophagus from Cashel, Co. Tipperary, which has finely-executed representations of Urnes-inspired beasts comparable with those on St Manchan's shrine.[99]

## Conclusion

Much of the work on Insular art has hitherto concentrated on trying to understand its origins and development together with the various influences which helped to create it. Considerable energy has also been expended on attempting to establish some kind of relative chronology and on arguments about where individual pieces of metalwork or manuscripts were made. But, in order to refine our ideas on such matters in the future, it is important to turn our attention in other directions.

First, there is still a great need to collect and collate material. In the case of ornamental metalwork detailed studies of specific objects, such as the Moylough belt-shrine,[100] the establishment of corpora, such as those of Insular objects from Viking graves and other sources in Scandinavia,[101] and collections of specific artefact types, such as penannular brooches or ringed pins,[102] have all greatly increased our knowledge. But much more work needs to be done along these lines, and there has been an understandable tendency to concentrate on the major pieces of the pre-Viking period. There has been a similar tendency with manuscripts. Detailed research on specific books, such as the Lindisfarne Gospels and the Book of Kells,[103] has greatly increased our understanding of the luxury manuscripts of the late seventh- to early ninth-century period and the kind of milieu in which they were written. But much less research has been done on the illumination of the pocket gospels, for example, or on

Insular manuscripts in libraries abroad and Irish manuscripts of the tenth to twelfth centuries. As far as sculpture is concerned a corpus of the material is desperately needed since much of it is located on remote sites where it is vulnerable to loss, destruction and weathering. Higgins' recent collection of the sculpture from Co. Galway[104] is an important contribution which indicates the extent of the work required elsewhere. He visited 600 sites and recorded 127 monuments, over a third of them for the first time. Much of the work on Irish sculpture has naturally focussed on the crosses but some still lack adequate recording, particularly of the Insular ornament; this is even truer of the other forms of sculpture.

Secondly, we need to examine individual objects more closely from a technical point of view. With metalwork, where this has already happened, in cases such as the analysis of the Ardagh chalice or the recent study of filigree techniques,[105] we have gained considerable knowledge. With manuscripts further study of the vellum or pigments might produce similar results. Research on the mechanisms, such as templates and constructional grids, by which the illuminated manuscripts were produced was pioneered by Bruce-Mitford in his work on the Lindisfarne Gospels and, though such techniques have now been used elsewhere, for example on the Durham Cassiodorus,[106] one suspects that they could be applied more widely. There has also been a growing interest in the design and layout of sculpture, particularly crosses and recumbent graveslabs. Again there is increasing evidence that in at least some instances templates and grids were used,[107] though whether such grids were as complex as their manuscript counterparts is arguable. Petrological analysis of the sculpture has yet to be undertaken and, though the great majority is thought to have been carved from local stone, it would be interesting to know how far they were prepared to transport it.

Lastly, the symbolic importance of the religious art is becoming increasingly apparent, not just in the iconography but also in the ornament.[108] The nature of this symbolism and its relationship to the liturgy needs to be more fully understood. It is only when all these avenues have been explored that we may be able to see the art of early medieval Ireland, not in terms of individual objects viewed in isolation from the society which produced them, but rather as objects which can tell us something about that society.

# CHAPTER 8

# The Vikings

This consideration of the Vikings in Ireland comes at a time of rapid change. Until comparatively recently our understanding of the nature of Viking activity in Ireland was largely dependent upon the documentary sources, such as the annals, and some linguistic and place-name evidence.[1] There were also periodic reports of archaeological discoveries, such as silver hoards and graves, including the important cemetery at Kilmainham/ Islandbridge, Dublin, but unfortunately such finds were rarely recorded adequately.[2] Over the last 30 years, however, interest in the Vikings in Ireland has grown immensely. This is because of the extensive excavations within the walls of medieval Dublin (92) which have uncovered the rich remains of the Viking town beneath. Dublin's location on the banks of the Liffey means that the archaeological deposits are waterlogged. Therefore a very wide range of organic material – structures, artefacts and environmental remains – has been preserved. Indeed, the wealth of the evidence far exceeds that from excavations in Viking towns elsewhere, such as York, Trondheim and Novgorod. Final reports on the Dublin excavations are now beginning to emerge but it will inevitably take many years for this vast project to be completed. Only then will it really be possible to consider Viking Dublin within its wider context, not only in Europe, but also as part of the broader sphere of Viking activity in Ireland.

But the richness of Viking Dublin contrasts sharply with the comparative lack of archaeological evidence from elsewhere in Ireland. Outside Dublin we are still too frequently largely dependent upon the documentary sources in our attempts to understand the course of the Viking raids and the extent of Viking settlement. In fact, with the important exception of the silver hoards, work in Dublin has, until recently, overshadowed research on other aspects of the Viking impact on Ireland.

## The Viking raids and settlement

Viking activity in Ireland should be viewed as part of the more general Viking expansion overseas. The Vikings who attacked Ireland were mainly from the western coastal regions of Norway. Their movement westwards began towards the end of the eighth century and the early raids on Ireland may be seen as an extension of Viking activity in the Northern and Western Isles of Scotland.

We can trace the course of the Viking raids and settlement in Ireland by a study of the documentary sources, particularly the annals. The first recorded raid in 795 was on the monastery at *Rechru* which is now generally regarded as Rathlin Island, Co. Antrim. Further sporadic activity is noted over the next quarter-century but after 820 it is possible to discern a gradual build-up in Viking aggression. Raids became more frequent and widespread but native opposition is also apparent and some Irish victories are recorded. After 830 there was a further escalation and the Vikings began to move inland. In 832 three raids are reported on the monastery of Armagh in a single month. In 836 Meath was overrun and Connacht devastated. In 837 a naval force is noted on the Boyne and a second fleet of 60 ships on the Liffey. In 838 the raiders were sailing up the Shannon and had penetrated Lough Erne. In 839 the first overwintering on Lough Neagh is reported, and in 841 the first permanent settlements, naval camps or *longphoirt*, were established, one at Dublin and one at *Linn Duachaill*, probably Annagassan, Co. Louth, on Dundalk Bay.[3]

There has been considerable disagreement about the seriousness of the Viking raids and the accuracy of their recording in the documentary sources. The early twelfth-century saga *The War of the Irish against the Foreigners*, which includes the colourful exploits of the legendary Viking leader, Turgesius, may largely be discredited as later propaganda concocted to extol the royal house of the Dál Cais (the O'Briens) and the career of King Brian Boru.[4] However, the contemporary, year-by-year record of the annals cannot be dismissed so lightly. The information given is undoubtedly terse and fragmentary and there must have been many raids which were never reported. However, the picture they present is vivid and leaves the clear impression that the Vikings were to be feared.

The annals include many references to Viking raids on monasteries. The destruction of such attacks has sometimes been played down and Lucas has suggested that the Irish were equally guilty of violence against the Church. However Hughes has shown that the violence of the Vikings may not have been exaggerated significantly in the annals and was undoubtedly feared more than native aggression, especially in the earlier part of the period. Before the advent of the Vikings there were native attacks on the Church but very few examples of indiscriminate plundering. In contrast, though the Vikings were not actively anti-Christian, as pagans they did not respect the tacit rules which had up to then protected the Church. Moreover, the major monasteries were clearly wealthy and largely un-protected. They were therefore highly attractive to the Viking raiders and easy prey. The annals make it clear that the Vikings were not just interested in plundering valuable metalwork, though their des-ecration of shrines and relics caused particular anguish. They were also keen to capture slaves, and there is some evidence to suggest that raids were sometimes carried out on Christian festivals when the major ecclesiastical sites were crowded with pilgrims. Other goods raided may have included food and other commodities owned by the surrounding lay population but stored in the monasteries for safe-keeping. It is only after the Vikings had begun to plunder and burn monaster-ies indiscriminately that there is evidence of a more general increase in native violence against the Church.[5]

What was the lasting impact of the Viking raids on the Irish Church? Repeated attacks on Iona off the coast of Mull in Scotland were sufficiently serious to be the most likely reason for the founda-tion of the major new Columban house at Kells, Co. Meath, in 807. Though Iona was never com-pletely abandoned, it ceased to be of international importance. The Viking raids probably also caused an increase in the number of Irish churchmen who went to pursue their studies on the Conti-nent. In general there is evidence for a decline in ecclesiastical income as a result of the Viking raids. Major monasteries, such as Armagh and Clonmacnois, with the backing of powerful royal patrons, maintained sufficient resources to recover from repeated attacks but many of the smaller foundations did not.[6]

Archaeological evidence for the Viking raids is more difficult to identify. Some of the buildings at the monastery of Nendrum, Co. Down, had been destroyed by fire and Lawlor suggested that this was caused by the Viking raid documented in 974, but it could equally have been a natural conflagration. Evidence of burning has also been noted at Iona but again it is impossible to equate it with a specific event. Hencken suggested that the construction of the final palisade around Lagore crannog, Co. Meath, was the result of a Viking raid in 934 but this cannot be proved either.[7] In fact the clearest archaeological evidence for the Viking raids comes from the Scandinavian home-lands, particularly the western coastal regions of Norway: Nord-Trøndelag, Sør-Trøndelag, Møre og Romsdal, Sogn og Fjordane, Hordaland, Rogaland, and Vestfold. Here many graves mainly datable to the ninth century have been found to contain Insular decorated metalwork. The objects are often fragmentary and have sometimes been adapted for secondary use· as brooches. Many, such as the Melhus house shrine or the plaque depicting the Crucifixion from Hofstad (Nord-Trøndelag), are clearly ecclesiastical but some objects, such as the brooches and harness fittings, are more likely to be secular and the purpose of many of the more fragmentary pieces is unknown.[8]

There has been considerable discussion about how these objects were acquired. It has been argued that at least some, for example objects found in the port of Kaupang (Vestfold), could have been bought as trade items rather than raided. It has also been noted that the Copen-hagen shrine, which came to light in a church in Norway, still contained its precious relics, which suggests some respect for the Christian religion.[9] While it is possible that some objects could have been acquired by peaceful means (and an inscrip-tion on the Copenhagen shrine suggests that it may have reached Norway some time after the raids of the ninth century), it seems unwise to ignore the documentary evidence. This makes it clear that the Viking raiders were interested in ornamental metalwork and ecclesiastics would hardly have handed over their treasures willingly to pagans; indeed the annals describe their efforts to hide them. The fragmentary nature of many of the objects also argues against their acquisition by peaceful means. It seems likely that panels of decorative metalwork were hurriedly removed from the objects they adorned or later divided amongst the members of a raiding party. Objects originally acquired by raid could even have found their way to ports like Kaupang and only then become trade items.

The provenance of many of the objects is also problematic because of the similarity of the Insular art style on either side of the Irish Sea in this period. Attempts have been made to isolate Anglo-Saxon material from the rest and it has also been suggested that it may be possible to recognize specifically Irish objects. These are concentrated in the region of Rogaland, and it has been postulated that many of the Vikings who raided Ireland in the ninth century came from this area.[10] Such close provenancing of much of the metalwork in this way is risky because of the overall similarity in style, which means that much of the material could equally well have come from Scotland. Yet the documentary sources do suggest that Ireland was the major Viking target during the first half of the ninth century and therefore a considerable proportion of the material is likely to be Irish.

With the foundation of permanent bases at Dublin and *Linn Duachaill* in 841 it was clear that the Vikings were in Ireland to stay. During the 840s the raids continued unabated and the Viking boats penetrated deep into Ireland's heartland and another fortification or *dunadh* was set up on Lough Ree in 845. Opposition was fragmented and the Irish began to intermarry and make alliances with the Norse against their native enemies. However the Viking settlers did not have it all their own way and during the 850s the raiding died down. There were some native victories and dynastic squabbles amongst the Vikings themselves. In 851 a fleet of Danish Vikings plundered Dublin and in the following year they inflicted a major defeat on the Norse at Carlingford Lough. The strength of the Norse was thus reduced and they began to concentrate their attention on the hinterland around Dublin. But after 873 dynastic feuds amongst the Dublin Vikings became more serious and resulted in secondary migrations to Iceland and across the Irish Sea. The native opposition was able to take advantage of this situation

and in 902 the kings of Brega and Leinster successfully destroyed the *longphort* at Dublin and expelled the Vikings from Ireland.

In 914, however, the Vikings returned and in 917 they re-established a settlement in Dublin. Again Viking fleets were active on the waterways of Ireland plundering and burning, and it has sometimes been suggested that they intended a total conquest of Ireland. But the real Viking achievement during the tenth century was to bring about the rapid growth of the trading ports, particularly Dublin, Limerick, and Waterford. These were the first towns in Ireland in the sense that we know them, and Dublin became one of the major international ports of the Viking world.

But the activities of the Vikings in Ireland during the tenth century have to be seen in relation to native Irish politics. The Uí Néill remained powerful in the north but in the south the strength of the Éoganacht waned and the Dál Cais, who originated in Co. Clare, came to the fore under the leadership of Brian Boru. In 980 King Máel Sechnaill of the Uí Néill won a significant victory against the Vikings of Dublin and the Isles at Tara, Co. Meath. Henceforward Dublin became a petty kingdom subject to a succcession of Irish kings who wished to benefit from its mercantile wealth. Thus well before the battle of Clontarf in 1014, later misleadingly portrayed as the final defeat of the Vikings by Brian Boru, Dublin had become fully integrated into Irish politics.[11]

## Hoards

Upwards of 120 Viking-age coin, silver and gold hoards are now known from Ireland (**88**). They represent the very considerable wealth of the Vikings in Ireland which was fostered by the establishment of the towns, particularly Dublin. By comparison only just over 30 hoards have come to light in Scotland where Viking settlement was dispersed and rural. Few of the Viking hoards from Ireland are recent finds. The majority were discovered during the nineteenth century or earlier, recorded to a greater or lesser extent by antiquarians, and then either dispersed or melted down.

**88** *Viking-age hoards:*
**a.** *distribution (after Briggs and Graham-Campbell 1976 and Kenny 1987 with additions);* **b.** *bar graph showing the number of hoards deposited per decade (after Graham-Campbell 1976 with additions).*

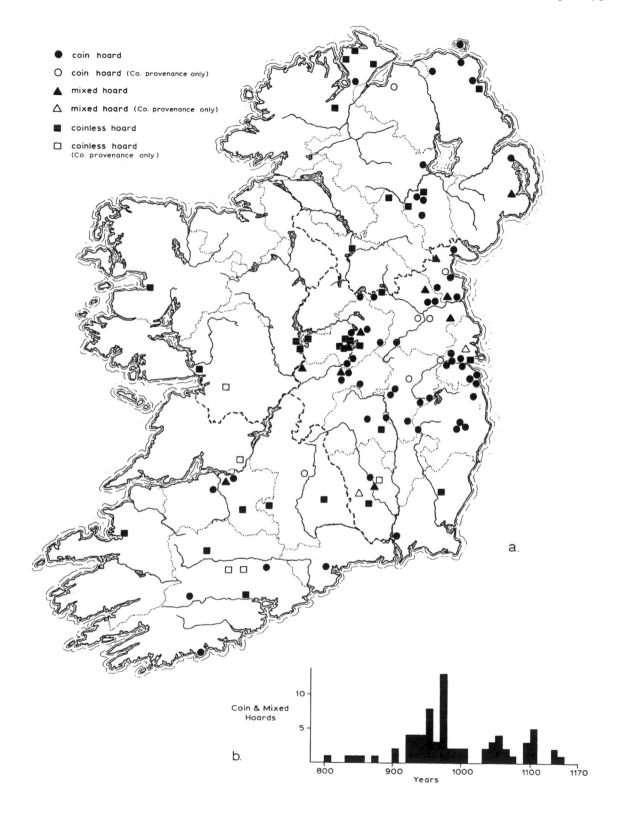

- ● coin hoard
- ○ coin hoard (Co. provenance only)
- ▲ mixed hoard
- △ mixed hoard (Co. provenance only)
- ■ coinless hoard
- □ coinless hoard
  (Co. provenance only)

a.

Coin & Mixed
Hoards

b.

Years

However painstaking detective work, particularly by Dolley and Graham-Campbell,[12] has enabled the contents of many of these hoards to be at least partially reconstructed and, where coins are present, it is usually possible to date them with some precision. The dated hoards are especially interesting because their content and date of deposition reflect various stages in the Viking settlement of Ireland.

Some 80 of these finds are coin hoards. The Irish had no coinage before the twelfth century[13] and the Hiberno-Norse only began to mint their own coins in Dublin c.997. Therefore before 997 all the coins were imported, either for use as bullion or as currency for trade. The majority came from England but in addition Carolingian coins are known from five hoards and Kufic coins minted by the Abbāsid caliphs and Sāmānid amirs of western and central Asia are represented in eight hoards. The latter were acquired by the Vikings in the lower Volga region and the Middle East and carried back to Scandinavia as bullion.[14] A dozen of the coin hoards also contain silver objects of which Dysart 4, Co. Westmeath, (c.905-10) is the most important since it is the only hoard with a wide range of objects. These include whole and fragmentary ingots and hack silver in the form of pieces of a bossed penannular brooch and a thistle brooch, Hiberno-Norse arm-rings and two small bits of Scandinavian metalwork, all of which had been cut up ready for the melting pot.

In addition over 40 coinless silver and gold hoards have now been reported, though the records of some are very uncertain, and, because they do not contain coins, they are difficult to date. They mainly consist of a variety of arm-rings and ingots and occasionally include neck-rings, finger-rings, and pieces of hack-silver. Some of these hoards were very large. For example, the unique lost hoard (No. 1) of mid-ninth- to mid-tenth-century date from Hare Island in the Shannon, Co. Westmeath, contained approximately 5kg (11lbs) of gold made up into ten arm-rings, some of which were very ornate. But in general silver is much more characteristic. For example, the Cushalogurt hoard, Co. Mayo, contained 25 arm-rings and various silver fragments including three ingots. Ingots in Viking-age hoards are usually rod- or finger-shaped though bun-shaped examples are also known. In addition two types which may be of native Irish manufacture, one oblong, the other much larger and boat-shaped, have recently been found in three hoards

(Carrick, Dysart 1 and 2) from around Lough Ennell, Co. Westmeath. A characteristically Hiberno-Norse form of silver arm-ring has also been identified. It consists of a thick penannular band, rectangular in cross-section and tapering towards the terminals, decorated on the outer surface with a variety of stamped vertical grooves often with a diagonal cross in the centre which is sometimes repeated near the ends (89).[15]

Hoards containing coins are mainly concentrated in Leinster and more particularly in a broad band some 48–113 km (30–70 miles) from Dublin with three main groupings in the ancient kingdoms of west Meath, north Brega and mid to north Leinster (88a). Such a distribution clearly indicates that substantial quantities of coin were entering Dublin, some of which was subsequently redistributed to the surrounding countryside. In contrast there are fewer hoards from the rest of Ireland and coinless hoards represent a greater proportion of the total. A regular sprinking may be noted across Munster while hoards in Ulster are concentrated along the coast and around Armagh. Hardly any hoards, and only one coin hoard, have been reported from the north-west, suggesting that Viking activity in this area was severely limited, though there is an interesting group from north-east Donegal.

By whom were these hoards deposited? Some, especially those found in the vicinity of the Viking towns and bases or around the coast and along inland waterways such as the Shannon, may best be interpreted as evidence of Viking activity, but others were deposited in contexts which suggest they may have been in native hands. For example, several hoards have come to light in major monasteries, such as Armagh and Glendalough, and others, for example Carraig Aille, Co. Limerick, Roosky, Co. Donegal, and Dysart 2, Co. Westmeath, have been found on secular settlements. Some of this silver may have been accumulated as a result of trade with the Vikings and hoards from major monasteries may well indicate commercial activity in adjacent markets. But other mechanisms are also likely. Silver might change hands as ransom or tribute and there is some evidence to suggest that certain hoards are the products of native victories or raids on the Vikings.[16]

As already mentioned the dated coin hoards reflect the course of Viking settlement in Ireland (88b). During the first phase (c.800-900) only five hoards have been noted. This is because no permanent settlements were established until 841 and therefore before this the raiders took their wealth back to Norway. The hoard from Mullaghboden, Co. Kildare (*c.*847) contained only Carolingian coins and probably reached Ireland in the hands of raiders who had also been active in Aquitaine. The others are made up of Anglo-Saxon coins and need not necessarily be Viking at all. It should be noted that neither the Vikings nor the Irish used coin during this period and therefore silver hoards are more likely to have been made up of objects which are more difficult to date.[17]

The hoards of the second phase, *c.*900-20, certainly reflect the expulsion of the Vikings from Ireland in 902 and their subsequent settlement in north-west Britain. Two major hoards datable to this period have been identified from Ireland. The first (*c.*905) from Drogheda, Co. Louth, is badly documented. It may, however, have contained 5,000 or more coins including Kufic *dirhams* and at least one penny possibly from the Viking kingdom of York. The second, the recently discovered hoard, Dysart 4, Co. Westmeath, (*c.*905-10), which contained Kufic *dirhams* and coins from Anglo-Saxon England, Viking York and possibly Carolingian Germany as well as ingots and a variety of fragmentary ornaments, has already been mentioned. It has been suggested that this important hoard may in part be derived from wealth captured by the Irish as a result of the sack of Dublin. Metal analysis of the silver in the Dysart

**89** *Part of the Cuerdale Hoard deposited* c.903 *on the banks of the River Ribble, Lancashire, north–west England (Copyright: the Trustees of the British Museum).*

4 hoard demonstrates close affinities with the nearby hoard from Carrick which contained 60 ingots together weighing over 31kg (68lbs), and it is possible that they are of a similar date.[18] Hoards outside Ireland also provide evidence of the Viking debacle. Graham-Campbell has shown that the massive Cuerdale hoard (89), which was deposited in a lead chest on the banks of the River Ribble, near Preston, Lancashire, *c*.903 is of likely Hiberno-Norse origin. It contained about 7,000 coins and over 1,300 pieces of silver which together weighed about 40kg (88lbs). The range of material, including Hiberno-Norse arm-rings and fragments of both bossed penannular brooches and thistle brooches, is closely comparable with Dysart 4. The slightly later hoard *c*.920 from Goldsborough, Yorkshire, also contains fragments of similar brooches and arm-rings.[19]

The main phase of datable hoard deposition is *c*.920-1000. This spans the return of the Vikings, their increased power in Leinster and Munster, the consequent upsurge in violence between native and Viking, warfare amongst the Irish and the rapid growth of Dublin as a trading port. The hoards reach a peak of deposition *c*.970 and Dolley has suggested this indicates rising violence prior to the Viking defeat in the battle of Tara in 980. The large number of coins minted in York in hoards dating to the early part of the period reflects the close political links between Viking York and Dublin, and the deposition of the Glasnevin hoard from just north of Dublin may be connected with the expulsion of the Hiberno-Norse dynasty from York in 927. Hoards between *c*.925 and *c*.975 are dominated by Anglo-Saxon coins minted in Chester demonstrating the importance of the trade route between Dublin and Chester and continuing Hiberno-Norse contacts with north-west England. But after *c*.975 the number of coins from Chester declines and the number from West-Country mints rises showing the growing importance of the Dublin–Bristol trade route. The amount of coin as a whole in the hoards of this phase indicates increasing familiarity with the use of coins for trade which finally resulted in the minting of the first Hiberno-Norse coins in Dublin; the earliest hoards of Hiberno-Norse coins from Dundalk, Co. Louth, and Clondalkin, Co. Dublin, were deposited *c*.997-1000.[20]

Hiberno-Norse coins were minted in Dublin between *c*.997 and the mid-twelfth century. The series is extremely complex but, as a result of pioneering work by Dolley, a chronology has now been established. The series may be divided into seven phases.[21] In the first phase (*c*.997-1020), as one might expect in the light of the importance of trade between Dublin and England, the Hiberno-Norse coins imitate Anglo-Saxon pennies. Some are straight imitations of coins with a profile portrait of Æthelred II, some substitute the name of Sihtric and the Dublin mint signature, and others are a mixture of both types. All the coins were struck for Sihtric Silkbeard, the son-in-law and stepson of Brian Boru. During Phase II (*c*.1020-35) the Dublin moneyers stop imitating English coins directly but instead imitate their own earlier issues. Most still carry the name of Sihtric but there is a gradual degradation in the lettering. In this period also the pennies cease to be the same size as their English counterparts. They gradually become smaller and lighter and consequently are used less overseas. Phase III (*c*.1035–65) sees a slight improvement in weight but on these coins the legends are completely illegible. In Phase IV (*c*.1055–65 or a little later?) two different types were produced. The first, like earlier issues has an imitation of the profile bust of Æthelred II; the second, unusually, has a facing bust. The dies in this phase are also unusual since they appear to be engraved rather than punched. Phase V (*c*.1065–95) is particularly complex because of the wide range of different types produced. Some are imitations of earlier Hiberno-Norse imitations of English models; some imitate a variety of English coins which were already obsolete when they were copied; a third group imitates contemporary Anglo-Norman pennies. It is also possible that coins from Denmark and the Ottonian Empire were used as models. The coins of Phase V are fairly consistent in weight at approximately two-thirds of their English counterparts but those of Phase VI (the first half of the twelfth century?) are considerably lower. In this phase we see a continuation of the type with the profile bust of Æthelred II first imitated by the Dublin moneyers over a century before. In the final phase (mid-twelfth century) the coins degenerate into thin semi-bracteates struck on both sides or bracteates struck on one side only. It is possible that some of the latter could have been struck outside Dublin by a native king such as Turlough O'Connor.

Dolley was able to build up a chronology for the Hiberno-Norse series by studying the contents of coin hoards in both Ireland and elsewhere. Dating was aided where Hiberno-Norse coins were found in conjunction with closely-dated English examples. There are fewer eleventh- and twelfth-century coin hoards in Ireland compared with the tenth century, perhaps reflecting the integration of the Hiberno-Norse into Irish politics. The latest hoard (*c.*1027) to include silver objects as well as coin is from Fourknocks, Co. Meath – it contained a single ingot – though the early eleventh-century hoard of 30 Hiberno-Norse coins from Clonmacnois, Co. Offaly, also included a fragmentary ornament of twisted gold wire and a copper-alloy ingot. Another important hoard from Dunbrody, Co. Wexford, which may be dated to *c.*1050, is unusually large. It was made up of more than 1,600 coins and both Anglo-Saxon and Hiberno-Norse examples are represented.[22]

## Towns

The greatest achievement of the Vikings in Ireland was the foundation of the coastal towns: Dublin, Limerick, Waterford, Wexford and Cork (**90a**).

**90 a.** *Viking towns: location map;*
**b.** *Viking Dublin and environs (after Ordnance Survey 1978; Simms 1979; Mitchell 1987).*

They had good harbours and easy access to inland waterways. Limerick, for example, was located on an island at the point where the Shannon broadens into its estuary, and Waterford harbour provided access to the Barrow, Nore and Suir. Although these settlements were established during the mid-ninth century, they only became important during the tenth. Archaeological evidence has up to now been confined to Dublin and Waterford; for the rest we are almost entirely dependent upon occasional references in the documentary sources.

### Dublin

The Vikings established their *longphort* near the mouth of the River Liffey in 841. They were attracted to Dublin, not only as a suitable place to beach their boats, but also as a focus of both land and water routes. The Liffey formed a natural boundary between the Kingdom of Brega to the north and Leinster to the south, and there was an important ford across the river probably located to the west of its tributary the Poddle (**90b**). The

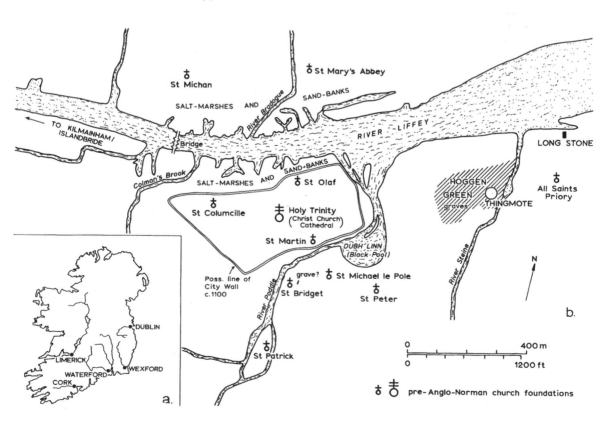

crossing seems to have been facilitated by rafts of hurdles deposited on the unstable ground of the river bed. This gives us one of the two Irish names for Dublin, *Áth Cliath*, the 'ford of hurdlework' and it has been suggested that the name could go back to a pre-Viking settlement located near the ford on the southern bank of the Liffey. There may have been a second pre-Viking settlement, possibly an ecclesiastical enclosure, on the east bank of the Poddle, one of a number of church sites in the lower Liffey Valley which included the important monasteries of Clondalkin, Finglas, Swords and Tallaght.[23]

We do not know the location of the ninth-century *longphort*. No trace of any ninth-century levels has been found under the tenth-century town and it is probable that it was sited elsewhere. The most likely position is 1.75 km (just over a mile) upstream somewhere in the vicinity of Kilmainham/Islandbridge, the site of the ninth-century cemetery, but an excavation on a possible site in the grounds of Kilmainham Hospital revealed nothing. Nor do we know what the *long-phort* looked like, though Wallace has plausibly speculated that it was Scandinavian in character and that, like Birka in Sweden, it may have consisted of a small fortress with an adjacent undefended trading settlement.[24]

The first Viking settlers in Dublin were buried on the south bank of the Liffey at Kilmainham/Islandbridge.[25] The cemetery was located in the area between the modern landmarks of Heuston Station and the Memorial Park. A few graves came to light during the early nineteenth century in fields overlooking the Liffey and adjacent to Kilmainham Hospital. However, the majority were found in the 1840s, 50s and 60s during construction of the railway at Kilmainham and as a result of gravel extraction in fields sloping down to the Liffey south-west of the village of Islandbridge. Five outliers were also uncovered during 1933–4 when the Memorial Park was set out (91). These were the only graves investigated by archaeologists and the records of earlier finds are fragmentary. Many of the gravegoods were eventually acquired by the National Museum but at the time they were discovered there was little understanding of what had been found. In 1866 Wilde suggested that the skeletons, which had been found with artefacts above and below them, represented Vikings left unburied on the battlefield and it was only in 1910 that it was realized that a proper cemetery had been uncovered. Because of this we have little idea of the orientation or layout of the graves and we are almost entirely depen-

*91   Viking grave find from Islandbridge, Dublin. These artefacts were found in 1933 together with parts of a skeleton. The four iron nails and two iron handles indicate that the body had been placed in a wooden coffin. The grave goods, denoting a male burial, consist of weapons, a sword, spearhead and axehead, together with a slotted-and-pointed object (Copyright: National Museum of Ireland).*

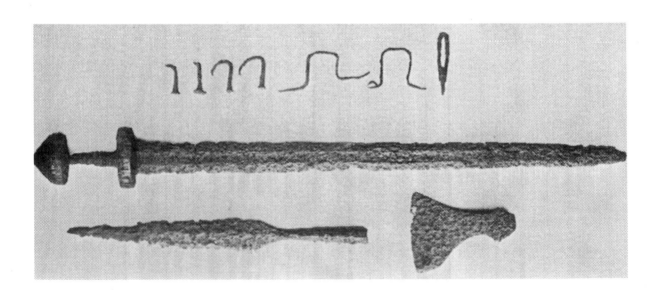

dent upon the gravegoods, which can seldom be linked to specific graves and which are yet to be comprehensively published, for our interpretation of this important site.

The burial customs indicate that the Viking population of ninth-century Dublin was pagan, though the cemetery was sited not far from a monastery at Kilmainham. The cemetery contained at least 40 graves and, although there is some evidence for cremation, the majority were

**92** *Excavations in Dublin 1960–86 (after the National Museum of Ireland).*

inhumations. Iron nails and handles indicate that some were buried in wooden coffins. Ringed pins of Irish type may have been used to fasten cloaks or shrouds. The artefacts, which indicate a prosperous community, are mainly of Scandinavian type and may be dated to the ninth century. One grave excavated in 1934 also contained the jawbone of a cow, an offering of food for the journey to the afterlife. The men were laid out with their weapons (**91**): swords, often with finely-decorated hilts, spears, long knives and occasionally battleaxes. They were also accompanied by shields but only the round or conical iron bosses now survive.

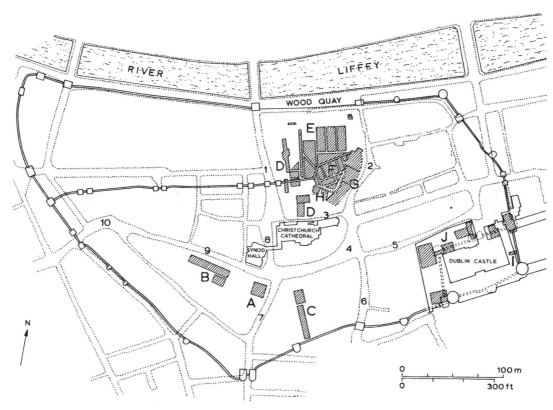

Key to excavations.

A. High St. I 1962-63
B. High St. II 1967-72
C. Christchurch Place 1972-76
D. Winetavern St. 1969-72
E. Wood Quay
F. Fishamble St. (the banks) 1976, 1977-78
G. Fishamble St. 1975-76, 1977-78
H. John's Lane 1978-79
I. Dublin Castle 1960-61
J. Dublin Castle 1984-86

Key to roads.

1. Winetavern St.
2. Fishamble St.
3. John's Lane
4. Christchurch Place
5. Castle St.
6. Werberg St.
7. Nicholas St.
8. St Michael's Hill
9. High St.
10. Cornmarket

The swords had sometimes been ritually bent or the shield bosses broken before they were interred. Some graves also included implements, such as hammer-heads, shears and a pair of metal-working tongs, indicative of craft-working. Scales and lead weights, including a fine set made from fragments of decorated Insular metalwork, represent trading activities. Female graves may be identified by pairs of oval brooches and glass beads and occasionally by household objects such as spindle whorls, a copper-alloy needle case, a whalebone ironing board and a black glass linen polisher. However, the number of artefacts which can definitely be linked with female graves is only a small proportion of the total. This suggests that far more men were buried in the cemetery than women, and it is therefore possible that only a few women accompanied their menfolk from Norway and native wives may have retained their Christian faith and been either buried elsewhere or interred without gravegoods.

Extensive excavations since 1960 have done much to reveal the later Viking and medieval town (90b, 92) which was situated on the southern bank of the Liffey to the west of its confluence with the Poddle. Near the mouth of the Poddle was a pool which formed a natural harbour. This was known in Irish as *Dubh Linn* or the 'Black Pool' and gave its name to the settlement. To the west of the pool was a ridge of boulder clay which ran parallel with the Liffey and rose to *c*.18 m (59 ft) above sea level. This was where the town grew up.[26]

In the tenth century the Liffey was much broader and shallower than it is now with sand banks and salt marshes along its margins. It was also tidal and subject to flash floods. This water-front area was uncovered in the Woodquay/Fishamble Street excavations (92E, F) revealing successive phases of Viking and medieval flood barriers, defences and land reclamation. There is some evidence that soon after the Vikings settled one or more low banks of boulder clay *c*.1 m (3 ft 3 in) high were constructed just above the high-water mark. These do not appear to have been defensive and were probably designed to prevent flooding. However Bank 2, built *c*.950, was defensive. It ran along the slope at high-water mark but towards the western end of the area excavated it appeared to turn uphill and away from the water-front. It may therefore have encircled the town. It consisted of an earth and gravel bank heaped around a pre-existing post-and-wattle fence and

was constructed on top of dumped refuse. The slope made it appear much higher externally than internally. At one point the outer face was protected by a post-and-wattle breakwater set into a channel and there was a cobbled pathway on the inner side; at another the outer slope was lined with planks and there was an external ditch *c*.2 m (6 ft 7 in) wide and 1.6 m (5 ft 3 in) deep. Bank 3, which replaced Bank 2 *c*.1000 or a little later, was on a much larger scale and topped by a timber palisade. It has been compared with late Anglo-Saxon town defences and with a similar bank in York. It was built on the riverward side of Bank 2 and in some places incorporated parts of the old bank into its structure. Bank 3 was made up of layers of gravel, stone and earth reinforced with brushwood and post-and-wattle hurdles. The outer slope was faced with a post-and-wattle breakwater and planks were driven into the fore-shore to provide further protection from erosion. To begin with a post-and-wattle fence ran along the top of the bank; later this was replaced by a stave-built wall and in its final stage the bank was covered with estuarine mud. The next and last Hiberno-Norse phase which can definitely be identified was the construction *c*.1100 of a stone wall which almost certainly encircled the town (90b), though whether it followed the line of the later medieval wall apart from the waterfront side is unknown. It was 1.5 m (4 ft 11 in) wide and possibly up to 3.5 m (11 ft 6 in) high and may have appeared higher on the river than the landward side. It was constructed of rubble with mortared stone facings partly standing on a drystone plinth. Such formidable defences led Irish writers to equate Dublin with a *dún* or stone fortress.[27]

The extensive area excavated at Woodquay/Fishamble Street also enables us to reconstruct something of the layout of the Viking town. Streets were not set out according to a grid-iron pattern but instead made use of the natural contours. One side of a street, probably the original Fishamble Street, was uncovered revealing ten tenements. These were roughly trapezoidal in shape with their broadest face fronting onto the street and their narrowest sloping down towards the waterfront. The plots

93 *Dublin, Viking-age timber buildings:* **a.** *Christchurch Place 356/1;* **b.** *High Street 9/1;* **c.** *Christchurch Place 6/1;* **d.** *Christchurch Place 85/1, Phase I (after Murray 1983).*

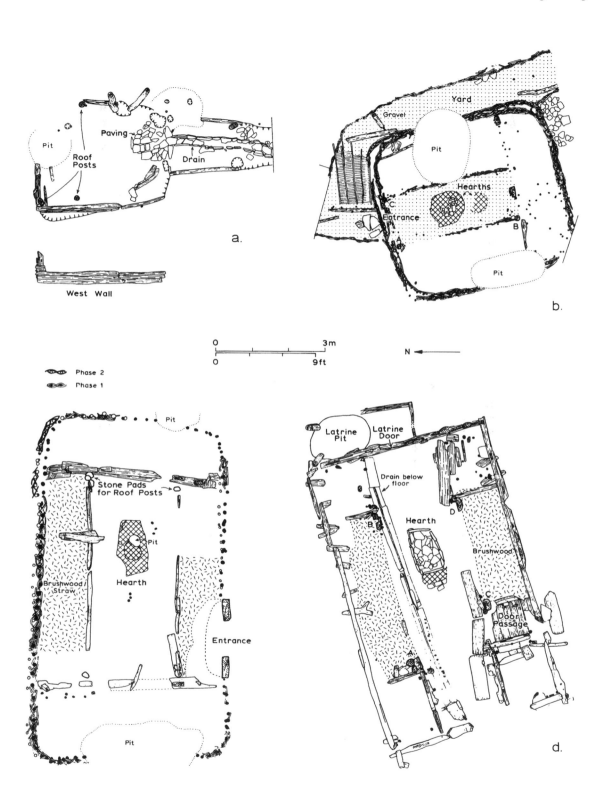

West Wall

a.

Yard

Gravel

Pit

Hearths

C

Entrance

B

A

Pit

b.

0        3m

0        9ft

N ←

Phase 2

Phase 1

Pit

Stone Pads
for Roof Posts

Pit

Brushwood/
Straw

Hearth

Entrance

Pit

Latrine
Pit

Latrine
Door

Drain below
floor

B

D

Hearth

Brushwood

C

Door
Passage

A

d.

Pit

Paving

Drain

Roof
Posts

were separated by post-and-wattle fences and the street would probably have been of a corduroy-timber construction. It is interesting to note that once the boundaries between the tenements had been established, they continued with only one change (possibly related to the construction of Bank 3) throughout the tenth and eleventh centuries. Indeed, there is some evidence that they were still in existence as late as the eighteenth century. But although the boundaries of the tenements were static, the buildings within them needed to be replaced regularly, perhaps approximately every 10–20 years, and their number, size and arrangement within individual plots varied considerably over time; in Fishamble Street 13 successive levels of buildings were uncovered.[28]

Waterlogging means that timber structures are well-preserved and about 200 tenth- and eleventh-century buildings have so far been excavated. These include examples from High Street, Christchurch Place, Winetavern Street and Fishamble Street.[29] Usually only the bottom of each building was recovered since the majority of the superstructure had normally been cut away before the next phase was built on top. The foundations remained *in situ* and were topped with a platform of turves to help give stability to the later building, but subsidence became an increasingly serious problem and from the late eleventh century onwards turves were sometimes replaced with either wattle rafts or planks. The dating of individual buildings currently depends upon the coin sequence. Although very large amounts of timber were preserved, ash rather than oak was the usual building material during the tenth and eleventh centuries in Dublin. Dendrochronological dating is therefore of little use and only one house from the Viking-age levels has so far been dated by this method.

The majority of buildings (93) were similar though they vary in size. They had a square or rectangular ground-plan with rounded corners. The roof, which was probably thatched with straw, was supported by four internal posts and the roof structure is likely to have been hipped. The walls would have been comparatively low, perhaps as little as 1.25 m (4 ft 2 in) high, and were almost always of post-and-wattle construction. At Christchurch Place changes in wall-construction techniques have been noted over time. During the late tenth and early eleventh centuries single post-and-wattle walls were used;

during the eleventh century double post-and-wattle walls were in fashion, but in the mid- to late eleventh century there was an influx of new techniques including one house of stave-built construction, one with plank-and-wattle walls and another with single thick post-and-wattle walls. The same influx has been noted in Fishamble Street in the same period. The interior was usually divided longitudinally into three parts though smaller houses were not always so rigidly organized. The central living area, which included the hearth, would have had more headroom, while the sides had benches for sitting and sleeping. Sometimes one or both ends were screened off or there were small corner rooms for sleeping or storage. In the larger houses doors were often located in both end walls thus providing a through passage; in smaller houses there was often a single door in one of the longer walls. The comparative uniformity of plan and construction, together with details repeated in several different contemporary buildings, indicate that they were made by professionals, and Wallace has suggested that the improvement in carpentry techniques witnessed during the late eleventh century was a result of native influence which had not been present earlier.[30]

Some of the constructional details may best be explained by examining a few buildings in more depth. High Street 9/1·(93b) was a small early eleventh-century house which measured approximately 4.5 m (14 ft 9 in) square internally. The walls were of double post-and-wattle construction and insulation material such as bracken fern would originally have been rammed into the intervening space. The door was in the north wall and there were traces of paving outside the threshold. Three of the four internal roof supports (A, B, C) survived. The southern end of the interior was partitioned off and the main part was divided into three with successive phases of hearth in the central area and wattle walls were used to retain the benches on the sides. Outside the house was a fenced yard.

Christchurch Place 6/1 (93c) was a much larger house of late eleventh- or early twelfth-century date. It was sub-rectangular in shape and measured approximately 5 x 9 m (16 ft 5 in x 29 ft 6 in) internally. There were two phases of single large post-and-wattle walls and in the second a mud daub had been applied to the wall surface. The entrance, at one stage at least, was located along the south wall and the roof posts were supported on granite pads to prevent rising damp. The interior was divided longitudinally into three and the ends had been screened off with plank partitions. There was a hearth in the central area, partially outlined by the remains of a stone kerb and the benches were retained by planks and built up with a thick layer of brushwood with straw on top. Christchurch Place 85/1 Phase 1 (**93d**) was a particularly well-preserved building of mid- to late eleventh-century date which demonstrates the introduction of more sophisticated carpentry techniques. It measured approximately 4.85 m x 8 m (15 ft 11 in x 26 ft 3 in) internally and was the only building so far discovered which had been constructed using the stave technique of setting vertical planks into horizontal sill beams. One piece of oak, which was probably originally part of the wall, has been dated by dendrochronology to c.1059. The roof was supported on four groups of timbers (A, B, C, D), each of which included a half-tree trunk. The door passage, which was lined with planks, was located off-centre in the south wall and a second door in the east wall led out to an adjoining latrine. The interior was divided longitudinally into three and there were also four small corner rooms screened off by plank walls set into sill beams. The central area was gravelled and had two phases of hearth; the second was stone-lined as well as having a stone kerb. Underneath the floor was a wooden drain. The benches were packed with brushwood which lay on top of a layer of fermenting organic refuse made up of wood, charcoal and sand which contained straw, grasses and rushes, probably originally used as bedding and for strewing on the floor, and food debris including charred cereal, hazelnuts and blackberry seeds; flax and the opium poppy were also present. Further examination revealed a variety of beetles attracted to such an environment including one species which lives on old animal bones and others which attack wood.[31]

A different type of building, of which only three examples have been found, may be illustrated by Christchurch Place 356/1 (**93a**). It consisted of a sunken-floored sub-rectangular chamber 3.4 m x 2.75 m (11 ft 2 in x 9 ft) approached by a passage, both of which had been lined with half logs. A stone drain ran the length of the passage with traces of a stone floor at its northern end. The roof was supported on vertical corner posts and there were further posts in the centres of the long walls. The buildings of this type all date to the mid- to late tenth century. They were not dwellings but

were probably used for storage. They have been compared with souterrains and tenth-century sunken-floored buildings have also come to light in York.

Some of the larger dwellings were also used for craft purposes, but many plots contained a number of ancillary buildings in addition to the house. Latrines were the most common, but animal pens, a byre, a workshop, and storehouses have also been located. Paths of woven wattles, planks or paving stones were found. Differences may also be noted between the various areas excavated. At the eastern end of High Street and in Christchurch Place there were larger houses and rich artefacts, clearly denoting a wealthy quarter. In contrast the western end of High Street was an artisan area of small buildings with large yards and there was considerable evidence for craft-working. The houses in Fishamble Street for the most part show little evidence of craft activities and their proximity to the waterfront may mean that they were inhabited by merchants.[32]

The wealth of Viking-age Dublin is clearly demonstrated by the variety and richness of the artefacts. These are now being studied, though almost none have been published finally, and for this reason it is only possible to provide a preliminary survey here. But it is already clear that the assemblage, which includes large numbers of organic objects preserved by waterlogging, is of great importance, not just to our understanding of Dublin as a craft centre and trading port, but also in a wider context. Indeed, the artefacts will ultimately tell us much about the relationship between the town, its hinterland and the native population, and the nature of contacts further afield with Anglo-Saxon England, Scandinavia and elsewhere.

A wide range of crafts were being practised in Viking-age Dublin and the evidence for woodworking is especially interesting. Like the majority of Irish the Vikings did not make their own pottery, and wooden vessels were therefore particularly important. Excavations in Winetavern Street indicate that in the eleventh to thirteenth centuries this part of Dublin was inhabited by wood-turners and coopers. Many lathe-turned bowls and platters were found, some unfinished, together with wooden staves. In High Street a stave-built bucket with a fixed lid with a central hole and spout was discovered in the tenth-century levels. It has been suggested that this was used to store water on board ship. Indeed, shipbuilding was clearly important and ships' timbers were sometimes re-used in other contexts. For example, a fragmentary carved prow of ninth-century date was re-used as the threshold to a mid-tenth-century house in Fishamble Street. Ship graffiti can also provide vital evidence for the types of craft in use. One example on a plank, which was re-used as a drain cover in an eleventh-century context in Winetavern Street, shows a ship of clearly Norse type. Toy ships complete with mast, sails and rigging were also popular as, for example, a boat found in a twelfth-century level in Winetavern Street.[33]

The Dublin excavations have produced a corpus of *c.*150 carved wooden objects including chair pommels and bench ends, crooks, handles, stoppers, and toggles (**94**). These are especially interesting, not only because carved wooden objects do not normally survive, but also because of the light they shed upon the eclectic nature of Viking-age art styles in Dublin and their ultimate influence on more conservative ecclesiastical art in the rest of Ireland (see p. 145). Lang has shown[34] that objects carved with Insular designs are found in the same contexts as those decorated with Viking-style ornament. We do not know

**94** *Carved wooden objects from Viking-age Dublin:* **a.** *weaving sword handle;* **b.** *stave or box-lid;* **c.** *crook;* **d.** *knife handle (after Lang 1988).*

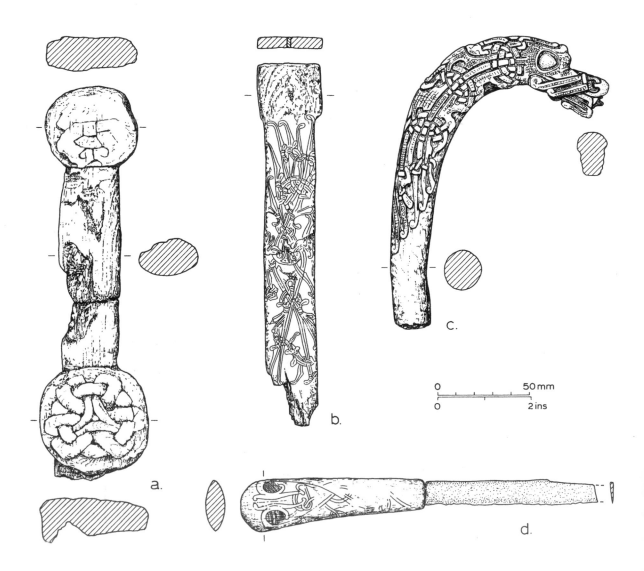

whether both were carved by the same hand but the Insular patterns clearly came to influence the way Scandinavian art styles were executed in Ireland. Contacts with Viking settlements in northern England and with Anglo-Saxon Wessex were also important and Lang has suggested a distinctively Dublin version of Ringerike style which drew upon late Anglo-Saxon art styles. Tenth-century objects may be exemplified by a weaving sword with a carved handle (94a), the lower pommel of which is decorated with an interlace knot reminiscent of Scandinavian Borre style but also influenced by Anglo-Scandinavian motifs in northern England. In the early eleventh century Ringerike ornament was beginning to filter in via Anglo-Saxon England and may be exemplified by a carved stave or box-lid (94b). Unlike Scandinavian Ringerike the central (hatched) animal is unimportant. Instead the design is dominated by long foliage tendrils comparable with a copper-alloy mount from Winchester, though Lang has suggested that their organization has been influenced by Irish art. Carved animals inspired by Ringerike style are also found in this period and may be exemplified by a crook which may have been used as a whip-handle (94c). Here the ornament has lost almost all its tendrils and the symmetry of the design clearly demonstrates the influence of Irish interlace. Only two objects with Urnes-style ornament have so far been found, including a late eleventh-century knife handle (94d) with a characteristically Irish-influenced design of elongated loops organized around a central crossing point.

The leather-working area seems to have been concentrated on High Street and it is clear that the workshops continued to flourish in the same place after the Anglo-Norman invasion. The waste indicates that the manufacture and repair of shoes was the major activity but finds from elsewhere show that other objects were also made, including sword scabbards decorated with Ringerike-inspired ornament. As one might expect the bone and antler workshops were located in an adjoining area of High Street and Christchurch Place. Evidence for the manufacture of long single-sided antler combs was particularly plentiful and included red deer tines, unfinished combs and large amounts of waste. The inhabitants of Dublin also adopted the native practice of trying out designs on motif pieces (see p. 91) and at least 40 examples have now been identified, but it is interesting to note that they were only found in the

Viking-age levels. They were usually of bone, though stone, wood and even leather examples are also represented, and the designs reflect the same eclectic tastes as the carved wood. Most were found in High Street and Christchurch Place and evidence for metal-working was also found in this area. In one part of High Street there was a workshop manufacturing copper-alloy ringed pins and stick pins. Numbers of small clay crucibles and heating trays also indicative of copper-alloy working have been found as well as a soapstone mould for casting Thor's hammer symbols. Iron slag suggests the presence of blacksmiths who would have produced a wide range of weapons, tools and fittings; gold, silver and lead were also worked. On Fishamble Street an amber and jet workshop has been uncovered. Lumps of unworked amber, waste chips and unfinished objects, mainly hemispherical and trapezoidal beads, but also cross-shaped pendants and finger rings, have been found together with jet bracelets. There is also evidence for glass bead production and drops of solidified glass have been found on the floors of some houses.[35]

We know from documentary and place-name evidence that in the twelfth century Dublin controlled an area of the hinterland called *Dyflinarskiri* which included modern Co. Dublin and parts of Counties Wicklow, Wexford, and Kildare.[36] The population of Dublin was dependent upon this area for the supply of most raw materials. For example, carefully-managed woodland was essential to provide the large amounts of timber needed and organized coppicing was practised to obtain wattles for building. Red deer tines were gathered in the woodland, as was moss for use in the latrines. Some animals, particularly pigs and goats, were kept in the town, but others were brought in from the countryside for slaughter. A sample of bones from Fishamble Street has shown that cattle were the chief source of meat. They were killed when mature and both cows and bulls were present. This shows that, in contrast with the native dairying economy, the cattle which were supplied to Dublin were being reared for their meat. The importance of grain, fish, and shellfish in the diet has yet to be studied, but the high incidence of fat hen and meld in samples which have already been examined suggests that they were grown in the town and the grains used for gruel or coarse bread. Hazelnuts, strawberries, apples, and sloes were also eaten.[37]

Above all the artefacts are beginning to indicate

the importance of Dublin as an international trading port of European significance. The importation of silver and coin and later the minting of coins in Dublin are indications of the trading process as are scales, steelyards and lead weights. Evidence for trade with the Irish hinterland is at present difficult to identify because of the similarity of much of the material culture, but souterrain ware has occasionally been found in late eleventh- and early twelfth-century levels and the Hiberno-Norse adopted the native taste for ringed pins and kite brooches. The annals suggest the importance of the slave trade. Evidence for foreign trade is however much more plentiful and links with England may be especially noted. Coin evidence suggests (see p. 178) that the route between Chester and Dublin was particularly important until *c*.975, but by the end of the century it was being replaced by the route between Bristol and Dublin. Late Anglo-Saxon cooking pots, for example, reached Dublin from north-west England during the tenth century and high-quality fabrics were imported as were luxury items such as a carved ivory plaque. Links with Anglo-Scandinavian York are also indicated by the import of raw jet from Whitby and possibly amber from the North Sea beaches. Contacts with other Viking areas are also detectable, particularly in the earlier part of the period. Amber may have been imported from the Baltic, walrus ivory and soapstone vessels from the North Atlantic. In the eleventh century trade with France became increasingly important and may be exemplified by the discovery of Andennes pottery from Normandy. More exotic items reached Dublin from further afield: preliminary research on the textiles, which include silks, suggests they may have come from as far away as Byzantium, Persia and central Asia.[38]

We know little of the Dublin Vikings' conversion to Christianity. The cemetery at Kilmainham/Islandbridge demonstrates that the inhabitants of the ninth-century *longphort* were predominantly pagan and some pagan graves may also be associated with the tenth-century town. The former name for College Green was Hoggen Green (**90b**) which derived from the Old Norse *hauge* meaning mound or tumulus. The destruction of the probable burial ground was recorded in 1646 and in the nineteenth century two swords, four spearheads, a shield boss and a silver buckle were found, which also suggest the presence of a Viking cemetery. A sword, spear-head and shield boss

found opposite St Bridget's Church in Bride Street south of the Hiberno-Norse town may indicate a further grave as may similar finds of weapons in Palace Row, Cork Street and Kildare Street. However, during the course of the tenth century, the growth of the town, the need to trade, eventual political domination by native rulers and, consequently, increasing contacts with the native population including intermarriage resulted in conversion, which was complete by the early eleventh century. In 1028 Sihtric, king of Dublin, went on a pilgrimage to Rome and in 1074 the death of the first bishop of Dublin is recorded. It is interesting to note that the see was subject to Canterbury, another indication of strong English influence. Holy Trinity Church, later Christ Church Cathedral, was a Viking foundation though the earliest surviving fabric, the crypt, is late twelfth-century. Another Viking church located in Fishamble Street was dedicated to St Olaf, the early eleventh-century king of Norway (though this may have superseded a dedication to the native saint Duilech) and traces of the church and adjacent cemetery were uncovered earlier this century. Other pre-Anglo-Norman foundations include St Michael le Pole located to the east of Bride Street, the round tower of which was still visible in the late eighteenth century.[39]

Another Viking-age land-mark which survived until relatively modern times was a mound known as the Thingmote which was located on Hoggen Green. In the late seventeenth century it was recorded as 83 m (240 ft) in circumference and 12.2 m (40 ft) high and a drawing indicates that it had a stepped profile. It may be compared with other Viking mounds, for example the Thing-wall on the Isle of Man, and was used for assemblies. The Long Stone, which stood on the bank of the Liffey to the north-east of Hoggen Green, is thought to have marked where the Vikings drew up their boats and took possession of the land.[40]

## Waterford

Recent excavations in Waterford have also revealed important evidence for the Viking and Anglo-Norman town which was located on the south bank of the River Suir. In High Street a plot with seven phases of Viking-age aisled houses similar to those in Dublin, represented by clay floors with central hearths and fragmentary post-and-wattle walls, have been uncovered. Two groups of post-holes, which have been interpreted as belonging to comparable structures, have also been exposed in Lady Lane to the south. One of these had been partially destroyed by the digging of a defensive ditch, which, at its northern end, was over 7 m (23 ft) wide. Metal-working slag had been dumped in the ditch together with sherds of eleventh- and twelfth-century pottery; animal and fish bones were also recovered.[41]

## Viking settlement outside the towns

At present we know almost nothing of Viking settlement outside the towns. However recent work on the twelfth-century and later documentary sources together with place-name evidence indicates that the towns controlled considerable hinterlands and also set up dependencies elsewhere. As we have already seen in the twelfth century *Dyflinarskiri* stretched north to the Skerries, south to Arklow and west to Leixlip. In the tenth century it may have included Co. Kildare as far south-west as Mullaghmast and parts of Co. Meath. Limerick controlled an area from the Bunratty river in the west to Plassey in the east, and from the Slieve Barnagh foothills in the north, possibly including Killaloe, to Ballyneety in the south, as well as the dependencies of Cashel and Thurles. The Viking cantred at Waterford consisted of the baronies of Gaultier ('land of the foreigners') and most of Middlethird, while that of Cork comprised the baronies of Kerrycurrihy and parts of Kinalea as well as much of the liberties of Cork. The hinterland of Wexford remains more difficult to reconstruct but probably included Rosslare to the south. In addition there are likely to have been isolated settlements along the coast, for example Annagassan, Co. Louth, and Larne Harbour (*Ulfrecksfjord*), Co. Antrim.[42]

We do not know the ethnic make-up of these urban hinterlands and archaeological evidence for a Viking presence within them remains elusive. No Viking rural settlements have been identified, even in *Dyflinarskiri*, though the presence of agricultural communities is attested by Old Norse words loaned into Irish such as *punann* meaning a sheaf of corn.[43] Considering the lack of archaeological evidence for Viking rural settlements in Britain outside northern and western Scotland, the failure to locate them in Ireland is not so surprising and we do not know to what extent Vikings living in the countryside may have adopted native settlement types.

Although few pagan Viking graves have been found outside Dublin, their distribution provides some clue to areas of Viking activity. A glance at the map (95) shows that, with two exceptions (Eyrephort, Co. Galway, and possibly Kinnegar, Co. Donegal), which may represent no more than temporary settlements or landfalls, the graves have an entirely eastern and mainly coastal distribution. Unfortunately, with the exception of Mayfield, Co. Waterford, none has been scientifically excavated and much potentially valuable information has been lost. The possible cemetery at Church Bay, Rathlin Island, Co. Antrim, is particularly interesting. The site was first used for burial during the early Bronze Age and at least some of the reported mounds and stone cists may be of this period. Other cists may have been Christian burials of early medieval date. Finds, including a penannular brooch, beads, a sword and possibly a copper-alloy vessel indicate the presence of three or more probably Viking graves. Whether they were placed within new or earlier mounds and/or within cists is unknown, but the grave containing the brooch and beads seems to have been marked by a standing stone. Another intriguing discovery at Mount Erroll, Donnybrook, Dublin, apparently consisted of a mound approximately 30 m (100 ft) in diameter and 900 mm (3 ft) high which contained the body of a Viking warrior accompanied by a richly decorated sword, a spearhead and three arrowheads. The skull showed that the man had died from a blow to the head and two skeletons without gravegoods laid beside his feet may indicate ritual killings. Between 600 and 700 other bodies were also found within the mound. Many showed signs of violence and the few artefacts discovered suggested that the bodies were Irish rather than Viking. All the burials appeared contemporary and it has been postulated that the mass grave could have been the result of retribution exacted on the native population for the murder of a Viking warlord.

Only one possible boat-burial has been identified at Ballywillin, Co Antrim. The rest are isolated graves. The finds at Ballyholme, Phoenix Park and near Arklow included jewellery, principally oval brooches, indicating female burials; while those at Larne, Cah, Eyrephort and Drakestown contained weapons indicating male graves. Although no diagnostic artefacts were found at Navan, Co. Meath, the rite indicates that the grave is also likely to have been a Viking warrior

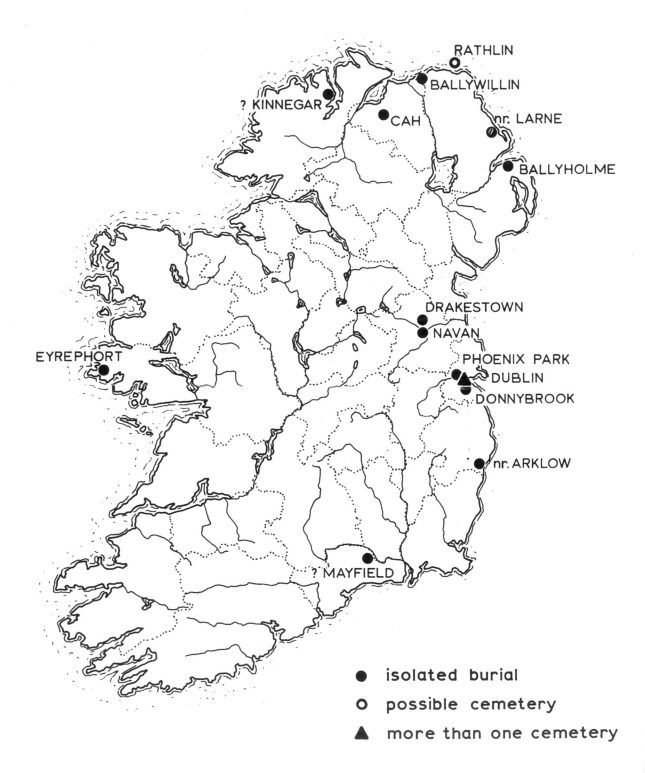

95  *Distribution of Viking burials (after Graham-Campbell 1976 with possible additions).*

burial. The body was accompanied by the skeleton of a horse and a set of Insular horse harness. The east/west oriented cist-and-lintel grave recently excavated at Mayfield is puzzling and may not be Viking at all. It was probably a child burial and the only artefact was a copper-alloy strap end found in the top of the grave fill. Its decoration is comparable with Anglo-Saxon Trewhiddle style. It has been suggested that it may be dated to the ninth or tenth centuries and could have been manufactured in the Scandinavian north of Britain. The relationship between the grave and nearby pits, one of which contained a possible Bronze Age pygmy cup, remains unclear. A cremation in a cist within a cairn reported from Kinnegar Strand on Lough Swilly may not be Bronze Age as originally thought. The recent discovery of a ringed pin in the vicinity has led to the suggestion that it could be Viking.[44]

The distribution of chance finds of Viking character, mainly weapons, is widespread. Many were found in rivers or lakes indicating the kind of waterborne activity well-attested in the annals though some objects, for example the sword from Ballinderry 1 crannog, are from native contexts. However, finds from Beginish, Co. Kerry, may point to the existence of a Viking settlement on the island. First, a cross-inscribed stone with a fragmentary inscription possibly dating to between 1000 and 1100 was found re-used as a lintel covering the entrance passage of a house on the eastern side of the island (see p. 47). The inscription tells us that Lir set up the stone while ?Munuikl carved the runes and it is interesting to note that the first name is Celtic while the second appears to be Viking. Secondly, a soapstone bowl of Viking type was found on the southern side of the island associated with a rectangular structure, though this was not investigated further.[45] Other Viking activity in west Kerry is suggested by the place-name Smerwick Bay near the end of the Dingle Peninsula, which comes from the Old Norse meaning 'butter bay', and by a runic inscription from the Great Blasket Island. Further eleventh- or twelfth-century runic inscriptions have been recorded from Killaloe, Co. Clare, Nendrum, Co. Down and Greenmount, Co. Louth. It has also been suggested that a group of grave-stones from south Co. Dublin decorated with cupmarks, herring-bone patterns, semi-circular loops and concentric circles are a characteristic Hiberno-Norse monument. A likely hogback grave cover of Viking type has been identified at Castledermot, Co. Kildare.[46]

## Conclusion

The advent of the Vikings in Irish waters at the end of the eighth century and their subsequent settlement during the ninth and tenth constituted the first foreign invasion of Ireland in the historic period. It remains almost impossible to estimate the amount of land the Vikings settled or controlled at any one time, but, putting the available historical, archaeological and linguistic evidence together, it seems that settlement outside the towns and their hinterlands was concentrated along the east coast with further littoral bases, perhaps particularly in the north-east, and along the inland waterways; there is comparatively little evidence of Viking activity west of the Shannon. Since much of Ireland remained unconquered, it is also extremely difficult to reconstruct the development of Hiberno-Norse relations over the period, though the ending of Dublin's political independence after 980 may be a turning-point which led to greater interaction detectable in archaeological terms by the inception of the Hiberno-Norse coinage and the influx of native carpentry techniques visible in some of the later tenth-century houses.

The destruction of the raids should not be forgotten but the lasting impact of the Vikings was more positive and wide-ranging. As we have seen the most important result of the incursions was the establishment of the Viking towns which functioned as centres of population and foci for administration, craft and trade. Before the Viking period the major monasteries may have fulfilled some of these functions but we do not know whether they would eventually have achieved urban status without the Viking intervention. For although it is clear that from the tenth century onwards some major monasteries did function as towns, 'it is impossible to treat either the Norse or the monastic town in isolation. Each thrived as a result of the existence of the other'.[47]

Initially the Viking raids had an adverse effect upon the native economy, but later the growing prosperity of the towns and the adeptness of the Vikings as traders resulted in an influx of wealth which ultimately benefitted both native and foreigner. The large number of silver hoards from Ireland and the wide range of imports from Viking-age levels in Dublin provide ample archaeological evidence for an expanding economy and the impact of Viking traders is also demonstrated by Old Norse loanwords into Irish such as *mogadh* meaning 'market'. The growth of international trade brought increased foreign contacts and the Dublin excavations have underlined the importance of links with parts of Anglo-Saxon and Anglo-Scandinavian England. Equally, research on the import of coin has emphasized the significance of the trade-route between Dublin and Chester in the early tenth century which was replaced after *c*.975 by the route between Dublin and Bristol. The expansion of contacts with southern England and France heralded a more general shift in geographical orientation, culminating in the Anglo-Norman invasion of 1169.

The impact of the Vikings on native technology should also be mentioned. As far as the archaeological evidence is concerned this is most clearly demonstrated in the sophistication of Viking smithing, especially in the manufacture of weapons. However, the Vikings also passed on their skills in boat building and navigation to the native population as indicated by Old Norse loanwords such as *stiúir* meaning 'rudder'.[48]

The coming of the Vikings also altered the development of Irish ecclesiastical art. The gradual intensification of raids on monasteries during the first half of the ninth century with the consequent pillaging of church treasures and the sapping of ecclesiastical wealth must have been a major factor in the abandonment of the rich polychrome designs typified by the Ardagh chalice and their gradual replacement with a simpler style exemplified by the 'Kells' crozier. It is also worth reiterating that, though Dublin seems to have acted as a melting pot for the fusion of Insular and Anglo-Scandinavian motifs, Scandinavian-inspired art styles do not begin to influence the conservative world of native ecclesiastical art until the eleventh century. But once assimilated they blended with a revival of earlier Insular techniques and motifs to produce the hybrid style associated with the late eleventh and early twelfth centuries (see p. 145).

In 1169 Ireland was again the object of foreign invaders, the Anglo-Normans. The incursion began after Dermot Mac Murrough obtained military assistance from a group of Welsh Marcher lords to regain the throne of Leinster. They quickly restored him to his kingdom and captured both Waterford and Dublin, but in 1171 Dermot died and one of their number, Richard de Clare, better known as Strongbow, who had married Dermot's daughter Aífe, succeeded him. Later that year Henry II arrived to take charge and Strongbow and the majority of Irish kings submitted to him.[49]

The Anglo-Normans never dominated Ireland completely. Nevertheless in the areas they conquered, principally Dublin and the lordships of Leinster and Meath, they built castles, founded many new towns, established a network of nucleated villages and added substantially to the number of stone-built abbeys, cathedrals and parish churches.[50] It is therefore they, much more than the Vikings, who were responsible for the gradual transformation of the medieval Irish landscape.

# REFERENCES

**1  The Roman impact** *(pages 1–5)*

1. Harbison 1988, 155–94; Raftery, B. 1984.
2. Tacitus *Agricola*, Ch. 24; Killeen 1976, 213–5.
3. Bateson 1973; 1976; Warner 1976, 285–6; Bradley 1981–2; Bélier 1981–2.
4. Jope and Wilson 1957; Jope 1960; Rynne 1976.
5. Bateson 1973, 45, 72–3; Warner 1976, 274–5, 277–8.
6. Tierney 1976; Tacitus *Agricola*, Ch. 24.
7. Carson and O'Kelly 1977.
8. Branigan 1977, 93–6.
9. Bateson 1973, 42–3, 63–4, 73–4; 1976, 171–3; Ó Ríordáin, S.P. 1947, 43–53.
10. Richards 1960; Thomas 1972a; 1973.
11. Laing 1985.

**2  Settlement: ring-forts** *(pages 6–33)*

1. Evans 1973
2. ibid; Freeman 1960; Orme 1970; Gillmor 1971; Pochin Mould 1972; Mitchell 1986.
3. Binchy 1954; Hughes 1972, 43–64; Kelly, F. 1988.
4. Ó Corráin 1978, 7.
5. Byrne 1971, 128–30; Kelly, F. 1988, 3–4.
6. Ó Corráin 1972, 28–48; Kelly, F. 1988, 7–15.
7. Ó Corráin 1978.
8. Kenney 1929, 62–4.
9. Wood–Martin 1886.
10. Westropp 1901.
11. Archaeological Survey of Northern Ireland 1966.
12. Lacy *et al* 1983; Stout 1984; Cuppage *et al* 1986.
13. Hencken 1950.
14. Hencken 1938, 2–3.
15. Hughes 1972, 99–146.
16. Raftery, J. 1981, 82.
17. Lynn 1985–6, 69–71; Warner 1985–6.
18. Raftery, B. 1972, 51–3.
19. Barrett and Graham 1975.
20. Hope–Taylor 1977.
21. Hencken 1950, 126; Lynn 1985–6, 71; Warner 1985–6, 76.
22. Lynn 1981–2, 120.
23. Lynn 1983a, 47.
24. Stenberger 1966, 51–3.
25. Ivens 1984a, 33, UB 2621, 2620, 2623.
26. Baillie 1982; 1985.
27. Ivens *et al* 1986; Williams 1985a, 75.
28. Baillie 1985, 22.
29. Hencken 1938, 55–8.
30. Archaeological Survey of Northern Ireland 1966, 108; Lacy *et al* 1983, 109–217; Stout 1984, 26–82.
31. Roy. Soc. Antiq. Ir. 1983, 10; Williams 1985a, 78; Barrett 1982, 85.
32. Collins 1961–2; Williams 1980.
33. O'Kelly 1970, 50–1; Ó Ríordáin, S.P. 1979, 30; Flanagan, D. 1980.
34. Archaeological Survey of Northern Ireland 1966, 108–12; Barrett 1980.
35. Archaeological Survey of Northern Ireland 1966, 109; Stout 1984, Fig. 19; Ivens 1984a, 9.
36. Stout 1984, 35–6; Ó Ríordáin, S.P. 1942, 79.
37. Lynn 1985, 81.
38. Lynn 1981–2.
39. ibid, 148–51, 167–8; Collins 1968b; Lynn 1985, 84–90; Hamlin and Lynn 1988, 38–44.
40. Stout 1984, 26; Barrett 1980, 43.
41. Archaeological Survey of Northern Ireland 1966, 116–7; Lynn 1981–2, 167–9; Waterman 1959a; Dickinson and Waterman 1960.

42. Archaeological Survey of Northern Ireland 1966, Fig. 72.2; Davies, O. 1947, 7–8; Lacy *et al* 1983, 119–54; Westropp 1896–7; Cuppage *et al* 1986, 186–214;Henry 1957.

43. Archaeological Survey for Northern Ireland 1966, 176–7.

44. Lacy *et al* 1983, 111–2.

45. Hencken 1938.

46. Davies, O. 1940a, 213–4; Proudfoot 1953, 42–4.

47. O'Kelly 1970, 51; Grogan and Eogan 1987; Kelly, E. 1974.

48. O'Kelly 1951; 1989, 219–22.

49. Ó Ríordáin, S.P. 1940, 110–2, 165–73, 176–8; Ó Ríordáin and MacDermott 1952; Caulfield 1981, 209; pers. comm. John Bradley.

50. Ó Ríordáin, S.P. 1949a; Raftery, J. 1944; Lynn 1983a, 48–50.

51. Ó Ríordáin, S.P. 1979, 31; 1982, 25–6; Selkirk 1970a, 304–11; Wailes 1974–5.

52. Caulfield 1981, 207, 212.

53. Lynn 1983a, 48, 54–7.

54. Mitchell 1986, 119, 153; Evans 1973, 57–8.

55. Proudfoot 1970, 41–3; Lynn 1983b, 79–81, 87–8.

56. Ó Cuileanáin and Murphy 1961, 80–1; Brannon 1981–2, 55, 58; Williams 1985a, 71; Manning 1986, 137–40.

57. Lynn 1983a, 50.

58. Proudfoot 1970, 41; Bersu 1940.

59. Thomas 1966, 87–91; Miles 1973.

60. Wainwright 1971; Jarrett and Wrathmell 1981; Edwards and Lane 1988, 68–9, 106–7.

61. Jobey 1972–4; Ritchie 1981, 108–10; Nieke 1983, 302–4.

62. Barrett and Graham 1975. For replies see Lynn 1975a; 1975b; McNeill, T.E. 1975; Davies, O. 1976.

63. Davison 1961–2.

64. Collins 1966, 124; Davies, O. 1940b, 342; Evans 1950; Proudfoot 1958; Warhurst 1967, 48; 1969, 96; Waterman 1967b, 52; 1958, 45–6.

65. Fanning 1973–4; Barry 1983, 304–5; 1987, 45–54.

66. O'Kelly 1962.

67. Rynne 1964.

68. Westropp 1896–7, iii, 120–2.

69. Flanagan, D. 1983.

70. Stout 1984, 31; Fahy 1969; Archaeological Survey of Northern Ireland 1966.

71. Ó Ríordáin, S.P. 1942, 78; O'Kelly 1962, 1–2.

72. O'Kelly 1963, 18–20, 22.

73. Stenberger 1966, 39–40.

74. O'Kelly 1967, 89–91; Fanning 1972, 173; Dickinson, C.W. and Waterman 1959, 70; Warhurst 1967, 44–6; Waterman 1959a, 143–4; Davies, O. 1940b, 338–40.

75. Davies, O. 1940a, 214; Ivens 1984a, 20–1; Ó Corráin 1983, 249; Hamlin and Lynn 1988, 39.

76. Brannon 1981–2, 54; Bersu 1947, 39.

77. Waterman 1972, 30; O'Kelly 1967, 91; Ivens 1984a, 20–1.

78. Department of the Environment for Northern Ireland 1983, 25, 93.

79. Ó Ríordáin, S.P. 1949a, 41–2; Lacy *et al* 1983, 111–2; Ó Ríordáin and Foy 1941, 90; Hencken 1938, 5–14.

80. Stout 1984, 28–30.

81. Ó Cuileanáin and Murphy 1961, 81.

82. O'Kelly 1963, 20–2, 115; Alcock 1972, 176–8; Waterman 1963, 63.

83. Ó Ríordáin, S.P. 1942, 79–84; Ó Ríordáin and Hartnett 1943, 5–9.

84. Lynn 1978b, 62–3; Collins 1968a, 56.

85. Ó Ríordáin, S.P. 1949a, 108; Lynn 1978b, 74.

86. Ó Ríordáin, S.P. 1942, 84.

87. Macalister and Praeger 1928, 100–8.

88. Collins 1966, 119–22, 127–9.

89. Ó Ríordáin, S.P. 1949b, 129–32.

90. Hamlin and Lynn 1988, 44–7; Lynn and McDowell 1988b.

91. Lynn 1978a, 37; Waterman 1956a, 76–83.

92. Lynn 1981–2, 86–93; Ó Ríordáin, S.P. 1949a, 44–52, Pls I, II; O'Kelly 1962, 6–7.

93. Ó Ríordáin and Foy 1941, 87–9.

94. Lynn 1978a.

95. Lynn 1981–2, 148.

96. Lynn 1978a, 36; Murray 1979.

97. Crew 1984; Lynn 1978a, 37–8.

98. Bersu 1947.

99. Collins 1968a, 56; Boal and Moffitt 1959.

100. Murray 1979, 87–9; Hamlin and Lynn 1988, 45–6.

101. Collins 1966; Waterman 1956a; Collins 1968b, Fig. 2.

102. Ó Ríordáin, S.P. 1949a, Pl. 2; Warhurst 1971, Fig. 1.

103. Lucas 1975, 168.

104. Warner 1979a, 103–11.
105. Lynn 1981–2, 86–92.
106. Warner 1979a, 107–10.
107. Waterman 1968.
108. Williams 1985a, 75–7.
109. Warner 1979a, 101–5; McCarthy 1983; Twohig 1976; 1971, 128–30.
110. Ó Ríordáin, S.P. and Hartnett 1943, 13–7.
111. Thomas 1972c; Ó Ríordáin, S.P. 1979, 70–1; Warner 1979a, 128–34.
112. Lucas 1975.
113. Ó Cuileanáin and Murphy 1961, 83.
114. Eogan and Bradley 1977; pers. comm. J. Bradley; Evans 1950, 8–16.
115. Thomas 1972c, 77.
116. Warner 1979a, 138–42.
117. Lynn 1981–2, 151.
118. Warhurst 1971; Williams 1985a, 75.
119. Lucas 1975, 181–4.
120. Waterman 1972, 33–4.
121. Lynn 1978b, 60–1; Warhurst 1969, 95; Ivens 1984a, 22–3.
122. Ó Ríordáin, S.P. and MacDermott 1952, 102–4; O'Kelly 1963, 99–101; Ó Ríordáin, S.P. 1942, 85–8.
123. Norman and St Joseph 1969, 38–72.
124. Ó Ríordáin, S.P. 1949a, 47–52; Waterman 1963, 69.
125. Lynn 1978b, 74; Ivens 1984a, 29–31.
126. Waterman 1972; Waterman and Collins 1952; Archaeological Survey of Northern Ireland 1966, 109.
127. Norman and St Joseph 1969, Pls 32, 34–5.
128. Ó Ríordáin, S.P. 1940.
129. MacNeill, E. 1923.
130. de Paor 1960, 79.
131. Ó Ríordáin, S.P. 1942.

## 3 Other settlement types *(pages 34–48)*

1. Hencken 1936; 1942; 1950; Collins 1955; Collins and Proudfoot 1959; Bradley 1982–3; 1984; 1985–6; Bourke 1986.
2. Hencken 1942, 1–29.
3. Davies, O. 1950; Ivens *et al* 1986.
4. Lynn 1983a, 53–4; Bradley 1982–3, 19; 1984, 86; 1985–6, 79–83; Collins and Seaby 1960; Williams 1978; Davies, O. 1941; Raftery, J. 1942–3; Ó Ríordáin, S.P. and Lucas 1946–7.
5. Raftery, J. 1957; 1972, 2–3, 6; Lynn 1983a, 53–4.
6. Wood–Martin 1886, 173; Lynn 1983a, 53.
7. Lynn 1983a.
8. Baillie 1982, 175–95; Ivens *et al* 1986, 102.
9. Lynn 1983a, 55.
10. Piggott 1952–3; Ritchie 1981, 111–4, K 1394, 2027; Morrison 1981.
11. Warner 1983.
12. Wood–Martin 1886, 147–54, 236; Crotty 1982; Hayes–McCoy 1964, Pl. V.
13. Hencken 1936; 1942; Rynne and MacEoin 1978, 51.
14. Pers. comm. J. Bradley.
15. Wood–Martin 1886.
16. Department of the Environment for Northern Ireland 1983, 27; Raftery, J. 1952, 182; Collins 1955, 45.
17. Lynn 1985–6.
18. Wood–Martin 1886, 26–7.
19. Hencken 1942, 30–3.
20. Hencken 1936, 107–18; Lynn 1985–6, 72–3.
21. Hencken 1950, 38–42; Lynn 1985–6, 69–72; Collins 1955, 49–51.
22. Lacy *et al* 1983, 104–6, 136–7.
23. Hencken 1950, 42–4; Lynn 1985–6, 70.
24. Hencken 1936, 107; pers. comm. J. Bradley; Mitchell 1986, 186.
25. Bradley 1984, 91; 1985–6, 82–3; pers. comm. J. Bradley; Hencken 1950, 44, Pl. I; Rynne and MacEoin 1978; Hencken, 1936, 119–21.
26. Bradley 1982–3, 20–4; 1984, 88–91; 1985–6, 83–5, Fig. 1; pers. comm. J. Bradley.
27. Hencken 1950, 41–2, 45–6; Hencken 1936, Pls XIV, XV, 122–6; Lynn 1985–6.
28. O'Kelly 1952b, 25, 35–54; Barry 1981, 306–7, UB 2216.
29. Childe 1936; Proudfoot and Wilson 1961–2; Liversage 1968; Barry 1981, UB 2215, 2217; Flanagan, D. 1980, 17; Department of the Environment for Northern Ireland 1983, 74.
30. Dark 1985; Thomas 1988.
31. Warner 1980–1, 48.
32. Eogan 1973; 1974, 68–111; 1977; Warner 1980–1, 48.
33. O'Kelly 1983, 149–79.
34. Warner 1971; 1972; 1973a; 1973b; 1974; 1975; 1979b; 1988; Scott 1983, 61, UB 844; O'Kelly 1989, Fig. 165.
35. Waterman 1956b.
36. Waterman 1971; Lynn 1974.
37. Williams 1983; 1984; Cuppage *et al* 1986, 396–7; Ó Ríordáin, S.P. 1949a, 57–62.

38. D'Evelyn 1933; Ó Ríordáin, S.P. 1935; Mallory and Woodman 1984; May and Batty 1948; Flanagan, L. 1966; Collins 1952; 1959.
39. Ó Ríordáin, B. and Rynne 1961; Lucas 1966b, 15–7; 1967b.
40. O'Kelly 1956.
41. Jackson, J.W. 1933; 1934; May 1943; Coleman 1947, 63–77; Movius 1935, 268–81; Molleson 1985–6.
42. Charles-Edwards 1984, 170–1; Evans 1973, 58–65.

## 4 Food and farming (*pages 49–67*)

1. Kelly, F. 1988, 99–110, 142–4, 273–7; MacNeill, E. 1923; Binchy 1981; Mac Eoin 1981; Charles–Edwards and Kelly 1983; Ó Corráin 1983; Kelly, F. 1976.
2. MacDonald 1984, 280–2; Connolly and Picard 1987, 24–5.
3. Kinsella 1970; Meyer 1892.
4. Hencken 1938; 1950; 1936; 1942.
5. Mitchell 1965; 1956; Case *et al* 1969.
6. Mitchell 1986; McCormick 1983; Monk 1985–6.
7. Irish National Committee for Geography 1979. Maps 30–4; Freeman 1960, 44–58.
8. Lamb 1981.
9. Mac Airt and Mac Niocaill 1983.
10. Mitchell 1976, 221–3; Freeman 1960, 59; Irish National Committee for Geography, Maps 24, 28; Mitchell 1986, 153.
11. Freeman 1960, 67–74.
12. Mitchell 1986, 117–21; Culleton and Mitchell 1976.
13. Baillie 1982, 175–95, 215–7.
14. Kelly, F. 1976; 1988, 99, 273–4; Mitchell 1976, 177–8.
15. Freeman 1960, 66–7, 74–5; Irish National Committee for Geography 1979, Maps 26, 36; Waterman 1972, 34; Proudfoot and Wilson 1961–2, 106.
16. Mac Niocaill 1971; Kelly, F. 1988, 274–5; Mitchell 1986, 166.
17. Mitchell 1986, 167; MacNeill, E. 1923, 286–7.
18. Hughes 1972, 51–2, 61–4.
19. Ó Corráin 1983.
20. Norman and St Joseph 1969, Pl. 35.
21. Williams 1983; 1984.
22. Cuppage *et al* 1986, 17, Pl. 52; Lynch 1981, 63, Gr N 9171; Caulfield 1983.
23. Ó Ríordáin, S.P. 1949a, 57–62.
24. Ó Ríordáin, S.P. 1940, Fig. 1, 139–45; Fowler, P.J. 1966–7; Fowler, P.J. and Thomas 1962, 69–80.
25. Case *et al* 1969; Mitchell 1986, 162–4.
26. Mitchell 1986, 160–2.
27. Lucas 1958.
28. Lucas 1958; Mac Niocaill 1981; O'Loan 1965, 175.
29. Irish National Committee for Geography 1979, Map 31; Duignan 1944, 140; Ó Corráin 1972, 53–5; Hughes 1972, 62–3; Kelly, F. 1976, 105.
30. Mac Airt and Mac Niocaill 1983.
31. Ó Corráin 1972, 55–6; McCormick 1983, 253–4; Lucas 1960, 19–30.
32. Lucas 1958; MacNeill, E. 1923; O'Kelly 1963, 120–5.
33. Proudfoot 1961, 109–10.
34. McCormick 1983; Lynn 1981–2, 153–4.
35. McCormick 1983.
36. Lynn 1978b, 73; Gaskell Brown and Harper 1984, 156.
37. Lucas 1960, 15–7; MacNeill, E. 1923, 288; O'Loan 1965, 173–4; Mac Airt and Mac Niocaill 1983.
38. MacNeill, E. 1923, 291; Ivens 1984a, 29.
39. Hencken 1942, 71; Proudfoot 1953, 51; O'Kelly 1967, 100; Lynn 1981–2, 158; Gaskell Brown and Harper 1984, 156; Lynn 1978b, 73.
40. O Corráin 1972, 57; Proudfoot and Wilson 1961–2, 105–6; Lynn 1981–2, 157–8.
41. Ó Corráin 1972, 57–8; Lucas 1960, 18–9; Hencken 1936, 233–4; 1942, 72; Henry 1965, Pl. 79; 1967, Pl. 102.
42. MacNeill, E. 1923, 291; Hencken 1950, 101–4; Eogan 1974, 97, Fig. 41; Hencken 1936, Fig. 15B, 137–8, Fig. 9c; Ó Ríordáin, S.P. and Hartnett 1943, 17–23; Armstrong 1922; Shetelig 1940, iii, 76, v, 33, Fig. 28.
43. de Paor and de Paor 1960, 88; MacNeill, E. 1923, 299; Hencken 1950, 225–6, 115–7; Scott 1978.
44. Lynn 1978b, 71 note 24; de Paor and de Paor 1960, 88; Henry 1967, Pl. 79.
45. Henry 1974, Pl. 120; Lucas 1960, 39; O'Loan 1965, 166; Proudfoot 1961, 111; Collins 1955, 77; Hencken 1950, 230.
46. Charles-Edwards and Kelly 1983.
47. Duignan 1944, 127; Proudfoot 1961, 104–9; Lucas 1960.
48. Binchy 1966.

49. Monk 1985–6, 33–4; O'Connell 1980, 314–6; Edwards, K.J. 1985, 213; Lynch 1981, 84, UB 2371.
50. Meyer 1892, 98; Binchy 1981.
51. Lucas 1970a, 99.
52. Edwards, K.J. 1985, 209–16.
53. Mitchell 1986, 143–4, 153–4; Lynch 1981, 127.
54. Duignan 1944; Rees 1979, (i), Share types 1b, 1c, 59–61.
55. Lucas 1972.
56. Gailey 1968; Hencken 1942, 47–8.
57. Duignan 1944, 140, Fig. 8.
58. Monk 1981, 216–9; Manning 1984, 242, 266, GU 1511; Ó Ríordáin, S.P. and MacDermott 1952, 103–4; Youngs *et al* 1984, 255–6; 1985, 214.
59. Lucas 1970b, 174; Mac Airt and Mac Niocaill 1983; MacNeill, E. 1923; Gailey 1970, 64–9.
60. Lynn 1974, 6.
61. Hencken 1938, Fig. 36; 1942, Fig. 31; Caulfield 1981, 210–1.
62. Lucas 1953; 1955; Wallace 1982, 264–5; Mac Eoin 1981; Baillie 1975; 1982, 177–95; pers. comm. M. Monk.
63. Ó Corráin 1972, 52–3; Binchy 1938, 27.
64. Kelly, F. 1988, 276–7; MacNeill, E. 1923, 304.
65. Henry 1965, Fig. 18, Pl. 92; Munro and Gillespie 1918–9; Flanagan, L.N.W. 1963, 109; Kelly, F. 1988, 107, 276.
66. Orme 1970, 97; Mitchell 1976, 184; Hencken 1950, 225; Proudfoot and Wilson 1961–2, 115; Hencken 1942, 67; Henry 1945, 136, 154; Anderson and Anderson 1961, 295; Lynn 1981–2, 81, 154; Collins 1955, 63; Kelly, F. 1988, 107.
67. Hencken 1950, 229–30; Proudfoot and Wilson 1961–2, 106; O'Kelly 1956, 193.
68. O'Kelly 1954.
69. Barfield and Hodder 1987; Ó Drisceoil 1988; Ryan 1976; Edwards, N. and Lane 1988, 96.
70. Woodman 1981–2, 182; Mallory and Woodman 1984, 55; Proudfoot and Wilson 1961–2, 106, 115; Childe 1936, 195; Went 1952, 114, 124, Pl. 20, A, B, E; Waterman 1971, 73–4; Ó Ríordáin, B. and Rynne 1961, 61; O'Kelly 1956, 179; Proudfoot and Wilson 1961–2, 106.
71. Hencken 1936, 121; pers. comm. M. Monk; Hamlin 1985, 279; Lucas 1960, 36–7;

Mallory and Woodman 1984, 55–6; Lynn 1981–2, 157–8; Hencken 1950, 51.

## 5 Craft, exchange and trade (*pages 68–98*)

1. Proudfoot 1961, 115.
2. Ó Ríordáin, S.P. 1942, 125–34; Radford 1956; Thomas 1959; 1976; 1981a; 1982; Peacock and Thomas 1967; Hayes 1972; 1980; Munn 1985; Campbell 1984; Keay 1984; Peacock and Williams 1986; pers. comm. E. Campbell.
3. Hodges, R. 1982, 67; Youngs 1986, 187; pers. comm. E. Campbell.
4. Bradley 1982–3, 24–5 (NB: The illustrated vessel is in fact a crucible, not E ware, pers. comm. E. Campbell.)
5. Warner 1979b.
6. Ryan 1973; Lynn 1978b, 65; 1981–2, 151.
7. Ryan 1973; Gaskell Brown and Brannon 1978, 83.
8. Proudfoot and Wilson 1961–2, 97–8.
9. Thomas 1968; Ivens 1984b.
10. Ryan 1973, 621; Brannon 1979, 29–33.
11. Jackson, J.W. 1933, 233; 1934, 107.
12. Ryan 1973; Ivens 1984a, 10–1, 24; Brannon 1981–2, 55–6; Ó Corráin 1972, 14; Barber 1981a, 358, Fig. 43; pers. comm. A. Lane; Raftery, J. 1941b, 306–8; Wallace 1985b, 125.
13. Ryan 1973, 628–9; Lynn 1978a, 36; Baillie 1986; Thomas 1968; Hutchinson 1979.
14. Bersu 1947, 51; Lynn 1978a, 36; 1981–2, 114; McNeill, T.E. 1977, 71–6; 1980, 109–13.
15. Hencken 1950, 126; pers. comm. E. Campbell; Fanning 1981a, 111–3, UB 2167.
16. Hencken 1950, 108–10; O'Kelly 1963, 45–7; Collins and Proudfoot 1959, 96–7.
17. Wallace 1982, 264–5; Collins 1955, 65–7, Fig. 14; Hencken 1950, 167–8; 1936, 110–2.
18. Kilby 1977; Jenkins 1981; Bradley 1984, 91.
19. Hencken 1936, 141–2; Bersu 1947, 53–4; Henry 1965, Pls 87, 91.
20. Morris 1982; Hencken 1950, 156–8, Figs 77, 84, W169, W173, W171; Bersu 1947, 54–5; Bradley 1984, 91; Collins 1955, 67, Fig. 14 (86).
21. Hencken 1936, 136–7; 1942, 58; Raftery, J. 1956.

22. Hencken 1936, 135, 175–86; Simpson 1972; Bell 1969, 45–6; Waterman 1969.
23. Hencken 1950, 151–2; McGrail 1976, 22–3; Baillie 1982, 240–1.
24. Hodges, H. 1976, 148–52; Stenburger 1966, Fig. 2, 47; Hencken 1950, 170, Fig. 86.
25. Lucas 1956, 366–88; Hencken 1942, 56–7; 1950, 180–1; Ivens 1984a, 26–8; Barber 1981a, 318–28; 1981b.
26. Bradley 1982–3, 28; 1984, 91; Webb 1965, 36; McGrail 1987, 3, 186.
27. Waterer 1968; Buckley 1915; Bruce-Mitford 1967, 2; O'Neill 1984, xiii.
28. Hencken 1950, 203–24.
29. Wild 1988, 21–2; Ó Ríordáin, S.P. 1949a, 110.
30. Eogan 1977, 74; Hencken 1938, 43–4; Patterson 1955.
31. Wild 1988; Lang 1988, Pl. XXI; Hencken 1950, 209–17, 194, Fig. 106 (673, 1479); MacGregor 1985, 188, 191–2; Proudfoot 1958, 30; Collins and Proudfoot 1959, 98.
32. Henry 1952.
33. Proudfoot 1953, 54; pers. comm. E. Campbell; Lynn 1989, 197.
34. Hencken 1950, Fig. 112, Pl. XIX (1).
35. McClintock 1950, 1–3, 11–4.
36. MacGregor 1985.
37. National Museum of Ireland Acc. Nos. B.17.18 – B.17.20.
38. MacGregor 1985, 55–72.
39. ibid, 73–95; Hencken 1950, 184–90; Eogan 1974, 100–2.
40. Lucas 1965, 101–2.
41. MacGregor 1985, 113–22; Hencken 1950, 190–4; 1942, Fig. 22 (2).
42. Gaskell Brown and Harper 1984, 125–8; Hencken 1942, 54–5; 1950, 195–7.
43. Eogan 1974, 103; Shetelig 1940, v, 71; MacDermott 1950; Raftery, J. 1941a, 149–50; Henry 1967, Pl. 82; Alexander 1978, Pl. 146; Hencken 1950, 181; 1942, Fig. 22 (790); Ó Ríordáin, S.P. 1949a, 82–3; Hencken 1938, 40–1.
44. Scott 1987.
45. Collins 1955, 71; Ó Cuileanáin and Murphy 1961, 90; Fanning 1981a, 108.
46. Tylecote 1986, 133–4; Fanning 1981a, 108–10.
47. Collins 1955, 71.
48. O'Kelly 1963, 99–103; 1952a, 32–5; Fanning 1981a, 105–8; Tylecote 1986, 141–2, 187; Williams 1985b, 96–101.
49. Scott 1983, UB 844; O'Kelly 1963, 56–7.
50. ibid, 41–65.
51. Scott 1978.
52. Roe 1966, Pls VII, VIII; Hencken 1950, 88–94; Rynne 1980; Ivens 1984a, 26.
53. Hencken 1950, 94–9; Alcock 1971, 329–31.
54. Hencken 1950, 240; Ó Ríordáin, S.P. 1942; Gaskell Brown and Harper 1984.
55. Hencken 1950, 234–41; O'Kelly 1963; Ivens 1984c; Bradley 1982–3; 1984; Warner 1973a.
56. Eogan 1977, 74.
57. Gaskell Brown and Harper 1984, 136–43; Curle 1982, 35–9.
58. O'Meadhra 1979; 1987a.
59. Ryan 1981; Bradley 1984, 91; Ivens 1984c, 95.
60. Ó Ríordáin, S.P. 1942; Hencken 1950; Harden 1956a, 151–2, 154; pers. comm. E. Campbell.
61. Bateson 1981, 87ff; Gaskell Brown and Harper 1984, 135–6.
62. Hencken 1950, 132.
63. Henry 1956, 85.
64. Warner and Meighan 1981; Guido 1978, 39–41.
65. Ivens 1984c, 98–100; O'Kelly 1963, 72.
66. Hencken 1950, 132–45.
67. ibid, 145–50; Eogan 1977, 75; Hencken 1938, 41–2; Kilbride-Jones 1937–8.
68. Hencken 1938, 55–62; 1950, 173; Ó Ríordáin, S.P. 1942, 107–16; O'Kelly 1963, 78–94.
69. Harper 1973–4, 37–9; Williams 1984, 41–5; Collins and Proudfoot 1959, 98.
70. Hencken 1942, 13–5; 1950, 150; Ó Cuileanáin and Murphy 1961, 86–7; Gaskell Brown and Collins 1984, 136–7.
71. Doherty 1980.
72. Evans 1966, 177–8.
73. Doherty 1980, 81–4.
74. Bruce-Mitford 1987, 32.
75. Doherty 1980, 77–8; James 1982.
76. Lynn 1984; Hillgarth 1984.
77. Blindheim, C. 1976; Doherty 1980, 81–2; Hodges, R. 1982, 50–1, 67.

## 6 The Church (*pages 99–131*)

1. Hughes 1966.
2. Thomas 1981b, 294–306.
3. Binchy 1962; Thomas 1981b, 307–46; Thompson 1985.
4. Hughes 1966, 45.
5. Lucas 1963.
6. Hughes 1966.
7. ibid; Chadwick 1961.
8. Davies, W. 1974; Sharpe 1984; Ó Corráin 1981b; Hurley, V. 1982.
9. Hughes 1966; Henry 1980; Ó Murchadha 1980.
10. Doherty 1985.
11. Hughes 1966; Gwynn 1968; de Paor 1967.
12. Sheehy 1980, 17–27; Petrie 1845.
13. Lawlor 1925.
14. Leask 1955; Macalister 1945; 1949.
15. Henry 1957.
16. O'Kelly 1958.
17. Archaeological Survey of Northern Ireland 1966; Lacy *et al* 1983; Cuppage *et al* 1986.
18. Norman and St Joseph 1969; Hurley, V. 1982, 314–21; Swan 1985.
19. Harbison 1970; Hamlin 1984.
20. Gaskell Brown and Harper 1984; Hamlin and Lynn 1988, 57–61; Ivens 1984c.
21. Jackson, K. 1953, 151–4; Macalister 1945, Nos 47, 277, 75; Thomas 1971, 94–7, 106; MacWhite 1960–1; Cuppage *et al* 1986, No. 971.
22. Charles-Edwards 1976.
23. Jackson, K. 1953, 152–4.
24. Hamlin 1982, 283–5.
25. Harbison 1975, 202–4; Killanin and Duignan 1967, 169–72.
26. Hughes and Hamlin 1977, 22–8; Leask n.d.
27. Ó Ríain 1972; Hughes and Hamlin 1977, 29–32.
28. Gaskell Brown and Harper 1984, UB 283; Rynne 1972, 80–3; Lynn 1988, UB 2437; McDowell 1986; 1987a; Lynn and McDowell 1988a; Hamlin and Lynn 1988, 57–61.
29. Hughes and Hamlin 1977, 29–32; Lucas 1963.
30. Doherty 1985, 53–60.
31. ibid; Nees 1983; Stokes 1905, xxiv–xxvi.
32. Thomas 1971, 32.
33. Swan 1973; 1985, 80–1, 95; Bradley 1980–1.

34. Lawlor 1925; Archaeological Survey for Northern Ireland 1966, 133–4, 292–5.
35. Hayes-McCoy 1964, 5–6; MacAirt and MacNiocaill 1983, 439, 457, 527; O'Donovan 1856, II, 797; Henry 1967, 39–43.
36. Norman and St Joseph 1969, Pl. 69; Gaskell Brown and Harper 1984, 111–7, UB 283, 285; Swan 1985, 84, Fig. 4.4; Lynn 1988.
37. Anderson and Anderson 1961, 109–16; MacDonald 1984.
38. Royal Commission on the Ancient and Historical Monuments of Scotland 1982, 14, 36–9; Barber 1981a, GU 1243.
39. Leask n.d., 30–2.
40. Hamlin and Foley 1983, 44–5.
41. MacDonald 1984, 293–7.
42. ibid, 284–93; Hamlin 1985, 286–8.
43. Royal Commission on the Ancient and Historical Monuments of Scotland 1982, 39–41.
44. O'Donovan 1856, II, 796–7, III, 50–1; Roe 1981, 76–8.
45. pers. comm. C.J. Lynn.
46. Lawlor 1925, 63, 106–8.
47. Gaskell Brown and Harper 1984; McDowell 1986, 12; Ivens 1984c; Royal Commission on the Ancient and Historical Monuments of Scotland 1982, 14, 41.
48. Charles-Edwards 1984; Royal Commission on the Ancient and Historical Monuments of Scotland 1982, 14.
49. Flanagan, D. 1984, 34–6.
50. Henry 1957, 101–4.
51. Hurley, V. 1982, 307–10.
52. Cuppage *et al* 1986, 257–346; Fanning 1981b; Henry 1957.
53. O'Kelly 1958.
54. Fanning 1981a, UB 2167.
55. de Paor 1955; Henry 1957, 113–29; Lecture, J. White Marshall, June 1987.
56. Wakeman 1893; Heraughty 1982, 16–35; Thomas 1971, 168–75.
57. Stout 1984, 92–6.
58. Manning 1984, GU 1511; 1986, GU 1781, 1782; Swan 1972; 1976; McDowell 1987b.
59. James 1981, 41–4.
60. Doherty 1984, 92–4; Bieler 1979, 186–7.
61. MacDonald 1981, 305–6; Hamlin 1984, 117–8; Henry 1974, Pl. 68.
62. Harbison 1982, 626; Herren 1974, lines 547–60.

63. Translation Bieler 1963, 28.
64. Harbison 1982, 627–9; Hamlin 1984, 123;
    Waterman 1959b; 1967a; O'Kelly 1975,
    20–2, HAR 1380; Thomas 1967, 138–40;
    Royal Commission on the Ancient and
    Historical Monuments of Wales 1976,
    14–5.
65. Harbison 1970; Leask 1955, 27–42.
66. Hamlin 1984, 118–20; MacDonald 1981,
    307; Harbison 1982, 620.
67. Harbison 1982.
68. Harbison 1970.
69. de Paor 1967; Stalley 1981a, 62–5, 80.
70. Harbison *et al* 1978, 80–4; de Paor 1967;
    Stalley 1981a, 65; Cuppage *et al* 1986,
    312–7.
71. Stalley 1980; 1987.
72. Petrie 1845, 380–96; Barrow 1979.
73. Hare and Hamlin 1986; Hamlin 1985, 288.
74. O'Brien 1984, 50.
75. O'Brien 1984; Raftery, B. 1981.
76. O'Brien 1984; Raftery, B. 1981; Grogan and
    Eogan 1987.
77. Doherty 1984.
78. Hamlin and Foley 1983.
79. Kendrick 1939; Howells 1941, 103–17;
    Lynn 1977; 1988, UB 2437;
    McDowell 1986; 1987a.
80. Brannon 1980; Hamlin 1985, 295;
    Sweetman 1982–3; Manning 1986;
    Mallory 1986, 4; Ivens 1987, 33–4; Hamlin
    and Lynn 1988, 27–9; O'Kelly 1967,
    74–83.
81. Thomas 1971, 132–66, 1981b, Fig. 60;
    Waterman 1960; Waterman and Hamlin
    1976; Hamlin 1985, 295–6.
82. Hamlin and Ní Chatháin forthcoming.

## 7 Art *(pages 132–171)*

1. Bain 1951.
2. Lynch 1983, 15.
3. Royal Commission on the Ancient and
   Historical Monuments of Scotland 1982,
   17; Lionard 1961, 145.
4. Ó hInnse 1947, 64–7; Lucas 1986, 17–20.
5. Edwards, N. 1985, 395–6.
6. Raftery, B. 1983; 1984; 1987.
7. Raftery, B. 1984, 328–30; Warner 1983;
   Fowler, E. 1963.
8. Warner 1987, 20.
9. Fowler, E. 1963; Laing 1975, 302–16;
   Kilbride-Jones 1980b; Dickinson, T.M.
   1982.
10. Fowler, E. 1963; Stevenson 1976; Smith
    1917–8.
11. Fowler, E. 1968; Longley 1975;
    Henry 1936; 1956, 79–83; 1965, 68–75;
    Bruce-Mitford 1987.
12. Doherty 1984.
13. Raftery, J. 1981, 82.
14. Backhouse 1981, 12–6.
15. Blindheim, M. 1984; Swarzenski 1954.
16. Hunt 1956; Bakka 1965, 39–40.
17. O'Kelly 1965.
18. Organ 1973; Henry 1965, 107–8.
19. Ryan and Ó Floinn 1983.
20. Harbison 1978; Cooney *et al* 1987, 43;
    Harbison 1984.
21. Holmqvist 1955; Mahr 1932, Pl. 30;
    Raftery, J. 1941a, 104–5.
22. Bourke 1980; Ryan 1987a.
23. Shetelig 1940, v, 83–111.
24. Smith 1913–4.
25. Henry 1965, 108–10; Stevenson 1974.
26. Fanning 1969; 1974–5; 1983.
27. Armstrong 1921–2.
28. Henry 1967, 111–32.
29. Ryan 1983, 3–15; 1987b, 68–73.
30. Bourke 1987.
31. MacDermott 1955; Bourke 1985, 154–62.
32. Graham-Campbell 1972; 1973–4; 1975;
    Johansen 1973.
33. Graham-Campbell 1983.
34. Fanning 1983, 327; Henry 1967, 128–31,
    Fig. 17.
35. Henry 1970; Ó Floinn 1987a.
36. Graham-Campbell 1987; Lang 1987; 1988.
37. Henry 1970; Ó Floinn 1983; 1987a; 1987b;
    Kendrick and Senior 1936.
38. Ó Floinn 1987a, 179.
39. Hughes 1972.
40. Armstrong and Macalister 1920; Lang
    1988, DW 25; Lynn 1985, 88; Gaskell
    Brown and Harper 1984, 132.
41. Alexander 1978, Nos 1, 4; Nordenfalk
    1947; Henry 1965, 59–65.
42. Alexander 1978, Nos 9, 17, 53–4.
43. Alexander 1978, No. 5; Nordenfalk 1947;
    1977, 15, 32–3.
44. Alexander 1978, No. 6; Henderson, G.
    1987, 19–55.
45. Stevenson 1981–2.
46. Roth 1987.
47. Alexander 1978, Nos 9–12.
48. Ó Cróinín 1982; 1984; Verey *et al* 1980.

49. Henry 1967, 68–95; 1974; Alexander 1978, No. 52; Henderson, G. 1987, 130–98.
50. Henderson, G. 1987, 168–74; Henderson, I. 1987.
51. Brown 1972, 234.
52. Nordenfalk 1977, 108.
53. Henry 1967, 69–70; 1974, 216–21.
54. Alexander 1978, 75.
55. Alexander 1978, Nos 44, 61.
56. Alexander 1978, No. 54.
57. Alexander 1978, Nos 45, 48, 53, 51.
58. Hughes 1958, 247–8.
59. Alexander 1978, No. 70; Henry 1967, 102–5.
60. Alexander 1978, No. 17; Bailey 1978.
61. Henry 1961; Alexander 1978, Nos 73–4.
62. Henry and Marsh-Micheli 1962; Henry 1970, 46–73.
63. Stalley 1981b, 185–6.
64. Henry and Marsh-Micheli 1962, 138–40; Gwynn 1977, 260–73.
65. Lang 1988, 4.
66. Edwards, N. 1985, 393–4.
67. Hamlin 1982, 286–93; Higgins 1987.
68. Hamlin 1982, 291.
69. Hamlin 1972; 1982; Fanning 1981a, 139–41.
70. Richardson 1987.
71. Henry 1965, 118–31.
72. Edwards, N. 1985, 395–6; Stevenson 1985; Harbison 1986.
73. Cramp 1965, 5.
74. Edwards, N. 1985, 397–402.
75. Henry 1965, 138–57; 1967, 133–94; 1970, 123–47.
76. Henry 1980; Ó Murchadha 1980; de Paor 1987, 140–3.
77. Harbison 1987a.
78. Hamlin 1987a.
79. Edwards, N. 1985, 402–6; Royal Commission on the Ancient and Historical Monuments of Scotland 1982, 17–8.
80. Henry 1930.
81. Henry 1965, 138–57; Hicks 1980; Edwards, N. 1983a; 1984, 57–9.
82. Edwards, N. 1986; forthcoming.
83. Roe 1966.
84. Henry 1965, 141–2, 149–50.
85. de Paor 1987.
86. Henry 1980; Ó Murchadha 1980.
87. Henry 1967, 138–9; Mac Airt and Mac Niocaill 1983, 377.
88. Roe 1981, 27–43.
89. Henry 1967, 159–88.
90. Flower 1954; Henry 1967, 140–59; Ó Carragáin 1987.
91. Henry 1967, 152–5, 158–9; Roe 1955; 1956; 1966, 44–54; 1981, 45–62.
92. Henry 1970, 125–7.
93. Henry 1970, 123–47; de Paor 1955–6; Stalley 1981b.
94. Ó Flionn 1987b.
95. Edwards, N. 1984, 59.
96. Harbison 1986; 1987b; Hamlin 1987b; Lionard 1961, 136–7.
97. Hickey 1985, 26–42.
98. Lionard 1961.
99. Henry 1970, 146–7, Pl. 89.
100. O'Kelly 1964.
101. Shetelig 1940, v; Wamers 1985.
102. Kilbride-Jones 1980b; Graham-Campbell 1972; 1973–4; 1975; 1983; Johansen 1973; Fanning 1969; 1974–5; 1983.
103. Kendrick *et al* 1960; Henry 1974.
104. Higgins 1987.
105. Organ 1973; Whitfield 1987.
106. Kendrick *et al* 1960; Bailey 1978, 12–7.
107. de Paor 1987, 153; Edwards, N. 1983b; Lang 1986, 155–6.
108. Stevenson 1981–2; Henderson, I. 1987; Ó Carragáin 1987.

## 8 The Vikings *(pages 172–192)*

1. Walsh 1922.
2. Shetelig 1940, iii.
3. Mac Airt and Mac Niocaill 1983, 250–99; Hill 1981, Fig. 46.
4. Ó Corráin 1972, 91–2.
5. Lucas 1966a; 1967a; Hughes 1972, 148–59; 1980, 24–7.
6. Royal Commission on the Ancient and Historical Monuments of Scotland 1982, 19–20; Hughes 1966, 197–214.
7. Hencken 1950, 7.
8. Shetelig 1940, v; Bakka 1963; 1965; Wamers 1983; 1985.
9. Blindheim, C. 1976; Graham-Campbell 1980, No. 314.
10. Bakka 1963; 1965; Wamers 1985.
11. Mac Airt and Mac Niocaill 1983, 302–3; Ó Corráin 1972, 89–131; Dolley 1966, 18–9.
12. Dolley 1966; Graham-Campbell 1976.
13. Kenny 1987, 508; Doherty 1980, 82; Dolley 1965, 31; 1966, 142–5.

14. Hall 1973–4; Kenny 1987, 521; Ryan *et al* 1984, 345–50.
15. Graham-Campbell 1974; 1976; Hall 1973; Ryan *et al* 1984.
16. Kenny 1987; Graham-Campbell 1976, 42–6; 1989; Gerriets 1985.
17. Graham-Campbell 1976, 47–8; Dolley 1966, 20; Hall 1973–4, 71.
18. Graham-Campbell 1976, 48; Dolley 1966, 26–7; Ryan *et al* 1984.
19. Graham-Campbell 1976, 51–4; Shetelig 1940, iv, 30–45.
20. Graham-Campbell 1976, 48; Dolley 1966, 28–9, 36–7; Kenny 1987, 509–10, 522.
21. Dolley 1966, 119–45; Heslip 1985, 29.
22. Graham-Campbell 1976, 48–9; Dolley 1966, 63–4, 67–8; Kenny 1987, 511.
23. Clarke 1977.
24. Mitchell 1987, 7; Wallace 1981a, 138–9.
25. Wilde 1866–9; Coffey and Armstrong 1910; Shetelig 1940, iii, 11–65; Briggs 1985; Wallace and Ó Floinn 1988, 9–10.
26. Mitchell 1987, 7.
27. Wallace 1981b, 110–3; 1985a, 114–7; 1981a, 134–5.
28. Wallace 1985b, 112–5.
29. Wallace 1985b, 116–9; Murray 1983.
30. Wallace 1982.
31. Murray 1983, 112–6, 91–7; Coope 1981; Mitchell 1987, 31–2.
32. Murray 1983, 54–6, 66–7; Wallace 1985b, 119; 1986, 212.
33. Ó Ríordáin, B. 1985, 142; Wallace 1985b, 121; National Museum of Ireland 1973, Nos 204, 245–6, Pl. 12; Lang 1988, 53; Christensen 1988.
34. Lang 1988.
35. Wallace 1985b, 123–4; National Museum of Ireland 1973; Ó Ríordáin, B. 1971; O'Meadhra 1979, Nos 22–63; 1987b.
36. Bradley 1988, 56–62.
37. Wallace 1985a, 133–5; McCormick 1983, 259–61; Mitchell 1987, 22–7.
38. Wallace 1985a, 132–8.
39. Haliday 1884, 153–5; 195–7; Shetelig 1940, iii, 65–8; Hughes 1966, 256–7; Wallace 1986, 203–4; Clarke 1978; 1985, 146, 150–1.
40. Haliday 1884, 151–2, 156–70, 179–80.
41. Hurley, M. 1988; Barry 1987, 34–5.
42. Bradley 1988, 62–6.
43. Greene 1976, 78.
44. Graham-Campbell 1976, 40–2, 59–61; Fanning 1970; Warner 1973–4, 61–3; Hall 1974; 1978; Sheehan 1987–8; Lacy *et al* 1983, 66; Gowen 1988, 162–9.
45. Graham-Campbell 1976, 42; Shetelig 1940, iii, 77–98; O'Kelly 1956, 171–5; 1961.
46. Bradley 1988, 66–7; Oftedal 1976, 132; Macalister 1916–7; Lawlor 1925, 70; Ó hEailidhe 1957; Lang 1971.
47. Doherty 1985, 68.
48. Green 1976, 79.
49. Frame 1981, 1–21.
50. Barry 1987.

# BIBLIOGRAPHY

**Abbreviations**

JCHAS    Journal of the Cork Historical and
         Archaeological Society

JRSAI    Journal of the Royal Society of
         Antiquaries f Ireland

Med. Arch.  Medieval Archaeology

PRIA     Proceedings of the Royal Irish Academy

PSAS     Proceedings of the Society of Antiquaries
         of Scotland

UJA      Ulster Journal of Archaeology

Other abbreviations follow the conventions of the
Council for British Archaeology.

Alcock, L. 1971 Arthur's Britain
    (Harmondsworth)
— 1972 "By South Cadbury, is that Camelot..."
    (London)
Alexander, J.J.G. 1978 Insular Manuscripts 6th to
    the 9th Century (London)
Almqvist, B. and Greene, D. (eds) 1976 Proceedings
    of the Seventh Viking Congress (Dundalk)
Anderson, A.O. and M.O. (eds) 1961 Adomnan's
    Life of Columba (Edinburgh)
Archaeological Survey of Northern Ireland 1966
    An Archaeological Survey of County Down
    (Belfast)
Armstrong, E.C.R. 1921–2 'Irish bronze pins of
    the Christian period', Archaeologia 72: 71–86
— 1922 'Some Irish antiquities of unknown use',
    Antiquaries J. 2: 6–12
— and Macalister, R.A.S. 1920 'Wooden book
    with leaves indented and waxed found near
    Springmount Bog, Co. Antrim', JRSAI 50:
    160–6

Backhouse, J. 1981 The Lindisfarne Gospels
    (London)
Bailey, R.N. 1978 The Durham Cassiodorus
    (Jarrow Lecture)
Baillie, M.G.L. 1975 'A horizontal mill of the
    eighth century AD at Drumard, Co. Derry',
    UJA 38: 25–32
— 1982 Tree-Ring Dating and Archaeology
    (London/Canberra)
— 1985 'Irish dendrochronology and
    radiocarbon calibration', UJA 48: 11–23
— 1986 'A sherd of souterrain ware from a dated
    context', UJA 49: 104–5
Bain, G. 1951 Celtic Art, The Methods of
    Construction (London)
Bakka, E. 1963 'Some English decorated metal
    objects found in Norwegian Viking graves:
    contributions to the art history of the eighth
    century AD', Årbok Univ. Bergen 1963 Hum.
    Ser. 1: 1–66
— 1965 'Some decorated Anglo-Saxon and Irish
    metalwork found in Norwegian Viking graves',
    Small, A. (ed.), 4th Viking Congress (London)
    32–40
Barber, J.W. 1981a 'Excavations on Iona, 1979',
    PSAS 111: 282–380
— 1981b 'Some observations on early Christian
    footwear', JCHAS 86: 103–6
Barfield, L. and Hodder, M. 1987 'Burnt mounds
    as saunas, and the prehistory of bathing',
    Antiquity 61: 370–9
Barrett, G.F. 1980 'A field survey and
    morphological study of ring-forts in southern
    Co. Donegal', UJA 43: 39–51
— 1982 'Ring-fort settlement in County Louth:
    sources, pattern and landscapes', J. Co. Louth
    Archaeol. Hist. Soc. 20: 77–95
— and Graham, B.J. 1975 'Some considerations
    concerning the dating and distribution of
    ring-forts in Ireland', UJA 38: 33–45

Barrow, G.L. 1979 *The Round Towers of Ireland* (Dublin)

Barry, T.B. 1981 'Archaeological excavations at Dunbeg promontory fort, Co. Kerry, 1977', *PRIA* 81c: 295–330

— 1983 'Anglo-Norman ringwork castles: some evidence' in Reeves-Smyth, T. and Hamond, F. (eds) 295–314

— 1987 *The Archaeology of Medieval Ireland* (London/New York)

Bateson, J.D. 1973 'Roman material from Ireland', *PRIA* 73c: 21–97

— 1976 'Further finds of Roman material from Ireland', *PRIA* 76c: 171–80

— 1981 *Enamel-working in Iron Age, Roman and Sub-Roman Britain. The products and techniques* (Brit. Archaeol. Rep. 93)

Bélier, A.-C. 1981–2 'A sherd of Terra Sigillata from Wood Quay, Dublin', *UJA* 44–5: 192–4

Bell, R.C. 1969 *Board and table games from many civilizations*, Vol. 2 (London)

Bersu, G. 1940 'Excavations at Little Woodbury, Wiltshire. Part I: The settlement as revealed by excavation', *Proc. Prehist. Soc.* 6: 30–111

— 1947 'The rath at Townland Lissue', *UJA* 10: 30–58

Bieler, L. 1963 *Ireland: harbinger of the Middle Ages* (London/New York/Toronto)

— (ed.) 1979 *The Patrician texts in the Book of Armagh* (*Scriptores Latini Hiberniae*, 10) (Dublin)

Binchy, D.A. 1938 'Bretha Crólige', *Ériu* 12: 1–77

— 1954 'Secular institutions' in Dillon, M. (ed.), *Early Irish Society* (Dublin) 52–65

— 1962 'Patrick and his biographers, ancient and modern', *Studia Hibernica* 2: 7–173

— 1966 'Bretha a Déin Chécht', *Ériu* 20: 1–66

— 1981 'Brewing in eighth century Ireland' in Scott, B.G. (ed.) 3–6

Blindheim, C. 1976 'A collection of Celtic(?) bronze objects found at Kaupang (Skiringssal), Vestfold, Norway' in Almqvist, B. and Greene, D. (eds), 10–27

Blindheim, M. 1984 'A house-shaped Irish-Scots reliquary in Bologna, and its place amongst other reliquaries', *Acta Archaeologica* 55: 1–54

Boal, F.W. and Moffitt, M.K. 1959 'A partly destroyed rath in Killarn townland, Newtownards, Co. Down', *UJA* 22: 107–11

Bourke, C. 1980 'Early Irish hand–bells', *JRSAI* 110: 52–66

— 1985 'A crozier and bell from Inishmurray and their place in ninth-century Irish archaeology', *PRIA* 85c: 145–68

— 1986 'Newtownlow', *Excavations* 1985, 40

— 1987 'Irish croziers of the eighth and ninth centuries' in Ryan, M. (ed.) 166–73

Bradley, J. 1980–1 'St Patrick's Church, Duleek', *Ríocht na Mídhe* 7 (1): 40–51

— 1981–2 '"Medieval" Samian ware – a medicinal suggestion', *UJA* 44–5: 196–7

— 1982–3 'Excavations at Moynagh Lough, Co. Meath 1980–81: interim report', *Ríocht na Mídhe* 7 (2): 12–32

— 1984 'Excavations at Moynagh Lough 1982–1983, interim report', *Ríocht na Mídhe* 7 (3): 86–93

— (ed.) 1985 *Viking Dublin exposed* (Dublin)

— 1985–6 'Excavations at Moynagh Lough 1984, summary report', *Ríocht na Mídhe* 7 (4): 79–92

— 1988 'The interpretation of Scandinavian settlement in Ireland' in Bradley, J. (ed.), *Settlement and society in medieval Ireland* (Kilkenny), 49–78

Branigan, K. 1977 *The Roman villa in south-west England* (Bradford-on Avon)

Brannon, N.F. 1979 'A trial excavation at an earthwork near Moira, County Down', *UJA* 42: 26–33.

— 1980 'A trial excavation at St John's Point church, Co. Down', *UJA* 43: 59–64

— 1981–2 'A rescue excavation at Lisdoo fort, Co. Fermanagh', *UJA* 44–5: 53–9

Briggs, C.S. 1985 'A neglected Viking burial with beads from Kilmainham, Dublin, discovered in 1847', *Med. Arch.* 29: 94–108

— and Graham-Campbell, J.A. 1976 'A lost hoard of Viking-age silver from Magheralagan, Co. Down', *UJA* 39: 20–4

Brown, T.J. 1972 'Northumbria and the Book of Kells', *Anglo-Saxon England* 1: 219–46

Bruce-Mitford, R.L.S. 1967 *The art of the Codex Amiatinus* (Jarrow Lecture)

— 1987 'Ireland and the hanging-bowls – a review' in Ryan, M. (ed.) 30–9

Buckley, J.J. 1915 'Some early ornamental leatherwork', *JRSAI* 45: 300–9

Byrne, F.J. 1971 'Tribes and tribalism in early Ireland', *Ériu* 22: 128–66

Campbell, E. 1984 'E ware and Aquitaine: a reappraisal of the petrological evidence', *Scot. Archaeol. Rev.* 3 (1): 35–41

Carson, R.A.G. and O'Kelly, C. 1977 'A catalogue of the Roman coins from Newgrange, Co. Meath and notes on the coins and related finds', *PRIA* 77c: 35–55

Case, H. J. *et al.* 1969 'Land-use in Goodland townland, Co. Antrim from Neolithic times until today', *JRSAI* 99: 39–54

Caulfield, S. 1981 'Some Celtic problems in the Irish Iron Age' in Ó Corráin, D. (ed.) 205–15

— 1983 'The Neolithic settlement of north Connaught' in Reeves-Smyth, T. and Hamond, F. (eds) 195–216

Chadwick, N.K. 1961 *The age of the saints in the early Celtic Church* (London)

Charles-Edwards, T.M. 1976 'Boundaries in Irish law' in Sawyer, P.H. (ed.), *Medieval Settlement* (London) 83–7

— 1984 'The church and settlement' in Ní Chatháin, P. and Richter, M. (eds), 167–75

— and Kelly, F. (eds) 1983 *Bechbretha. An Old Irish law-tract on beekeeping* (Dublin)

Childe, V. G. 1936 'A promontory fort on the Antrim coast', *Antiq. J.* 16: 179–98

Christensen, A.-E. 1988 'Ship graffiti and models' in Wallace, P.F. (ed.), *Miscellanea* 1 (Medieval Dublin Excavations 1962–81, Ser. B, Vol. 2, fascicule 3, Dublin) 13–26

Clarke, H.B. 1977 'The topographical development of early medieval Dublin', *JRSAI* 107: 29–51

— 1978 *Dublin c.840–c.1540: the medieval town in the modern city* (Dublin)

— 1985 'The historian and Wood Quay' in Bradley, J. (ed.), 144–53

— and Simms, A. (eds) 1985 *The comparative history of urban origins in non-Roman Europe* (Brit. Archaeol. Rep. S255, 2 vols)

Coffey, G. and Armstrong, E.C.R. 1910 'Scandinavian objects found at Islandbridge and Kilmainham', *PRIA* 28c: 107–22

Coleman, J.C. 1947 'Irish cave excavations', *JRSAI* 77: 63–80

Coles, J.M. and Simpson, D.D.A. (eds) 1968 *Studies in ancient Europe* (Leicester)

Collins, A.E.P. 1952 'Excavations in the sandhills at Dundrum, Co. Down, 1950–51', *UJA* 15: 2–26

— 1955 'Excavations at Lough Faughan crannog, Co. Down', *UJA* 18: 45–81

— 1959 'Further investigations in the Dundrum sandhills', *UJA* 22: 5–20

— 1961–2 'An earthwork at Craigboy, Co. Down', *UJA* 24–5: 116–8

— 1966 'Excavations at Dressogagh rath, Co. Armagh', *UJA* 29: 117–29

— 1968a 'Settlement in Ulster, 0–1100 AD', *UJA* 31: 53–8

— 1968b 'Excavations at Dromore ring-work, Co. Antrim', *UJA* 31: 59–66

— and Proudfoot, B. 1959 'A trial excavation at Clee Lakes crannog, Co. Down', *UJA* 22: 92–101

— and Seaby, W.A. 1960 'Structures and small finds discovered at Lough Eskragh, Co. Tyrone', *UJA* 23: 25–37

Connolly, S. and Picard, J.-M. 1987 'Cogitosus: Life of Saint Brigit', *JRSAI* 117: 5–27

Cooney, G. *et al.* (eds) 1987 'National Museum gets tough', *Archaeol. Ireland* 1 (2): 43

Coope, G.R. 1981 'Report on the coleoptera from an eleventh-century house at Christ Church Place, Dublin' in Bekker-Nielsen, H., *et al.* (eds), *Proceedings of the Eighth Viking Congress Århus 24–31 August 1977* (Odense 1981) 51–6

Cramp, R. 1965 *Early Northumbrian Sculpture* (Jarrow Lecture)

Crew, P. 1984 'Rectilinear settlements in Gwynedd' in Edwards, N. *et al.* 'The archaeology of early medieval Wales: conference summary', *Bull. Board Celtic Stud.* 31: 320–1

Crotty, S. 1982 'A discussion of the material from Ardakillen and Strokestown crannogs, Co. Roscommon' (unpublished University of Wales BA dissertation, UCNW Bangor)

Culleton, E.B. and Mitchell, G.F. 1976 'Soil erosion following deforestation in the early Christian period in south Wexford', *JRSAI* 106: 120–3

Cuppage, J. *et al.* 1986 *Archaeological survey of the Dingle peninsula* (Ballyferriter)

Curle, C.L. 1982 *Pictish and Norse finds from the Brough of Birsay 1934–74* (Society of Antiquaries of Scotland Monograph 1, Edinburgh)

Dark, K.R. 1985 'The plan and interpretation of Tintagel', *Cambridge Medieval Celtic Stud.* 9: 1–18

Davies, O. 1940a 'Excavations at Lissachiggel', *Co. Louth Archaeol. J.* 9 (3): 209–43

— 1940b 'Excavations at Corliss fort', *Co. Louth Archaeol. J.* 9 (4): 338–43

— 1941 'Trial excavations at Lough Enagh', *UJA* 4: 88–101

— 1947 'Types of rath in southern Ulster', *UJA* 10: 1–14

— 1950 *Excavations at Island Mac Hugh* (Suppl. Proc. Belfast Natur. Hist. Phil. Soc.)

— 1976 'Ring–forts and mottes', *UJA* 39: 72–3

Davies, W. 1974 'The Celtic church', *J. Religious Hist.* 8: 406–11

Davison, B.K. 1961–2 'Excavations at Ballynarry, Co. Down', *UJA* 24–5: 39–87

de Paor, L. 1955 'A survey of Sceilg Mhichíl', *JRSAI* 85: 174–87

— 1955–6 'The limestone crosses of Clare and Aran', *J. Galway Archaeol. Hist. Soc.* 26: 53–71

— 1967 'Cormac's Chapel: the beginnings of Irish Romanesque' in Rynne, E. (ed.), 133–45

— 1987 'The high crosses of Tech Theille (Tihilly), Kinnitty and related sculpture' in Rynne, E. (ed.), 131–58

de Paor, M. and L. 1960 *Early Christian Ireland* (2nd ed., London)

Department of the Environment for Northern Ireland 1983 *Historic Monuments of Northern Ireland* (6th ed., Belfast)

D'Evelyn, A.M. 1933 'A sandhill settlement, Maghera, Co. Donegal', *JRSAI* 63: 88–100

Dickinson, C.W. and Waterman, D.M. 1959 'Excavation at a rath with motte at Castleskreen, Co. Down', *UJA* 22: 67–82

— 1960 'Excavations at Castle Skreen, Co. Down', *UJA* 23: 63–77

Dickinson, T.M. 1982 'Fowler's Type G penannular brooches reconsidered', *Med. Arch.* 26: 41–68

Doherty, C. 1980 'Exchange and trade in early medieval Ireland', *JRSAI* 110: 67–89

— 1984 'The use of relics in early Ireland' in Ní Chatháin, P. and Richter, M. (eds), 89–104

— 1985 'The monastic town in early medieval Ireland' in Clarke, H.B. and Simms, A. (eds), 1: 45–75

Dolley, R.H.M. 1965 *Viking coins of the Danelaw and of Dublin* (London)

— 1966 *The Hiberno-Norse coins in the British Museum* (London)

Duignan, M. 1944 'Irish agriculture in early historic times', *JRSAI* 74: 124–45

Edwards, K.J. 1985 'The anthropogenic factor in vegetational history' in Edwards, K.J. and Warren, P. (eds), *The quaternary history of Ireland* (London) 187–220

Edwards, N. 1983a 'An early group of crosses from the kingdom of Ossory', *JRSAI* 113: 5–46

— 1983b 'Some observations on the layout and construction of abstract ornament in early

Christian Irish sculpture' in Thompson, H. (ed.) *Studies in Medieval Sculpture* (London) 3–17

— 1984 'Two sculptural fragments from Clonmacnois', *JRSAI* 114: 57–62

— 1985 'The origins of the free-standing stone cross in Ireland: imitation or innovation?', *Bull. Board Celtic Stud.* 32: 393–410

— 1986 'The South Cross, Clonmacnois (with an appendix on the incidence of vine-scroll on Irish sculpture)' in Higgitt, J. (ed.) 23–48

— forthcoming 'Some crosses of County Kilkenny' in Nolan, W. (ed.), *Kilkenny: History and Society* (Dublin)

— and Lane, A. (eds) 1988 *Early medieval settlements in Wales AD 400–1100* (Bangor/ Cardiff)

Eogan, G. 1973 'A decade of excavations at Knowth', *Ir. Univ. Rev.*, Spring 1973: 66–79

— 1974 'Report on the excavation of some passage graves, unprotected inhumation burials and a settlement site at Knowth', *PRIA* 74c: 11–112

— 1977 'The Iron Age and early Christian settlement at Knowth, Co. Meath, Ireland' in Markotic, V. (ed.), *Ancient Europe and the Mediterranean, studies in honour of Hencken* (Warminster) 69–76

— and Bradley, J. 1977 'A souterrain at Balrenny near Slane, County Meath', *JRSAI* 107: 96–103

Evans, E.E. 1950 'Rath and souterrain at Shaneen Park, Belfast, townland of Ballyaghagan, Co. Antrim', *UJA* 13: 6–27

— 1966 *Prehistoric and early Christian Ireland. A guide* (New York)

— 1973 *The personality of Ireland* (Cambridge)

Fahy, E.M. 1969 'Early settlement in the Skibbereen area', *JCHAS* 75: 147–56

Fanning, T. 1969 'The bronze ringed pins in the Limerick City Museum', *North Munster Antiq. J.* 12: 6–11

— 1970 'The Viking grave goods discovered near Larne, Co. Antrim, in 1840', *JRSAI* 100: 71–8

— 1972 'Excavation of a ring-fort at Narraghmore, Co. Kildare', *J. Kildare Archaeol. Soc.* 15 (2): 170–7

— 1973–4 'Excavation of a ring-fort at Pollardstown, Co. Kildare', *J. Co. Kildare Archaeol. Soc.* 15 (3): 251–61

— 1974–5 'Some bronze ringed pins from the Irish midlands', *J. Old Athlone Soc.* 1: 211–7

— 1981a 'Excavation of an early Christian

cemetery and settlement at Reask, County Kerry', *PRIA* 81c: 3–172

— 1981b 'Early Christian sites in the barony of Corkaguiney' in Ó Corráin, D. (ed.) 241–6

— 1983 'Some aspects of the bronze ringed pin in Scotland' in O'Connor, A. and Clarke, D.V. (eds), 324–42

Flanagan, D. 1980 'Common elements in Irish place-names: *dún, rath, lios*', *Bull. Ulster Placename Soc.* 2nd ser. 3: 16–29

— 1983 'Some less frequently attested Irish placename elements of archaeological interest', *Nomina* 7: 31–3

— 1984 'The Christian impact on early Ireland: place-names evidence' in Ní Chatháin, P. and Richter, M. (eds) 25–51

Flanagan, L.N.W. 1963 'Belfast Museum: archaeological acquisitions of Irish origin for the years 1960 and 1961', *UJA* 26: 105–11

— 1966 'Dark Age sites in Ballymacrae Lower, Co. Antrim', *UJA* 29: 115–6

Flower, R. 1954 'Irish high crosses', *J. Warburg Courtauld Institutes* 17: 87–97

Fowler, E. 1963 'Celtic metalwork of the fifth and sixth centuries A.D. A reappraisal', *Archaeol. J.* 120: 98–160

— 1968 'Hanging bowls' in Coles, J.M. and Simpson, D.D.A. (eds), 287–310

Fowler, P.J. 1966–7 'Ridge-and-furrow cultivation at Cush, Co. Limerick', *North Munster Antiq. J.* 10: 69–71

— and Thomas, A.C. 1962 'Arable fields of the pre-Norman period at Gwithian', *Cornish Archaeol.* 1: 61–84

Frame, R. 1981 *Colonial Ireland 1169–1369* (Dublin)

Freeman, T.W. 1960 *Ireland* (2nd ed., London)

Gailey, A. 1968 'Irish iron–shod wooden spades', *UJA* 31: 77–86

— 1970 'Irish corn-drying kilns' in McCourt, D. and Gailey, A. (eds), *Ulster Folklife* 15–6: 52–71

Gaskell Brown, C. and Brannon, N.F. 1978 'The rath in Hillsborough Fort, Co. Down', *UJA* 41: 78–87

— and Harper, A.E.T. 1984 'Excavations on Cathedral Hill, Armagh, 1968', *UJA* 47: 109–61

Gerriets, M. 1985 'Money among the Irish: coin hoards in Viking Age Ireland', *JRSAI* 115: 121–39

Gillmor, D. 1971 *A systematic geography of Ireland* (Dublin)

Gowen, M. 1988 *Three Irish Gas pipelines: new archaeological evidence in Munster* (Dublin)

Graham-Campbell, J.A. 1972 'Two groups of ninth-century Irish brooches', *JRSAI* 102: 113–28

— 1973–4 'The Lough Ravel, Co. Antrim, brooch and others of ninth-century date', *UJA* 36–7: 52–7

— 1974 'A Viking Age gold hoard from Ireland', *Antiq. J.* 54: 269–72

— 1975 'Bossed penannular brooches: a review of recent research', *Med. Arch.* 19: 33–47

— 1976 'The Viking Age silver hoards of Ireland' in Almqvist, B. and Greene, D. (eds), 39–74

— 1980 *Viking artefacts* (London)

— 1983 'Some Viking-Age penannular brooches from Scotland and the origins of the 'thistle-brooch'' in O'Connor A. and Clarke, D.V. (eds), 310–23

— 1987 'From Scandinavia to the Irish Sea: Viking art reviewed' in Ryan, M. (ed.) 144–52

— 1989 'A Viking-age silver hoard from near Raphoe, Co. Donegal' in MacNiocaill, G. and Wallace, P.F. (eds), *Keimelia* (Galway) 102–11

Greene, D. 1976 'The influence of Scandinavian on Irish' in Almqvist, B. and Greene, D. (eds), 75–82

Grogan, E. and Eogan, G. 1987 'Lough Gur excavations by Seán P. Ó Ríordáin: further Neolithic and Beaker habitations on Knockadoon', *PRIA* 87c: 299–506

Guido, M. 1978 *The glass beads of the prehistoric and Roman periods in Britain and Ireland* (Soc. Antiq. London Rep. Res. Committee 35, London)

Gwynn, A.O. 1968 *The twelfth century reform* (History of Irish Catholicism, 2, i: Dublin)

— 'Tomaltach Ua Conchobair coarb of Patrick' *Seanchas Ard Mhacha* 8: 231–80

Haliday, C. 1884 *The Scandinavian kingdom of Dublin* (2nd ed., repr. 1969, Shannon)

Hall, R. 1973 'A hoard of Viking silver bracelets from Cushalogurt, Co. Mayo', *JRSAI* 103: 78–85

— 1973–4 'A check list of Viking-age coin finds from Ireland', *UJA* 36–7: 71–86

— 1974 'A Viking grave in the Phoenix Park, Co. Dublin', *JRSAI* 104: 39–43

— 1978 'A Viking-age grave at Donnybrook, Co. Dublin', *Med. Arch.* 22: 64–83

Hamlin, A. 1972 'A Chi-rho-carved stone at Drumaqueran, Co. Antrim', *UJA* 35: 22–8

— 1982 'Early Irish stone carving: content and context' in Pearce, S.M. (ed.), 283–96
— 1984 'The study of early Irish churches' in Ní Chatháin, P. and Richter, M. (eds), 117–26
— 1985 'The archaeology of the Irish church in the eighth century', *Peritia* 4: 279–99
— 1987a 'Crosses in early Ireland: the evidence from written sources' in Ryan, M. (ed.), 138–40
— 1987b 'Some northern sundials and time-keeping in the early Irish church' in Rynne, E. (ed.), 29–42
— and Foley, C. 1983 'A women's graveyard at Carrickmore, Co. Tyrone, and the separate burial of women', *UJA* 46: 41–6
— and Lynn, C.J. (eds) 1988 *Pieces of the Past* (Belfast)
Harbison, P. 1970 'How old is Gallarus oratory?', *Med. Arch.* 14: 34–59
— 1975 *Guide to the National Monuments in the Republic of Ireland* (2nd ed., Dublin)
— 1978 'The Antrim cross in the Hunt Museum', *North Munster Antiq. J.* 20: 17–40
— 1982 'Early Irish churches' in Löwe, H. (ed.), *Die Iren und Europa im früheren Mittelalter.* I (Stuttgart) 618–29
— 1984 'The bronze Crucifixion plaque said to be from St John's (Rinnagan), near Athlone', *J. Irish Archaeol.* 2: 1–18
— 1986 'A group of early Christian carved stone monuments in County Donegal' in Higgitt, J. (ed.), 49–86
— 1987a 'The Carolingian contribution to Irish sculpture' in Ryan, M. (ed.), 105–10
— 1987b 'The date of the crucifixion slabs from Duvillaun More and Iniskea North, Co. Mayo' in Rynne, E. (ed.), 73–91
— 1988 *Pre-christian Ireland* (London)
— Potterton, H. and Sheehy, J. 1978 *Irish art and architecture* (London)
Harden, D.B. 1956a 'Glass vessels in Britain and Ireland, A.D. 400–1000' in Harden, D.B. (ed.), 132–67
— (ed.) 1956b *Dark-Age Britain* (London)
Hare, M. and Hamlin, A. 1986 'The study of early church architecture in Ireland: an Anglo-Saxon viewpoint with an appendix on documentary evidence for round towers' in Butler, L.A.S. and Morris, R.K. (eds), *The Anglo-Saxon church* (Council Brit. Archaeol. Res. Rep. 60) 130–45
Harper, A.E.T. 1973–4 'The excavation of a rath in Crossnacreevy townland, Co. Down', *UJA* 36–7: 32–41

Hayes, J.W. 1972 *Late Roman pottery* (London)
— 1980 *A supplement to late Roman pottery* (London)
Hayes-McCoy, G.A. (ed.) 1964 *Ulster and other Irish maps c.1600* (Dublin)
Hencken, H. 1936 'Balinderry crannog no. 1', *PRIA* 43c: 103–239
— 1938 *Cahercommaun, a stone fort in Co. Clare* (*JRSAI* special volume)
— 1942 'Ballinderry crannog no. 2', *PRIA* 47c: 1–76
— 1950 'Lagore crannog: an Irish royal residence of the seventh to tenth century A.D.', *PRIA* 53c: 1–248
Henderson, G. 1987 *From Durrow to Kells. The Insular gospel-books 650–800* (London)
Henderson, I. 1987 'The Book of Kells and the snake-boss motif on Pictish cross-slabs and the Iona crosses' in Ryan, M. (ed.), 56–65
Henry, F. 1930 'L'inscription de Bealin', *Revue Archéologique* 5 ser., 32: 110–5
— 1936 'Hanging-bowls', *JRSAI* 66: 209–46
— 1945 'Remains of the early Christian period on Inishkea North, Co. Mayo', *JRSAI* 75: 127–55
— 1952 'A wooden hut at Inishkea North, Co. Mayo', *JRSAI* 82: 163–78
— 1956 'Irish enamels of the Dark Ages and their relation to cloisonné techniques' in Harden, D.B. (ed.), 71–88
— 1957 'Early monasteries, beehive huts and dry-stone houses in the neighbourhood of Caherciveen and Waterville (Co. Kerry)', *PRIA* 58c: 45–166
— 1961 'Remarks on the decoration of three Irish psalters', *PRIA* 61c: 23–40
— 1965 *Irish art in the early Christian period to A.D. 800* (London)
— 1967 *Irish art during the Viking invasions (800–1020 A.D.)* (London)
— 1970 *Irish art in the Romanesque period 1020–1170 A.D.* (London)
— 1974 *The Book of Kells* (London)
— 1980 'Around an inscription: the Cross of Scriptures at Clonmacnois', *JRSAI* 110: 36–46
— and Marsh-Micheli, G.L. 1962 'A century of Irish illumination (1070–1170)', *PRIA* 62c: 101–65
Heraughty, P. 1982 *Inishmurray* (Dublin)
Herity, M. and Eogan, G. 1977 *Ireland in prehistory* (London/Henley/Boston)
Herren, M.W. 1974 *The Hisperica Famina: 1, The A-text* (Toronto)

Heslip, R. 1985 'Reflections on Hiberno-Norse coinage', *UJA* 48: 25–30

Hickey, H. 1985 *Images of stone* (2nd ed., Fermanagh)

Hicks, C. 1980 'A Clonmacnois workshop in stone', *JRSAI* 110: 5–35

Higgins, J.G. 1987 *The early Christian cross slabs, pillar stones and related monuments of County Galway, Ireland* (2 vols., Brit. Archaeol. Rep. S375)

Higgitt, J. (ed.), *Early medieval sculpture in Britain and Ireland* (Brit. Archaeol. Rep. 152)

Hill, D. 1981 *An atlas of Anglo-Saxon England* (Oxford)

Hillgarth, J.N. 1984 'Ireland and Spain in the seventh century', *Peritia* 3: 1–16

Hodges, H. 1976 *Artifacts* (2nd ed., London)

Hodges, R. 1982 *Dark Age economics* (London)

Holmqvist, W. 1955 'An Irish crozier-head found near Stockholm', *Antiq. J.* 35: 46–51

Hope-Taylor, B. 1977 *Yeavering* (London)

Howells, W.W. 1941 'The early Christian Irish: the skeletons at Gallen priory', *PRIA* 46c: 103–219

Hughes, K. 1958 'The distribution of Irish scriptoria and centres of learning from 730 to 1111' in Chadwick, N.K. *et al.*, *Studies in the early British church* (Cambridge) 243–72

— 1966 *The church in early Irish society* (London)

— 1972 *Early Christian Ireland: introduction to the sources* (London)

— 1980 'Introduction' in Otway-Ruthven, A.J., *A history of medieval Ireland* (2nd ed., London) 1–33

— and Hamlin, A. 1977 *The modern traveller to the early Irish church* (London)

Hunt, J. 1956 'On two 'D' shaped objects in the Saint-Germain museum', *PRIA* 57c: 153–7

Hurley, M. 1988 'Recent archaeological excavations in Waterford City', *Archaeol. Ireland* 2 (1): 17–21

Hurley, V. 1982 'The early church in the south-west of Ireland: settlement and organisation' in Pearce, S.M. (ed.), 297–332

Hutchinson, G. 1979 'The bar-lug pottery of Cornwall', *Cornish Archaeol.* 18: 81–103

Irish National Committee for Geography 1979 *Atlas of Ireland* (Dublin)

Ivens, R.J. 1984a 'Killyliss rath, County Tyrone', *UJA* 47: 9–35

— 1984b 'A note on grass-marked pottery', *J. Ir. Archaeol.* 2: 77–9

— 1984c 'Movilla Abbey, Newtownards, County Down: excavations 1981', *UJA* 47: 71–108

— 1987 'Dunmisk fort, Dunmisk' in Cotter, C. (ed.), *Excavations 1986* (Dublin) 33–4

— *et al.* 1986 'Excavations at Island MacHugh 1985 – interim report', *UJA* 49: 99–103

Jackson, J.W. 1933 'Preliminary report on excavations at the caves of Ballintoy, Co. Antrim', *Ir. Naturalists' J.* 4: 230–5

— 1934 'Further excavations at Ballintoy Caves, Co. Antrim', *Ir. Naturalists' J.* 5: 104–14

Jackson, K. 1953 *Language and history in early Britain* (Edinburgh)

James, E. 1981 'Archaeology and the Merovingian monastery' in Clarke, H.B. and Brennan, M. (ed.), *Columbanus and Merovingian monasticism* (Brit. Archaeol. Rep. S113) 33–55 (eds), *Ireland in Early Mediaeval Europe* (Cambridge) 362–86

— 1982 'Ireland and western Gaul in the Merovingian period' in Whitelock, D. *et al.* (eds), *Ireland in Early Mediaeval Europe* (Cambridge) 362–86

Jarrett, M.G. and Wrathmell, S. 1981 *Whitton: an Iron Age and Roman farmstead in South Glamorgan* (Cardiff)

Jenkins, J.G. 1981 *The cooper's craft* (Welsh Folk Museum, St Fagans)

Jobey, G. 1972–4 'Excavations at Boonies, Westerkirk, and the nature of Romano-British settlement in eastern Dumfriesshire', *PSAS* 105: 119–40

Johansen, O.S. 1973 'Bossed penannular brooches. A systematization and study of their cultural affinities', *Acta Archaeologica* 44: 63–124

Jope, J.M. 1960 'The beads from a first century AD burial at 'Loughey' near Donaghadee, a supplementary note', *UJA* 23: 40

— and Wilson, B.C.S. 1957 'A burial group of the first century AD from 'Loughey' near Donaghadee', *UJA* 20: 73–94

Keay, S. 1984 *Late Roman amphorae in the western Mediterranean* (Brit. Archaeol. Rep. S136)

Kelly, E. 1974 'Aughinish Island, sites 1 and 2', *Excavations* 5: 21

Kelly, F. 1976 'The Old Irish tree-list', *Celtica* 11: 107–24

— 1988 *A guide to Early Irish Law* (Dublin)

Kendrick, T.D. 1939 'Gallen Priory excavations, 1934–5', *JRSAI* 69: 1–20

— and Senior, E. 1936 'St Manchan's shrine', *Archaeologia* 86: 105–18

— *et al.* 1960 *Evangelorum quattuor Codex Lindisfarnensis* (2 vols., Olten/Lausanne)

Kenney, J.F. 1929 *The sources for the early history of Ireland: ecclesiastical* (New York)

Kenny, M. 1987 'The geographical distribution of Irish Viking-age coin hoards', *PRIA* 87c: 507–25

Kilbride-Jones, H.E. 1937–8 'Glass armlets in Britain', *PSAS* 72: 366–95

— 1980a *Celtic craftsmanship in bronze* (London)

— 1980b *Zoomorphic penannular brooches* (Rep. Res. Committee Soc. Antiq. London 39)

Kilby, K. 1977 *The village cooper* (Aylesbury)

Lord Killanin and Duignan, M.V. 1967 *The Shell Guide to Ireland* (London)

Killeen, J.F. 1976 'Ireland in the Greek and Roman writers', *PRIA* 76c: 207–15

Kinsella, T. (trans.) 1970 *The Táin* (Oxford)


Lacy, B. *et al.* 1983 *Archaeological survey of County Donegal* (Lifford)

Laing, L.R. 1975 *The archaeology of late Celtic Britain and Ireland 400–1200 AD* (London)

— 1985 'The Romanization of Ireland in the fifth century', *Peritia* 4: 261–78

Lamb, H.H. 1981 'Climate from 1000 BC to 1000 AD' in Jones, M. and Dimbleby, G. (eds), *The environment of man: the Iron Age to the Anglo-Saxon period* (Brit. Archaeol. Rep. 87) 53–66

Lang, J. 1971 'The Castledermot hogback', *JRSAI* 101: 154–8

— 1986 'Principles of design in free-style carving in the Irish Sea Province: *c*.800 to 950' in Higgitt, J. (ed.), 153–74

— 1987 'Eleventh-century style in decorated wood from Dublin' in Ryan, M. (ed.), 174–8

— 1988 *Viking-age decorated wood. A study of its ornament and style* (Medieval Dublin Excavations 1962–81 Ser. B, vol. 1, Dublin)

Lawlor, H.C. 1925 *The monastery of Saint Mochaoi of Nendrum* (Belfast)

Leask, H.G. 1955 *Irish churches and monastic buildings. I. The first phases and the Romanesque* (Dundalk; repr. 1977)

— n.d. *Glendalough, Co. Wicklow* (Dublin)

Lionard, P. 1961 'Early Irish grave-slabs', *PRIA* 61c: 95–169

Liversage, G.D. 1968 'Excavations at Dalkey Island, Co. Dublin 1956–59', *PRIA* 66c: 53–233

Longley, D. 1975 *The Anglo-Saxon connexion* (Brit. Archaeol. Rep. 22)

Lucas, A.T. 1953 'The horizontal mill in Ireland', *JRSAI* 83: 1–36

— 1955 'Horizontal mill, Ballykilleen, Co. Offaly', *JRSAI* 85: 100–13

— 1956 'Footwear in Ireland', *J. Louth Archaeol. Soc.* 13: 309–94

— 1958 'Cattle in ancient and medieval Irish society', *O'Connell School Union Record 1938–58* (Dublin)

— 1960 'Irish food before the potato', *Gwerin* 3 (2): 8–43

— 1963 'The sacred trees of Ireland', *JCHAS* 68: 16–54

— 1965 'Washing and bathing in ancient Ireland', *JRSAI* 95: 65–114

— 1966a 'Irish-Norse relations: time for a reappraisal?', *JCHAS* 42: 62–75

— 1966b 'National Museum of Ireland: archaeological acquisitions in the year 1963', *JRSAI* 96: 7–27

— 1967a 'The plundering and burning of churches in Ireland, 7th to 16th century' in Rynne, E. (ed.), 172–229

— 1967b 'National Museum of Ireland: archaeological acquisitions 1964', *JRSAI* 97: 1–28

— 1970a 'Paring and burning in Ireland: a preliminary survey' in Gailey, A. and Fenton, A. (eds), *The spade in northern and Atlantic Europe* (Belfast) 99–147

— 1970b 'Notes on the history of turf as fuel in Ireland to 1700 A.D.' in McCourt, D. and Gailey, A. (eds), 172–202

— 1972 'Irish ploughing practices', *Tools and Tillage* 2: 52–62, 67–83

— 1975 'Souterrains: the literary evidence', *Béaloideas* 39–41: 165–91

— 1986 'The social role of relics and reliquaries in ancient Ireland', *JRSAI* 116: 5–37

Lynch, A. 1981 *Man and environment in south-west Ireland 4000 BC–AD 800* (Brit. Archaeol. Rep. 85)

— 1983 'Excavations at the base of St Patrick's cross, Cashel', *N. Munster Antiq. J.* 25: 9–18

Lynn, C.J. 1974 'Ballywee', *Excavations* 5: 4–6

— 1975a 'The dating of raths: an orthodox view', *UJA* 38: 45–7

— 1975b 'The medieval ring-fort – an archaeological chimera?', *Ir. Archaeol. Res. Forum* 2: 29–36

— 1977 'Recent excavations in Armagh City: an interim report', *Seanchas Ard Mhacha* 8 (2): 275–80

— 1978a 'Early Christian period domestic structures: a change from round to rectangular', *Ir. Archaeol. Res. Forum* 5: 29–45

— 1978b 'A rath in Seacash townland, Co. Antrim', *UJA* 41: 55–74

— 1981–2 'The excavation of Rathmullan, a raised rath and motte in Co. Down', *UJA* 44–5: 65–171

— 1983a 'Some 'early' ring-forts and crannogs', *J. Ir. Archaeol.* 1: 47–58

— 1983b 'Two raths at Ballyhenry, Co. Antrim', *UJA* 46: 67–91

— 1984 'Some fragments of exotic porphyry found in Ireland', *J. Ir. Archaeol.* 2: 19–32

— 1985 'Excavations on a mound at Gransha, County Down, 1972 and 1982: an interim report', *UJA* 48: 81–90

— 1985–6 'Lagore, County Meath and Ballinderry No. 1, County Westmeath crannogs: some possible structural reinterpretations', *J. Ir. Archaeol.* 3: 69–73

— 1989 'Deer Park Farms', *Current Archaeol.* 113: 193–8

— 1988 'Excavations in 46–48 Scotch Street, Armagh, 1979–80', *UJA* 51, 69–84

— and McDowell, J.A. 1988a 'Muirchú's Armagh', *Emania* 4 (Spring 1988) 42–6

— 1988b 'A note on the excavation of an early Christian period settlement in Deer Park Farms, Glenarm, 1984–1987', *The Glynns* 16: 3–16

MacAirt, S. and MacNiocaill, G. (eds) 1983 *The Annals of Ulster (to A.D. 1131)* (Dublin)

Macalister, R.A.S. 1909 *The memorial slabs of Clonmacnois, King's County* (Dublin)

— 1916–7 'On a runic inscription at Killaloe Cathedral', *PRIA* 33c: 493–8

— 1945, 1949 *Corpus inscriptiorum insularum Celticarum* 2 vols. (Dublin)

— and Praeger, R.L. 1928 'Report on the excavations at Uisneach', *PRIA* 38c: 69–127

McCarthy, J.P. 1983 'Summary of a study of County Cork souterrains', *JCHAS* 88: 100–5

McClintock, H.F. 1950 *Old Irish and Highland dress* (Dundalk)

McCormick, F. 1983 'Dairying and beef production in early Christian Ireland: the faunal evidence' in Reeves-Smyth, T. and Hamond, F. (eds), 253–68

McCourt, D. and Gailey, A. (eds) 1970 *Studies in folklife presented to Emrys Estyn Evans: Ulster Folklife* 15–16

MacDermott, M. 1950 'Terminal mounting of a drinking-horn from Lismore, Co. Waterford', *JRSAI* 80: 262

— 1955 'The Kells crozier', *Archaeologia* 96: 59–114

MacDonald, A. 1981 'Notes on monastic archaeology in the Annals of Ulster' in Ó Corráin, D. (ed.) 304–19

— 1984 'Aspects of the monastery and monastic life in Adomnán's Life of Columba', *Peritia* 3: 271–302

McDowell, J.A. 1986 'Scotch Street Armagh' in Cotter, C. (ed.), *Excavations 1985* (Dublin) 12

— 1987a 'Scotch St, Armagh' in Cotter, C. (ed.), *Excavations 1986* (Dublin) 11–2

— 1987b 'Doras' in Cotter, C. (ed.), *Excavations 1986* (Dublin) 33

MacEoin, G. 1981 'The early Irish vocabulary of mills and milling' in Scott, B.G. (ed.), 13–9

McGrail, S. 1976 'Problems in Irish nautical archaeology', *Ir. Archaeol. Res. Forum* 3 (1): 21–31

— (ed.) 1982 *Woodworking techniques before A.D. 1500* (Brit. Archaeol. Rep. S129)

— 1987 *Ancient boats in N.W. Europe* (London/New York)

MacGregor, A. 1985 *Bone antler ivory and horn* (London)

MacNeill, E. 1923 'Ancient Irish law: the law of status or franchise', *PRIA* 36c: 265–311

McNeill, T.E. 1975 'Medieval raths? An Anglo-Norman comment', *Ir. Archaeol. Res. Forum* 2: 37–9

— 1977 'Excavations at Doonbought Fort, Co. Antrim', *UJA* 40: 63–84

— 1980 *Anglo-Norman Ulster: the history and archaeology of an Irish barony 1177–1400* (Edinburgh)

MacNiocaill, G. 1971 'Tír Cumaile', *Ériu* 22: 81–6

— 1981 'Investment in early Irish agriculture' in Scott, B.G. (ed.), 7–9

MacWhite, E. 1960–1 'Contributions to a study of ogham memorial stones', *Zeitschrift für celtische Philologie* 28: 294–308

Mahr, A. 1932 *Christian art in ancient Ireland. Volume I* (Dublin)

Mallory, J.P. 1986 'Ulster archaeology in 1985', *UJA* 49: 3–6

— and Woodman, P.C. 1984 'Oughtymore: an early Christian shell midden', *UJA* 47: 51–62

Manning, C. 1984 'The excavation of the early Christian enclosure of Killederdadrum in Lackenavorna, Co. Tipperary', *PRIA* 84c: 237–68

— 1986 'Archaeological excavation of a succession of enclosures at Millockstown, Co. Louth', *PRIA* 86c: 135–81

May, A.McL. 1943 'Portbraddon cave, Co. Antrim', *UJA* 6: 39–60

— and Batty, J. 1948 'The sandhill cultures of the River Bann estuary, Co. Londonderry', *JRSAI* 78: 130–56

Meyer, K. (ed.) 1892 *Vision of MacConglinne* (London)

Miles, H. and T. 1973 'Excavations at Trethurgy, St Austell: interim report', *Cornish Archaeol.* 12: 25–30

Mitchell, G.F. 1956 'Post-boreal pollen diagnosis from Irish raised bogs', *PRIA* 57b: 185–251

— 1965 'Littleton Bog, Tipperary: an Irish agricultural record', *JRSAI* 95: 121–32

— 1976 *The Irish landscape* (London)

— 1986 *The Shell Guide to reading the Irish landscape* (Dublin)

— 1987 *Archaeology and environment in early Dublin* (Medieval Dublin excavations 1962–81 Ser. C, Vol. 1, Dublin)

Molleson, T.I. 1985–6 'New radiocarbon dates for the occupation of Kilgreany cave, Co. Waterford', *J. Ir. Archaeol.* 3: 1–3

Monk, M.A. 1981 'Post-Roman drying kilns and the problem of function: a preliminary statement' in Ó Corráin, D. (ed.), 216–30

— 1985–6 'Evidence of macroscopic plant remains for crop husbandry in prehistoric and early historic Ireland: a review', *J. Ir. Archaeol.* 3: 31–6

Morris, C. 1982 'Aspects of Anglo-Saxon and Anglo-Scandinavian lathe-turning' in McGrail, S. (ed.), 245–61

Morrison, I.A. 1981 'The extension of the chronology of the crannogs of Scotland', *Int. J. Nautical Archaeol.* 10 (4): 344–6

Movius, H.L. 1935 'Kilgreany Cave, Co. Waterford', *JRSAI* 65: 254–96

Munn, M.L.Z. 1985 'A late Roman kiln site in the Hermonid, Greece', *American J. Archaeol.* 89: 342–3

Munro, R. and Gillespie, P. 1918–9 'Further notes on ancient wooden traps – the so-called otter and beaver traps', *PSAS* 53: 162–7

Murray, H. 1979 'Documentary evidence for domestic buildings in Ireland c400–1200 in the light of archaeology', *Med. Arch.* 23: 81–97

— 1983 *Viking and early medieval buildings in Dublin* (Brit. Archaeol. Rep. 119)

National Museum of Ireland 1973 *Viking and medieval Dublin* (Dublin)

Nees, L. 1983 'The colophon drawing in the Book of Mulling: a supposed Irish monastery plan and the tradition of terminal illustration in early medieval manuscripts', *Cambridge Medieval Celtic Stud.* 5: 67–91

Ní Chatháin, P. and Richter, M. (eds) 1984 *Irland und Europa, Die Kirche im Frühmittelater* (Stuttgart)

Nieke, M.R. 1983 'Settlement patterns in the first millennium A.D.: a case study of the island of Islay' in Chapman, J.C. and Mytum, H.C. (eds), *Settlement in North Britain 1000 BC–AD 100* (Brit. Archaeol. Rep. 118) 299–325

Nordenfalk, C. 1947 'Before the Book of Durrow', *Acta Archaeologica* 18: 141–74

— 1977 *Celtic and Anglo-Saxon painting* (London)

Norman, E.R. and St Joseph, J.K.S. 1969 *Early development of Irish society: the evidence of aerial photography* (Cambridge)

O'Brien, E. 1984 'Late Prehistoric-Early Historic Ireland: the burial evidence reviewed' (unpublished M.Phil. thesis, Nat. Univ. Ir., Univ. Coll. Dublin)

Ó Carragáin, E. 1987 'The Ruthwell Cross and Irish high crosses, some points of comparison and contrast' in Ryan, M. (ed.) 118–23

O'Connell, M. 1980 'The developmental history of Scragh Bog, Co. Westmeath and the vegetational history of its hinterland', *New Phytologist* 85: 301–19

O'Connor, A. and Clarke, D.V. (eds) 1983 *From the Stone Age to the 'Forty Five* (Edinburgh)

Ó Corráin, D. 1972 *Ireland before the Normans* (Dublin)

— 1978 'Nationality and kingship in pre-Norman Ireland' in Moody, T.W. (ed.), *Nationality and the pursuit of national independence* (Historical Studies 11, Belfast) 1–35

— (ed.) 1981a *Irish antiquity* (Cork)

— 1981b 'The early Irish churches: some aspects of organisation' in Ó Corráin, D. (ed.), 327–41

— 1983 'Some legal references to fences and fencing in Early Historic Ireland' in Reeves-Smyth, T. and Hamond, F. (eds), 247–52

Ó Cróinín, D. 1982 'Pride and prejudice', *Peritia* 1: 352–62

— 1984 'Rath Melsigi, Willibrord, and the earliest Echternach manuscripts', *Peritia* 3: 17–49

Ó Cuileanáin, C. and Murphy, T.F. 1961 'A ring-fort at Oldcourt, Co. Cork', *JCHAS* 66: 79–92

O'Donovan, J. (ed.) 1856 *Annala Rioghachta Eireann. Annals of the Kingdom of Ireland, by the Four Masters, from the earliest period to the year 1616* (2nd ed., 7 vols., Dublin)

Ó Drisceoil, D. 1988 'Burnt mounds: cooking or bathing?', *Antiquity* 62: 671–80

Ó Floinn, R. 1983 'Viking and Romanesque influence 1000 A.D.–1169 A.D.' in Ryan, M. (ed.), *Treasures of Ireland* (Dublin) 58–69

— 1987a 'Schools of metalworking in eleventh- and twelfth-century Ireland' in Ryan, M. (ed.) 179–87

— 1987b 'Irish Romanesque crucifix figures' in Rynne, E. (ed.) 168–88

Oftedal, M. 1976 'Scandinavian place-names in Ireland' in Almqvist, B. and Greene, D. (eds), 125–34

Ó hEailidhe, P. 1957 'The Rathdown slabs', *JRSAI* 87: 75–88

Ó hInnse, S. (ed.) 1947 *Miscellaneous Irish annals* (A.D. 1114–1437) (Dublin)

O'Kelly, M.J. 1951 'An early Bronze Age ring-fort at Carrigillihy, Co. Cork', *JCHAS* 56: 69–86

— 1952a 'St Gobnet's house, Ballyvourney, Co. Cork', *JCHAS* 57: 18–40

— 1952b 'Three promontory forts in Co. Cork', *PRIA* 55c: 25–59

— 1954 'Excavations and experiments in ancient Irish cooking places', *JRSAI* 84: 105–55

— 1956 'An island settlement at Beginish, Co. Kerry', *PRIA* 57c: 159–94

— 1958 'Church Island near Valencia, Co. Kerry', *PRIA* 59c: 57–136

— 1961 'A stone bowl of VIking type from Beginish Island, Co. Kerry', *JRSAI* 91: 64–8

— 1962 'Beal Boru', *JCHAS* 67: 1–27

— 1963 'The excavations of two earthern ringforts at Garryduff, Co. Cork', *PRIA* 63c: 17–125.

— 1965 'The belt shrine from Moylough, Sligo', *JRSAI* 95: 149–88

— 1967 'Knockea, Co. Limerick' in Rynne, E. (ed.), 72–101

— 1970 'Problems of Irish ring-forts' in Moore, D. (ed.), *The Irish Sea province in archaeology and history* (Cardiff) 50–4

— 1975 *Archaeological survey and excavation of St Vogue's church, enclosure and other monuments at Carnmore, Co. Wexford* (Dublin)

— 1989 *Early Ireland* (Cambridge)

— and O'Kelly, C. 1983 'The tumulus of Dowth, Co. Meath', *PRIA* 83c: 135–90

O'Loan, J. 1965 'A history of Irish farming – part 3', *J. Dept. Agriculture and Fisheries* 62: 131–97

O'Meadhra, U. 1979 *Motif-pieces from Ireland* (Theses and papers in North-European archaeology 7, Stockholm)

— 1987a *Motif-pieces from Ireland 2. A discussion* (Theses and papers in North-European archaeology 17, Stockholm)

— 1987b 'Irish, Insular, Saxon and Scandinavian elements in the motif pieces from Ireland' in Ryan, M. (ed.) 159–65

Ó Murchadha, D. 1980 'Rubbings taken of the inscriptions on the Cross of the Scriptures, Clonmacnois', *JRSAI* 110: 47–51

O'Neill, T. 1984 *The Irish hand* (Portlaoise)

Organ, R.M. 1973 'Examination of the Ardagh Chalice: a case history' in Young, W.J. (ed.), *The application of science in examination of works of art* (Boston) 238–71

Ó Riain, P. 1972 'Boundary associations in early Irish society', *Studia Celtica* 7: 12–29

Ó Ríordáin, B. 1971 'Excavations at High Street and Winetavern Street, Dublin', *Med. Arch.* 15: 73–85

— 1985 'Excavations in Old Dublin' in Bradley, J. (ed.), 134–43

Ó Ríordáin, B. and Rynne, E. 1961 'A settlement in the sandhills at Dooey, Co. Donegal', *JRSAI* 91: 58–64

Ó Ríordáin, S.P. 1935 'Recent acquisitions from County Donegal in the National Museum', *PRIA* 42c: 145–91

— 1940 'Excavations at Cush, Co. Limerick', *PRIA* 45c: 83–181

— 1942 'The excavation of a large earthen ring fort at Garranes, Co. Cork , *PRIA* 47c: 77–150

— 1947 'Roman material in Ireland', *PRIA* 51c: 35–82

— 1949a 'Lough Gur excavations: Carraig Aille and the 'Spectacles'', *PRIA* 52c: 39–111

— 1949b 'Lough Gur excavations: three marshland habitation sites', *JRSAI* 79: 126–39

— 1979 *Antiquities of the Irish countryside*, 5th and revd. ed. by de Valera, R. (London/New York)

— 1982 *Tara* (Dundalk)
— and Foy, J.B. 1943 'The excavation of Leacanabuaile fort, Co. Kerry', *JCHAS* 46: 85–99
— and Hartnett, P.J. 1943 'The excavation at Ballycatteen fort, Co. Cork', *PRIA* 49c: 1–43
— and Lucas, A.T. 1946–7 'Excavation of a small crannog at Rathjordan, Co. Limerick', *North Munster Antiq. J.* 5: 68–77
— and MacDermott, M. 1952 'The excavation of a ring-fort at Letterkeen, Co. Mayo', *PRIA* 53c 89–119
Ordnance Survey 1978 *Dublin c.840 – c.1540: the medieval town in the modern city* (Dublin)
Orme, A.R. 1970 *The world's landscapes – Vol. 4 Ireland* (London)

Patterson, R. 1955 'Hand distaffs from Lough Faughan, Lagore and Ballinderry crannogs', *UJA* 18: 81–2
Peacock, D.P.S. and Thomas, C. 1967 'Class E imported post-Roman pottery; a suggested origin', *Cornish Archaeol.* 6: 35–46
Peacock, D.P.S. and Williams, D.F. 1986 *Amphorae and the Roman economy – an introductory guide* (London)
Pearce, S.M. (ed.) 1982 *The early church in western Britain and Ireland* (Brit. Archaeol. Rep. 102)
Petrie, G. 1845 *The ecclesiastical architecture of Ireland* (Dublin)
Piggott, C.M. 1952–3 'Milton Loch crannog I: a native house of the second century AD in Kircudbrightshire', *PSAS* 87: 134–52
Pochin Mould, D.D.C. 1972 *Ireland from the air* (Newton Abbot)
Proudfoot, V.B. 1953 'Excavation of a rath at Boho, Co. Fermanagh', *UJA* 16: 41–57
— 1958 'Further excavations at Shaneen Park, Belfast, Ballyaghagan townland, Co. Antrim', *UJA* 21: 18–38
— 1961 'The economy of the Irish rath', *Med. Arch.* 5: 94–122
— 1970 'Irish raths and cashels: some notes on origin, chronology and survivals', *UJA* 33: 37–48
— and Wilson, B.C.S. 1961–2 'Further excavations at Larrybane promontory fort, Co. Antrim', *UJA* 24–5: 91–115

Radford, C.A.R. 1956 'Imported pottery found at Tintagel, Cornwall' in Harden, D.B. (ed.), 59–70

— 1977 'The earliest Irish churches', *UJA* 40: 1–11
Raftery, B. 1972 'Irish hill forts' in Thomas, C. (ed.), 37–58
— 1981 'Iron Age burials in Ireland' in Ó Corráin, D. (ed.) 173–204
— 1983 *A catalogue of Irish Iron Age antiquities* (Marburg)
— 1984 *La Tène Ireland: problems of origin and chronology* (Marburg)
— 1987 'La Tène art in Ireland' in Ryan, M. (ed.) 12–8
Raftery, J. 1941a *Christian art in ancient Ireland, Volume 2* (Dublin)
— 1941b 'Long stone cists of the early Iron Age', *PRIA* 66c: 299–315
— 1942–3 'Knocknalappa crannog, Co. Clare', *N. Munster Antiq. J.* 3: 53–74
— 1944 'The Turoe stone and the Rath of Feerwore', *JRSAI* 74: 23–52
— 1952 'Crannog finds at Lough Gara', *JRSAI* 82: 182–3
— 1956 'Wooden bucket from Co. Louth', *Co. Louth Archaeol. Soc. J.* 13 (4): 395–8
— 1957 'Lake dwellings in Ireland', *Scientific Service* 4 (3): 5–15
— 1972 'Iron Age and Irish Sea province: some problems for research' in Thomas, C. (ed.), 1–10
— 1981 'Concerning chronology' in Ó Corráin, D. (ed.) 82–90
Rees, S.E. 1979 *Agricultural implements in prehistoric and Roman Britain*, 2 vols. (Brit. Archaeol. Rep. 69)
Reeves-Smyth, T. and Hamond, F. (eds) 1983 *Landscape archaeology in Ireland* (Brit. Archaeol. Rep. 116)
Richards, M. 1960 'The Irish settlements in south-west Wales', *JRSAI* 90: 133–62
Richardson, H. 1987 'Observations on Christian art in early Ireland, Georgia and Armenia' in Ryan, M. (ed.) 129–37
Ritchie, G. and A. 1981 *Scotland, archaeology and early history* (London)
Roe, H.M. 1955 'Antiquities of the archdiocese of Armagh, Co. Armagh', *Seanchas Ard Mhacha* 2: 107–12
— 1956 'Antiquities of the archdiocese of Armagh, Co. Tyrone', *Seanchas Ard Mhacha* 3: 79–88
— 1966 *The high crosses of Kells* (2nd ed., Dublin)
— 1981 *Monasterboice and its monuments* (Co. Louth Hist. Soc.)

Rohan, P.K. 1975 *The climate of Ireland* (Dublin)

Roth, U. 1987 'Early Insular manuscripts: ornament and archaeology, with specific reference to the dating of the Book of Durrow' in Ryan, M. (ed.) 23–9

Royal Commission on the Ancient and Historical Monuments of Scotland 1982 *Argyll Volume 4, Iona* (Edinburgh)

Royal Commission on the Ancient and Historical Monuments of Wales 1976 *Glamorgan Volume 1: Part III The Early Christian Period* (Cardiff)

Royal Society of Antiquaries of Ireland 1983 *Monuments in danger* (Dublin)

Ryan, M. 1973 'Native pottery in early historic Ireland', *PRIA* 73c: 619–45

— 1976 'Fulacht fiadh at Rath More townland, Rathmore', *J. Kerry Archaeol. Hist. Soc.* 9: 11–5

— 1981 'Some archaeological comments on the occurrence and use of silver in pre-Viking Ireland' in Scott, B.G. (ed.) 45–50

— (ed.) 1983 *The Derrynaflan hoard. I. A preliminary account* (Dublin)

— 1987a 'The Donore hoard: early medieval metalwork from Moynalty, near Kells, Ireland', *Antiquity* 61: 57–63

— (ed.) 1987b *Ireland and Insular art A.D. 500–1200* (Dublin)

— and Ó Floinn, R. 1983 'The paten and stand' in Ryan, M. (ed.) 17–30

— *et al.* 1984 'Six silver finds of the Viking period from the vicinity of Lough Ennell, Co. Westmeath', *Peritia* 3: 335–81

Rynne, E. 1959 'Souterrain at Donaghmore, Co. Louth', *Co. Louth Archaeol. Hist. J.* 14 (3): 148–53

— 1964 'Ring-forts at Shannon airport', *PRIA* 63c: 245–77

— (ed.) 1967 *North Munster studies* (Limerick)

— 1972 'Celtic stone idols in Ireland' in Thomas, C. (ed.) 79–98

— 1976 'The La Tène and Roman finds from Lambay, County Dublin: a re-assessment', *PRIA* 76c: 231–43

— 1981 'A classification of pre-Viking Irish iron swords' in Scott, B.G. (ed.) 93–7

— (ed.) 1987 *Figures from the past* (Dun Laoghaire)

— and Mac Eoin, G. 1978 'The Craggaunowen crannog: gangway and gate–tower', *N. Munster Antiq. J.* 20; 47–56

Scott, B.G. 1978 'Iron "slave-collars" from Lagore crannog, Co. Meath', *PRIA* 78c: 213–30

— (ed.) 1981 *Studies in early Ireland* (Belfast)

— 1983 'An early Irish law tract on the blacksmith's forge', *J. Ir. Archaeol.* 1: 59–62

— 1987 'The status of the blacksmith in early Ireland' in Scott, B.G. and Cleere, H. (eds), *The craft of the blacksmith* (Belfast) 153–6

Selkirk, A. and Selkirk, W. 1970a 'Dun Ailline', *Current Archaeol.* 22: 308–11

— 1970b 'Navan fort', *Current Archaeol.* 22: 304–8

Sharpe, R. 1984 'Some problems concerning the organization of the church in early medieval Ireland', *Peritia* 3: 230–70

Sheehan, J. 1987–8 'A reassessment of the Viking burial from Eyrephort, Co. Galway', *J. Galway Archaeol. Hist. Soc.* 41: 60–72

Sheehy, J. 1980 *The rediscovery of Ireland's past: the Celtic revival 1830–1930* (London)

Shetelig, H. (ed.) 1940 *Viking antiquities in Great Britain and Ireland. Parts III–V* (Oslo)

Simms, A. 1979 'Medieval Dublin: a topographical analysis', *Irish Geography* 12: 25 41

Simpson, W.G. 1972 'A gaming board of Ballinderry type from Knockanboy, Derrykeighan, Co. Antrim', *UJA* 35: 63–4

Smith, R.A. 1913–4 'Irish brooches of five centuries', *Archaeologia* 65: 223–50

— 1917–8 'Irish serpentine latchets', *Proc. Soc. Antiq. London* 30: 120–31

Stalley, R.A. 1980 'Mellifont abbey: a study of its architectural history', *PRIA* 80c: 263–354

— 1981a 'Three Irish buildings with West Country origins' in Coldstream, N. and Draper, P. (eds), *Medieval art and architecture at Wells and Glastonbury* (Brit. Archaeol. Ass. Conference Trans. 4) 62–80

— 1981b 'The Romanesque sculpture of Tuam' in Borg, A. and Martindale, A. (eds), *The vanishing past* (Brit. Archaeol. Rep. S111) 179–96

— 1987 *The Cistercian monasteries of Ireland* (London/New Haven)

Stenberger, M. 1966 'A ring fort at Raheennamadra, Knocklong, Co. Limerick', *PRIA* 65c: 37–54

Stevenson, R.B.K. 1974 'The Hunterston brooch and its significance', *Med. Arch.* 18: 16–42

— 1976 'The earlier metalwork of Pictland' in Megaw, J.V.S. (ed.), *To illustrate the monuments* (London) 245–51

— 1981–2 'Aspects of ambiguity in crosses and interlace', *UJA* 44–5: 1–27
— 1985 'Notes on the sculptures at Fahan Mura and Carndonagh, Co. Donegal', *JRSAI* 115: 92–5
Stokes, W. (ed.) 1905 *Félire Óengusso Céli Dé: The martyrology of Oengus the culdee* (Henry Bradshaw Soc. 29, London)
Stout, G.T. 1984 *Archaeological survey of the Barony of Ikerrin* (Roscrea Heritage Soc.)
Swan, L. 1972 'Fennor, Co. Meath', *Ríocht na Mídhe* 5 (2): 64–9
— 1973 'Duleek, an early Christian site', *Annals of Duleek* 3: 12–20
— 1976 'Excavations at Kilpatrick churchyard, Killucan, Co. Westmeath', *Ríocht na Mídhe* 6 (2): 89–96
— 1985 'Monastic proto-towns in early medieval Ireland: the evidence of aerial photography, plan analysis and survey' in Clarke, H.B. and Simms, A. (eds), 77–102
Swarzenski, G. 1954 'An early Anglo/Irish portable shrine', *Bull. Museum Fine Arts Boston* 52: 50–62
Sweetman, D. 1982–3 'Souterrain and burials at Boolies Little, Co. Meath', *Ríocht na Mídhe* 7 (2): 42–57

Thomas, C. 1959 'Imported pottery in Dark-Age western Britain', *Med. Arch.* 3: 89–111
— 1966 'The character and origins of Roman Dumnonia' in Thomas, C. (ed.), *Rural settlement in Roman Britain* (Council Brit. Archaeol. Res. Rep. 7, London) 74–98
— 1967 'An early Christian cemetery and chapel on Ardwall Isle, Kircudbright', *Med. Arch.* 11: 127–88
— 1968 'Grass-marked pottery in Cornwall' in Coles, J.M. and Simpson, D.D.A. (eds), 311–32
— 1971 *The early Christian archaeology of north Britain* (London/Glasgow/New York)
— 1972a 'The Irish settlements in post-Roman western Britain, a survey of the evidence', *J. Roy. Cornish Inst.* 6: 251–74
— (ed.) 1972b *The Iron Age in the Irish Sea Province* (Council Brit. Archaeol. Res. Rep. 9, London)
— 1972c 'Souterrains in the Irish Sea province' in Thomas, C. (ed.), 75–8
— 1973 'Irish colonists in south-western Britain', *World Archaeol.* 5 (1): 5–13
— 1976 'Imported late Roman Mediterranean pottery in Ireland and western Britain', *PRIA* 76c: 245–55
— 1981a *A provisional list of imported pottery in post-Roman western Britain and Ireland* (Inst. Cornish Stud., Special Rep. 7, Redruth)
— 1981b *Christianity in Roman Britain to A.D. 500* (London)
— 1982 'East and west, Tintagel, Mediterranean imports and the early Insular church' in Pearce, S.M. (ed.), 17–34
— 1988 'Tintagel castle', *Antiquity* 62: 421–34
Thompson, E.A. 1985 *Who was St Patrick?* (Woodbridge)
Tierney, J.J. 1976 'The Greek geographic tradition and Ptolemy's evidence for Irish geography', *PRIA* 76c: 257–65
Twohig, D.C. 1971 'Souterrains in Cos Cork and Louth', *JCHAS* 76: 128–33
— 1976 'Recent souterrain research in Co. Cork', *JCHAS* 81: 19–38
Tylecote, R.F. 1986 *The prehistory of metallurgy in the British Isles* (London)

Verey, C.D., *et al.* 1980 *The Durham gospels* (Early English manuscripts in facsimile, vol. 12, Copenhagen)

Wailes, B. 1974–5 'Excavations at Dun Ailinne, near Kilcullen 1974', *J. Co. Kildare Archaeol. Soc.* 15 (4): 345–58
Wainwright, G.J. 1971 'The excavation of a fortified settlement at Walesland Rath, Pembrokeshire', *Britannia* 2: 48–108
Wakeman, W.F. 1893 *Survey of the antiquarian remains on the island of Inismurray* (JRSAI special vol. 1892, London/Edinburgh)
Wallace, P.F. 1981a 'The origins of Dublin' in Scott, B.G. (ed.) 129–42
— 1981b 'Dublin's waterfront at Wood Quay: 900–1317' in Milne, G. and Hobley, B. (eds), *Waterfront archaeology in Britain and northern Europe* (Council Brit. Archaeol. Res. Rep. 41) 109–18
— 1982 'Carpentry in Ireland AD 900–1300 – the Wood Quay evidence' in McGrail, S. (ed.), 263–99
— 1985a 'The archaeology of Viking Dublin' in Clarke, H.B. and Simms, A. (eds), 103–45
— 1985b 'A reppraisal of the archaeological significance of Wood Quay' in Bradley, J. (ed.), 112–33
— 1986 'The English presence in Viking Dublin' in Blackburn, M.A.J. (ed.), *Anglo-Saxon monetary history* (Leicester) 201–21

— and Ó Floinn, R. 1988 *Dublin 1000. Discovery and excavation in Dublin, 1842–1981* (Dublin)

Walsh, A. 1922 *Scandinavian relations with Ireland* (Dublin)

Wamers, E. 1983 'Some ecclesiastical and secular Insular metalwork in Norwegian Viking graves', *Peritia* 2: 277–306

— 1985 *Insularer Metallschmuck in wikingerzeitlichen Gräben Nordeuropas* (Neumünster)

Warhurst, C. 1967 'Excavations at Drumee Rath, Co. Fermanagh', *UJA* 30: 44–8

— 1969 'Excavations at Rathbeg, Co. Antrim', *UJA* 32: 93–100

— 1971 'Excavation of a rath at Shane's Castle, Co. Antrim', *UJA* 34: 58–64

Warner, R.B. 1971 'Clogher demesne', *Excavations* 2: 23–4

— 1972 'Clogher demesne', *Excavations* 3: 27–8

— 1973a 'Clogher demesne', *Excavations* 4: 25

— 1973b 'The excavations at Clogher and their context', *Clogher Record* 8 (1): 5–12

— 1973–4 'The re-provenancing of two important penannular brooches of the Viking period', *UJA* 36–7: 58–70

— 1974 'Clogher demesne', *Excavations* 5: 27

— 1975 'Clogher demesne', *Excavations* 6: 18

— 1976 'Some observations on the context and importation of exotic material in Ireland, from the first century B.C. to the second century A.D.', *PRIA* 76c: 267–89

— 1979a 'The Irish souterrains and their background' in Crawford, H. (ed.), *Subterranean Britain* (London) 100–44

— 1979b 'The Clogher yellow layer', *Medieval Ceramics* 3: 37–40

— 1980–1 'Fortification: observations on the beginnings of fortification in later Iron-age Ireland', *Bull. Ulster Place-name Soc.*, 2nd ser., 3: 45–52

— 1983 'Ireland, Ulster and Scotland in the earlier Iron Age' in O'Connor, A. and Clarke, D.V. (eds), 160–87

— 1985–6 'The date of the start of Lagore', *J. Ir. Archaeol.* 3: 75–7

— 1986 'Comments on "Ulster and Oriel souterrains"', *UJA* 49: 111–2

— 1987 'Ireland and the origins of escutcheon art' in Ryan, M. (ed.) 19–22

— 1988 'The archaeology of Early Historic Irish kingship' in Driscoll, S.T. and Nieke, M.R. (eds), *Power and politics in early medieval Britain and Ireland* (Edinburgh) 22–46

— and Meighan, I.G. 1981 'Dating Irish glass beads by chemical analysis' in Ó Corráin, D. (ed.) 52–66

Waterer, J.W. 1968 'Irish book-satchels or budgets', *Med. Arch.* 12: 70–82

Waterman, D.M. 1956a 'The excavation of a house and souterrain at Whitefort, Drumarood, Co. Down', *UJA* 19: 73–86

— 1956b 'An excavation of a house and souterrain at Craig Hill, Co. Antrim', *UJA* 19: 87–91

— 1958 'Excavations at Ballyfounder rath, Co. Down', *UJA* 21: 39–61

— 1959a 'Excavations at Lismahon, Co. Down', *Med. Arch.* 3: 139–76

— 1959b 'White Island church – note on a recent excavation', *UJA* 22: 65–6

— 1960 'An early Christian mortuary house at Saul, Co. Down', *UJA* 23: 89–96

— 1963 'Excavations at Duneight, Co. Down', *UJA* 26: 55–78

— 1967a 'The early Christian churches and cemetery at Derry, Co. Down', *UJA* 30: 53–75

— 1967b 'A pair of raths at Glenkeen, Co. Derry', *UJA* 30: 49–52

— 1968 'Note on a destroyed rath and souterrain at Killyglen, Co. Antrim', *UJA* 31: 67–70

— 1969 'An early medieval horn from the River Erne', *UJA* 32: 101–4

— 1971 'A marshland habitation site near Larne, Co. Antrim', *UJA* 34: 65–78

— 1972 'A group of raths at Ballypalady, Co. Antrim', *UJA* 35: 29–36

— and Collins, A.E.P. 1952 'The excavation of two raths at Ballywillwill, Co. Down', *UJA* 15: 71–83

— and Hamlin, A. 1976 'Banagher church, Co. Derry', *UJA* 39: 25–41

Webb, J.F. (trans.) 1965 *Lives of the saints* (Harmondsworth)

Went, A.E.J. 1952 'Irish fishing spears', *JRSAI* 82: 109–34

Westropp, T.J. 1896–7 'Prehistoric stone forts of northern Clare', *JRSAI* 26 142–57, 363–9; 27: 116–27

— 1901 'The ancient forts of Ireland', *Trans. Roy. Ir. Acad.* 31: 579–726

Whitfield, N. 1987 'Motifs and techniques of Celtic filigree: are they original?' in Ryan, M. (ed.) 75–84

Wild, J.P. 1988 *Textiles in archaeology* (London)

Wilde, W.R. 1866–9 'On Scandinavian antiquities discovered near Islandbridge, Co. Dublin', *PRIA* 10c: 13–21

Williams, B.B. 1978 'Excavations at Lough Eskragh, Co. Tyrone', *UJA* 41: 37–48

— 1980 'Excavation of a tree-ring at Gallanagh, Co. Tyrone and some observations on tree-rings', *UJA* 43: 97–101

— 1983 'Early Christian landscapes in Co. Antrim' in Reeves-Smyth, T. and Hamond, F. (eds) 233–46

— 1984 'Excavations at Ballyutoag, Co. Antrim', *UJA* 47: 37–49

— 1985a 'Excavation of a rath at Coolcran, Co. Fermanagh', *UJA* 48: 69–80

— 1985b 'Excavations at Ballyvollen townland, Co. Antrim', *UJA* 48: 91–102

Woodman, P.C. 1981–2 'Sampling strategies and problems of archaeological visibility', *UJA* 44–5: 179–84

Wood-Martin, W.G. 1886 *The lake dwellings of Ireland* (Dublin)

Youngs, S.M., *et al.* 1984 'Medieval Britain and Ireland in 1983', *Med. Arch.* 28: 203–65

— 1985 'Medieval Britain and Ireland in 1984', *Med. Arch.* 29: 158–230

— 1986 'Medieval Britain and Ireland in 1985', *Med. Arch.* 30: 114–98

# Index

DISCARD